THE LIVING LIGHT DIALOGUE

Volume 10

THE LIVING LIGHT DIALOGUE

Volume 10

Through the mediumship of
Richard P. Goodwin

Living Light Books

The Living Light Dialogue Volume 10
Copyright © 2018 Serenity Association

Through the mediumship of Richard P. Goodwin.

All rights reserved. Printed in the United States of America. No portion of this book may be reproduced—electronically, mechanically, or via internet transmission—without advance, express written permission of the publisher except in the case of brief quotations embodied in critical articles and reviews. No derivative work—games supplemental material, video—may be created without advance, express written permission of the publisher. For information address Living Light Books, P.O. Box 4187, San Rafael, CA 94913-4187.

Cover design copyright © 2018 by Serenity Association
Cover photograph by Serenity Association, 2018; copyright © 2018 by Serenity Association.

www.livinglight.org

Library of Congress Control Number 2007929762

FIRST EDITION

This volume of teachings is dedicated to the spirit friends who brought to Earth the Living Light Philosophy. With eternal gratitude, we pray that we may demonstrate these principles and continue to bring to publication these teachings.

CONTENTS

Acknowledgement ix
Preface xi
Introduction xv
Church Lectures
  CL 82 – Faith, The Power that Frees our Soul 3
  CL 83 – The Lighted Path 9
  CL 84 – A Working Philosophy 18
  CL 85 – A New Dawn 27
  CL 86 – Review and Renewal 35
  CL 87 – The Winds of Change 42
  CL 88 – Our Ship of Destiny 49
  CL 89 – Looking Ahead 57
  CL 90 – Our Journey Inward 65
  CL 91 – Reaping the Harvest 69
  CL 92 – Fulfillment 73
  CL 93 – A New View 78
  CL 94 – World of Spirit 87
  CL 95 – Gratitude, The Faculty of Fulfillment 93
  CL 96 – Looking Ahead 98
  CL 97 – A Year of Fulfillment 104
  CL 98 – Ninth Anniversary Service 119
  CL 99 – Tenth Anniversary Service 126
  CL 100 140
  CL 101 – [The Continuity of Organization] 148
Church Questions and Answers
  CQA 1 160
  CQA 2 174
  CQA 3 184
  CQA 4 196

CQA 5	203
CQA 6	211
CQA 7	220
CQA 8	237
CQA 9	246
CQA 10	257
CQA 11	268
CQA 12	281
CQA 13	289
CQA 14	301
CQA 15	313
CQA 16	323
CQA 17	332
CQA 18	345
CQA 19	356
CQA 20	368
CQA 21	376
CQA 22	385
CQA 23	394
CQA 24	412
Appendix	423

ACKNOWLEDGMENT

Grateful acknowledgement is made to the many friends and associates for invaluable aid in compiling this book, for their helpful suggestions, for their loyal interest and encouragement.

Special acknowledgement is due to those who painstakingly and selflessly transcribed and proofread the text.

PREFACE

It was through the mediumship of the Serenity Association founder, Mr. Richard P. Goodwin, that a philosophy known as the Living Light was given in more than 700 classes over a twenty-five-year period.

To be specific, the philosophy was imparted through Mr. Goodwin by a magistrate who had lived on Earth some 8,000 years ago. The former magistrate is known to Living Light students as "the Wise One," and he narrated the journey of his soul on the other side of life, the experiences—especially the difficulties—he encountered in having to face himself, as well as the teachings he earned to help himself through the realms in which he traveled. It was his decision to share the teachings with souls on both sides of "the curtain."

Prior to the advent of the Wise One, Mr. Goodwin had prayed for a teacher from the realms of light. Mr. Goodwin, since age fourteen, had been the instrument through which spirit was able to communicate with those seeking help. But he saw that his mediumship brought only temporary solace, because the people he was trying to help soon became fascinated with the phenomena and ignored the help that spirit was imparting. He prayed for someone who would bring forth teachings that would benefit any soul seeking a path to a greater awareness of himself and of God.

His prayers were answered in 1964 when the Wise One came through for the first time. Mr. Goodwin, at first apprehensive about what this new teacher would impart, was taken into deep trance and not able to control what was being revealed through him. Upon hearing the recorded classes afterward, however, he became convinced of the goodness of the teacher and of the value of the simple, beautiful teachings. This, then, was the beginning of the Living Light Philosophy given to Earth through the mediumship of Richard P. Goodwin.

In carrying out the request of the Wise One and Mr. Goodwin, students of the Serenity Association transcribed from audiotape the classes that had been brought through. Because most are in the form of teacher–student interaction, the classes became known as *The Living Light Dialogue;* and the students were instructed to publish the classes as a multi-volume set of the Living Light Philosophy. *Volume 1* was published in the autumn of 2007.

The present book, *Volume 10,* continues the Church Lectures series of classes, which were delivered by Mr. Goodwin on the first Sunday of the month during the devotional services of the Serenity Spiritualist Church, and begins the next series of classes, the Church Questions and Answers, which were also delivered as part of the church services. *Volume 10* includes the lectures from CL 82 through CL 101, as well as CQA 1 through CQA 24 covering the time period of October 1, 1978, through March 7, 1982.

The foundation of the classes—the foundation of the Living Light Philosophy itself—is the Law of Personal Responsibility which states, in part, that we are responsible for all our experiences, and that our experiences are the return of the laws that we have established with our thoughts, acts, and deeds. Through greater awareness of our thoughts and by exercising our divine right of choice, we may choose to establish laws of greater harmony and goodness.

The Living Light Dialogue teaches that we have come to Earth to learn the lessons that are necessary to free us from the dictates and limits of our own thoughts and judgments, which are the mental patterns that we follow through our own lack of awareness and are so very potent, forceful, and limiting. These teachings guide us in making the necessary changes in our thinking in order to free ourselves from those patterns and to express our soul consciousness.

The choice of guiding the direction of our life, as stated by the Wise One when he speaks of being with a person, place, or thing, is, in essence, of being in this world and not a part of this world. He further explains that no matter what experiences we encounter, no matter what we do or do not do, we—our spirit—may view the experience in objectivity from a soul level of consciousness where peace reigns supreme.

The teachings of this volume help us to restore harmony or balance in our life by flooding the consciousness with spiritual affirmations and prayers, a few of which can be found in the appendix. When reason is restored, by balancing our sense functions with our soul faculties, we will consciously experience peace. Without annihilating our ego or our sense functions, we will find a pathway of expression for our soul. Where there was once disturbance, now there is acceptance. Where there was disease, now there is poise. And where there was hopelessness and despair, now there is reason, divine neutrality; and peace shows the way.

If you make the effort to apply these laws, such as, "If man is a law unto himself, what are you doing with the law that you are?", and demonstrate the wisdom of patience, the truth of this philosophy will be your living demonstration.

As the teacher states in CC 130, "My journey of many centuries and much experience has brought me here to Earth to share with you these simple teachings that have come as the effect of a long, long, long journey. Let not your journey be so long in the realms of illusion. For it is not necessary for you. For in your evolution, you have earned an awakening. But it is up to you to do something that is constructive and worthwhile."

INTRODUCTION

[This introduction was written by Mr. Goodwin and originally appeared in The Living Light, which were the first teachings of the Living Light Philosophy published in book form. The entire text of *The Living Light* was republished in *The Living Light Dialogue, Volume 1.*]

> "Think, children. Think more often
> and think more deeply."

The teachings in this book were given as a progressive series of lessons to a group of four students who were sitting for spiritual unfoldment with me beginning in January of 1964. The communications were regular until October of that year, when nearly a seven-year silence ensued, and resumed in 1971 to the present. They were received in three ways by me as a channel. The main text was taped from a direct control of my voice in deep trance at special sittings of our group, during which I had no experience of the voice or what was being transmitted. A few scattered verses were given independently when I was privileged to see and hear our teacher clairvoyantly. I have also been a channel for this communicant when speaking from the podium at church and in answering difficult questions at our public seminars.

Nearly all we know about our teacher is contained in the lectures. He reports that he had tried for sixteen years to break through an interference barrier that the channel had to deep trance. When our conditions were in resonance with his patient wisdom, he came through ready to teach his understanding. I have seen him as an old man dressed in white with long flowing white hair. He has blue eyes, slightly smiling and deeply compassionate. I have always called him the Old Man. The students liked to call him the Wise One. He is surely one of those often called a Teacher of Light. I do not know his country, although he indicated at one time that he was from 6000 B.C., and a form of a judge in his time.

The text is often difficult, but it is complete, having been transcribed word for word from the original tapes recording the trance voice. It is presented with a minimum of punctuation to be freer for the individual interpretation of each reader. The lessons given before the long silence are phrased with many allegories often paradoxical. There are repetitions and renewals of theme, but it is explained that if an understanding is not perceived, compassion dictates that it be said again. Some of the topics have but a simple mention with little development but all are revealed, we are told, according to merit.

The Old Man is a fine teacher. He has in a hundred ways intertwined his allegory, progressive explanations, unfolding exercises, and timely references to reach a multitude of levels of individual understanding. A notable change is his more direct style of presentation beginning in 1971.

There is an endearing intimacy of person that can be felt through his lectures, a meaningful and loving encounter with a wise friend. Like an old man, he makes a mistake and conscientiously corrects himself a few paragraphs later. He listens often and carefully to our earnest discussions of his words. He consults with a group of experts on evolution and cites their learning in his lesson. His use of the direct address "children" or "my children" is not patronizing but infinitely loving and supportive.

A word must be said about the teachings. The Old Man makes clear that his lessons are not dogma, a creed or a narrow way, but simply his own understanding offered to us as a form of instruction to aid us in our own individual progression. When he speaks of Laws, he does not refer to man–made rules or moral traditions but to the cosmic and atomic way–things–are, the natural world of what–is, the universal laws of life, part of the original creative design and through which creation is fulfilled. These laws are beyond the possibility of being changed, suspended, transcended, or destroyed but they are ever a tool of mankind, not his master. First, through our awareness of the universal laws and then slowly through our developed understanding, the powers of creation are accessible to us. Not power over men's minds or circumstances, but power over whatever is selfish and imperfect in ourselves is the way up the eternal ladder of progression. When the Old Man cautions us concerning the Law of Responsibility or gives us a thinking exercise to explore the Law of Identity in a dynamic manner, he prepares us to take another step. And all move in accordance with the Law of What Can Be Borne.

Our teacher shows us how the two worlds are drawn together. In his realm, he describes, there is a great diversity of thought, many schools of understanding; but the Light is always known by the Light. Because of the interdependence of the two realms, listening to our discussions helped to clarify his teaching to others on his side of the curtain. His love and gratitude he humbly equates with ours.

The lessons to be perceived are not new, they are very old, but they are new to certain levels of our being. I would personally advise the reader, after reading this volume of discourses in full, to make a daily habit (or when there is a feeling or need) to sit quietly with the book. Open it at random and be guided to the Light by the passage that is there for the day. This technique is still used by the original students who were given the lessons and by many students after them who have studied in unfolding classes with me through these teachings.

Go beyond the words into feeling, into the immediate meanings for you. Touch into the inspiration that flows into the form of this book. It is from the Divine.

RICHARD P. GOODWIN
San Geronimo, California
June, 1972

CHURCH LECTURES

Church Lecture 82

Faith, The Power that Frees Our Soul

In speaking with you today on, "Faith, the Power that Frees Our Soul,"—the word *faith*, usually associated with religion, so vastly misunderstood in the world. Without faith, we do not move, we do not breathe. Without faith, we do not walk, we do not see, we do not hear. That is what faith really is. As we come to this the earth realm, under the power of faith we entered the forms—the human form—of this planet. This word, *faith*, reveals a power of the Infinite Intelligence, called God. As we encourage ourselves in any endeavor, we open the door of faith to this great power.

In our experiences here on the Earth planet, there are many things that we wish often to change. And when we make the effort to make those changes in our life, we often become discouraged and soon we quit before the victories. Whatever it is in life that you choose to change, we must remember that it not only requires the power of faith, the intelligent Energy, known as God, but it requires the door to that power to be opened. And the door to that power is the soul faculty of encouragement. The great struggle and difficulty that we find in making these efforts to change experiences and to change the attitudes and the patterns of mind of yesterday is because we are lacking in encouraging ourselves.

We go out into the mundane world and we see and we hear and we experience so much discouragement. Because there have been so many experiences in peoples lives, because they have quit just before the victory, they easily share with us, in their discussions, the discouragement of their own experiences. When we open this door to this intelligent power, known as faith, we must remember that we and we alone will have to make the effort to encourage ourselves.

Whenever you start on any endeavor of your choosing, it has been stated that the secrets of the universe are never given to the blabbermouths. When you speak forth into the universe what you are making an effort to accomplish, you expose your effort to all of the negativity, to all of the discouragement that others have experienced in their lives. Therefore, you have a greater struggle, for you must not only use great effort to accomplish what you have chosen to accomplish, but you must utilize great effort to overcome your own acceptance of the discouragement, that is a level of consciousness within all of us. If the little babe is not encouraged to walk, then it will crawl for a long, long time. And so we see in our education here, just on this earth realm, that it does require a great deal of encouragement to get anything worthwhile accomplished. It also requires a great deal of encouragement to get things accomplished that we find in our lives and decide are not worthwhile. These patterns, so tenacious, that we have directed so much faith to, can only be overcome by directing an equal amount of energy and encouragement to our new patterns of mind, to our new attitudes in life, and new experiences.

It is faith that brought us to the earth realm, and it is faith that will take us to the next and the next and the next. Man cannot experience anything in his life that he does not have faith in. If he has faith in destructive things, then that is the only thing that he, in his experience, can encounter. If you have faith in the abundant good in life, if you have faith in your divine, eternal right to experience it, then indeed that is what you will experience.

There are many philosophies that constantly teach a positive attitude of mind, but they only work if you and you alone make them work. Nothing can work for us unless we permit it to work for us. There are many things that we know. There are few things that we apply when it comes to making a change.

It is not that we are left in this world in darkness. It is not that we don't know the way. Each and every soul upon this planet knows the way to the eternal light. As sure as the sunflower turns its face to the light of truth, so does the soul of each and every one of us ever turn towards the light. We know the way. Whether or not we are applying the way that we know is something that is a struggle between our mind and our own conscience. No one has to tell us which way to go. We in truth know the way. There are many paths that lead to the eternal light of truth, but there are not so many who are consistently making the daily effort to follow the path that they truly know.

Someday we will all arrive in consciousness; we will all go back home. Back home is a place in consciousness called by man heavenly heights. They are heavenly heights in the sense that they are realms of consciousness of peace and abundant goodness. The harmony in our life that we permit is revealed in the health and the wealth in our life. Some philosophies in ages past taught that it was a sin to be without the abundant good of life. And in a sense, if you mean by the word *sin*, error or mistake, then indeed it is, in that sense, a sin. We know the true and only source of our supply, for we have wandered from that true and only source of our supply. It is known as God or Infinite Intelligence. God did not dictate for us to wander from that source. Our minds, gaining slowly, but surely, over the untold eons of evolution, began to rise and to dictate what was the source of goodness, happiness, and health and wealth in our life. As our mind rose up to dictate what was the source, it wandered farther and farther away from the source. And so the mind says "I have happiness subject to . . . " And our mind is always subject to the errors of its own experiences.

When we—and we can this moment—choose to return to the source from whence we have wandered, there we will have all that our heart could possibly desire. It is but an error in our own thinking that we have judged we are without. We are without only because we have faith in the dictate of our own mind. And our mind makes these ever-changing dictates dependent upon the experiences that it has already encountered. It is indeed a most unreliable source, our human mind. It does not even recall with any degree of accuracy, if it recalls at all, the untold centuries of experiences that it had encountered prior to this earth realm. And because it does not recall, if at all, those experiences, then it dictates to us those experiences did not ever exist.

We know that we are ever limited by what we identify with. Because in the very process of identifying with anything, through that Law of Identification, we are directing the intelligent Power through the faculty of faith. So if we permit our minds to identify with the limitations and the sufferings, which are but the experiences of the errors of our own mind, then, my friends, that's all that we can have, for that is all we are allowing ourselves.

All of life is dependent upon our own willingness to identify, to direct this power of faith. We know that God sustains whatever thought we choose to entertain. So if you are having experiences that you are not pleased with, if they are experiences that you find are depriving you of the basic goodness of freedom, the goodness of life, then remember, it is only a matter of redirecting your own thought. But in that process of redirecting your thought, remember, it takes a great deal of daily and constant encouragement. For we are where we are because we are who we have permitted ourselves to be. It took much encouragement to put us where we are today and it's going to take much encouragement to put us where we want to be.

The teaching to place your attention, which is the vehicle through which this great power of faith is directed, to place our attention upon what we desire to become, to remove our attention from what we have chosen to overcome is a very basic and wise truth. For as long as we permit our mind to think of the obstructions in our life, we will never find the way. As long as we insist upon fascinating with the causes of our experiences, we will remain in those experiences, for we are insisting upon directing this great power of faith to those causes.

Let us move today, let us move in our consciousness. Move forward, ever onward and upward, that we may truly, fully, and completely enjoy what this planet has to offer. For if we cannot enjoy the goodness that this planet, Earth, has to offer, then do not delude yourself with what the next planet has to offer. For if we do not find it here, we are not going to find it here after we leave the physical body.

Many people seem to misunderstand on the spiritual path of evolution. They seem to entertain the belief that all of the physical and material things that this planet has to offer should be disregarded; that they should spend their time in contemplation and meditation. I assure you that man, designed by the infinite, intelligent Architect, is no greater, nor is he any lesser, than the little insect known as the ant that crawls the ground. They all have within them and flowing through them the intelligent, infinite Energy. And you notice how the little ant, he crawls and he works—a great organization of society. And look at the beaver. How he works for that that he receives. Man is no less in God's sight. He has been designed to move, to be motivated. Designed to encourage himself to find the true love of life, known as work made manifest. That's what our life eternal is all about. We are here—and we will be there soon—to be doers. Because without doing, we simply become grounded within our own limited thought patterns and we lose the beauty, the goodness, and the joy of life itself.

Stop and think, my friends, when you are not active, when you are not doing, what is your mind thinking about? Are you thinking in those moments of how great life is? Or are you thinking how miserable life is, how little you have, and how much you need?

Many people have said when the going gets tough, the tough get going. We all have the substance, the toughness that is necessary to get us through any obstruction in life that we alone have created. We know that nothing outside stands in our way. So let's look where that something is that is standing in our way. It's only in our thought. It is not dependent upon the government. It is not dependent upon the world. Why, it isn't even dependent upon God, the Infinite Intelligence. It's dependent on what we alone choose to think.

How many times during the course of our day do we choose to think how great life is? How many times during the course of our day do we choose to think about how wealthy, how healthy we truly are? When you have a seeming health condition, do you place your attention upon something besides the condition, to redirect the intelligent Energy? Because if you do, my friends, the healing will be spontaneous. When we put our attention upon the obstruction—be it a problem of health or of wealth—we simply feed more energy to it. We make it stronger until someday it becomes a great mountain for us to climb. Let us, as we all know, encourage our self on the way of peace and happiness. Remember, the great demonstrable truth that that which disturbs us controls us. So let us stop and think. If it disturbs us, redirect our thought, and we will no longer be controlled by it.

Thank you.

OCTOBER 1, 1978

Church Lecture 83

The Lighted Path

Speaking with you today on the subject of, "The Lighted Path," I would like to review for a few moments the basic teachings of the Living Light Philosophy, the philosophy of this church. This philosophy teaches that our denials in life become our destinies, that acceptance, total acceptance, is the will of the Divine. So let us, for a few moments, examine our daily experiences in our life, for then we shall clearly see that as we dictate by our minds that we are without the things that we desire in life, we establish these very laws of denial. And therefore, we continue on the path, the destiny of our own limited minds.

We all know, for we have all experienced at some time here in our earth life, that there is something greater than what our minds have already offered to us. But to experience that something greater, we must make our own effort to rise above and beyond the dictates of our human mind.

Our mind is likened to a programmed computer and so it experiences only what we feed into that computer by our own thoughts, by our own feelings. And so we are constantly in a process of judgment, constantly in a process of denying and therefore we go on the treadmill, the so-called karma, of continuous experiences that we know is contrary to our true desire to be free from this old duality of creation.

When we say we have not what we desire and we continue on in the mental realms of experience, we prove to our self, by our own thought, by our own belief, by the greatest power ever known in the universes, the power of faith, that we have not. To say that we have and to experience the opposite causes us to falter, we think, in our faith. But, my good friends, our experiences are only in keeping with our faith. We have faith in the shortage of what we desire and, therefore, we experience the shortage of what we desire. But that same power, called faith, we can redirect at any moment that we choose to redirect it. But that's up to us. That is not up to what we call God. God is the sustaining power of the universe. God is not going to change your thought, for God is already sustaining the thought that you already have chosen. If you wish your life to change, then only you can change it. God will sustain the change that you choose to make, but God will not change it for you, for that is contrary, *contrary* to your very divine birthright of free choice.

In order to make these changes that we say we want to make, to improve our lives for the better, to experience the goodness that we know deep within us is our right, in order to do that, we must accept the very basic teaching of all philosophies known in our world: the very basic teaching of personal responsibility. We must ask our self, if we truly wish to awaken from this slumber, we must ask our self how often in the course of any given day do we say unto our self, "I am responsible for this thought. I am responsible for this feeling. I am responsible for the world in which I live. And, being responsible, I and I alone can change my thought. I can change my life. I can change my feeling"? Not until we accept the Law of Personal Responsibility in our life can we bring about the transformation of our life and enjoy the world that is here for us to enjoy.

The smallest of creatures, the birds, the animals, and the insects—we call it instinct within them, but they demonstrate the Law of Personal Responsibility. All of creation, with one exception, demonstrates the full acceptance of personal responsibility. What happened to the animal called man? What happened in the evolution of that species on our planet that he and he alone demonstrates the direct opposite of natural law, that man alone dictates to the universe that he is exempt from the responsibilities of his own thoughts, his own feelings, his own acts, and his own deeds? It is because man, awakening to what is called free choice, that man lives in an illusion of self-created thought.

Because these thoughts that man alone has created are his children and no one else's, it is very natural to his mind to protect that which he has judged is his. Therefore, the child, to the parent, can do no wrong if the parent is emotionally attached to the child. And so man, emotionally attached to his own thoughts and feelings, permits those thoughts and feelings to cause his life to be restricted and limited. But that restriction and limitation is sustained and maintained by the great power, the same power, that will free him, known as the power of faith.

We demonstrate the great power of faith each and every moment of our life. We have the faith in whatever thought we're entertaining and sustaining over a period of time. It takes this power of faith to support the judgments that we make each moment of our life. So why not direct this great power—which we are already using anyway, in obviously (from our demonstrations) a negative way—why not direct this same power called faith in a positive way to bring about all the good that we are seeking? For it is natural for us to experience good, for we are, our true being, the very principle of good. Being an inseparable part of the united whole, we are the God of which we speak, that God being that very principle of goodness. Whenever we support in our mind thoughts that are obstructions to natural, divine flow, then we are aware of restriction and limitation. But it is only our thought. It's not someone else's. It is ours. And because it is our thought, we can do something with it.

When we dictate that we are in such a circumstance and condition because of something beyond our control, something beyond the power that is within us to transform, then in that moment do we become the victim and in that moment do we become the slave of circumstances, of something outside. The something outside, my friends, is only the veil of illusion; the veil that all of us on the lighted path must someday pierce. We are moving slowly, but surely, in that direction. And as we move in that direction, the world that we experience moves in that direction.

Slowly, but surely, we are going home in consciousness, for that is where everything is—everything that we could possibly desire. Again and again it has been stated, everything is right where we are. And so in following that demonstrable truth, that everything that we desire in life and everything that we seek in life is right where we are, we must make the effort to ask ourselves, "Where am I? If everything I think I need is right where I am, then where am I?" That is the question, my friends, to ask each day. That *is* the question. When you feel a financial struggle, when you feel the health problems and the plagues that beset your human mind, ask yourself in that moment, "Where am I?" And when you ask yourself that question—the question, to the mind, presupposes and guarantees no less its answer—an answer will rise up into your conscious mind and you will be very surprised what that answer will be. For as you receive that answer from within your own being, you will find your mind is quickly changing. For no one likes to be in those levels of consciousness. No one truly wants to give away the very precious gift of free choice, but each time we place the blame and the cause for anything in our experience, each time that we project outside the cause, we sacrifice our most precious gift of all: that precious gift of free choice.

We like to believe that we think for our self, but unless we ask our self more frequently where we are, then we can be assured, my friends, we're not thinking very much for our self.

We are where we are in life because of the way we have thought in life. There is no law that dictates to us that we must think a certain way—only the law that we have created. Those laws, of course, are an effect of our inner needs to be needed and to be wanted, to be liked. Each time we think and do anything for someone else, then we must put upon the brakes of reason. For we cannot grant to another what we have not first granted unto our self. And this is why the Bible teaches, "O physician, heal thyself." We must first qualify our self. If we have granted unto our self freedom, then we are qualified to be an instrument to demonstrate that freedom to others, for the demonstration is the revelation. To speak forth one thing in life and to manifest its opposite is an absolute guarantee of failure.

If you have experienced failure in business or in any area of your life, then take an honest look at the laws that you have set into motion. No man can speak forth one thing and demonstrate the other and experience success. Success is an effect; it is an effect of effort. It is a direct effect of consideration.

If you are lacking in anything—if you think you are lacking in anything, then ask yourself, in the very thing that you think you are lacking, have you accepted personal responsibility? If you have truly accepted personal responsibility, then you will see you are not lacking at all. But if you have given your free will, your free choice, if you have given it to the realms of delusion that your joy in life and your happiness is dependent upon anything, then you are the servant, the slave, and the victim of the very thing you have given that power to.

Spiritualism is not a popular religion in our world today, but many religions before Spiritualism were not popular religions in their day. When man grows a bit more and he takes that which is rightfully his and accepts responsibility for the taking, then Spiritualism, its philosophy and demonstration, will become more popular in the world.

When you tell a child that their experiences are the effect of their own thoughts, when they don't like their teachers and they don't like this and they don't like that and you tell them that is their choice and if they wish to be miserable, continue to support that choice, then the child awakens and grows up to be a responsible adult in society.

When we look at the world of politics and we look at the world of finance and we look at this material realm, we see an untold variety of thoughts and experiences. But in that seeing and in that viewing, we have the birthright to choose that which we will permit our minds and our lives to experience.

When you want to change and the change involves another, remember, don't try to change the other, for you are denying that which is rightfully yours. You're denying the responsibility and the power that is within you. Change you and that that you wanted changed, it will grow or it will go. There's nothing you have to do outside. If you are not happy in your marriage, change your thought concerning your marriage. If you are not happy in the job that you have in life, if you are not happy with your business, change your thought and your business will change. For your business, your marriage, your job is an effect of your thought. It's not an effect of someone else's thought. It is an effect of your thought, of your act, and your deed. Therefore, it is your right to change it when you choose to do so. To give away this precious birthright is a sad experience. To give it to a partner in marriage, to give it to a business, and to give it to a job is a very sad, sad way. And I'm sure all of us will surely, in the light of reason, agree to that.

Let us take back that which we have so foolishly given out in errors of ignorance. Let us no longer cast our pearls before the swine, for in so doing the pearls are no longer pearls. It's up to us. You can search the universes over, you can believe in anything you choose to believe in, but remember, it is your faith that is doing the work. It is that power that is within *you* that is doing it. It's not someone else. It's not a church. It's not a religion. It is not a philosophy that is doing it. You, your attitude, your thought, and your effort is what is doing it. When we accept that demonstrable truth, our lives will indeed become more successful; more abundant good will flow through our universe, for abundant good is the demonstrable law, the natural law of life itself. The meadows are not short of grass, nor are our forests short of trees, nor is the sky forever without clouds. Look all around you and see the constant multiplication of creation. It ever multiplies. It ever increases.

And that's what your thoughts do. They are seeds that you plant in fertile soil. They grow and grow and grow. All we need to do is to choose what seeds we plant, but that choice must be a conscious choice, a daily choice. You may plant the seeds that bring you all the things your heart could possibly desire, but then you must care for the seed that you plant. And first, above all, you must plant the seed in fertile soil. What is the fertile soil of the mind? There are two types of soil in the human mind: the fertile soil and the barren soil. The fertile soil is in the realm of total acceptance, the will of God. The barren soil is in the desert of denial, the human will. And so when you plant a seed, remember, you are planting it either in barren or fertile soil. So choose wisely in which soil you will plant the seeds of your thought. And you will indeed reap the harvest as you water it and you care for it and the years pass and you learn the beautiful soul faculty that wisdom lives in the realm of patience.

Patience is the key word to experience the continuity of goodness in anyone's life. If you are patient and you have planted your thoughts, your seeds, in fertile soil, you will live in that beautiful harvest forever and ever and ever in keeping with your own effort.

When you look at a tree—you purchase it for your home or your garden—and you see how beautiful it is. We all know it will only remain that way if someone, somewhere makes the effort. Well, we are the ones that chose the tree. We are the ones who are enjoying the tree. And so we must accept the responsibility of it or it won't stay beautiful very long. Well, that's the way our thoughts are. We ofttimes plant them and they are beautiful and they do land in fertile soil of acceptance, but then we get distracted with a multitude of other desires and we don't care for that little seed. And the day comes that it dies, it transforms, and it passes on. Look at the desires of yesterday. Are they all in keeping with our desires of today? Is there any demonstration of continuity, of single purpose? Is there a lifeline that we are working with? Do we have a goal in life? Do we really—consciously, are we aware of our goal? Or have we created so many goals that that word no longer is important in our life? Or do we look back and say, "Well, if I hadn't made that mistake and that mistake and the other mistake, then I would have what I want today." That's fine, my friends, if you want to live in rejection and the pity of yesterday, if you wish, and it is your choice to live that way.

Ofttimes, when we're faced with the things that we have done in life, our mind is so quick to justify. "Well, that happened because of so-and-so. And I did this because someone else did that." Remember, there is no way, there is no way that two wrongs can make a right in our life. So if you permit your mind to say that "I do this and I do that because someone else did something else," you're not going to find any peace and happiness and joy that way. For you didn't sell your birthright, you gave it away freely. You cast it to the swine. Those pearls, those precious gems that are yours, you threw away. And then you guarantee the day when your feelings of hurt and the injustices that have been cast upon you are unbearable. The injustices in life, friends, are what we judge them to be.

We are responsible for our life. And if each and every one of us accept that demonstrable responsibility, we won't have to be so concerned about what's happening outside. We won't have to worry about what someone else did, because we will be so active taking care of our own lives, about what we're doing, and enjoying life. We won't have to worry so much. We won't have to live in regret. We won't have to live in self-pity. We won't have to live in struggles of financial shortages. We won't have to worry about everything outside, because we're taking care of the joy of living, the job that's inside.

Thank you.

NOVEMBER 5, 1978

Church Lecture 84
A Working Philosophy

In speaking today on, "A Working Philosophy," we all are aware, I am sure, of the numerous philosophies available to us in our world today. Whatever your search takes you into, we must always remember, no philosophy presented at any time can work for us unless we work with it. All philosophies available to us today have the essence and the grain of truth within them. Many of them reveal some of the demonstrable laws of life that, once applied, can work for us harmoniously, as we work with them, to improve our lives, to bring about a more abundant and joyous good into our experiences.

It seems that in the study of philosophies and the practice of religions that we often falter on the path when we meet the strong desires of our mind and they are contrary to the way that we are trying to go. A house divided—meaning oneself—cannot stand. Not until we make the effort to bring unity, through harmony, into our minds can we move forward peacefully and joyously.

In spite of our own desires, change, through which the Law of Evolution is made possible, is ever with us. Whatever our thoughts of the moment are, they are in a process of evolution; they are in a process of change. If we will only make the effort frequently to remember whatever our desires and thoughts and feelings are, they are growing, they are evolving, they are changing. A philosophy of today must be a growing, changing, evolving philosophy or it will falter and die, because that is the way of evolution.

Working with the human mind, our own mind, and becoming aware, becoming aware that all of our experiences are effects, that so often when we encounter what our conscious mind considers to be a new experience, that so-called new experience is ever subject to the judgments, the denials, and the acceptances of similar past experiences. It is said that there is nothing new under the sun and, indeed, there is not. When we understand that we are on a path of evolution, that our life experience did not begin with the Earth planet and will not end with the Earth planet—when we look at the eternal moment of now, ever pulled by the magnetic and emotional pull of the past experience, ever driven forward by that divine discontent which is absolutely indispensable to the evolution in creation.

No matter what it is that we become involved with, the eternal search is never filled. As long as we have an awareness of creation, as long as we have an individualized soul, as long as we have a mind to think, the search will never end. Because the search did not begin in creation, the search is not subject to the beginnings and endings of forms and thoughts. It is this eternity that rises up in our consciousness; that is what drives us ever upward and ever onward. We can move with this evolutionary process in a harmonious, peaceful, and joyous way or we can fight and we can buck the tides of creation.

This philosophy does not teach a passive attitude toward creation; it teaches a harmonious understanding and a movement through creation. We, our eternal being has earned in its evolution a mind, a form, a body through which to express itself. Our difficulties begin when we forget that the mind that we have earned in evolution is [in] a constant process of change; the form is in a process of change. And when we become objective in our thinking, then we can see clearly and beyond a shadow of any doubt that our experience of the moment is an effect, that it changes when we choose to change our thought.

Our thought, in this earthly realm, is the most important vehicle through which our eternal being is expressing. Our physical world is the effect of this mental vibration or thought. Now our thought, we all like to believe, is what we are constantly, consciously choosing. But upon thorough analysis we quickly learn that it is not, any longer, what we are consciously choosing. It is what we have chosen yesteryear.

We are controlled by the patterns of our mind, the ones that are the strongest. Those patterns of our mind have taken years to become firmly established within our consciousness. How does man, then, free himself from all of the dictates and all of the judgments of yesteryear? It is when we think of self that we become the victims of past experience. When we think of self, the throne of judgment, with all of its negative effects, with all of its prejudices and discriminations, rises up and takes control. We are free in the moment of our choice to be free, but we cannot be free until we choose the freedom of objectivity: to become objective and not controlled by those patterns.

You see, my friends, a thought never dies; it only goes to sleep. Why does it not die? Because thought, the principle of thought, is not something that had a beginning. It is not something that has an ending. Now its form and its effect has its beginning and ending within our consciousness, but the principle of thought is something that is as eternal as the spirit itself. Its expression, as I said, begins and ends.

So we want to be free from these chains that bind us to yesterday. We want to be free that we may have a more abundant, a happier, a more joyful experience today. Then I assure you, my friends, as every great philosophy throughout the ages has taught, free yourself from self. For example, when you are thinking of you, you are controlled by every experience of yesterday that *you*, as you, have associated with. For example, when you want to get a new car or you want to go on a journey or you want to fulfill some other desire of your mind, if you are thinking of you, then all of the limitations, all of the judgments, all of the prejudices, all of the denials, they rise up and take control of your thought, your act, and your activity. To begin any endeavor in life with the thought of self is to guarantee the continuity of yesterday's experiences. If we have gone into business or some profession in our life and we choose to make a change, in that choosing if we think of self, we will only repeat the experiences that we have already had. Oh, they will take a different form. We will meet different people. We will have what appears to be different experiences, but when we look with the light of reason and common sense, we will see, though the people are new, though the experiences *appear* to be new, it's the same old thing all over again.

Many times in our lives many people, starting off with a burning desire to be successful in something, they choose a business or something else and they seem to [be] becoming successful. But then something happens and failure—which is success, the negative effect of success—failure takes hold in their life. And so they walk away from that negative success and they feel badly for a time. And they attract into their life another endeavor and they're going to try again. Because they have not freed themselves from the thought of I, from the limited computer of yesterday's experiences, the law fulfills itself and there is a repetition of the negative success: another failure. As the experiences continue and failure follows failure, the mind becomes firmly established in the belief that in that particular area of their life they are a guaranteed failure. That very belief becomes the king of their world. And so, no matter what one says, no matter how hard someone may try to help, that created form of negative success becomes their god in the mental realms of experience.

But in our lives, because of the divine, eternal principle of search—and we are constantly searching—we don't all know for what we are searching, but we are searching. That principle in our world is a beautiful, daily demonstration. Look at the department stores and look at the things available for sale in our material world. If man wasn't searching, the manufacturers would not produce so many trinkets for us to find. But they know that principle, of course, in business, and so regardless of what the masses think about economy, the purchasing, the *searching* keeps going on. And we search and search and search.

Now it may seem that purchasing of objects to fulfill our desires is not a search, but that is not true. It is simply that that principle, that eternal principle of searching, is expressing in that particular way.

I have often said, in over thirty-eight years of this work, that man does not need to concern himself with being psychic or mediumistic; he doesn't need to concern himself with the principle of prophecy. All he needs to do is to pause and think. Because if he will pause and think, he will observe. And if he will observe objectively, he will know what's going to happen, for he will see the inevitable, demonstrable laws of life working constantly. You can tell what a person is going to do when you make the effort to know what you're going to do, for we are inseparably a part of one united whole, of one consciousness. When we know our self, then we know the world and everything that is in it. But first we must make some effort, daily effort, to know our self. To know why, in one moment, we desire one thing and in a few moments later, we reject the very thing that we desire.

Why do we desire and then reject what we desire? Because we have censored desire. We have censored what is known as the divine expression for that, the principle of desire, that is what it is. We have censored it by our own judgments. We have limited it. So whenever we have a desire—and as long as we're in self we will desire constantly—as long as we have a desire, we are constantly censoring it. So what happens to all of this divine expression that wells up within our consciousness? It rises up, all of the judgments of past experiences rise up, and we push the desire back down. We suppress it. Day after day and year after year we suppress all of these multitudes of desires. Until we begin to experience what the psychologists call frustration. It has been said by many that we live in a very frustrated society.

The teaching of freedom and liberty is not the teaching of license. License simply means to do what you want to do, when you want to do it, how you want to do it, without any concern for the effect or anyone else. That is license. And when we are in license, we are not considering our whole being. We are only considering a limited, momentary desire. But when there is law with desire, the light of reason shines. We can look clearly inside. We can see our patterns of mind and we know beyond a shadow of any doubt not only what it is we desire, but why we desire it. That is what is so important to all of us. To desire is the way of things. To know why we desire, why we express the divine principle in a particular way, that is what's important in life. To find the cause of anything is the first step and guarantee of its own cure.

Why should we limit this great power that is flowing through us? We only limit it by an error in our thought. But it is our thought. It is our error and we can change it. It is said that man is the effect of his own beliefs and how very true that is. Why should we believe in poverty and destitution? Why should we believe in lack and limitation when we have been given the divine power to believe in the goodness and the abundance of everything?

You see, my friends, a working philosophy is what you apply and you can only apply it when you believe it. And how does man believe something? How does man believe a seeming new experience in his life? That depends on how free he is from self, how free he is from all of those patterns and experiences of yesterday. In our world it appears that many have turned their back on religion, that many have turned away from the philosophies of old. But we must ask, if we have turned away, did we ever apply, did we ever really believe? Because if we didn't apply and we didn't believe, we couldn't experience what was there for us to experience.

The human ego serves a beautiful, constructive purpose when the light of reason is in control of it. For without the drive of the human ego, there would not be progress, change, and evolution in this world of creation. Therefore, because it was designed to serve constructive good, is it not sad when, through our errors, it serves the opposite? Man gains—if you can call it gain—success in his life in keeping with his efforts not to be controlled by the negative, limited aspects of yesterday.

It is stated in many philosophies that all things are possible to he who believes. How often do we ask our self that question? Do we ask our self, "Are all things to me possible?" Do we really stop and think? When we desire so many things, do we ask our self if it's possible? Do we become aware of what it is within our mind that says it is not? Do we make the effort on the inward journey to go inside to trace that thought pattern to its original cause? If we would simply do that, if we would say to our self, "All of my experience I know is taking place within my own head. It's my choice. Do I believe that all things are possible? If I do believe and I am not happy with this thought and I am not happy with this experience, then let me change it. Let me go, in the light of reason and common sense, and find the cause of my thought and find the cause of my feeling, for it is mine; it's taking place within my mind." My friends, if we would simply do that often each day, we could lay aside the philosophies of the world, for they would not be needed, for the truth lies within us. The philosophies of the world, including this, the Living Light Philosophy, is simply making the effort to show you a way to go inside of yourself, for that's where your freedom, your truth, and everything that is worthwhile truly exists.

The error is when you permit your mind to tell you that the experience, the cause of the experience is outside of your mind, that the cause is another person, a circumstance, a place, or thing. The moment you do that, you have lost the power of your own freedom. Your God becomes the false god of creation in that moment. Think of that, my friends. Think more often and more deeply whenever you permit your mind to blame, to dictate to you that you don't have what you desire because—the word *because* is the problem, for that's the first step that sends your little mind into the delusion of the past and gives your precious freedom to a thought form.

How often in the course of a day, how often we do that. We're doing it all the time. We give that precious power to our employers. We give it to our husbands, our wives, our relatives, our friends, our enemies. We give it to the government. We give it to society. We throw it away. The Bible teaches us: "Cast not thy pearls before the swine." And here we cast this precious freedom constantly before the swine of the errors of thought. Each time we do that, we go into bondage. Fear, known in this philosophy as negative faith, becomes supreme. We then become the slave of this created master in our own head. Be not with fear, for we are the creators of things. Fear, we created. We can put it to sleep.

We can move onward into a positive attitude of mind, for it's such a beautiful world in which we live. Each time you tell yourself that truth, each and every time, that pattern of mind becomes stronger in your life and your world gets more beautiful each and every moment. But, you see, we've got to tell our self those simple truths so often because we've told our self the opposite for so many years.

Life, after we leave this physical world, it's not heaven, it's not beautiful, it's not even hell, unless that's what you have this moment. The moment you leave this world, you won't find heaven unless you have heaven now. And you won't find hell unless you have hell now. For your mind will not go through some miraculous change. It doesn't work that way, I can assure you from personal experience. If your thoughts are heavenly today, then you are in heaven, and life is beautiful. And if you leave your physical bodies this moment, that's where you will be. For our world is ever as we are within. If our world within is filled with judgment, if our world within is filled with fear, then that is the world that we are in. Those are the type of people we will attract unto us, for like attracts like and becomes the Law of Attachment. We won't attract anything different until we make the difference by a little change inside our self.

What have we truly to fear? We only fear what we don't understand, and we don't understand what we make no effort to understand. So if you want to be free from fear, then make some effort to understand: to understand how your mind works, to understand the way of things, to understand the purpose and the principle of life. For the truth is ever available to you. The truth is inside of you.

The religions and philosophies of the world are designed to help guide you back inside of yourself. We've only lost the way when we think that the cause of anything in our life is outside. If you want to speak of lost souls, those are the only lost ones that I have ever found: the ones who blame outside for what is going on inside. Let us remember that outward manifestations are revelations of inner attitudes of mind. Let us grow in this moment. Let us grow up. We don't need a mommy and a daddy to blame our experiences on. We are adults. Let us face personal responsibility. Then we can see what a great life this truly is. There's nothing outside that you ever need, unless you believe that error of thought.

Thank you.

DECEMBER 3, 1978

Church Lecture 85

A New Dawn

Speaking with you today on the topic of "A New Dawn," we all realize, I am sure, that we cannot experience to the fullest anything that is new until we let that which has passed go from our consciousness. Each moment that we face this life eternal, which is the now, the moment of now, we are guided and controlled by the experiences of our past. When we make this conscious effort to let those experiences that have passed in our life to truly pass and not guide and control and dictate our tomorrows, then we can live in the eternal moment. Then in that eternal moment, we have the fullness and the goodness of the new experiences and the new lessons that are waiting for us to learn.

We look over the world and are ever seeking something. That something we call by many names. Each time we find what we thought we were seeking, it does not fulfill our life. And so we go on this eternal search, ever looking outward for the beauty, the goodness, and the heaven that is residing within us at all times. When we accept that all of life is taking place within our own consciousness, that it is not dependent upon anything outside of us, then we begin to truly live, and we begin to fulfill the purpose of our soul's journey here on this Earth planet.

Because we hold to things, to the things of the mind—we hold to our thoughts, we hold to our feelings—we stunt, so to speak, our own growth. Yesterday is not where the goodness of life exists, for the goodness of life cannot exist in that which has passed, which is returning to the source from whence it came. As a thought held in consciousness is composed of a mental substance and that mental substance is an ever-flowing source, we have the responsibility not only to our self, but to the worlds in which we live, to let freely return to the source that which has come from it.

And so in our relations with people and this material world, we soon realize, as we make the effort to awaken within, that everything, everything in our life and everything that we think is not yet in our life, is dependent upon our own thought. It is our thought. And because it is our thought, it is a child that we alone have created. We are responsible for the growth of that child. We are responsible to release it when it matures. For all things, they are born, they grow, they mature, and they return to their source. Our physical bodies and all physical things, we easily view as growing and returning. But how many of us accept that the thoughts of our mind, that we alone create, are born and grow and they must pass? When it is their time of maturity, their time to return to the source from whence we have garnered them and we insist upon holding to them, we begin to decay inside. We decay with that which by the very laws of evolution is in a process of decay and return.

And so we quickly see that our problems in life are only the things that we are holding to beyond the purpose which they were born to serve. For example, when we think of how good yesterday was and yesterday has grown and matured and is in the process of returning to its source, then a part of us, a part of our emotional and mental body attached to that thought and to that feeling, is decaying. And then we feel discouraged. We feel discouraged because we no longer experience the enthusiasm that we think we experienced in our youth. Youth is an attitude of mind. It is not dependent upon a physical form. And so it is our attitudes that are ever in a process of change or if not, we soon lose the enthusiasm that we once thought we had.

To look to life in the spirit of joy is to be a part of the fulfillment of life. To look to life with the negativity of discouragement and disgust, to look to life with hopelessness is not to look to life at all. Let go of that which has matured and by the very law must return unto its source. When we stop living in yesterday, we will truly start enjoying today. But we cannot enjoy today as long as we hold to those thoughts and feelings, to those attitudes that have long ago served their purpose.

We hear so much in our world today about the freedom—the freedom of minorities, the freedom of this and the freedom of that. Freedom is not something that is outside of your grasp. I assure you, in keeping with the law that like attracts like and becomes the Law of Attachment, that all of these outward experiences, like a great magnet, we are pulling into our lives. If you have and entertain a negative attitude about anything, you will call forth from the universe everything to support it.

So there we find ourselves, not only with a great weight of responsibility for our own life, but a responsibility, through indirection, of all the lives around and about us. Not only the human lives, but the life in nature, the life in the animals and the birds and the insects. We are an inseparable part of that stream of consciousness. If our attitudes are negative, that that is around and about us—be it plant or human—responds accordingly. When we wonder, as so many do, why we don't have what they call a green thumb, all we have to do is ask our self the question, "Do I love this plant as much as I love myself? For if I do, I will care for it accordingly." It is our feelings that all of life is receptive and responsive to.

If we are so overly concerned with our self-thought, then there is no room for us to experience the universality of goodness which is all around and about us. We stand in our own light and, therefore, cannot find the way. When we begin to think of something beyond our limited thoughts that flood our consciousness from day to day, then we begin to free our self from our self.

A successful life is a life that is harmoniously in the eternal stream of consciousness, ever changing, ever growing, ever prospering. When we think that we are not successful or prosperous in any endeavor that we have chosen in life, we can be rest assured that we are holding to the decaying process. Therefore, we are not receptive, nor can we see, that which is being born. When we view the night, we think we do not see the light, but what we see in truth is a lesser light. And if we are grateful for the crumb of a lesser light, then we guarantee, through the Law of Gratitude, the greater light. But if our needs are such that we must have the greater light and we do not have the patience for the natural process of birth and growth of the lesser light, that greater light will ever elude us, for we stand in the midst of it and, therefore, we cannot see.

In this new year, it will be as prosperous, it will be as abundant, it will be as good as you alone choose to accept it in your thought. If you find difficulty in accepting the principle of success, it simply reveals to you, as a personal demonstration, that you are not yet ready, willing, nor able to let go of that which has passed. And because we, perhaps at times, are not willing to let go of that which has served its purpose in our evolution, we do not move forward and cannot see the greatness and the beauty of life that is here and now.

When we listen to the news and we hear so much disaster and destruction, so much negativity that the world seems to be flooded with it, we must remember that that is someone's viewpoint. It does not have to be ours. But if we choose to make that viewpoint ours, then in that choosing we must accept the responsibility of what it will bring into our life.

Our life is not dependent upon anything outside until, through the error of ignorance, we make it so. For everything necessary for our joy and happiness exists within us. It is our error in thought that makes the judgment: for us to experience success and happiness, we must go beyond and outside of what is within us. I can assure you, you may search the universes over, incarnation after incarnation, you will not find home by going away from home, for your home is wherever you are. So it's up to you where you choose to be. If you choose your home to be one of a harmonious flow of beauty and goodness, then it's totally dependent on guarding your own thought. You see, my friends, thought is the cause. The effect or experience is dependent upon your thought. It is your thoughts that create your attitude and it is your attitude of mind that establishes the law in your life. For in this mental and material-physical world we are a law unto our self. And until, through the use of common sense, we choose to use the law for the benefit of our self, then we are going to experience the opposite. For no man, in this world or any world, is qualified to help another until they have first helped themselves. The Bible teaches that great truth when it states very simply "O physician, heal thyself," for only in so doing can you be qualified to heal another. And so it is that truth is taught through indirection, demonstration, and example. You cannot, and are not—none of us—qualified to help another to the success and the goodness of life if we are not doing so for our self. We cannot change others. We never will. It is contrary to the natural Law of Personal Responsibility. We can change our self and, in so doing, in keeping with the law that like attracts like, be an instrument through which another chooses to change themselves.

Along the spiritual path in life, it takes, indeed, a great deal of effort, for it took, indeed, a great deal of effort to create the problems that we find in our life. They just didn't happen by so-called accident, for there are no accidents in truth. So whatever it is that you think you face in this moment, in this year ahead, remember that it is in keeping with what you alone choose to set into motion.

So often in the study of this, the Living Light Philosophy, a student will say that they have tried and the months have passed and perhaps even the years, but there's been no change. There's been no change in the level of consciousness from which they speak, for no effort in that level of consciousness was ever made. Now there is no question that effort was made in other levels of consciousness and when, from those levels of consciousness, they speak, they readily and willingly admit the changes that have taken place for the better in their lives.

We all know from our own personal lives that we have many levels of consciousness, for one moment we find our self with certain attitudes towards life, only in the next moment to find ourselves in totally different attitudes of mind to life. These represent and express the various levels of consciousness through which our eternal soul is moving and expressing.

It is a matter, then, of gaining control of one's vehicle of expression, known as the human mind, not to let it wander around in the universe in any level that it so chooses. It is a ship of which, by the very laws, *you* are the captain of. You certainly would not want your suit that you wear or your dress to tell you where you are going, to tell you that it's taking you here and there, whether you like it or not. No one wants to think that they are so controlled by a vehicle designed for them to use for their own eternal good, but I assure you that Life herself—our personal lives—reveal day after day, experience after experience, that that is exactly what the vehicle of our eternal soul is so often doing to us.

We all have had experience in our life when we found it most difficult to still our thought, when certain feelings rose up and we lost control of our mind, that we said and did things that a moment later we sincerely wish we had not. What does that reveal? It reveals the various levels of consciousness. It reveals a lack of control. And because of this lack of control we experience regret, we experience sorrow, and we experience these many negative functions. We don't need to experience those things. It is not necessary for us to suffer to be free. By our divine birth, we already are free. We *are* free. It is when our minds, without control of the faculty of reason—which is an expression of our eternal soul—our minds take us into these many different things. That's when we experience what we know deep within our self is bondage.

That we have difficulties at times in changing our thoughts and our feelings, that we experience fear—any man true to himself cannot experience fear. It is not possible to experience fear when you are true to yourself. For when you are true to yourself, you are not dependent upon anything outside of yourself and, therefore, have nothing, but nothing, to fear. It is when we become dependent on the great error of ignorance, which is the dependence on something outside of our own universe, that we experience fear. Fear, it is stated in this philosophy, is a function of the human mind. It is known as the control of the mind over our eternal being. It's negative faith. We do not have to live that way. There is a better way. The way that we all know: to go deep within, beyond the disturbing waters of thought, to find our true home.

Some of us, I'm sure, believe that this earth life is a new experience for them, but that's only the illusion of the mind, for each of us are evolving throughout these universes. This is not the first physical experience on a physical planet. It surely is not the last. And because we are, in truth, the circle and because there is, in truth, no escape from being, then let us choose to be that which brings the great power of peace into our life. Let us not permit our minds to any longer delude us that we need anything. For it is in that type of thinking that we begin to chase the rainbow, that we have to move from place to place, ever searching for a home that our little minds are keeping us running away from.

When you find difficulty in being still, when the thoughts rise up without your conscious choice of calling them forth, then awaken, my friends, for they have control of you. They are no longer serving their true purpose. They are designed for you to consciously choose them into your experience. They were not designed to rise up whenever they felt like doing so.

So take a few moments each day and every day and be perfectly still. If you have awareness of thoughts that you haven't chosen to experience, then you know how much work is yet to be done. But if, in your efforts to be still a few moments each and every day, you are truly still—no thought rises in your consciousness, no feeling—there you have entered the perfect void of your divine birth. And there, because in that great divine void, you are the cause of everything, that you are inseparably the essence of all things, there are no ripples of the water. There is the perfect peace, which is in truth your being.

Thank you.

JANUARY 7, 1979

Church Lecture 86
Review and Renewal

In speaking on this topic of, "Review and Renewal," we look at the many experiences that we have already had in our lives and we often think and place our attention upon the seeming mistakes and errors that we have made. However, as we review our life and the many things that we have already allowed ourselves to experience, there is always the renewal of hope. For no matter how difficult things may seem to be, or have been, experience has already revealed to us that hope, indeed, springs eternal within us.

In this evolution that we are in, when we willingly accept the changes in our life—for indeed they are many—then we can move more harmoniously along the evolutionary path.

We all know that something does not come out of nothing and I am sure that none of us consider ourselves to be nothing. So it is that coming from something—that that comes from a thing is destined by the law to return to it. And as we go out into this world and we see the many things that distract our minds for a time, we always return to that source within. That's where our true home really is. No matter how long a time we wander, we shall forever and ever return within, to the source and to the true cause of life itself.

Whenever we permit ourselves to encourage ourselves we begin to find that life takes on a more positive, a more joyous meaning for us. It is in those times that we permit our thinking to be discouraging, to be negative, to look at our lives and think that it's not worth it—and in a sense, of course, the present experience may not, to our conscious minds, be worth it, but it has been brought to us by us in order that we may grow through it and find the something greater that is indeed within us.

If we have spent our lives looking outside to gather and to garner in the hopes that it would bring us happiness, peace, and the goodness of life, then by that very thinking and judgment we guarantee the necessary experiences that we may free our self from that error in our thinking.

And so it is time and time again the philosophies of our world have taught, it is indeed inside. It's all deep within us. All our hopes and all our fears, all our joys and all our sadness is created by a thought, an attitude of mind that we permit to exist within our own consciousness. We don't have to do that, for we know from experience already that there are moments when we feel the goodness and greatness of life itself. So it is indeed a conscious choice. Although we may think we are not aware of consciously choosing to be miserable, of consciously choosing to be sad, that choice is, in truth, a conscious choice that we have made. If that conscious choice, which usually is made very early in life—there is no law of nature or law of man that dictates it cannot be changed. For we are all aware of changing many of our attitudes from what they were in our earlier days on this planet. And so this great Law of Evolution, that clearly reveals that change is indispensable to the inevitable Law of Evolution, is indeed taking place within us.

Because we often cannot see the reason and the purpose of a lesson that we are in does not in any way detract from its value and its necessity for us. These lessons of life and these growth steps are not created by some intelligent being in some universe somewhere. It has not been done by any force or any power outside of our self. We alone have chosen the experience and we and we alone are the only ones who can, and will, grow through it. Once accepting that demonstrable, simple truth, we can indeed encourage ourselves, for we can review the many lessons that are already passed. And we can clearly say, "Yes, that did pass me by. Yes, indeed, I am today free from that type of thinking, free from that attitude, and free from that judgment." And so it is that this faculty, this hope constantly is with us.

Ofttimes a person will become so discouraged they look for an avenue of escape, but all of life clearly shows us there is no escape. Death is not an ending; it is a continuation of your present thought, your present attitude of mind. And so it is in this philosophy those who have truly accepted it are not so foolhardy to attempt to escape from themselves. We cannot escape from the laws that we alone have established. We can, however, awaken to those laws. We can awaken to the reason why we set them into motion and, in so doing, take corrective measures in our own attitude and change the forthcoming experiences.

This philosophy teaches that repetition is the law through which change is made possible. And so we see that Law of Repetition everywhere around and about us and within us. We know very well that when we are feeling discouraged that the thought continues to repeat itself within our mind. But sooner or later, the thought changes, for that is the Law of Repetition.

And so, my friends, as you find these ofttimes irritating experiences and you look at your life in review and you see that certain experiences have continuously repeated themselves year after year, day after day, and month after month, be of good cheer. For when that repetition has reached its saturation point, the change will come about.

It will come about much quicker and much sooner if you will allow your mind to accept the Law of Personal Responsibility. When you permit yourself to accept that simple light of demonstrable truth, what you do is awaken your own soul. For it is our soul that knows that truth. It is difficult for our mind to accept it. Anyone who has had experience with so-called accidents knows very well that their mind has found the cause to be outside. Someone ran into their car while they were driving on the freeway; but it wasn't someone else who made the choice to be on that particular freeway at that particular moment in order for the experience to take place for us. It was we and we alone who made that choice. We may justify that we were on our way to work. We may justify that that was the logical route that we had always taken. We can justify anything at any time to suit a particular level of consciousness that we find our self in. But when we pause in all of that and when we truly accept that we, our soul, chose this earth in keeping with the laws it had already demonstrated, that it knew beyond a shadow of any doubt the experiences that were—and lessons—that were ahead of it, then we can see more clearly.

There is no need to question the tomorrow when we know the today. You see, the day is our day; we view it the way we choose to view it. Circumstances and so-called accidents, they're only effects. We chose the family in which we were reared. We chose the country. We chose the race. We chose that. There was no accident that brought us to earth. There is no accident that's going to free us from earth. If we entertain for a moment that we can escape the lessons that we are facing, you may be rest assured your physical body returns unto physical elements, but you have identified with a mental body, that that you have created. Your physical body is the effect of that mental body and your mental body does not return to the physical elements of this Earth planet. It is composed of mental substance. It is not a physical substance; it is energy. You have identified with that body of energy, and within that body of energy is every experience you have ever had in all of evolution, is every attitude and every thought and every feeling that you have ever experienced. And so to try to escape is not only foolhardy, it is impossible by simply discarding the physical body.

You've heard much, I am sure, about spirits in the realms of heaven and so-called spirits bound to earth. What is it that binds us to anything? It is our own identification with it. As we believeth, indeed, shall we becometh. And so if we identify with the good in life, we are identifying with the goodness that is within us. And it is that that is within us that attracts its kind in the world in which we live. If we choose to see the abundant good of life, then that abundant good of life, that exists in potential within us, will be the strongest vibration emanating from our aura or energy field. Therefore, if you find in your lessons in life, if you find that you attract unto you things that are not pleasant, beneficial, or good, stop in that moment. Because that experience is not only taking place inside your own mind, it is being created by your own mind.

It is not someone else that makes us happy or sad. If we think that it is, then we have lost the most precious gift known to the eternal, human soul: the so-called gift of freedom. For that which disturbs our mind reveals the greatest truth: that is what controls our mind. And so if you permit yourself the error of thinking that something else—be it a person, place or thing—brings you goodness, brings you joy, and brings you the things that you desire, in that thinking you are the victim of that person, place, or thing.

Surely that bondage is not something that we would reasonably, consciously choose. For when you find yourself believing that way, remember that you are controlled by that vibration. When you find yourself so attached and bound to another person or place or thing, whenever that person, place, or thing, in keeping with the Law of Evolution, changes its vibration in the slightest degree, so are you affected, so are you controlled and victimized.

That gift of freedom—to freely choose, to be free in the depths of our being—is not something any of us wish to consciously cast aside. But we do it so frequently. We do it in the jobs that we have, for we give power to our employer. We do it with the finances of the country in which we live, for we give power to all those things. And because we give away that great power, we are controlled by those we have given it to. That, I assure you, is not the purpose of this the Living Light Philosophy.

But we must be consciously, constantly aware of what we are doing to our self. We must ask our self the question, "Can we live and live fully without the things that we think we have to have?" If our answer is in the affirmative, then we are free in that area of consciousness. But if we believe that we have to have this, and so much of it, and we have to have that, and so much of it, then we are bound; we are controlled. No one outside did it. An error that we permitted in our thought has done it to our self.

You see, my friends, it's called negative faith and negative faith to our world is one word, known as fear. And so it is said, "The thing I fear the most has befallen me." And how true and how demonstrable. For that that we fear the most, we tenaciously believe in. We don't have to fear. There is no law of nature that says that we must fear, for we have the choice to direct this great power, this great power called faith. We have the choice to direct it to the limits of our mind and experience what is known as fear or negative faith, or we have the choice to direct it back to the source from whence it came and experience the true fullness of life.

No one cares to choose to believe in a God that is limited, that is partial, that is stingy. No one consciously cares to believe in that type of God. But we must ask our self the question, "How often do we express, how often do we demonstrate our belief in that type of a limited god?" Those are the false gods so often spoken of by the prophets of old, for they are the gods created by our mind. Whenever we give power to anything over our life, we have, in that moment, created that type of god. It doesn't matter whether or not it is a political god, it is a money god, or any other type of god. Our minds are limitless in their creation. And so we create many gods. Those are the gods that must fall in order for us to be free.

Whatever stands between you and your freedom, your fullness of life, whatever you think is the obstruction, you may be rest assured that is the false god that will fall someday, that you may know beyond a shadow of any doubt the peace that passeth all understanding, that is not dependent upon form, and, therefore, the true purpose of life is fully expressed.

Thank you.

FEBRUARY 4, 1979

Church Lecture 87
The Winds of Change

In speaking with you today on this topic, "The Winds of Change," so often we find, in our lives, the intense desire to bring about certain changes in our life that we find distasteful. But we do not, at those times, consider that by the very thought and desire to make some change in certain areas of our life we have established the very law to bring about those changes. In all of our experiences we see this evolutionary process taking place. Change is inevitable. And so it is only a matter of viewing, from an objective vantage point, what is really taking place in our lives. We find the things that we hold so dearly to us, sooner or later, they leave us. They go through a process of birth, a process of growth, and decay.

Whatever in life is form is brought about from the formless into the mental world of form. The effect thereof is what we know as a physical world. From an idea of the Divine Spirit, we experience these untold numbers of things in the universe. But they, being form, are temporary. They are not lasting, nor enduring. And so it is with the thought of man. A thought is a form composed of mental substance. It will only be with you for a time. That time, of course, is ever dependent upon the energy that is directed to it to keep it with you.

And so it is in these things that we want to change in our life, that we think so much about. Each thought releases energy to continue the experience that we no longer desire.

So often we think that the experiences we're having were not a conscious choice that we had consciously made, but that is only our lack of understanding the law by which all things take place in our life. We cannot think of the good without experiencing the good. We cannot think of love without experiencing love. But our minds have limited and have judged what love is, have judged what all things for us should be. To free our self from these errors of ignorance in our evolution is the true purpose of our soul's evolution.

We have, each moment in this great eternity, the golden opportunity, the golden opportunity to be the instrument of the Divine. This foundation upon which all of us, in truth, stand—the foundation of personal responsibility—is not something that we can, this moment, consciously choose or not choose. It is something that in our eternal evolution we have earned; we and we alone have merited. And so it is by these laws of divine, free choice, by that very law, man has become responsible to all his thoughts, to all his acts and activities.

And so it is that we find in these winds of change, we find the storms of life. And when we wonder when they're going to pass, they seem to continue to go on and on and on.

This philosophy clearly teaches that we have a tendency to become whatever we place our attention, our thought upon. And so in these changes that all of us, in truth, are desiring, we must remember whatever our attention is upon, we, by the law of directing that energy to it, are guaranteeing its continuity. They say that it is human to forgive, to give forth; that it is divine to forget. And indeed it is the Divinity within us and only that Divine Spirit, by the Law of Total Acceptance, that can move freely onward and forget the multitude of experiences that we have already encountered. When we permit ourselves to be discouraged, when we permit ourselves to be disappointed with the way our lives are going, we guarantee the continuity of the discouragement and the continuity of the disappointment.

All philosophies, in truth, teach that whatever we believeth, we and we alone becometh. It is a matter of becoming aware—aware each and every moment of our life. What is it that we believe? Do we believe in poverty? Do we believe in the lack? Do we believe in a God that is partial or do we believe that we are an inseparable part of a Divine Source? If we truly believe that we are an inseparable part of a Divine Source, that man calls

God, and that to this Divine Source all things are possible, then we shall experience the possibility of all things in our life. It is only our limited thinking that stands between us and the very source of our life.

So whatever it is that you want in life and if you want it from the Divine Source and do not dictate that it must come from another, then you have established the law to experience that which you, by the law of divine, free choice, have a right to have. It is when we permit our mind to dictate how we will experience what we choose to experience, that is when the mental law becomes established for us. When a mental law is established, it is limited by whatever the mind has accepted prior to our experience.

Because man's memory is not as infallible as he would like to think that it is, he does not see clearly the mental law or man's law that he is establishing with the desires of his mind. For example, when we desire these changes, that we want success and we want the things that our minds tell us are outside of us, in that moment, by entertaining that thought and that desire, it travels through our mind into the deep recesses of our so-called subconscious and every similar experience—similar in principle—that we have ever had, not only in this short earth life but in all evolution through the mental worlds, rises up and establishes the mental law by which it may come into our life. For we have denied, by the desire, we have denied the true source which brings it to us.

Desire, we understand in the Living Light Philosophy, is the expression of the Divine. We also understand that desire is blind. Now that seems, at first glance, to be a contradiction. If desire is divine and divine means God, then how can it be blind? Desire is blinded by the thought of man. It is blinded the moment that man decides how he will experience the fulfillment of the desire. That is the blindness that man and man alone, through his own errors, has established in his own life.

Whatever it is, whatever change you desire, if you will only remember the source that brings it to you and you will not permit your mind to judge and to dictate when it will come, from who it will come, and how it will come, if you will only remember and keep your mind still, then your waiting will not be as long as your mind likes to think it will.

The years for all of us, here on earth, they pass very quickly. None of our minds know the exact moment when we will leave permanently this physical, earthly realm. But we are in the very process of going, for we are in the process of evolution and when we have reached that point in so-called time to be freed from the shackles of this physical world, we'll take everything that's in our mind with us. You see, we *do* take it with us, for it is our mind, which is the vehicle through which our little soul is expressing, that goes on. It's not composed of physical, earthly clay; it is composed of mental substance. So all of our thoughts, our attitudes, our feelings, they go with us. There is no dramatic change in consciousness at the moment of so-called death. There is only the experience of leaving the physical body, of being lighter and freer, as though a heavy weight had been removed from us. But our thoughts, they are the same, until we alone make the effort to change them.

If we believe that the world to which we are going is filled with roses and angels playing harps, then we create that in our mind. And as long as we are experiencing our limited mind, then that's what we will experience when we leave the physical body. But we won't stay in that realm, that mental realm forever. For nature has already revealed to us we do not stay in this physical world forever.

With so much investigation in this day and in the century past into the religion and science of Spiritualism, so many spirits, so many mediums have given so many different descriptions of the world of spirit. But does not man give so many different descriptions of this old earth of ours on which he travels? And so is it not understandable, when he leaves this physical world and he still has this so-called free choice and independence, that he would describe his abode a bit differently than the one next to him. And so it is as this veil is lifted between this physical world and these other dimensions—there are many dimensions.

How does man enter the world of spirit? Why, he enters it when he has a spiritual vehicle in which to travel to it. We don't automatically go from this physical world into a world of spirit unless we have entered that world of spirit with a spiritual body that is altogether and ready to go to it here and now. Spiritualism is not a religion of pie in the sky, of a heaven that is hereafter, if the pie in the sky and the heaven is not here and now. For heaven is not a place that we're going to unless we've already grown to it today. So let us grow to this heavenly state of consciousness by making some effort to bring harmony, the divine law, into our life in its fullness. How do we experience harmony, unless we're making some effort to bring about a unity within our own mental, emotional realm of consciousness.

It is said that which disturbs us is that which controls us. Now we're all seeking to be free, to be free from so many things, our mind tells us. But all we have to do is to pause and to think. "What in my life is controlling me? Do I have thoughts and feelings that I find uncomfortable, that when I experience them, they cause me anger and cause me to be miserable and sad? If I have those thoughts, those feelings, and those attitudes, then I know what is controlling me in my life." Once we know the thoughts and attitudes that are controlling us in our life, then we can go to work on bringing about a change. If a thought repeats itself in your mind and that thought is not bringing you the fullness of joy in your life, then you may be rest assured that it is that thought that's controlling your life. But do not be discouraged, for discouragement will only guarantee the continuity of that negative thought. You can change by redirecting the divine, neutral, infinite, intelligent energy to any other thought that you choose to entertain in your mind.

I have never, in these thirty-nine years in this work, found a God that dictates that any of his children must be without. That is not the type of God that I have found in my life. That does not mean that I have not experienced the errors of ignorance and been without. But in all experience there is some good. If you will look for the good, no matter how disastrous the experience seems to be to you, if you will look for the good that lies within it, then you will gain from the experience and you will move on to greater good. In the seeming worst experience, there is good, for it is this God that is sustaining all of life, and that means the little ant that crawls the ground, as well as the angel that works in heaven. There is no difference to the intelligent, infinite Energy, known to man as God, that sustains everything.

The heaven and the hell, the duality in our beliefs in God, is created by our mind. If you find that your God has deprived you of anything, then you can be rest assured that your god is a created god of which the prophets of the Bible have spoken so long ago. Those are the gods, the idols, that must fall, for they all have clay feet.

When we pray for changes to come about, we are not consciously aware, all of us, that in our very prayer is a mental judgment and dictate to the Divine to whom we are beseeching a change to take place in our life. Do we pray for an understanding of the natural, demonstrable laws of life? Do we pray that we may awaken and see these infallible laws and be inspired to follow them to their inevitable destiny of success and joy in our life? Or do we pray for things? Do we pray that changes be taking place with our self and with others, totally disregarding the natural laws of life through which those things, those changes could be brought about? If we pray for things, then we are yet to be freed from things, and then we are still controlled by the god created by our own mind.

Think, my good friends, the choice is ever within our hands. At any moment we can, by the very law of divine choice, we can choose the beauty of life. We can choose to see the good, or God, in everything, for whatever we place our attention upon, in time, we do become. Now we don't want to become miserable. We don't want to become the struggle in evolution, for we all know, deep within our very being we all know that there is something greater. And indeed that something greater we cannot find in our tomorrows unless we are making some effort to find that something greater today.

This is your, and my, eternity for this is the moment of which we are consciously aware. If we do something with this eternity, which is the moment of our awareness, all concern about tomorrow will disappear and all of those haunting feelings of yesterday, they will disappear.

The fullness of life is restricted by our thought, which creates our attitude. We cannot have the fullness of the moment of which we are consciously aware as long as we insist upon concerning our self with the tomorrows that may never come or with the yesterdays that have long gone. This is our moment and in this moment is the power of God. To realize that is a very small and simple effort: to *be* in the moment of now. To concern ourselves about depressions and recessions, to concern our self about the experiences that have already passed us by is not only a waste of time and energy, but it is so detrimental to experiencing the fullness of life, which is ever in the moment of now. To worry about your job, which may or may not change, to worry whether or not you're going to live alone the rest of your life traps us in mental realms. And in so doing we continue on the karmic wheel, that wheel of constant repetition of the same experience. But be not without hope, for it is, in truth, through the Law of Repetition that change is indeed made possible.

Thank you.

MARCH 4, 1979

Church Lecture 88
Our Ship of Destiny

In speaking with you today on the topic, "Our Ship of Destiny," we understand that our ship, its course, is ever the effect of how we accept the life that we are experiencing. For example, each time that we encounter a denial of the right of God to express, each time that we permit our minds to become superior in our thought to the divine, neutral, intelligent Energy, called God, that is sustaining all life, that is, in truth, all life, each time we rise through our errors of ignorance to dictate the rights and the wrongs of others, we set the law into motion to guarantee the experience that we cannot tolerate another in to befall us. That is known in this philosophy as the first triune soul faculty: the faculty of duty, gratitude, and tolerance.

It is clearly stated in the Living Light that what we cannot tolerate in another we have yet to educate within our self. We are all a part of the so-called human race. We are inseparable from that vibration of humanity of which we are a part. When we look at our world and we see so much struggle and so much difficulty, we are viewing our world from a level that is unwilling to change. As long as we can entertain our thought in our mind how difficult it is to gain what we are seeking to gain, to attain the fulfillment of the desires in our life, as long as we permit our mind to dictate how difficult it is to attain, we establish that law, so that the attainment comes to us at indeed a very heavy, heavy payment. The attainment and payment balance law is in keeping with our own acceptance.

Surely we all realize that we do not get something in life for nothing. The air we breathe, our lungs, they work, they pay for, for they make the effort. And so it is that for everything we desire, some effort is extracted from us. It is a matter of our own willingness. We all have willingness. We all have this divine right of will. There is no one who doesn't have enthusiasm.

There is no one who doesn't have will. It is simply that we do not recognize the direction that someone may be placing their enthusiasm in life.

Whatever you see in another, you may guarantee, for the law is impartial, that it exists within you. So the intolerance to what you see in others reveals the intolerance to that very level that exists within you. If you feel that you do not act the way others act and that you cannot tolerate the way they act, it is only that you have yet to recognize that very thing expressing within yourself. And so it is as we awaken the first soul faculty of our being, that faculty of duty, gratitude, and tolerance, we begin to free our self from the control and the enslavement of these errors of ignorance.

We all are seeking something. The something that we are seeking seems very different to different people, but in truth and in principle, we're all seeking to go home in consciousness to where peace and harmony reigns supreme. That is possible, of course, for all us, for we all came from the same source and we are all on our journey returning to that same source. As we pause in our thought and we make that small degree of effort to know within us—for there is a part within us that knows beyond a shadow of any doubt—to know within us that there is a guiding light, that there is an intelligent Energy, that we, by our very divine birth, have the right to use it to benefit the world. For a man does not benefit the world unless he first benefits himself. You cannot teach another what you have yet to teach yourself because it will fall on deaf ears. And so it states clearly in the Bible, "O physician, heal thyself."

So let us, as we face this year before us, which passes so very quickly, let us, in our daily activities, make some effort to help our self to levels of peace and harmony that are waiting for us to accept. But I assure you, my friends, as long as your thoughts are thoughts of intolerance, as long as your thoughts are dictates and judgments of what others should and should not be doing, then you're far, we're all far, from the freedom and the beauty and goodness that we all are seeking.

The world before us is in keeping with our attitude. Now some may say, "Well, that's not reality." But what, in truth, is reality? Reality is simply a conscious awareness of passing events. Now our conscious awareness is limited by our own dictates of our own thoughts. We look at the day and we may say it is beautiful—to some. It is ever dependent upon what level we are looking through. We all know how we feel better when we experience anything of beauty, for that is the revelation and the demonstration that beauty, in truth, is the smile of God. So let us remember to smile inside, for only with the smile inside, with the experience of the beauty of the awakening of our own eternal soul faculties can we truly sail our ship of destiny upon a course that will bring good unto the world and unto our self.

So often we want things to change, but when it comes to making the effort to involve our self to help the things we want to change to change, we seem to be too busy doing something else. We firmly believe in this church and religion that work is love made manifest and that love, in truth, is the Divine Intelligence, called God. So when we find the opportunity, which is ever before us, to do some work, let us not look at that word as some drudgery in life, for without work, we could not love, we could not fulfill the purpose of our journey on this planet. So whatever it is in life that you want changed, you must first think, "Is that a high enough priority in my life? Am I willing to involve myself and to demonstrate the Law of Continuity or is it a desire that I want some other to have the responsibility to fulfill?" It is so easy to criticize, to be intolerant to the work of others when we are not making the effort to involve our self to do the work that's being done. We can always look outside and find something wrong. But it is not often that we pause in a moment of honesty to look inside to see what changes are necessary in our own attitudes in life.

I assure you, my friends, life indeed is an effect of attitude. It is our attitude that is ours and being ours, we can always change it. But it is a constant job. It is a job that must be worked at each day, each morning, each afternoon, and each evening. To first become aware of how we feel and to accept the truth that how we feel is the effect of how we think. But we can think whatever way we choose, for the way we are thinking this moment is the way we have chosen to think. But we don't have to continue to think that way.

There is something better when you accept the possibility that there is. But there is nothing better in life, until you first accept its possibility. Man flies because enough people accepted the possibility. Man enjoys what he enjoys today because people accepted the possibility. It is that first crumb that is so very important: to accept the possibility of something better, no matter what your experience may or may not be, is to establish the law that will take you to the fulfillment of what you alone are accepting. We are already experiencing what we have already accepted. And if it is something better than what we have that we want—and I know of no one in the sound of my voice that doesn't want something better. Although life is as good to us as we choose to make it, it can always be better.

We are in a constant process of changing. So let us accept that demonstrable evolution, that law that is infallible and inevitable. We are changing whether we want to change or not. Let us accept the possibility that that changing is bringing us ever closer to the home that is ours, to the fulfillment that is, in truth, the real purpose of our being.

The years are very short. We know not the hour, nor the moment, when we leave this physical earth. But we do know our mind does not change because we leave the physical body. Whatever your attitude, that is what goes with you. So it's our own thinking. And when we say the struggle is too great, remember, the priority of making the change is not yet very high on our list of priorities. When you feel that the struggle is so great, when you feel there is a shortage of the things you desire, when you feel that someone else has what you really want, remember that in that moment and in that thinking, you are denying the very God that is waiting to bring it into your life, for you are looking with a limited mind, you are looking in the mental realm, you are looking how you can have what you want instead of accepting that the great, intelligent God is ever waiting to fulfill your desires in life. You cannot accept until you first take control of the human mind, the limited vehicle that stands between our soul and the divine, eternal truth. When we still this vehicle of ours, when we bring it into a perfect harmony—for that's what stillness really is—then we will see and we will know beyond a shadow of any doubt that it is only our self that is standing in our own light.

Let us enjoy the short journey that we have here on earth, for that indeed is the will of the Divine. Let us, by the enjoying of this journey that we have, fulfill the true purpose of our being. We know what we're doing. No one needs to tell us that, for in the moment that we pause, we see very clearly. But let us, in that pause, declare our divine right to the fullness of life. Let us dethrone the false gods, created by our mind, of fear, for they bring us no goodness in truth. Any thought that your mind has that denies you the right of beauty, goodness, and peace and the fullness of life is a false god created in errors of ignorance by a limited mind.

Remember, there is no God anywhere at any time that denies anyone anything. This intelligent Energy is constantly flowing around us, about us, and through us. Every experience that we have is an effect of our directing this intelligent Energy. If those experiences have been experiences that we do not enjoy, it is not God, for God is sustaining what we have chosen to think.

So let us think thoughts of beauty. Let us think the goodness of life and in so doing, if we are consistent, if we make just a little effort, we will see the so-called miracle of change before us.

For no matter what your mind thinks about anything, there is always the possibility of change. Things get better when man accepts that they will. And things get worse when man accepts that they will. We are already the living demonstration of how things can get worse. And by viewing that objectively, seeing the inevitability of the law of our own choice, let us choose how things can get better.

When we have so many of these negative experiences we immediately think, "Because of what someone else did, I am having this negative experience and difficulty." So in those seeming rare moments when something good takes place in our life, we forget completely that we gave the credit for the negative experience to someone else, and now that something good is happening, all of a sudden we did it all our self. Now, my friends, that's not the way life really is. True, we made the effort to have the negative experience. And true, we made the effort to have the positive and good experience, but something greater sustained and supported our choice. So let us never forget that. That something greater is waiting for you to use, not to abuse, but to use.

We know the negative experience, in truth, is an effect of our thought, and so is the positive experience. So why not enjoy the goodness of life by flooding your consciousness with a positive acceptance of what it is you choose to desire as long as you do not judge that it must come from another? For the moment you judge that your goodness in life must come from a person, place, or thing, you deny the very intelligent Energy that will sustain it and, therefore, become a victim not only of the thoughts of others, but first of the thoughts of yourself.

So, my friends, as long as we're on earth using this mental and physical body, this automobile that we're driving around by our thoughts, well, let's drive it where we want to go. Let us put the brake on and tell this mind of ours, which is like a car, "That's where I'm going on my ship of destiny. You will no longer tell me where you want to go. I will tell you where I want to go."

It is only this great delusion, known as the king I, the thought of I, that stops us from enjoying life. Because in the thought of I is the denial of God. The moment your mind says "I," you separate yourself from the eternal Source, from the intelligent Energy, known as God, that is flowing through everything and, in so doing, are totally dependent upon a mental realm, a mental substance. In that moment you have stepped down from the light of the spiritual realms. The faculty of reason, the faculty of patience, of tolerance, and all of the soul faculties, in that moment, are closed. It is known—that thought of I—it is known as the great delusion of self-reliance.

It is interesting to me to note that in this coming year of 1980 that the American Psychiatric Institute will debate whether or not what they call narcissism will be an official mental disease. Now this so-called narcissism is what they understand to be people who are so controlled by the thought of self that they are mentally ill. The question indeed rises and is so interesting: in the debate to reach a decision of whether or not these thoughts of self are a mental disorder, who or what will be making the decision? It will indeed be a most interesting year ahead.

However, it does reveal to us the beautiful progress that is being made in the medical field. For slowly, but surely, they are beginning to accept ancient, indeed, very ancient truths. Though the words may be different, the principle remains the same. Man is the cause and he is also the cure of all his discomfort, of all his discord, of all his disease. Disease is a discord, a lack of harmony between the mental and spiritual body, and the physical body is the effect. When we make the effort to bring about a peace and harmony between our mental attitudes and our spiritual soul aspirations, we will experience the beauty, the wonder, and the goodness of so-called perfect health. We all realize, I'm sure, that none of us are so perfect that we do not experience some discord and, therefore, experience some so-called disease.

Let us place our attention, as we move forward in time, upon what it is we have to do, and do it joyously. No matter what your job in life is, it is an important job. It is important to you. It is what your eternal soul has merited. And in the job, there is much that you can do, much more than you've already done. We limit ourselves by our own thinking. But we have the jobs that are right for us at the time that we have them. So let us be a light into the world, for in so being the Light, the world will be so much brighter for us.

Thank you.

APRIL 1, 1979

Church Lecture 89
Looking Ahead

Today, to us here in Serenity, is indeed a most important day marking the completion of eight years of this church and its weekly Sunday services. The title chosen for today, "Looking Ahead," is indeed, of course, interesting and important to all of us. For as we attempt to look ahead with hope and anticipation of things being better in our lives, we are pulled ever backward to yesterday. It is the backward pull of our own emotions that limit and obstruct our view of the present and the tomorrows. And so it is as we look ahead to the years that we will pass on through and the centuries yet to come, we very quickly realize that it is always and forever our attitude, our hopes, our faith, or our fears that direct us.

So often there are so many things that we want to do, and it is so often difficult for us to maintain and to sustain the wisdom of patience to accomplish them. Many centuries we have already, in eternity, passed through. We do not easily nor often recall those experiences of centuries ago because we are so filled with the seeming problems and difficulties of today. When we make the daily effort to pause, when we stop to think, then we can view this great world with an objective, impartial, and unemotional view of progression.

Whatever the seeming obstructions, struggles, and difficulties that our mind thinks today is offering us, we can turn them around in our thought. [With] each seeming disaster, lying deep within that disaster, [is] the golden opportunity to make a turnaround in our consciousness and bring into our lives the good that we truly are seeking. If we will pause in our thinking and turn around these seeming struggles and problems, if we will make, truly, the effort to view the opportunity, the golden opportunity that lies deep within each and every experience, we will soon find that this great negative fear, this cloud that so often obstructs our view to the beauty of life will quickly disappear.

As we leave this physical body, we enter a world which is indeed so familiar to us. There is no surprise on leaving this earth realm unless we permit our self to be surprised at the thoughts and the feelings that we have entertained for this earthly life. For we are, the moment we leave, the very same as the moment before we go. Time and time again the spirit has revealed there is no drastic change on leaving your physical world. There is only the shedding of a physical suit of clothes. Your mind does not change. No mind, anywhere, changes quickly. It is a slow and progressive process.

If our mind is filled with pain, then we are ever seeking its opposite, known to us as pleasure. If our mind is filled with discord, then we are ever seeking peace. But seldom do we think that they are, in truth, one and the same, the opposites on two ends of the same pole. It is our view that brings about the change.

And so, my friends, the work to be done for all of us, in looking ahead, is not what's out there: a something or someone that we have no control over. It is looking within. It is our view. Our view we can change at any moment. And the most important thing about changing our view is when we change our view, we literally change the laws that we and we alone have established. Therefore, no one, in truth, is lost forever. We are only temporarily lost in the error of our own ignorance of the laws that we alone are establishing.

But we can change that this moment. We can see the good, if we choose to do so, no matter what the experience is. I can assure you after thirty-eight years this year in this spiritual work that with a multitude of seeming negative experiences, that it is worthwhile to stop and see the good. For in so doing we establish new laws in a mental realm in which we and we alone individually are living. Because it is our world, because it is ever in keeping with the way we view it, the cure is in, of course, the cause. So let us make that effort to view this moment in ways that we will feel the goodness and the joy of life. And when we find that our view is changing and we are not feeling the God or goodness in our life, let us stop and make that small effort to change our thought.

It has been stated that heaven is not a place we are going to; that it is, in truth, a state of consciousness that we are growing to. We can grow quickly to that state of consciousness by the willingness to change our view.

I look forward to life, for life, to me, is the greatest wonder of all. I cannot image what so-called death is possibly like. For that that is known as dead is supposedly lifeless, yet we view all the universe and we see that everything is filled with the spirit of life. When we fill our minds with that enthusiasm, with that spirit of life, then we experience all the goodness that it has to offer.

So many millions of souls passing from this earthly, physical realm open their eyes and ears only to hear the echoes of their own thoughts and unfulfilled desires. I do not mean to imply by that demonstrable truth that there are not millions in what we know as heavenly realms, but I do mean to say that there is no intelligence that I have ever been aware of, or am aware of, that brings about an automatic freedom from the thoughts that we alone choose to have. Each day we are preparing for our tomorrows. And because that is a living demonstration, does it not behoove us to prepare more wisely that we may enjoy more fully our tomorrows?

It has been said that luck is a loser's excuse for a winner's position. I do not believe in luck. I believe that man and man alone, as an inseparable part of the Infinite Intelligence, establishes all the laws in his life; that those laws are fortunate, if we care to view them that way, but there's no luck, good or bad, for any of us. Let us not spend our lives in the superstitions of yesterday. For we live in an enlightened age, though we may not think, sometimes, that we do, this is, in truth, the golden age. And there are untold millions of souls in physical bodies that are awakening and accepting the greatest magic wand, if you wish to call it that, that we could possibly have: that great wand of personal responsibility. None of these multitudes of gods of superstition to blame our seeming bad luck upon, no armies of spirits to cast our responsibilities upon, but that wonderful, magic wand of personal responsibility.

And in accepting personal responsibility, let us not forget that our ability to personally respond to anything is sustained by the infinite Divine Intelligence, known as God. For no man is an island unto himself, for no man of and by himself can create life itself. But we can create many things. And we are moving forward in this great golden and scientific age, we are moving quickly forward to the creating of the vehicles or forms through which life expresses. And as we face this great scientific dawn, let us never forget, though man is the creator, let us not be deceived or deluded, ever, into thinking that he is the sustainer, that he in and of himself can create the life force. That he will never, ever, ever do, for he has never, ever had that great power, which is reserved exclusively and forever to the Divine Intelligence, known as God.

So as we travel through the universe in our spaceships, as we become awakened to the many forms that man and his great intelligence is creating, remember, it's not the life, but only the vehicle through which the life is temporarily expressing that man in his great knowledge is creating.

They say that knowledge knows much, but wisdom knows better. So in our choice between wisdom and knowledge—knowledge, which is restricted by limited desire, and wisdom, which is expanded by total consideration. One (knowledge) offers the love of self; the other (wisdom) offers the love of all.

And so, my friends, looking forward each day, looking forward each year, we not only improve our own life, we not only improve and refine the conditions around and about us, but as the demonstrable law that like attracts like and becomes the Law of Attachment, as that immutable law moves over the land, we see the great changes and the good that is ahead.

As we concern ourselves with our mundane and material world over the cost of living, as we concern ourselves with the seeming limited supply of energy and gasoline, we do not stop to think that from this negative experience great good is being born. For already we are hearing of new ways not only of conserving energy, but we hear of new discoveries of seemingly new types of energy. I assure you beyond a shadow of any doubt that this country and this land will not experience a so-called depression equal to that of years gone by, that we will experience a mild recession and from that a greater awakening shall take place for the people of our world, a greater interest in our natural resources, a greater consideration for all of God's children.

Our greatest asset, our greatest benefit, our greatest wealth is our health, our spiritual health, which reflects in our mental health, which reflects in our physical health. If we find our self lacking in this, the greatest asset we know (our health), then let us go to work diligently and religiously upon our thoughts, our attitudes of mind, and what we are doing to our self. For we alone, with the sustaining power of God, can bring about the transformation. For it is in truth our divine right to experience the health, which is the wealth and happiness, that life has to offer. If we, at any time, find our self short in those areas in life, then remember it is only an error in our thought. And because it is an error in our thought, we can change it. We can bring about that transformation.

I have never experienced in my life any God in any universe that denies man his health, wealth, and happiness. It is not God that is the doer, for God is the sustaining power. It is man and his own errors that denies himself. It is also a great and compassionate divine, intelligent Power, called God, that permits us the free choice to deny the goodness of life that is our divine right. Let us never forget that.

For whenever we permit our thinking to dictate to us that we are experiencing the lack of health, wealth, and happiness because of something or someone else, then we have created the false gods who must crumble. The false gods born in error, born in superstition. And we must cast the light of reason upon our mind that we will no longer depend on a rabbit's foot or some other superstition to bring us so-called good luck in life.

Spiritualism, in 131 years this March, has worked diligently to bring a religion, a philosophy of common sense and reason to humanity. There is no need for any of us to have what is called blind faith. There is no need for us to analyze the smallest insect in order to prove to our mind that God exists, for we are the living demonstration of that truth. And as man knows himself, he knows that truth, and he is freed from those errors and those superstitions of yesteryear.

Here in a country with the finest colleges and universities to teach the students, we still find the great battle between superstition and plain old common sense. But that, too, is in a process of change. Many people still will not reside in a hotel if it has a thirteenth floor and rare would be the hotel you could find with a thirteenth floor. Because they're in business and they couldn't rent a room on a thirteenth floor if they had a thirteenth floor. And so they don't mark it number thirteen, for the plain, old, common business sense of renting it. Now we must ask our self why, in this the twentieth century, [is it] that we still permit our mind to control us with superstition. That, surely, is long ago outdated. If you believe that Friday the thirteenth is a day of bad luck, stop and create the so-called good luck, if you still need to hang on to those worn out superstitions of yesteryear.

If you believe there is an end of this world that is coming in some great Armageddon, then believe that it is an end of the world of negativity that you have already been experiencing. For man becomes his own belief. Our world is as it is today because we believe the way we believe. We are impatient and unhappy because we have yet to fulfill our goals in life, because we believe we have yet to fulfill our goals in life. So whatever it is as you believeth in your heart, so shall you becometh. I simply say you have the divine right of choice to believe in that that brings the goodness in your life. And once making that effort to believe, then make the constant effort to sustain the belief that you have chosen.

My good friends, it is not something new for you to do. It is not some added effort, some extra work, for we are already doing those things and our life is telling us what we're doing. We already believe. And if we find that our experiences are negative, then all we have to do is take a look and see that's what our thoughts are.

It's our thoughts that are so important because we are so familiar with our mind and with our mental world. And so it is simple and reasonable that we should study that which we are most familiar with that we may view it with some degree of objectivity. Why concern ourselves so much with our spiritual body when so much of our energy is going into our mental body? Let us first find out what we are doing with our mental body, then we can prepare our self to investigate and study intelligently these other more refined bodies through which our soul is at present expressing.

Therefore, let us look forward with that that is the divine choice within us. Let us choose the path that is joyous, for that is obviously and evidently the intent of the Divine Intelligence. I never saw a sparrow cry. I never saw an animal filled with frustrations. I never saw a little ant crawling along the ground worried about whether the sun was going to shine or it was going to rain. They don't try, those little insects and animals and plants and trees, they don't try to take over the job that belongs to the Divine Intelligence. They have more common sense than to do such a silly thing. So why should we make so much effort to run God's universe, when we've yet to make an ounce of effort to run us, our own universe, with a little more reason and a little more common sense?

Thank you.

MAY 6, 1979

Church Lecture 90
Our Journey Inward

In speaking on the subject this evening, "Our Journey Inward," we find that many of us have investigated so many different philosophies and so many different forms of meditation and contemplation. And we have tried these different ways, many of us, and yet we still seek because we have yet to find that which we believe works for us. And, of course, in any endeavor that which works for us is what we make the effort to make work for us. We all, I'm sure, will agree from our view of this world, this physical world that we see, that there is some type of system and order. The planets, they revolve in space and so do all things move through a progression. And in viewing that in nature, we cannot help but accept the possibility of some intelligent and infinite energy in the universes.

We ofttimes find our self obstructed by the word *God*. We find this obstruction from the disappointments that we have encountered in our own past. But because we have ofttimes been disappointed in our efforts and endeavors is no reason that we should stop in our investigation to find the true purpose of our being.

And so it is this journey inward, which is, in truth, taking place all of the time. We become aware of this journey inward that we are on at all times when we make the conscious effort, the conscious effort to still our mind that we may have an awareness, an inner awareness of our true being. Now there are many, of course, systems and techniques that have been designed to serve that purpose. But like all things in life, it is our motive that establishes the law that we alone must follow. If our motive is pure, then the manifestation for us is right. And so we first must become aware of what our motive is in entering into any endeavor in life, for by becoming aware of our true motive, we know beyond a shadow of any doubt what the outcome will be. For the law is impartial and the law is inevitable.

So often we seek to be satisfied, our senses, and we judge what will bring about for us that satisfaction. But satisfaction without irritation is contrary to the very laws of evolution. We are all in a constant process of change. So often the changes that we are experiencing are not the ones that we consciously think we should be experiencing. But they are only the effects. They are the effects of the mental laws that we alone have set into motion.

And so it is on this journey inward, there is something above and beyond the limited human mind. Indeed, we spend much of our time in the mental worlds. We spend much of our time in our disappointments and in our satisfactions. For every joy that we experience, there's always the guaranteed sadness. For every high, there is the low. For every gain, there is the loss. And that's the way it is in a mental and material, physical world. There's always this Law of Duality and it serves a good and just purpose, for in time it helps us to look for something greater than what the physical and mental worlds have to offer.

It is in that search for something greater that we become consciously aware of this inward journey. If you think this journey is a journey that ends, then stop in that thinking, for it is a journey that did not begin and therefore, it cannot end. We entered this earth and we have this present identity, but that is not something that is eternal, for it had a beginning. Like all things of form that have beginnings, they all have endings.

And so it is the things that we attach our self to that cause us the greatest struggles and the greatest difficulties in life. Each of us knows our own attachments. We know what they are and we know how strong those attachments, in our lives, have become. For when they leave us without our conscious choice, we know how strong they are from the struggle and the suffering and the discouragement when they pass. But if we look at life objectively and we see that all things of form, they come to us, and by those simple laws of coming to us, they all pass from us. So to attach ourselves to anything of form is to guarantee this Law of Duality and all that it has to offer. To use that which is here to be used and not to abuse it is to be freed from it. It is through our error of ignorance that we abuse the things of form in our life, and we abuse them by our attachment and possession of them. And that is when our true struggle really begins.

So let us make a little effort to pause each day a little more often, perhaps, than we have, for in so doing we're going to find that great peace that is within us, that has always been within us, and that always will be within us. It's never out there. That's not where we will find it. In all of our searching, in all of our gathering, and in all of our garnering, we will not find that great peace, nor that great freedom [outside].

So often I have heard from students and members their great drive to be free. Freedom is something that we know deep within our self is our divine, eternal birthright. But when we transgress the simple laws of freedom, then we experience what our mind tells us is bondage. And the greatest transgression of the principle of freedom is the denial of the Law of Personal Responsibility. Whenever we permit our mind to dictate that our problems and our struggles are caused outside by something or someone else in the universe, we deny the Law of Personal Responsibility and place our self in the bondage of our own errors of ignorance.

Personal responsibility is a very easy word to say, but we find it difficult, frequently, to apply. But if we will make that daily effort, that constant effort to truly accept the demonstrable Law of Personal Responsibility, we will be freed from the bondage of our errors. We will no longer need to be concerned about the drives to fulfill our desires, for the principle of desire is the divine expression. We will no longer dictate how things will come, how long they will stay, and when they will go. And in so being freed from those dictates, we will know beyond a shadow of any doubt, consciously, the peace that passeth all understanding and the freedom that is, in truth, our birthright.

Thank you.

JUNE 3, 1979

Church Lecture 91
Reaping the Harvest

In speaking with you today on this topic, "Reaping the Harvest," when we hear those words of reaping a harvest, our minds immediately react. They either react in a positive way or they react in a negative way. It is, of course, ever dependent upon how we judge our experiences of the moment. This philosophy clearly teaches to put God into all our thoughts or to forget them, for a very simple reason. Man, we understand, is a law unto himself. And so a wise man pauses in all of his daily experiences and asks himself the simple question, "What am I doing with the law that I am?" Our experiences, throughout the course of our life and each of our days, are revealing to us, constantly, what we are doing with the law that we are.

In order for us to truly become the captains of our ship and the masters of our destiny, we must first demonstrate the simple Law of Personal Responsibility. Each and every time that we permit our thoughts and our minds to tell us that the cause of the goodness in our life, the cause of the difficulties and struggles in our life are the fault of anything or anyone outside of our self, in that moment the law of slavery, for us, is established. We, in that moment, become the victims of the denial of truth and, in so doing, live in the struggles and in the falsehoods that it offers to us.

However, when we declare that we and we alone are truly responsible for our feelings, that we and we alone are truly responsible for whatever we are seeking in life, when we flood our consciousness with that simple, clear light of common sense and reason, we free our self. We are no longer the slaves and the victims of this error of thinking. We are, in that moment, truly free spirit. We are, in that moment, filled with the goodness throughout our entire universe and we live, from that moment, and see its direct effect in the experiences in this world around and about us.

No matter what our mind may say to us—what a great struggle it is or what a great disaster has befallen us—if we will simply make the effort in that moment, in that type of thinking, and say to our self, "It seems to be a disaster. I feel that it is, but it is only because I do not see yet the good that is in it." Every experience in our life is absolutely necessary for our own evolution because we are a law unto our self. The experiences that we have that continue to repeat themselves in our life do so in order that we will make the effort to change our attitude, to change our thinking, to be free from the bondage that we have, in our errors of thought, created for our self.

Whatever stands between us and the goodness of life shall crumble and fall. It may not seem to be doing so as we keep our eye upon the obstruction, for in so doing we keep the obstruction in our consciousness between us and the Divine Intelligence.

This great infinite Divine Intelligence sustains and supports our right of choice. As we choose to blame outside for our refusal to make necessary changes inside, we continue on this karmic wheel of delusion. Whatever it is that we want to do, opportunity, like the hands of the clock, meets ever so often. And that meeting is taking place when you are ready, willing, and able to view it, for there is nothing that your eyes can view, nor your ears can hear, nor your senses feel that does not offer to you an opportunity to change, to grow, and to thoroughly enjoy the wonder and the beauty and the goodness of life.

Unfortunately, we ofttimes look to others for a better way. We look to see how good we think they are doing. And in so doing we don't have to make the effort to do so "good" our self. Because we view outside and then we excuse the reasons why someone else is doing good to luck or to chance or to circumstance, we deny personal responsibility: that we are the creators of circumstance.

So in order to reap a harvest that is not only filled with abundant good, but peace and harmony and the joy of life, we must first accept that we are the creators. We are the creators of the good in our life. We are the creators of the so-called bad in our life. We are the creators of unfulfilled desires, as we are the creators of fulfilled desires. This Divine Intelligence, known as God, supports whatever you choose to do. So it is indeed up to us what we choose. May we truly make the effort to choose more wisely, to become aware of what we are doing with the law that we are.

All things in our life can be turned around to serve a greater good. And we and we alone are the ones who can turn the circumstances around. So often, I know, some of my students have told me of the difficulties and the struggles that they have. Because their attention is constant upon the obstruction, the way for them, though it's right in front of their nose, they cannot see. We cannot see what we choose not to see. And if we choose to see the struggle, we cannot find the way of peace. But let us ask ourselves, why, why, when we know—and we know deep inside of our heart—why do we choose the struggles of life when we know the path of peace? What do we get from the struggle? Do we receive the attention and the energy of the friends and acquaintances around and about us? Do we receive their pity and their sympathy because our lot in life is such a struggle? And in so receiving their pity, their attention, and their sympathy, do we feel better in those moments?

Let us be honest with our self. We have a great struggle in life if we choose to have a great struggle in life. We have the highs and lows in life, if that is what we choose.

When we accept that we always get what we really want—for we all know the truth of that—when we accept that we always get what we really want and we are experiencing what our minds say is such a struggle in life, then we will find inside of our self what we are getting from the struggle we are creating.

Let us no longer delude our self with blaming God, for that is a false god, and that god has not brought us any good to this moment. Those are the false gods of clay feet; those are the images, the gods we have created. And when those false gods, they crumble and fall, then we begin to live the life that the infinite Divine Intelligence has designed for all forms of life. But the false gods will not crumble and the false gods will not fall for us until we accept that all that we experience we have created. It's not someone else's fault. Someone else didn't do it to us. We did it to our self. And because we did it to our self, we can do something better. When we truly accept that demonstrable truth, then we will start being a friend to our self and no longer an enemy of ignorance.

Thank you.

JULY 1, 1979

Church Lecture 92
Fulfillment

In speaking with you on this topic of "Fulfillment," we find often in our lives this great need to fulfill the multitude of desires that we experience each day of our life. And so our mind ever dictates the way to the fulfillment of that which it seeks. Because it is the mind that is doing the seeking for the fulfillment of its desires, then it is, of course, in keeping with the law that it would be our mind that would judge and dictate the way. This philosophy, the Living Light, clearly shows that desire is the divine expression. And being divine, its fulfillment is ever present. And so it is that when we still our mind, when these desires rise up into our conscious awareness and when we still the mind, in that moment do we awaken to the demonstrable, eternal truth that the fulfillment of everything is ever within us. Because we have, in our education and our upbringing, been trained that it is our mind that must work, that must find these many devious ways to attain and to fulfill whatever it seeks, we have grown to rely upon a vehicle that was designed to be used by our eternal soul and spirit and never was designed to be the master of our ship of destiny. Sooner or later in these multitude of experiences that we encounter in life, sooner or later we slowly and gradually awaken to that simple truth that though our mind can do many things, it cannot, and will not, do everything, for it was never designed for that purpose.

And so it is so important to pause more often in our daily thoughts and activities. When we encounter these problems that we encounter, when we encounter these seeming great struggles, when we have tried with our minds to do all that we think we can do, then it's time to give it to something, something that is greater than the limited vehicle of our mind, something that has the power to sustain all our thought.

So often you hear of the benefits of learning to think positive, of the detriments of thinking negative. And so it is that when these positive thoughts and their counter-balancing negative thoughts have had their heyday, so to speak, in our life, they neutralize each other, and at that moment, we give up the dictates of the mind and begin to experience the humble joy of our eternal being.

The lessons of life are hard or soft depending on how you look at life. And how you look at life establishes your own attitude of mind. If you will make the effort to see the good in everything, to see the good in all thought, to see the good in all experience, then you will, by seeing the good, first have risen the good within your own consciousness.

Remember, my good friends, there is no power anywhere, there never has been any power at any time that is greater than the power that is within you. For God is not some intelligence that is working to you and for you. God is an Intelligence, infinite, eternal, that is ever working through us, not to us. So many people seem to misunderstand that simple truth of Spiritualism. God can only do for you what you allow this Infinite Intelligence working through you to do for you. For it is a neutral Divine Intelligence. It will sustain and it will support any thought you choose to entertain in your mind. That is known as the free will, the divine, free will that man in his evolution has earned. And having earned this free will of choice, with it came the weight of responsibility: the ability to respond intelligently to every experience that we attract in our life.

So often when we have these so-called negative experiences, we immediately blame causes or forces outside and beyond our control. The reason that we do that is very simple: whatever we can blame outside as the cause of our problem, we do not have to face personal responsibility for it. And therefore, we have to make no changes in our attitude, no changes in our thought, no changes in our feelings. So, my friends, the moment that we stop blaming outside for what is truly going on inside, in that moment will we stop denying the demonstrable, eternal truth, which is known as personal responsibility. For when we deny truth, we deny God. And when we deny God, we deny the experience of abundant good in our life.

We know that acceptance is demonstrably the divine will, the will of God, for there is no experience, there is no thought, there is nothing in all of the universes that is not sustained by the Infinite Intelligence. There is neither good or bad; there is only undeveloped good. It ever depends on our evolution and our view point. If God does not judge man—and Life herself reveals that truth—then who is man to judge first himself and then another? Remember, he who judges another has first judged himself.

And so it is, my friends, the more we judge ourselves, the more we judge another, ever in keeping with that simple law that we cannot grant to another what we have not first granted unto our self. If you find yourselves intolerant with others, be rest assured you are equally intolerant with yourself. And that intolerance deprives you of the happiness and the joy of living. You don't have to be intolerant, for the greater your intolerance, the less your success in life, the greater your judgments, the greater your denials of God. We don't have to live that way. It is only an error of our own ignorance. For each time we express intolerance, remember, that very expression controls our own life.

Acceptance, the divine will, is what truly keeps us free from these many so-called traps in creation. Whatever it is that you are working your way through, if you will accept that great truth that by the law of coming to you, it shall go, for that is the Law of Evolution. And as it has been attracted to you ever in keeping with the law that you alone have established, so it shall serve its purpose and pass on. Coming to you as a lesson necessary for you that you—all of us—may awaken that life, in truth, is ever as we take it and it's just the way that we alone choose to make it. We have that wonderful, divine birthright of choice.

Let us be more consciously aware of each moment. Let us look at the experience and choose the good that is in it. Let us not spend so much time trying to analyze how it got to us, until it has passed from us. For energy follows attention. The more attention you place upon the obstructions in your path in life, the more obstructions shall you have, for he who sees the obstruction never finds the way. It is our attention that is directing this God-energy that is flowing through us. And being divine energy, it can be used by us for a greater, more beautiful evolution or a difficult and seeming disastrous one. Every lesson, every experience, being the effect of our willingness or unwillingness to change. There is nothing your mind can view in all of creation that is not in a process of constant change. Our minds are an inseparable part of creation and being an inseparable part of creation, their very nature is change.

It is when we hold to our thoughts and when we hold to things, that's when our struggle begins. So often in these years in this teaching I have heard students say how difficult it is for them to let go. But we can look at our life and we can clearly see, it is only difficult to let go of the things that we choose to be difficult to let go. For there are many things in our life that we have let go of so very easily. So what we really mean to say is there are certain things that we have judged, somehow, to be of value to us—be they thought or thing—and those thoughts or things are difficult to let go of.

Think of nature, God's demonstration before our eyes and senses, day in and day out. Do you let your breath go easily? If you do, you will have no difficulty in getting it. For what comes with great difficulty goes with great difficulty. This ever-moving Intelligence, regardless of our thought, will ever continue to move. If we choose to move with it, we, indeed, will sail serene on the sea of time. We will see many things upon the shore, but none will hold us from our eternal destination: a return home to where the peace that passeth all understanding is waiting this moment for us.

For this spiritual abode, from which we have wandered, is not something that we will automatically go to at so-called death, when we leave our physical body. We go to it now. We make that effort today or we do not find it tomorrow. For all of our experiences this day are establishing the laws of our tomorrow. It is entirely up to us. We can make it as great, as wondrous, and as beautiful as we alone choose. And if we will remember that it is in keeping with that Law of Personal Responsibility, that it is up to us—not some spirit somewhere, not some God far off in space. That will never do it for us, for this so-called God is within us. Don't blame God for your lack of effort, for God gave you that divine choice to make no effort, if that's what you want to do. But that very same God, in its infinite wisdom, will support whatever you choose to do.

Thank you.

AUGUST 5, 1979

Church Lecture 93
A New View

Speaking on "A New View," in order to attain a new view of anything, we must release the view that we already have. And so it is as we go along this path in life and our experiences continue to repeat themselves in our lives and now and then we seem to get a few moments break from those experiences that we don't care for. We must never forget they are only effects. They are necessary effects for us only because we have made them so.

So many people in our world today have varying views of what we call God. But the God, the "Santa Claus god" is not a god of Spiritualism. It never has been and it never will be. For to have a "Santa Claus god," you must first deny the demonstrable truth of personal responsibility. In other words, some God somewhere in the universe is going to hear your prayer, give you what you're praying for, and you have to make no effort and no changes in your thinking. That is not the God of Serenity and of the religion and philosophy of Spiritualism.

Our belief is very clearly demonstrable: a God that sustains everything in the universe and whatever thought you choose. By the very law of your birth, you have that divine right of choice. That is an impartial God. That is a true God. These gods that are supposed to be giving us whatever we want when we want it are the false gods created by our own superstitions, created by our own minds. They give to us when we honor them and they take away from us when we do not. That is not the God of reason or intelligence or truth.

Whatever it is in life that we want, we must always pay the price to attain it. Now often we may say, well, we want this or that, but we don't know what the price is. To know what your price is for the fulfillment of your own desires and choices, all you have to do is look objectively at the struggles in your life. Those struggles are the obstructions created by our mind. For whatever we think—as all philosophies of truth will teach, and do teach—whatever it is, it is ever, ever and forever within us.

We have, on the positive side, that wonderful choice: to choose and to have a new view of our present situation. But to have that new view, we must let go of the past. We must let go of the patterns of mind that have created the view that we presently have. That, of course, is going to take some effort on our part. We cannot expect, in a few moments a day of directing our thought and our attention to a new view, to completely bring about the demonstration of the change for us when our old view took so many untold thousands of hours to bring into being. Let us be reasonable in our efforts to attain a new view of this moment of now.

When you ask a person to make some effort to forget the past, which is troubling them and bringing them so much grief in life, they don't like to hear that. Because to hear that means a change in our thought must take place. But think, my friends, every experience that you have already had in life has already demonstrated to you that it's an effect of thought. And thought you can change whenever you choose to change it. Thought has brought us where we are and thought will take us on. We don't give much attention to our thought. Perhaps, it is because we cannot see our thought physically. We cannot—most of us—hear our thought physically. We cannot sense it with the five physical senses, but we certainly do feel its effect. We do see its effect, but we don't yet see it when we're thinking.

Sometime ago it was given in this philosophy to think and think and think more deeply. We get up in the morning and our minds are filled with many thoughts. Sometimes they are so filled with so many thoughts, if someone asked us what we were thinking about, we would tell them nothing—thinking about absolutely nothing. Well, that's just about what it amounts to, because it's like a record that's stuck in a groove and the thoughts continue to repeat themselves. We know already from past experiences that repetition and only repetition is the law through which change is made possible. So if you have not recently had any changes in your life that you feel are beneficial to you, then you can be rest assured that the thoughts of yesterday and yesteryear are still playing their tune in your mental universe.

We don't have to stay where we are if we don't wish to remain there. We don't have to because, in truth, we know how we got there. And whenever you know how you got any place in life, you know how to get back out again. You know how to open a door to enter. And by that law of knowing how to open a door, we also know how to close it.

This philosophy emphasizes greatly the importance of our thinking. It does so because our thinking not only affects our life here in this earthly realm, it affects our life in the realm that we go to when we leave this physical body. All of us at sometime in our life have entertained the thought, the possibility of escaping from the situations that we alone have placed our self in. And we have tried many mental gymnastics to escape from those situations we found our self in. And we have also already proven to our self there is no escape. The Law of Personal Responsibility is an impartial law. We all are under its control whether we like it or we do not.

You can travel over the universes. You can go to many schools of thought. You can study many religions and many philosophies. They will not change your life. You and only you can do that. God will not change your life; God will only sustain what you choose. So in the final analysis, sooner or later we pause and really begin to think.

A church, a teaching, a philosophy may or may not be instrumental in you awakening to the light of reason within yourself, but only you can bring about the transformation. If you believe that someone else can do it, if you are yet controlled by those false beliefs, you will have the temporary experiences in keeping with those false beliefs. For example, if you believe by getting married you will change your life for the better and you set those laws into motion and you have a few experiences that life is better, you guarantee the total opposite because you have made a judgment, which is the Law of Creation: for every white, there is a black; for every day, there is a night. Those are the false gods, those are the gods created by our beliefs, by our own mind. They do not, and cannot, sustain our life, for they are not the true God of all life.

We can do whatever we choose to do. But it's up to us to do it. If you permit your thinking to depend on anything outside of you, *anything* outside of you to bring you what you desire, you will make the payment for your attainment. But there is a simple and a greater way: to accept that Divine Intelligence that is within you, to know beyond a shadow of any doubt that it is sustaining you and to ever be alert, awake, and aware that you are, in truth, a law unto yourself; to take hold, through a little discipline, self-discipline, knowing that you are a law unto yourself to choose wisely each moment in each day what you are doing with the law that you are.

We have within us everything that is necessary for the joy, the happiness, the abundance, the fulfillment in life itself. If we permit our minds to deceive us and to tell us that our fulfillment is dependent upon something that we have no control of, then we pay the price of misery year after year after year. Whenever we allow our mind to dictate that our goodness is dependent on things beyond our control, we shall suffer. And we shall suffer until we learn the lesson that that type of thinking is an error in our own thought. For some of us, it only takes a few years to learn that truth, and for others, it shall not be learned in this earthly incarnation. That, of course, is ever dependent on how much it really means to us.

Have you not already noticed, my friends, whoever depends on things beyond their control suffers greatly? They rise to the heights of their thinking, only to descend back down to the depths, only to rise again, only to descend again. Someday we will, indeed, become weary of this rise and fall. Someday we will see more clearly that that is the Law of Duality, that it is the Law of Creation, that we are, in truth, above and far beyond creation, that we are using it as you use your car—that's the only value that it really has. But that is a great value for this earthly realm, because without it we could not identify.

Why, we must ask ourselves more often, why do we choose the struggles of life? Why do we choose those things that we alone create? What value to what level of our mind do they have? Let us ask our self that question. Are we in need of love? Then it is obvious we are not expressing it. If we are in need of anything, all we have to do is stop and think. The law is clear: like attracts like and becomes the Law of Attachment. So when your minds say you need something, be rest assured whatever your mind tells you that you need, you are lacking in giving. Because if you were giving, then you would have no need.

The greatest gift we will ever give in all of eternity is the gift of self. But how many of us know what this is, this thing called self that we have created? And so we find ourselves each day filled with a multitude of needs. They're telling us, as lessons of life, wherever those needs are directed by our mind that within us we have closed the door and we are not giving.

You see, my friends, so many of us, we loan, and we loan many things. There's a vast difference between a gift, a givingness, and a loaning. A loan has the chains of thought connected to the gift. It has all the concern that the mind has to offer of what has been done with it. That is a loan. It draws interest and, sooner or later, it returns to us in full. But a gift, a gift is that which we free from our own universe, from our mental thought, recognizing beyond a shadow of any doubt that it has passed through us. It did not come from us. It did pass through us. Think, now, of your thoughts. The ones identified with so-called self. Do you believe that they are you? If you do, you cannot give, you can only loan. But if you awaken to the truth that, as an instrument of a Divine Intelligence, they pass through you and slowly, but surely, this vehicle becomes more illumined. That is the purpose of evolution: a refinement of the many forms that your eternal being is passing through.

You are not the flesh. Look at it constantly changing. You are not even the thought, for it, too, is changing. You are that which sustains the thought and you are that which keeps the form. But it is passing. Surely we would not attach ourselves to something that we knew beyond a shadow of any doubt would not endure. Surely we are not that foolhardy. Eternity is exactly that: eternity. It does not change. Only the forms that your eternal being are using, those are the only things that change. The infinite, Divine Spirit, the true you, cannot, and does not, change. Your mind changes; your many bodies change. They're constantly in a process of refinement. But you, the true you, doesn't change.

To separate truth from creation is the great personal responsibility of mankind. Now truth is the same today as yesterday and tomorrow. Being truth, it is changeless, for it is formless. It is only our expression of truth that changes. You cannot change truth; it is beyond that law. So what is changing is the vehicle that you're using. And if you have identified and over-identified with the form in which the true you is now expressing, then you experience the pain and pleasure of form and its final decay. It's a snowball going downhill. And so you find at certain ages in the human beings, they become concerned—concerned about age, concerned about their looks. Because no matter how they think, the change *is* taking place. And if we become over-identified with this form that we are using, we're going to pay the dear price of its decay.

How does man identify with something greater? By first becoming aware of his thought and then choosing wisely what type of thought he wants to entertain. Not just now and then.

When the disasters come into your life, they're not now and then disasters when you are having the experience. To you, they are very real. They are as real as you have attached yourself to them by the Law of Identification.

A new view is ever dependent upon what you choose to identify with. This day is a great day, if that's what you choose it to be. Every experience in your life can be a great experience, filling your life with the joy of living, if you choose to view it that way. However, if you choose to look out in the world to find support for your misery, you will only be more miserable. But if you look out into the world and you choose to share the joy that is within you, then you will become more joyous. There's one thing about pity: it will not long endure if it does not have a listening ear. No one will remain miserable very long if they can't find someone to share the misery with.

One of the greatest purposes of this church is to bring into the awareness of those who participate in it the way to freedom: personal responsibility. When you mention the words *personal responsibility*, people don't seem to like that very much, unless they've just experienced some bonanza of some type in their life and then they smile from ear to ear because *they* were personally responsible for it. Usually, however, they scorn and they frown and they get very emotional and irritated because the little mind is thinking about how things aren't going the way they want it to go. But once in a while someone is joyous about hearing the truth, called personal responsibility. It does happen.

Now, friends, life is so simple and our thoughts, so complicated that it's difficult, I know, to try to see our way clear. But, remember, everything for us is within us. If you do not first accept, if you do not first recognize—for you must recognize that it really is inside of you, everything that you're looking for. If you will only accept that, you will establish the simple law necessary, known as like attracts like and becomes the Law of

Attachment; you will start on the first step. But you must accept it within yourself first. If it is happiness you are seeking, then you must accept that it is within you. Usually what happens, when a person says, "I am looking for happiness and have not found it," if you tell them that it exists within them, instantaneously the judgment rises to dictate the experiences that they have already encountered. You cannot get a new view that way, for you are blinded by the attachment of yesterday's experiences. To truly accept that all that we seek is within us, we must first remove, by rising to higher levels of consciousness, the judgments, the dictates, and the experiences of yesterday.

It's like a man in business. Not happy with the business that he has, so he makes a change of business. That proves to be like the business before. So you make another change. And that proves like the last business and you make another change. But slowly, but surely, it begins to dawn within the mind, "Something's got to change inside my head. It's not outside. That's the effect. I've got to make a change in my attitude." It's like a woman that marries one husband after another and every one of them do her dirt, because she did it—the dirt—to herself. How do we do it to our self? As I said earlier, by making the false belief that our happiness is dependent upon—the moment you say that the goodness of your life is dependent upon, you establish the law and you pay the price. There's a vast difference between the mind's dictate of "dependent upon" and accepting, a simple acceptance that you have it.

When you accept you have it, you will experience it with your whole being, if you have the wisdom of patience. How long will it take you? That depends. Each one knows how long it's going to take them. And how do we know how long it's going to take us? It's very simple: just look at your life and see how readily you make changes in your thinking. How readily, how quickly, and how easily do you give up judgments, prejudices, discrimination, and go down the list. If you give them up easily, then you can be rest assured whatever it is you choose to want is not far away. You will not have to wait long, for you have already learned the greatest lesson of life: Wisdom lives in the faculty of patience.

Thank you.

SEPTEMBER 2, 1979

Church Lecture 94

World of Spirit

Speaking with you today on this topic, "World of Spirit," is not something or someplace that we are going to after this so-called death. World of spirit is something that we are in, in this very moment, for spirit *is* the essence of God. And so we move and breathe in this divine essence this very moment. The only difference with some of us is that some are aware; through a disciplining of their mind, they have some awareness of this spiritual essence and this world of spirit in which we are this moment.

As we place our attention upon anything, we, sooner or later, become that upon which we have placed our attention. And so it is we have—most of us—placed a great deal of our attention upon this physical, mundane, and material world in which we move in a material body. The awareness of that which moves this physical world is not only possible for all of us, but it is, in truth, our divine birthright.

That which is beyond question is known as truth. And it is beyond question because it is beyond the contradictory, dual, mental capacities. Many people, throughout the ages, have struggled with what is known as faith. Not seeming to understand that we all have an abundance of faith, but it is the direction in which we place our faith. For we have faith that we shall breathe, and so we breathe. We have faith in many things in this mundane world, and we experience those things.

As we make a little effort each day to still and to quiet our minds, we will slowly, but surely, become aware of dimensions in which we are moving that we have yet to be consciously aware of. When we place our attention through concentration upon spiritual values, those spiritual values, they grow and increase in our life. To give thought to the effects of things in no way brings about a change in our life. We readily see the effects from our thoughts, our motives, from our attitudes, but rarely do we pause long enough to see the causes that are behind those effects.

They say that experience is not only a great teacher, but that it is a great preacher. Experience indeed is a great preacher: it is a preacher to those of us who are unwilling to accept the lessons that we experience. When we begin to accept these lessons as the direct effects of our own attitudes in life, then we begin to bring about the changes in our thinking that will reap a harvest more in keeping with our true desires. For none of us consciously choose to suffer and to be deprived of the good things of life, for they are available to all of us if we are willing to accept that availability for us.

But when man first begins to make the effort to accept the possibility of a better life than he has already experienced, these patterns of our mind that have been so reinforced throughout the years by placing our attention upon them, they rise up strong within our mind. And it takes great effort of our will to bring about a balance, to look to the eternal moment of the now—the only moment that we will ever have any power to do anything. We cannot change yesterday. We cannot change the moment that has just passed. We can only change the moment in which we are moving now. We can change our thought now. We cannot change it for yesterday, but we can do it now. In so doing we reach these states of consciousness known as harmony or heaven. It is, in truth, always dependent upon our own willingness to see life with a different perspective.

If we have yet, in this earth life, to experience the multitudes of so-called angels and unseen beings around and about us, that is no guarantee that it will always be that way for us. But we must look to this moment. This philosophy clearly teaches that acceptance is the divine will, that it is the will of God. Now we all have acceptance, and we all have plenty of it, but it is what we choose to do with our acceptance—whether we choose to limit it to certain rigid patterns of our past or we choose to broaden it in the light of reason here and now. When we choose to broaden our acceptance of the divine right of all, then we move into what is known as a godly state of consciousness. For every thing, every being, every creature, every thought, and every attitude is sustained impartially by the infinite Divine Intelligence, known as God. When we broaden our acceptance and accept the right of all existence, of all expression, we not only move into that godly state of consciousness, but we move in what is known as the divine eternal flow.

Whenever you experience obstructions to the fulfillment of your aspirations in life, remember, the obstruction—its cause—is never outside of your universe no matter how it appears to you. The way for you, for all of us, is always and forever dependent upon our willingness to accept the possibility of experiencing those aspirations in our own life. Whenever man accepts the possibility, he directs this great power within him, that is flowing through him, he directs it to what is known as a positive faith.

Everything that we have ever desired has either taken place in our life, or is in process, or is about to be, for man, in truth, is a law unto himself. The only question that arises with that statement is, "What are we doing with the law that we are?" God is not our obstruction. No force in the universe, nor power, is our obstruction—only our thought, only our attitude, only our lack of the wisdom of patience, for all things that are good shall come to pass. And because all things are sustained by the divine intelligent Power, known as God, there is no such thing as "bad." There are only varying degrees of good.

And so we must consider what type of a God is our faith directed to. Is our God a judge that is in a constant process of judging us, that is in a constant process of giving to us and taking from us? I assure you, those gods are the gods of ancient history, known as the false idols created by the errors of ignorance by the minds of men. There is no god that punishes, and there is no god that brings pleasure, but there is an Infinite Intelligence that sustains whatever you choose to entertain in your thought. That, however, does not exempt us from the first law of the universe—the first law known as personal responsibility. For whatever we think and whatever we do, it shall return to us, for that is the law of the universe. Everything shall return to the source from whence it has wandered, including our thought, our feeling, and our attitude. When we feel that we are uncared for, unloved, and unwanted, we can be rest assured that we were the instruments, in days of error, to cause another to feel the same way. Whatever it is that we find difficulty in tolerating in life reveals to us that wonderful truth: we have yet to educate that in our self.

When we open these soul faculties of duty, gratitude, and tolerance, we begin on the path of spiritual illumination. One need not study a book—or books—to be spiritual. For some, that is a path for them, but for millions it has not, and is not necessary. We must consider, my friends, we didn't come to earth without a history, for we have expressed for untold ages in untold places. And we all came to earth bringing with us our record book, bringing with us the lessons that we had to learn in this earthly journey. And I assure you, the more difficult you find your lessons in life is a true revelation of how many times you flunked them in the past. If your lessons are easy, then it hasn't had to be repeated to you in your evolution so many times. And so it is these difficult lessons that offer to us the greatest possibility of growth and freedom. That which you find so difficult to tolerate is a golden opportunity for you to free yourself from the throne of judgment. For think, my friends, of the payment of judgment, when the very Intelligent Energy that sustains our very life and breath and word does not judge that which it sustains. Think of what we do when we rise supreme to God in our thought and judge anyone or anything.

What is it that causes us to make so many judgments in our life? It's known as pride. Some people have spoken of false pride. I only know of one pride, unless you consider it to be false—a pride that is born and created in realms of darkness of our own human mind, lacking the light of common sense let alone reason, born in a realm of need. And let us understand what we mean by need. When we say that we need anything, we deny that we have it, because we cannot need what we already have. And, therefore, we must first deny in order to need. And what do we deny? We deny the great intelligent Power, called God, that has given us everything. In an error in our thought, we deny that we have it in our life. Remember, my friends, what we already have we have first accepted in our mind and then it has entered in our material, physical world. So to say that we need anything is to deny that we have it, and to deny that we have it, we keep it from us. And this is why we see in our world today that the cry of man is the constant need of what is called money. Therefore, we can be rest assured that we are denying it in our life, for we are not experiencing its effect.

This is such an important teaching and lesson for all of us. To take stock of our thought, to see how we keep from us the good that we seek. To deny is to separate, to be out of the stream of consciousness, of the wholeness, and the unity that is everywhere in all universes. But remember, my friends, we cannot deny until we entertain the thought of I. Because the God that we understand has denied nothing, no one, ever, then it is a full God, a whole God, a complete God, a Totality. We are fulfilled when we free our self from the error of denial, when we flood our consciousness with a broadening of our acceptances in life.

Pause in your daily activities; become aware of the things that you deny, for they are your destiny. And none of us look forward to a destiny of need and want. It doesn't have to be that way. It was not designed by the Goodness of Life Itself to be that way. The birds of the field do not hunger, for they do not deny. They do not tell their Great Creator, "I will only feed in this pasture or that, that I will only live in this tree or that." Only man in his error does those things in his judgments.

And so the greatest lesson in spiritual awakening is the freedom from the error of judgment that we may no longer deny—for we cannot deny until we have judged, and we cannot judge until we have separated our self with the illusion of the thought of I, until we have separated our self from the universal whole known as God or goodness. Let us no longer separate our self from the abundant good that is our home and our birthright. Let us broaden our acceptance and free ourselves from the error of the past. For this is a new moment, but it is only new to those who let the past go. For they can do nothing about that which is past, but we can do everything about that which is present.

Thank you.

OCTOBER 7, 1979

Church Lecture 95
Gratitude, The Faculty of Fulfillment

In speaking to you today on, "Gratitude, The Faculty of Fulfillment," I know that all of us have experiences in our life for which we are truly grateful. As we place our mind, our thought, our attention upon those experiences that we have already had for which we are truly grateful, we increase the Law of Fulfillment. For whatever it is that we place our attention upon, we, in truth, do have a tendency to become. And so it is that life, the great mirror of all experience, reveals to us in a multitude of ways that whatever goes out from our universe shall return unto us.

As we, in this journey through a multitude of lessons that are offered to us in this earthly experience, consider the value of these experiences, that we, through them, are awakening slowly, but surely, to the fulfillment of the true purpose of our life's journey here on earth. So often we hear it said in this life that many seem to be weary and tired of this earthly journey and are waiting and willing to go on to the new dimensions. But, my friends, let us consider. New dimensions we experience only when we are ready. And that simply means that we cannot, and do not, experience what we have not yet accepted. And so to leave this physical world and to expect a great transformation of new experiences, to expect a better life the moment after we leave earth than we had the moment before leaving earth is not only foolhardy, it is contrary to the demonstrable law that life, in truth, is an effect. Our minds go with us, for they are the vehicle through which our soul is traveling through this earthly journey and they are the refined vehicle to take us to the mental worlds when we shed this physical piece of clay.

We can talk about spiritual realms and spiritual worlds, but we cannot experience those dimensions and those worlds until we have a vehicle capable of receiving the spiritual emanations from those worlds. Now this vehicle, known as a spiritual body, is like any body in the sense that it is created. We know our physical body is created. We see physical bodies being created all around and about us. And we know that our mental body is created. All form, all bodies are created. The only thing that is eternal, that is everlasting, without beginning or ending, is the formless and the free, known as the Infinite and the Divine Spirit.

We are aware of any body that we are expressing through as long as we identify with it. It is our identification with anything that brings to us an awareness of it. The man who does not investigate or identify with the possibility of eternal life cannot experience that possibility. But someday all of us, in keeping with this evolutionary path of constant change, will experience all that is waiting for us to experience.

As we feel this faculty of gratitude in our hearts, we become more receptive to a greater flow from the Divine Source. And so it is that man's success of fulfillment, that man's experiencing of abundant good is ever dependent upon his receptivity to it. For we cannot experience anything that we are not receptive to. And so the slightest change in our thinking brings about the changes that we are seeking in our experiences, for he who knows beyond a shadow of any doubt establishes the Law of Fulfillment. We see so often in seeming negative ways, how beautiful, how positive the law works for us to have negative experiences. But the identical same law that brings back to us the negative also brings back to us the good and the positive.

And so no matter where we go and no matter what we do, we have, inherent within us, the infinite, divine, eternal truth: that whatever it is in life eternal, in any phase of our journey, is ever available and waiting for us to receive it. When we make this slight change in our thinking—that all that we seek is within us—we will begin to experience whatever it is that we seek.

For to God, we know, all things are possible. And that God is not something that we have to look without to find, for looking without, we will never find. It lies within us. It is ever ready and waiting, for God, the Infinite Divine Spirit, is the greatest servant of all. It is beyond doubt and beyond question that the Infinite Intelligence, demonstrable in our view, is serving everything for it is sustaining everything. Whatever you choose to think, this neutral, intelligent Energy is sustaining for you. So you may choose the good in your life by constantly being aware of its possibility within you. There is no power without. There is no power beyond your control, unless you, in your thinking, make it so. The Divine Intelligent Energy is always available to you. It is up to you what you choose to do with that power that is flowing through you.

Accept the possibility, no matter what your experiences are, or are yet to be, accept the possibility that they are changing for the better. For nothing in life is ever so good that it cannot be better. As you accept the possibility of something better, you become receptive to that vibratory wave and, through your own directed faith, shall experience it. In our day when there is so much talk and fear, of fear of this and fear of that, let us do our part by knowing beyond a shadow of any doubt whatever the experience is, it has come into our thought, it shall leave our thought, and, in truth, things *are* getting better.

When you talk to people and you listen to the disasters in their life and you listen to these negative expressions, unless you speak, you support that negativity within you. For you, by your own choice, have attracted unto you that negative expression. Therefore, having, by your own choice, attracted it to you, you have a responsibility to yourself to declare the truth during that expression.

I know there are not many, yet, who truly accept that there are no accidents in the universe. An accident is merely a lack of understanding the immutable, divine Law of Attraction. We have this responsibility to declare the truth for our self, for man cannot grant to another what he has not yet first granted unto himself. Therefore, when you look out in the world and you see others who are experiencing what you judge to be good, do not deny their right. For if you do, you deny that right to experience that good for yourself. Our denials, indeed, are our destinies, and acceptance is, in truth, the divine will.

We, in truth, cannot help but agree that there is nothing in all the universes that we have viewed or experienced that is not sustained by the Infinite Intelligence, known as God. If we wish more good, then we must grant, to our self, more good. And that goodness begins in our heart, for that is where it truly lives. And as it grows deep within our own heart, the vehicle through which our soul on earth is expressing, then it lights our mind with what is known as the light of reason. As we keep faith with this light of reason, it begins to transform us, and we begin to experience the true purpose of our journey here on earth.

There is no one and no thing that is outside of the Infinite Divine Intelligence. Therefore, it is not possible for anyone to be without until they make the judgment by their mind, the judgment of denial. When we judge that what we need is dependent upon anything, we establish for us in our mind the false gods that must be dethroned before we can experience the fullness and the abundant good of life. If we will pause each day in our thinking and become aware of the many times in the course of a single day that we establish the laws of denial by the error in our thinking that our goodness is dependent upon, if we will only make that small change in our thinking, we will be freed from the bondage and the slavery of the ignorance of our own mind. Our health, our wealth, and our abundant good is not dependent upon anything that our mind can think of, until by our own belief, by the direction of our own faith, we make that a law for our self.

Let us free ourselves from these errors in our thought. Let us accept our divine birthright to the goodness that this world has to offer, but before we can experience the fullness of that goodness, we must first accept our right to it. And accepting our right to it, we must know that it is that goodness within our self. And whenever we make that mistake by our thought of dictating to the Divine Intelligence that that abundant goodness is dependent upon anything, when we make that error and slip from truth into creation, let us pause and remind our self that our divinity is a perfect harmony, that health, wealth, and happiness is, in truth, an effect of that perfect harmony, or God, within us.

Thank you.

NOVEMBER 4, 1979

Church Lecture 96
Looking Ahead

In our experiences throughout our life, we are ever faced, in the eternal moment, of looking backward or looking forward. And so it is we find ourselves in a constant state of consciousness of associating with experiences that have already passed in our life. As all experiences in life are a direct effect of levels of consciousness or attitudes of mind, those experiences which have passed in our life have come to us in keeping with the Law of Attraction, have served their purpose, and gone from us, if we will permit that to be. Unfortunately, in our day-to-day activities, we frequently associate the present experience with that which has passed, and in so doing we make a judgment concerning the experience we are presently facing. By establishing that judgment within our consciousness, we come under the law that governed the experience of yesterday. And so it is that we go on in life repeating again and again and again the experiences of the past. However, as we grow in the light and understanding of how these laws work, we should be filled with the vibration of hope and goodwill for the efforts that are being made by levels of consciousness within us that we are not often consciously aware of.

As we repeat these multitudes of experiences of yesterday, through the Law of Repetition, change is made possible. And so, ofttimes in spite of our self, change is taking place. We are in truth evolving, for we are an inseparable part of all nature and all nature is evolving and refining. But we can make this evolution—that in spite of our thought will continue to evolve—we can make it more harmonious and more joyous and more filled with peace and goodwill for our self by first recognizing and then accepting the simple laws that govern our own universe.

As material science is moving forward in their understanding of the electromagnetic field in which all forms are moving and breathing, as medical science, in its early stages, is using electricity to help certain diseased parts of our physical body, they will soon discover that each and every thought that man entertains in his consciousness releases from his own aura electrical impulses that have either a beneficial or a detrimental effect upon his own body, which is a part of nature, and upon all of nature as a whole. As each thought releases this electric energy and each feeling associated with it releases a magnetic vibration into the universe, so the law is ever demonstrated for all of life's form: that like attracts like and becomes the Law of Attachment.

For any of us to change any experience at any time, we must first accept that the experience is an effect that we and we alone, in our own errors in our thought, have set that experience into motion by our own attitude of mind. When we begin to recognize and accept that simple truth, we then become the masters of our destiny and the captains of our ship. That, my friends, is our divine birthright.

The only thing that controls us is what we permit to control us in our own thought and in our own belief. To be in the world and never a part of the world, to be with anything and never a part of the thing is known as true freedom. That freedom is the fullness and the goodness of life itself. But that does not come to us easily because long ago it did not leave us easily. Ignorance is born in strife and struggle; reason and common sense is born when we are still and at peace that we may see objectively the simple laws that govern, not only our life, but that govern all of life.

It is the very purpose of the founding of this church and the Serenity Association to bring to all mankind, who are seeking a better way in life, to bring them the revealed laws of nature. But it's up to each and every one to make the effort to understand them and to apply them. To study any law of life and not to apply it is of no benefit to any of us. But to become aware of the law being set into motion at any moment by our own mind is to mark a course in the universe that will bring us home to that state of consciousness known as heaven in the here and the now. For no matter where we go in life, we will never go away from what we have created. But we can create something new and more beautiful; it is up to us. We establish the law for our day by the first thought and attitude of mind that we awaken to. Think of what we have within our grasp. It's ever up to us.

Self-control is truly freedom. The ability to control that which is our divine right to control: the vehicle that our soul is using in this earthly experience. This vehicle, this human, physical, and mental body, is not the responsibility of anyone else. It's our responsibility. It is ours. We have earned and merited it through untold stages of evolution prior to this earth experience. And it is up to us to keep it working in the way in which the divine laws of nature intended it to work. It is the effect, our physical body, of our own attitude. And if we are not happy with the body that our soul merited in this earthly experience, it is only because we have yet to understand the laws that we established in the many incarnations prior to this one.

Looking ahead is only possible through the faculty of hope. And so man is always hoping for something. But hope, without the effort to establish the laws to fulfill it, is of no value. We can hope for many things and the many things for which we hope, they do not appear in our universe because the laws we have established are contrary to our hopes and aspirations. But we can change those laws, for that is the divine, free will that we have merited in this earthly experience.

As we make this effort when we awaken each day to set the law into motion to bring us the fullness, the goodness, and the joy of life that day, and as we close our eyes in so-called sleep and we make the effort to establish the level of consciousness which is an effect of our attitude of mind, we may rest in the peace that is our right. So often we think when we go to sleep that we are unconscious in some state of limbo, but science gradually is becoming more and more aware. We are not in some state of limbo when we are experiencing what we call sleep. We are very active in different dimensions and we enter those dimensions by the law, the attitude of our own mind.

It is said whatever we place our attention upon, we have a tendency to become. So we must start with our own thought, our own feelings, what we believe, and why we believe it. Is the thought that we have in this moment, is it our thought or are we only receiving sets receiving the strongest thought being broadcast at any moment in the universe? Think of that, my friends. You know the effect upon your lives of so-called advertising, but are you aware, yet, of the effect upon your lives from not being aware of yourself and knowing from whence cometh your own thoughts? Are they bringing you what you are seeking or are they bringing you the opposite? Will the new year be a year of goodness and greatness for you? That, of course, is up to all of us. It will be for us, what we will allow it to be.

Our life is ever in keeping [with] what we will allow. It is our denials in life that establish our destiny. And so as we deny the right of another, we in truth deny our self. As we look to others and seek what they have earned, we deny what is waiting for us that we have earned. Let us look within and not without. Let us rise up within our own consciousness and firmly declare the principle of life, of love and light—for that is our true birth—that we may, once again, take control of our destiny, that we may truly, once again, be the captains of our ship through the universes. For time on earth is very short. The days go quickly and the years pass very fast. And before we blink, we find our self in another world. Oh, it's not so different than the one we're in. The only difference is we're not limited by a physical body to try to move around in the universe. We're just limited by our own thought, as we are here. We limit our self, in no matter what we seek, by our denial of our right to it. We have many mental justifications why we have not yet attained the success that we have sought. We have many excuses why we don't have what we have worked so hard for and those are the things that are keeping us from experiencing it.

It is stated by all true philosophies that all things are possible to God. But as long as we believe in a God that is somewhere off in the universe someplace, that gives to one and takes from another, then we are controlled by that false belief. All things are possible to all people who accept their divine birthright that God is within them. But because God is within us, the God within us is only limited by our thought. The God within someone else is not limited by your thought, but by that person's thought.

I assure you the only obstruction to the absolute awareness of the simplicity of truth, the *only* obstruction is the judgments of our own mind based upon the experiences of our own past. There is no other limitation. There is no other obstruction. It is only our thought. But because it is our thought that has created the veil between us and the eternal life that is here, this moment, because it is our thought that has done it, because it is ours, we can change it. We have the right to change that which is ours and our thought *is* ours. No matter what anyone says, no matter what anyone does, remember, it's your thought. And because it is your thought, you can do something with it. You are no longer the helpless victim of circumstances. You are no longer the victim of the politics of the world or the financial decisions of anyone. Because it's your thought. And you can do with your thought whatever you choose to do. But first you must accept your right to your thought.

If someone came to you and gave you a list of thoughts that you would be permitted to have in the course of any day, you would very soon rebel that someone beyond your power and control would dictate to you what thoughts you could have in the course of a day on any subject. Yet, we sadly, willingly, and in error of ignorance permit experiences of our own past to dictate to us constantly that we may only have these types of thought in any particular area of our life. That, my friends, is what we have done to our self. But we don't have to continue on doing that. Just remember, those experiences of yesterday can only dictate what thoughts you can have as long as you let those experiences keep control of you. They only have control of us in the darkness and the errors of our own ignorance. Because we are not stopping and pausing to think, "Why do I feel this way this moment?" And then we will see very clearly why we feel the way we feel. Through the Law of Association, which is a natural law to the human mind, we relate all experiences to what has passed. And so we repeat those experiences again and again and again.

The moment you pause to think, the moment you declare the truth—that it's your thought and you may do with your thought what you choose to do by the very law of free will—in that moment, you will experience a great freedom. You will continue to experience that great freedom as long as you remind yourself, moment by moment, that it's your thought and your feeling, and no one else, but you, can change it.

Thank you.

DECEMBER 2, 1979

Church Lecture 97
A Year of Fulfillment

As our chairman has stated, this morning's topic [is], "A Year of Fulfillment." Speaking with you today on that topic, we are speaking of that which is now, this the year of 1980, and that which is ahead of all of us.

Because of the great interest today in the events in our world, I wish to take a few moments with you and share an understanding of these current events. Because these events, we have permitted in our thinking, we have permitted these events to disturb us and, by disturbing us, to control us. For only that which disturbs us can control us and rob us of the peace that passeth all understanding. However, before sharing with you an understanding of these worldly events today, I wish to make it clear to all within the sound of my voice that the religion of Spiritualism, of which this church is a chartered auxiliary, does not judge nor discuss any particular position or judgment of these worldly events. The Serenity Church and Association does not take any particular position or stand on these events, nor does its philosophy, the Living Light. I share with you this morning an understanding, not only my own, personally, but those of my guides and teachers in the spirit world.

Our reality is, of course, what we make it. And it appears to us, to many of us, as we enter and are in this decade of the eighties—and as was stated in our forecast last Sunday [which was the Sixteenth Annual World Forecast], a decade, a year of fulfillment, a year of totality. And so it is as we look at the so-called crises in the world in which we spend most of our time, we seem to view discord, shortages, disasters, and misunderstanding.

The events in the Middle East and in particular the countries of Iran [and] Afghanistan are events that are effects, effects of errors of ignorance on the part of ourselves as individuals and as a body of people, as a nation, as a country. It has only been an error of over twenty years standing. An error in not expanding our consideration of what would take place in the years ahead, not only politically, but in reference to the great consumption of energy that we, as people, are using. None of us, of course, like the word *shortage* or *shortages*. None of us seem to appreciate hearing the word *conservation*, but we all will agree that efficiency, true, pure efficiency is what we are seeking. For efficiency is the handmaiden of success and all of us are seeking success in something in our lives. So let us change our thought for a moment from shortages and limitations and conservation to efficiency, energy efficiency.

Now where does one begin when they desire a change in their reality? We look out at the world and we see it ever from our own vantage point and therefore, we create our reality. If you take a dozen people and you ask them what their reality is, they will give you many different answers. Some of those answers will be harmonious and in accord with the others, and some will not.

And so it is [if] in our desire to have efficiency and its effect, success, in our life and we are not presently experiencing it, then we must begin within, where the cause truly lies. How, then, does man become more efficient? If we will pause for a few moments this moment, and the moments yet to come, and become aware of how much energy we are using inside this little house, called the human body, in which our eternal being, known as the soul, resides. We all, I am sure, will agree that there are no shortages and there are no limits. And some of us even believe that there is no conservation with the abundant supply of energy from the Divine Source, known as God. But we must look at nature, and we see that nature does not waste. Nature does not waste. The trees, they fall. They turn into mulch upon the ground and once again their energy serves the new tree or to keep the present one in healthy condition.

So we do see clearly that there are no shortages or limitations to God, the divine, infinite Eternal Flow. But there is what we know as energy efficiency.

Man has a limitless supply to this Divine Source. The limits that he experiences are only the limits and so-called shortages created by an error in our thinking. Therefore, as we face the truth within us of how much of our energy is being used efficiently and constructively in our own body, in our own little universe, how much is being used efficiently and how much we are wasting in our own body, in our own thinking, then we will clearly see whether or not we are efficient and successful.

We have an understanding in the Living Light Philosophy which clearly states, "I speak my word forth into the universe knowing that it shall not come back to me void, but accomplish that which I send it to do." How does that work? So many times in the philosophies that we have read or read, we see that the philosophies tell us of all these beautiful things, but do not show the way to attain them. Whenever we speak our word, we must unite, with that word, our thought. It is the unity between the thought and the spoken word that permits the entrance and the flow of the divine, eternal, spiritual energy to go out through us to the universe. If we are what is known as clear channels for the flow of this energy, it will indeed accomplish that which we send it to do. For we all know we have the right of choice.

Let us, then, in this decade and in this moment, choose wisely that we may be successful in our life by using to its fullest the soul faculty of efficiency. I am aware that to many of you that awareness [is new]: that efficiency, like gratitude and compassion, is a soul faculty. For efficiency, the effect of which is success, carries with it the light of reason and the stability of understanding.

As we make this change today and we accept personal responsibility for our reality, personal responsibility for our thoughts, acts, and activities, personal responsibility for where we are because we are who we are, who we have made our self, then we qualify our self to bring about a great change in our world today.

They say—and have said for so many centuries—that charity, another soul faculty, begins at home. Let us be more charitable with our self, for in so doing we serve a great and beautiful, selfless purpose in life. As has been stated, "O physician, heal thyself," that you may be qualified by your own demonstration to be the instrument through which another may be healed. And so we can only grant unto another what we have first granted unto our self. And so I ask you once again, let us become more charitable with our self, then, indeed, shall we, as a group, as a community, as a state, and as a nation, and as human beings on the planet Earth, become the living demonstration that there are no limitations, there are no shortages, there are no impossibilities, for to God, of which we are an inseparable part, all things are possible.

In viewing the many events to take place in this year and this decade, in being privileged to see some of the great changes that are just ahead of us, I am indeed filled with the spirit of joy and happiness, filled with the spirit of gratitude for the beautiful and wonderful changes that are taking place in our world today. It seems that many of us do not yet understand that from the mud of earth the lotus of heaven does grow. And that, my friends, is what is taking place. Not only in the Middle East, not only in Asia and Africa, but throughout the United States and our world today. We listen to the news media and we read the papers and we see and we hear so much discord, so much pain, and so much suffering. Without pain, the pleasures of life cannot be realized. Without night, the day cannot be appreciated. Without sadness, we cannot experience the fullness of joy. And so as we view these events of these so-called crises and difficulties, let us remember, in those moments, that we are viewing the pains of birth. We are only viewing the process through which a greater and brighter day is dawning for all of us.

As I said earlier, our error of over twenty years standing in this seeming energy crisis is in process of being corrected. We are, I assure you, being freed from the dependence upon foreign resources in our world. This is not something that's going to take another decade or two. I am aware that it does seem easier to be negative and pessimistic than it does to be positive and optimistic, seemingly, in the world today.

This, my friends, is a decade of light. It is a decade not only of spiritual light, it is a decade of physical, material light, for it was a great, illumined soul, Thomas Alva Edison, that was the instrument to bring to our world light that we may find our way in the physical, material darkness of creation. And we celebrate at this time the greatness, the wonder, and the goodness of the Divine Spirit, known as God, that sent a soul to our planet and to our country to lift up the souls who were stumbling along the way. I am aware that some may think, "And what does a physical light have to do with the eternal, spiritual light?" My good friends, all the inventions that we are aware of today came to us from the realms of spiritual light that our lives may be more fulfilled, that our joy may be, yea, even greater in its expression, that we may all know beyond any doubt that goodness is what we really are, that any other thought is an error and transgression to our divine Source. For we are the goodness in life. When we accept the reality of what we *really* are, these problems will pass into the nothingness; they will be a thing of the distant past.

The situation today in Afghanistan is in the best interest not only of the United States, but of the world today. It is in the best interests of the United States and its allies because it is an instrument through which the spirit of understanding and unity could bring millions of people together to stand up for what they believe is right and just. Whether it is right or just, each one of the millions know, for we all have a spiritual consciousness. It knows right from wrong; it does not have to be told. And I assure you from this condition in the Middle East, a greater unity is growing throughout the world. The Russian bear shall bow its head in humbleness. If you do not recognize the bow of the bear, it is because you do not understand the ferociousness of the bear. Pause and think and open your eyes and let three months from this day pass and you will see, if you are, yourself, freed from rejection, freed from retaliation, freed from revenge; if you yourself free yourself from those things, you will see the goodness that has already been born and is growing each and every day.

Last Sunday it was revealed to me that in our forecast they had stated that methanol was the energy salvation—one of them—in the United States. Within the coming five years, methanol will be used to fuel over 30 percent of our energy consumption. That I assure you. That may seem to be too soon to many. It may not be pleasant to the ears of those who are interested solely and exclusively in solar energy, but methanol, like solar energy, will take its place in our world today.

A new friendship, born from much sadness, disaster, discord, and misunderstanding, is growing day by day with the nation of China. Arms—not yet—will be supplied to that country, but all technology is already, *already* in the hands of their leaders. Of that we will be aware before we come to summer, to June. We should not be concerned or fear what is being done in Asia, the Middle East, or Africa, for it is necessary to bring to all of us the goodness that we seek. The path that is necessary for us, we may not agree with, but it is the path that, from our own error, we alone have chosen.

Let us then, as we conclude this moment, let us then give daily thought, and, by daily thought, increased energy, to efficiency in our own personal life. As we do that, we will find ourselves, being what some of us like to call more conservative, let us be more efficient. We don't have to drive so fast to feel pleasure and enjoyment. We don't have to drive big cars that accommodate five people and only have one. We don't have to do those things and if we will accept that, we will enjoy doing other things. I know you've heard those stories so many times. I think they call them carpools. Every single drop of energy that you use efficiently is one bullet less in our back.

My friends, we do have choice. And today, beginning this new decade, is our choice. For every ounce you save, for every ounce, though it be the smallest crumb, it is what is necessary to create the loaves from heaven. Now we all want these loaves, this manna from heaven. I'm only sharing with you an understanding and a way to get it. Bring about these changes in your life, your reality, the effect of your life and your thoughts, your reality will bring a new light of abundant good for you.

I am a firm believer in physician, heal thyself. I do not feel saintly, because I don't know how a saint is supposed to feel. I have not yet made that judgment. I hope I stay free from it. I do not, of course, in any way feel perfect. I do not even feel like I am the most efficient person in the community. I do, however, feel that I am making some effort and because I am making some effort, I am experiencing some success.

No one makes effort without experiencing success. Even though, through error, it is negative success, success is success. What is negative to one, what is negative success to one and called failure is positive to another and called success. They are one in the same of the same pole. Positive and negative. Let us be neutral. Let us keep both things in balance. My friends, without the negative, there would be no positive. Without the day, there would be no night. Believe me. So when we look at the negative and we begin to feel upset and emotional, let us pause, let us stop and let us say, "I see the negative side of this. Now I choose to see the positive side and, in so doing, bring myself into what is called neutrality and enjoy the world in which I live."

I know some of you have been thinking, "He hasn't mentioned anything, really, about those Iranians and the hostages. Hasn't mentioned, really, anything about the economy and the gold and the silver and all those things." They were mentioned last Sunday. They are available on cassette tape at our book table today. But I wouldn't want you to think that I direct my energy exclusively and efficiently to a commercial world. And so I'll share a bit more, in a few moments, for those of you who do not feel at this time—what is it they call it?—extremely flush.

And so what am I talking about? Iran. Yes. Iran. Yes! It was stated there would be a change in vibration and attitude on the sixty-third day of the holding of the hostages in Iran. I believe that yesterday was the sixty-third day. I'm sure that many of you, had you viewed the news, would all agree "Why, it's just the opposite. There was nothing positive in the hostages being freed. It was definitely the opposite side of the coin." Well, there's one thing about the coin of creation: it does flip. And, unfortunately for many of us, we don't see it when it flips. And that's how come we seem to lose so much in our lives, in our material world. My friends, the change is already, since yesterday, in process.

For over twelve years the Union of Soviet Socialist Republics—many of its officials—have not only been aware of the so-called world energy problem—oh, they've been aware for forty years, long before many of our public officials. But for the last twelve, they have made great effort not only to understand the world energy problem, but to find solutions. Why, my friends, for years they used our grain—and still use our grain, if we can call it ours because we've sold it. We didn't loan it. We've sold it. They used US grain to fuel their vehicles, long before most of our people, in public office, gave it any serious thought. But they realized, over these past twelve years, that they were, in a very microscopic way, becoming dependent upon US grain. Now you know how all of us feel about being dependent on what they call OPEC oil. Well, how do you imagine those poor Russians felt when they began to think of their dependency upon the United States government? My friends, there are two sides to all coins, and creation is indeed a dual vehicle. Well, they weren't happy. The bear got furious and though the bear did not speak to us in those days and years about energy and giving them more wheat that they may make more fuel, it expressed itself and its anger in many other ways.

And so their government made a decision long ago, a good eight years ago. And now, for twelve years they've been fully aware and making effort. For forty years they've been aware; for twelve years they've been making effort. For eight years, they've really gotten serious. And so a political plan was brought about by the various officials—and military—of what they would do to save their country. And they looked across the world and they saw, as we all see today, where the energy we know, called oil, comes from. And when that was truly brought to the awareness of all those officials, a very old dream started to play in their minds. A dream of owning all these countries in the Middle East, that surround them, not only giving them a warm-water port, but giving them energy independence. Energy independence—the very thing that we are crying for today the officials of that republic did not cry for twelve years ago, but they demanded the change eight years ago.

Now we may or we may not agree with the tactics that are being used. Personally, for myself, I share with you I don't fully agree. I don't fully disagree. I don't fully agree. I do not disagree because we all have a right to energy efficiency. I do not fully agree because I have certain restrictions on how I will fulfill my rights, and it doesn't include invading another country. However, from all of that—and I should conclude because I know you are in hopes I [will] still do some billets, I guess. I'll do my best.

The longest lecture I ever gave, my friends, outside of colleges and other churches. *[Many in the congregation laugh.]* It's the longest lecture I have ever given in my thirty-nine years in this work. And so bear with me just a few more moments, maybe nine maximum. I'll see if I can see the clock; it's difficult.

Where was I? Well, anyway, energy—oh, let's move to money. *[Some of the congregation laugh.]* Because, you see, money is the effect of directed energy. Now we all know that's all that money is. Money is the effect of directed energy. Now because it's an effect of something we have directed, namely energy, we don't need money, because we're the ones that direct it. It needs us. Don't you understand? See, money needs us because money is the effect of energy, we direct the energy, and that that is directed by needs what it is directed by. Now I hope you understand that. If you don't, we'll have to listen to the tape. And I hope he's getting it recorded. *[The vice president of the Serenity Association was responsible for recording the lectures.]*

Anyway, money. It was stated here last Sunday, I believe, yes, last Sunday, that gold would reach and go over the so-called 600 mark. No problem. But it would drop and what a drop it would take. Now it's not going to go down to $40 an ounce tomorrow. And I'm not saying it's going down to $40 an ounce in ten years. I am saying it's going to take some mighty big $40 jumps down.

So, what have so many done? From fear—and what is fear? Fear is nothing more nor less than a lack of faith in the power of God. It is faith in what our computer, called our mind, our brain, has to offer us only from past negative experiences and a few, hopefully, positive ones. So they go and they buy gold coins and silver coins and all of those things. That's fine for the speculators. They like to gamble; that's their right. It is sad, I'm sure we'll all agree, for young people, for families, for those who have saved, perhaps a hundred, five hundred, a thousand, maybe three, maybe even six thousand, to take money that they have set aside, bit by bit, to go out and to buy a commodity, to buy gold or silver or any of those metals at such an unbelievable, exorbitant price and a few days later to lose it all. I assure you, do what you want, for it's your right. As long as you do not step on another's toes, indeed, it is your right, but let's be reasonable. Let's be filled with a little common sense.

You feel that you need more money? That's the first error. That's the first mistake. Because when we feel we need more money, we deny what we already have. Now, you see, my friends, you say, "Well, let's see, I've only got $10 and I need to do several things. I'd like a new coat, etc. That's going to cost me $30—no, I mean about $130." But anyway, the changes are so fast nowadays. And we think and we make all these—what we think are decisions. They're really judgments, you know. You see, the difference between a decision and a judgment: a judgment, we make it. It's very rigid. It won't change without a lot of emotional trauma, when we've made a judgment, because it has the emotional body in it. It doesn't have the light of reason or common sense. Oh, no. A decision has the light of reason and common sense. A decision—it's very simple. You choose this instead of that. And while you are making the choice, you consider and totally accept the possibility that you may change. You may change that decision. Now, you see, there's your difference between decision and judgment. A judgment binds you to the prison house of the eternal soul. A decision frees you to express God's manifestation, known as variety. But unless you have that consideration and the acceptance of the possibility and the willingness that you are ready to change from whatever decision you have made, you're bound. We're all bound, you see?

And so it is, yes, we're talking about silver, a little gold, too. Someone asked the other day if we'd ever return to the gold standard. I told them exactly what was revealed to me: not in my lifetime nor the lifetime of those eternal spirits that are over there. Because that's what they told me. Not this country.

Now, you will, however, see the day—not on earth—when the countries of your world will no longer be on any kind of gold standards. Oh, yes, that is inevitable. Believe me. But that's so far away, don't worry about your gold investments. Please don't worry about your gold mines either. Because that's so far away. We'll all be on the other side by then.

I must finish up. Economy?!—is doing beautiful. Now I know you don't agree. What's the inflation rate? Thirteen, 14 percent. It's supposed to be 6 or 7. It's supposed to be 3, if you want to know the truth about the matter. And the spirit has told me repeatedly—[for] your economy—that inflation should be about 3 percent and it would be very stable. But it's not. Our President says that it's 7 percent! Everybody else says it's about 14, but he says it's 7. That other 7 belongs to OPEC. *[Many in the congregation laugh.]* So, I mean, it depends [upon], of course, how we look at things, don't you see? Well, because I feel better with 7 percent, that's my reality. I mean, if everybody else wants to talk about 14, that's fine, but I will stay with 7. I like the number 7. It happens to be my birth number. So I will stay with 7 percent and hold on for dear life with absolute faith that my reality is my infinite, divine right.

But still, I must listen to, hopefully, some common sense, because you never know from what mouth it's going to reach you, you know. And so I will try to be practical with my 7 percent, you see. And if you want to do the same thing, then life in this year, in this decade, for you, is just going to be great!

Now I am aware, and so is everyone else, that in '79 we had a little session there of a shopping spree because everybody was passing the word, "Buy it now. It'll be double by March." Well, wait 'til March. There are going to be some changes. And it won't be as low as you like it, but it's sure not going to be as high as you keep telling yourself that it is. Believe me.

Now the dollar bill? Poor thing. It certainly has grown through humility. And—*[Most of the congregation laughs.]*—but it's working its way up. It's working it's way up. I wish that everyone would take a look at the dollar bill. It reveals some great spiritual truths, you know, not just the color. No, no, no.

Green means eternal, and so one could call that spiritual, I'm sure we'll agree. But much more than the color, look at the symbols on the back of the dollar bill. They tell you a whole story of what, in this world, they seem to like to call mysticism. Well, I spent my life trying to get the mist out of mysticism. Because I like to see things clearly. Now I like the fog, if I'm not out driving in it. But who wants to drive in a dense, mystic fog? You can't see. I like to see where I'm going and give a little thought to where I've been, as a comparison, whether or not I'm moving ahead. Now our minds all have to have comparisons. So let's get the mist out of mysticism and let's look at that for a moment for what it really reveals: the all-seeing eye of eternity, the great triangle of eternal truth. Count the blocks on the triangle and count the arrows in the claw of the eagle. All these things, they're not just telling you about thirteen colonies. My friends, that's coincident with the great spiritual truth that's contained on that little piece of paper.

Now it's been tattered and torn. It's been in pretty sad shape. I heard someone the other day—and I shouldn't say it in church, but I'll say it anyway because I'm so independent. You know, I believe in saying what I want to say. And I hope God will forgive me—that some people were using toilet paper—I mean, using the dollar bill for the bathroom. Well, they can pour them in my bathroom anytime they want. *[The congregation laughs.]*

No, the dollar bill is going up. It's going up. Wait 'til the end of April. Give yourself a little chance. Oh yes, it's going to inch its way microscopically up the ladder. Because it has so much determination. You know, the dollar bill is the most determined currency ever known in the history of the planet Earth! There is no currency with more determination. There is no currency with more ego and pride—because it's paying its price today, you know, for that ego and pride. There is no currency ever known to mankind stronger, more determined, more tenacious, filled with more ego and pride than the American dollar bill. Now, any, *any* vehicle, whether it's a piece of paper, a human being, a dog, a cat, or an ant, any vehicle—and a dollar bill's a vehicle, through which energy is expressed—any vehicle with the soul faculty of determination, with the sense function of pride and ego, with the soul faculty of strength, cannot help but survive the onslaught of jealousy in the material world this past sixty-two years. Think about it. Just think about it, my friends. The dollar bill doesn't need Fort Knox with twenty zillion trillion more blocks of gold. It doesn't need that. It has the American public. It has the forefathers of America behind it. It has all the energy, all the determination, all of the tenacity, all of the ego, and all of the strength and all of the pride and a little bit of humility in it!

Now it has been gaining humility for several years. I never saw a successful man, or woman—I don't want to be prejudiced—that didn't express in the things they desired the most a little bit of humility. Believe me, they all do. Because without a tiny bit of humility, you can't have energy efficiency and you can't have success. Because you've got to be humble with some of those driving, demanding, blind desires. All right. And so it is with the dollar bill. It's coming up. In spite of all the envy, in spite of all the jealousy, in spite of all the disloyalty, in spite of all the Benedict Arnolds in our world today, the dollar bill is coming up. And it's going to take its rightful place, once again, in the planet Earth and in our world. We are not going to print new currency, called yen or pesos or something else. No, the government's not going to do that. The dollar not only will survive, but if you are interested in your own survival, stop and accept with the fullness of all that is right that you know that is within you that no vehicle, be it a dollar bill or a ruble, that has had so much faith and honesty, determination and goodness poured into it is going to die from this planet, because it is not.

Many things change. The American flag will not.

I promised you nine minutes and please forgive me for not being aware of the delusion and illusion called time. So, I accept the forgiveness within me, for making a promise of delusion. *[The congregation again laughs.]* And I do hope you will accept my apology for that delusion in the first place. All right, I finish. I do bless you all in God's name as I accept that blessing from God for myself. I only share that with you. And I do hope you will be patient. We'll get to the next part of our service—I mean, after all, you know, I could complain and go into self-pity and rejection because this is the first Sunday of the month and I'm supposed to book appointments and I haven't even had my brunch yet. *[The congregation laughs loudly.]* And—but I'm going to have that before I take any appointments. And it's always kind of a heavy day for me, but I don't want to think about it too much because if I do I get kind of dizzy, I feel real sick, and I might need an Alka-Seltzer, which I don't take anyway.

Thank you very much.

JANUARY 6, 1980

Church Lecture 98
Ninth Anniversary Service

Indeed it is a pleasure to speak to you today on the "Ninth Anniversary Service" of this church. I know that some of you were expecting our regular first of the month Questions and Answers, but I hope in discussing the nine years of the work and efforts of this church and its people that you will find something of value and benefit to take with you in your own personal lives.

I know many of you are not aware that one of my greatest adversities in life was being in a church, let alone being the founder and pastor of one. And so I speak to you from personal experience that our adversities in life, indeed, do become our attachments. It's only a matter, of course, of time.

But it was in the month of February in 1971 that the spirit that I have worked with over these many years prior to this church requested that a church be opened in this county. And at that request, which happened to be given to me on the morning of my birthday, I was very unhappy indeed and determined that they had made a mistake and were speaking to the wrong person. However, needless to say the request was that the doors be opened not later than the first Sunday of May. Well, that gave me from February 22nd to the first few days of the month of May, which was certainly a very short time to gather up twenty-five people, to sign a charter, to apply to a national organization and a state organization so that our church could be opened and incorporated. Needless to say, in my adversity I was indeed so busy I forgot quite frequently the adversity I had entertained for so long.

However, I have watched these past nine years with great interest. And, of course, we know that like attracts like and becomes the Law of Attachment and Serenity certainly has attracted some very strong-willed people. However, our teachings—and independent people—our teachings do not state that we should annihilate our ego, for it serves a wonderful purpose once we make some degree of effort to get it educated.

And so it is that Serenity has offered for nine years, and continues to do so, has offered a way to use our ego in an intelligent way with a faculty of reason, that it is, indeed, necessary, that we do have a purpose in life to serve, that to each and every individual all things indeed are possible. Whether we like those things or we don't, all things *are* possible. And so it is when we entertain in our mind the possibility of fulfilling anything that we choose or have chosen to do, if we will first entertain the possibility of its fulfillment, then, of course, we will set the law into motion. That law that is necessary for its own fulfillment.

And so it is that the people of this church have [made], and continue to make great effort with their own personal lives, because to teach one thing in life and to demonstrate its opposite, of course, is an absolute guarantee of failure. So whatever it is you want another to do in life, be sure that you first do it yourself. Whether it's an adversity you're growing through or it's effort that you are making to have a more peaceful and abundant life, remember, friends, the physician must first "heal thyself," because we are not qualified to tell another and show them the path if we are not first walking upon it ourselves.

And so I can assure you when I talk to people who have great difficulty in wending their ways to any church, I know exactly how they feel, considering I felt that way for most of my own life. You see, I never felt it was necessary to go to a church because God was everywhere and God, being everywhere, there was no place for me to go because wherever I was, there God would be. And, of course, that is true. But it's like learning to play ball or any other sport. He who associates with one who is learning about any particular path supports his own efforts. And so those who are interested in improving their lives, in finding a more spiritual awakening within themselves, of course, it is to their own best interest that they make some effort to associate with people who are making the same effort.

You know, it's really interesting because it brings to mind about the reformers in life. I don't think I was adverse to that attitude of mind called reforming, because it doesn't seem to be of interest to me to reform anyone. But it is interesting to note the attitude of the reformers in life. It's like a person, you know, for some reason or other they've made a decision that they must stop eating certain foods or they must stop doing certain things or they must stop smoking or they must stop something and they go ahead and they do it. The very first thing that you see taking place is they go out on a bandwagon to force everybody else to do what they forced themselves to do. I bring this up because it's so much in keeping with the Living Light Philosophy. Whenever we force a suppression of any desire that we have in consciousness, we guarantee someday for it to rise again. And our teaching has always been never to suppress the desires in your mind, but to fulfill or to educate them. Because, you see, my friends, if you suppress a desire of your own, your mind will dictate that that same desire, whenever you see it expressed in another, must be suppressed. And so that's the mark of these instantaneous reformings in life.

The spiritual path I have found in these past thirty-nine years is not a path of miraculous change. It doesn't work that way. Repetition is the law, and the only law, through which change is made possible. And so when we start on any type of a self-improvement program or any type of a spiritual path, we don't have a spontaneous, miraculous change that takes place in our life. It's a very slow, gradual process, that is, if you make daily effort. If you make spontaneous weekly or monthly effort, then, of course, it's more of a snail's pace and it does, indeed, from what I have viewed, take many, many centuries.

But whenever we seek to change, to bring about a change in our life, we always face the obstruction of the patterns of mind that we already have. We want to make changes from the way we have experienced our life—that is, certain changes. I don't know of anyone that wants to change their whole life. But there are certain things in their life that they would like to change. Now when you think about those changes, you must remember that you have certain patterns of mind that are very strong from directing energy to them over a period of many years. And so you must face, in your interest in bringing about changes in your life, you must face the emotional trauma and the experience of the other patterns revolting against your thought of bringing about a change.

But like everything in life, whether we like it or not, change is inevitable in evolution. And our eternal soul is expressing through forms that are constantly changing and evolving. We have accepted most of the natural changes in evolution. The problem is we don't want to accept the possibility of changes in our mind and in our mental attitude. And so that's where we seem to have most of our struggle.

Whenever your mind is so filled with things that you find discordant, robbing you of the peace that passeth all understanding, then it's a very simple step to go beyond it. But when man thinks, "Well, what's beyond my mind?" then he's still *in* the mind. So it is a matter of gaining control of the mental process and shutting it off, at least for a few moments. That comes, of course, with daily effort. And the best time to make some effort to still the mind, which most people call meditation, is early in the morning before it becomes so extremely active and so involved with all of the variety of creation.

I want to thank all of you, especially the people who have come to our church over these many years and the membership of this church, who have made so much effort to continue to serve God and the ministering angels of the spirit world, that those people, who wend their way here—and sometimes we don't see again for many years—they come and whether or not they believe or disbelieve is not really what's important. What is important is they have been exposed to this understanding and in that exposure, it is recorded in their memory par excellence. And someday in this great eternity in time of need, I know it will serve them very well.

And I hope that all of you will remember, as I remind myself, in your thoughts of judgment in life, remember, they lead quickly to adversities and from those adversities to long-lasting attachments. But if we will make friends with the things in life that we seem to think that we are adverse to, then we won't have to have them attached to our lives. You see, my friends, it serves a wonderful purpose in the expanding of duty and gratitude and tolerance. As I have often said, without tolerance, there is no success in life. And if you look at anyone that is successful in any field, you can be rest assured they are very tolerant in that particular field of their interest.

So we all want to be successful in something. And I hope you'll remember that success doesn't necessarily mean making money, because to be successful is to be successful within, for only what is within you will go with you when you leave this old physical world. So if your interest is being only successful in money and the material world, you have to leave all of that behind. But you do take the thought with you. But what good is the thought of it, when in the world we're all going to there's nothing to purchase and there's nothing to sell?

You see, my friends, whatever you think within is what manifests for you without. And when you leave this physical world, you will see that so very clearly. If you have not made the effort to concentrate, to gain control of the human mind, when you leave this physical body and you think of a rose, a rose will appear. But the next second, you're thinking, perhaps, of a weed, and a weed will appear. And so it is, you see, the outward revelation—the outward manifestation is the revelation of the attitude within. Here we have a physical buffer and we do not see it as readily happening to us. But all of our experiences in life are the direct effects of our thoughts and of our attitudes. And when we shed this physical body and we express in the next world—the astral, the mental, or the spiritual—whatever thought you have in your mind, that is what you experience. So does it not behoove us to gain some degree of control of our mind here and now?

I assure you, in these many years, it has been revealed to me thousands of times: that's the way the world really is. If you have thoughts of goodness and joy and harmony and peace, then you will experience those realms ever in keeping with your own merit in life. But if you do not gain control of the mind, if you do not make some effort to place your mind pointedly and fixedly upon the object of your choice until only the essence remains, then you will have a constant panorama of things to view and to experience.

Time and again the Friends have stated to be in the world and never a part of the world, to learn to be with a person, place, or thing and never a part of the person, place, or thing. That's when you truly express your individuality. That's when you truly experience freedom.

So often we go out into this world and we say we're feeling fine until we met such and such a person. We were feeling fine until such and such a thing happened. But we didn't have to meet that person, we didn't have to have that experience, if we had some degree of control of our own mind. Life, and our reality of life, is dependent on whatever we choose. So if you choose to make your reality one filled with the joy and beauty and wonder of life itself, then that's the way your life will ever be. But if in thinking of the possibility of accepting that new way of thinking you say, "That's fine, except" or "but"—when you make that statement, you are not able to create your own reality consciously by your own volition and experience that goodness of life.

There is but one obstruction between us and the infinite, eternal, spiritual realms: the only obstruction is the mental world. It is our mental world, our thoughts that are filled with so much contradiction, so much discord, and so much variety that we cannot see clearly to those higher realms of consciousness. That is the only obstruction between us and the eternal realms: the unwillingness of making the effort to still the human mind. There is, I assure you, no other obstruction between you and your eternal spirit.

Thank you.

MAY 4, 1980

Church Lecture 99
Tenth Anniversary Service

I have been granted permission to be seated during our talk. I hope you don't think I'm lazy. I just like to feel a bit more relaxed.

Now I know that many of you have attended our services for a number of years. Some of you are a bit new to the Serenity Church, but what is important is that you come when you feel that you would like to come. I have always felt, and still feel, that vibration is much more important than the physical body, because it is vibration and vibration alone that brings the peace that passeth all understanding. And so it is in this church for these ten years to this day that we have always emphasized the importance of coming to church when you feel like coming to church. And, of course, the few members that we have, I have tried to make great effort that they always feel like attending on Sunday morning *[Many in the congregation laugh.]* because it's not possible, of course, for one person to do everything.

Sometime ago the teacher of our philosophy in the spirit world brought to me a little saying, which has, over these years, brought me some degree of comfort and it clearly states, "A wise teacher suffers well the growth pains of his students." And so it is when I thought that something was intolerable or unbearable, I reminded myself that I didn't care to be a stupid teacher. Therefore, it did help me, hopefully, in some degree of tolerance.

We all seek in this life success in whatever endeavor we choose to involve our self. Once we make a decision of what we want to do in life, the easiest thing in the world is to attain it, if we know the way. Having made a decision of what to do—even though in reference to this church I felt it was forced upon me. For those of you who are not aware, I never wanted a church. Obviously, I had created some type [of] an adversity for it certainly grew into some degree of attachment. However, what is, is. And so it is when we truly decide on anything, if we, in that decision, not only accept the possibility of change in how it shall be attained, but we accept fully the Law of Personal Responsibility, then attainment is not only assured, it is absolutely guaranteed.

In making decisions in life, it is the judgments of our mind that dictate how we will attain what we desire to attain. That is where the struggle and the payment and all of the disasters are given birth. Having made a decision in life with the acceptance of responsibility for our decision and working daily with our mind to keep us free from mental laws established by judgments (how something shall be accomplished), then that that is for us—in the good and the best interest—shall take place. And so it is with the Serenity Church.

[On] the founding day of this church, ten years ago this day, the spirit stated very clearly many will enter our doors, some will stay and grow, and many will go. But that's what a church—this church—is all about. Serving the purpose for which it is founded: to share with those who are truly seeking what it has to offer. And those who are ready for what it has to offer will stay; they will come and grow with it. I have never been and, hopefully, will never be, one who is interested in growing numbers and membership rolls. Because, you know, my friends, the gift without the giver is absolutely worthless and has no value and no good in it. And what is the gift without the giver? So often, you know, in life we think we give something and we're constantly plagued with what the person we gave the item to has done with the item. So we clearly see and quickly see, it never was a gift; it was only a loan because we're still attached to it.

Freedom, of course, is dependent upon the control of the mind, which establishes the laws of bondage. We all know that creation is form or limit. We also know that limit is bondage; it has a boundary. So to be free and to express the truth that is ever available to us, we must make the effort at what is known, by all philosophies, as self-discipline: a degree of control of our own mind—not someone else's mind, but our mind.

Remember, my friends, it's never in life what someone else has done to us. It is always in life what we're doing to our self. It is our thought and our judgment, our emotion and our feeling concerning another place, person, or thing that causes us our problems. Because it's our thought, because we alone have fathered and mothered it, because we are the only creator of it, we are still the captain of that ship of thought. We can still do something about it. If we have a thought that we are lost without a certain person, as long as we choose—our minds—to entertain that thought, indeed, indeed we are lost. But we created the thought. We can send the thought back to the universe.

We can be freed from the thought that we alone have created. None of us want to live with the multitudes of thoughts or creations that we have given birth to. Why, we give birth to thoughts of colds and sickness and limitation and poverty. We don't want to keep those thoughts, but because we gave birth to those thoughts, it's up to us to give them back, to let them go from our universe and, in so doing, to be free. But, of course, we all know that that takes some degree of control.

I sat here this morning and I asked myself, "Who is this new person on our Healing List called 'That's it'?" I hadn't heard of that person before. And, of course, I'll speak to our chairman after service is over. Considering the principle that the healing is an important part of our service, if there's such a person called "That's it," I want to meet them here or hereafter. So, you see, it isn't, my friends, just the word of someone called "That's it." It's the control of the mind. Now wouldn't you find it interesting if I picked up your billet, your identification is read, and I said, "That's it." And go to the next person or the next. I know humor is the salvation of our soul. I'm sure my chairman, a student, like the rest of my students, is benefiting tremendously. *[At the end of the healing portion of the church service, the chairman read a list of names of those who were unable to attend, but whose names had been submitted for absent healing. The list of names was called the Healing List. At this service, the last "name" the chairman said was "That's it."]*

We have one basic philosophy here: that is the Law of Personal Responsibility and exposure frees our soul. Now what does that really mean?

We understand that embarrassment is an attachment to a level of consciousness that we are unwilling to change. And so, we all know that change is indispensable to the Law of Evolution. We all know that everything is evolving. Only a fool holds to that that cannot grow and change, because that [that] we hold binds us and that that we hold controls us. It binds and controls us in our mental world. Things are not the way they were yesterday, and only a fool tries to make them that way. This service, today, is not the same as it was last week. It certainly is not the same that it was ten years ago.

We opened these church doors with almost a hundred members in a very short time. And slowly, but surely, we grew, and now we have about eighteen active ones and twenty-seven total ones. And that, to me, is great growth. Because the ones we do have, the majority—and a majority is important—they work very hard. In fact, the parents of one of our members said here just at our last dinner social, "You must have some kind of a special power to get these people to work so hard." I said, "Well, I'll tell you this: none of them are killing themselves." *[Many people in the congregation laugh.]* I am a firm believer to grant to others what I grant unto myself. If I didn't grant the love and blessing of work to myself, I would certainly not be able to grant it to anyone else.

My friends, it is the freedom from the illusion called the thought of I that is our only problem. When we entertain this thought, this illusion called the I, we separate our self from the universal whole. Now say, for example, a person feels they're a little on the broke side—either broke in health, broke in money, broke in something. We always seem to be broke in something. Well, of course, we're broke in something because in that particular area of consciousness we are totally separated by the illusion of the thought of I. Let us move into the divine flow by thinking less of the I and more of the whole, then we can experience more of the whole. You see, our obstructions are nothing more and they are nothing less than our lack of understanding of the natural Law of Divine Flow. We limit the abundant good by the dictate of how it shall enter our life.

It's like a person that wants to get married. Well, is it that they want to get married or they have a mold created in their mind for a soul to fit that particular mold in that particular way? It isn't that they want to get married. No. No, that's what they *say* they want. Usually what they want—they have created in their mind a certain mold. "Now this person's going to look like this, be like that, and give me the security, the comfort, the happiness, the joy, and everything that I desire." Only God can grant you that. So much to expect from a human being. *[Many in the congregation laugh.]* There's no human being I've ever seen to fulfill those shoes. No one, ever, in creation could be that perfect. So if you're seeking marriage, you want security, financial, emotional, and go down the list, go to the source. You're deluded to look for a man to fill those shoes. One may come along your way, that's fine, but will never completely fill the multitude of desires that enter your human mind. That is not possible.

Pause for a moment; become aware of the many desires in the human mind. Look at them honestly and see if they agree. I can assure you they do not, unless you have made the effort in concentration, the key to all power, to remain in one, and one only, level of consciousness for a moment. Considering there are demonstrably eighty-one levels of consciousness through which the eternal soul is expressing itself, pause for one moment: you will find your desires at war, demanding their fulfillment and few, if any, will agree with each other. It's called the war within. And it is the war within us that needs the effort by our self to gain control over, that we may not be deluded by reflections from within and think that the war is all around us. My friends, we all know, in honesty and truth, that the war around us is a reflection of the war within us. We cannot have peace, abundant good, health, wealth, and happiness unless that's where our head is in space. Now we can put our self there, in space, if we want to make the effort. Or we can be haunted and driven into the psychiatric institutions in our world from judgments and attachments of the past.

Whenever we put a thought, a judgment in our mind, in a priority in consciousness higher than God, we pay a very dear price. We are not limited to a year or two in the payment of that price. Because we have created a false god, we must suffer the deterioration of that false god in consciousness. Search your consciousness. Ask yourself honestly if there is a desire in your mind that has greater value to your consciousness than God. [If there is,] then you are serving the false gods of which the Bible and many philosophies have taught for untold centuries. And he who serves the false gods must suffer with the false gods.

How do we know when we are serving the false gods? We know when we pause to think. When we ask our self, "What does God mean to me? Does God mean a limitless, abundant good, a feeling of peace and harmony? Is that what my God is?" If that is what your God is, then you have found the true God and you will live in the peace and harmony which *is* the true God. But if your God is one who answers the dictates of your mind when you demand to have this and have that, when you demand for people to do this and do that, be rest assured that is not the god that can free you for that's not the God of truth. That is the mental god our minds have created. That is the "Santa Claus" that brings you the gifts when you demand them. That's the god that gives and takes. That god, created by our minds, will keep us for centuries in bondage.

The God of truth is the God of freedom. It is an infinite intelligent Energy, without beginning or ending, expressing, sustaining everything. It is the mental gods that dictate what is good and what is bad. It is the mental gods that have no tolerance, that have no understanding, that are limited by the desire of the moment that desire enters the mind. You see, my friends, desire, the expression of the Divinity, becomes judgment when the mind, controlled by the illusion of the thought of I, experiences the Divinity and limits the expression of God. Because Nature herself is the constant revelation of an Infinite Intelligence, sustaining all things everywhere, we can see moment by moment. And if we so desire to experience the God within anything, we must first be still to experience the God within our self, for God communes with God, as like attracts like and becomes the Law of Attachment.

If we want to be free from the attachments that we, in our days of ignorance, have created, then we must recognize within our self and be honest with the defect in our character. When we know the weakness within our self, we can go to work to strengthen it. But if we will not be honest with our self, we can never see it and, not seeing it, continue to be the victim of its control.

Self-control, we all know, is what our soul impinges upon our consciousness—the control of our mind. If we are freed from the illusion of the thought of I, then we go to work on the control of our mind within our self. If we are not freed from the illusion of the thought of I, we dictate and try to control others. But in our efforts in life to try to control others, we become the very victims of the people we try to control. Look at a mother or a father; if they have made the effort to educate themselves and to share that education with their children, not only will their children grow and prosper and be free but they (the parents) will continue to grow and prosper and be free. But if, in their error of ignorance, they have strived to control another soul, they will be the victim of that error in consciousness. And they will continue to be the victim as long as they dictate the need to control a soul who belongs only to the Divine, to the Divinity. Remember, my friends, possession is the pain of a very, very, very deep hell. For what we strive to possess in life, in truth, is possessing us. Surely we do not try to possess the grass that grows in the field, though sometimes in our error of ignorance we don't like the way it looks. And if we're not careful, we soon become possessed by it.

These attachments are nothing more nor less than an error in our thought. It is only our uneducated ego that enjoys the so-called feeling of being important. The most important soul is the one that knows it's not important. You see, my friends, we don't have to have the need to be important, if we accept the God that sustains us. It is not important whether people like or dislike us. I had to face that. My little pride had to have some education years ago. All you have to do is serve the public for forty-some years and you'll very soon learn you've got to give up this illusion and delusion that people like or dislike you. That's not important when you know what you're supposed to do.

It isn't important whether they like you or they don't like you. I sit here to do my work; some people [think,] "Well, when's he going to stop talking?" That's not important. You know, they think it's such a blessing to be a medium. Well, it has its blessings and that that has a blessing has its curse. Don't kid yourself. You know, you take the good with the so-called opposite. That's just the way that it is. But I look at things a little differently. I didn't come here to sit down and be controlled by people who want me to shut up and get on to the next stage of the service. Because if I did, I'd be in something else. Maybe I'd be selling shoes or whatever, you see. That's not the way to live. You don't have to live that way. You don't have to live being worried and concerned whether this person's going to like you or that person's going to like you. You don't have to live being concerned whether your children will love you, because all you've got to do is sell out and give them whatever their mind wants. And be rest assured they'll hate you with a passion and you'll live to see the day when they never want to see you again. Because something inside of them knows the thing they needed the most you didn't care enough to give them: that's called discipline.

When you give a person things, it doesn't matter whether its a two-legged human or a four-legged animal, it doesn't matter, my friends, you can't buy love. You can't even sell it. But you can buy and you can sell the delusion called possession, but you cannot buy and sell love. It is not controlled by the mental world nor the thought of man. When the mind thinks it has love or it doesn't have love, just tell it to be still, for it is not within the domain of the human mind to even know what love is.

The mind knows what control is. The mind knows what possession is. The mind knows what attachment is. It's only the soul and the heart, that expresses the soul, that experiences love. Don't delude yourself that your mind knows what love is. It calls possession, control, attachment, and doing what *it* wants, it calls those *things* love.

Let us free our self from that illusion, because when you have the same feeling in your heart looking at a sunset as you do looking at a cat or a dog or a person and you have that same upliftment, you are experiencing what you know in your heart is love. It doesn't have want, need, and desire. Control and possession have want, need, and desire. Love has all the soul faculties. It has the light of reason. It has freedom. It has non-attachment. It has the all; therefore, it cannot experience need. That's the mind that has need.

You see, my friends, there's a part of us religionists call the soul. Now that has expressed itself for untold ages. It didn't begin with the birth of your physical body. It won't end with the so-called death of your physical body. It has always been. The Infinite Spirit is God. It will always be. No beginning and no ending. It is an eternal stream of consciousness. This moment, through the illusion called I, you identify. You've given yourself a name. You think someone gave it to you, but they didn't. You gave yourself a name. You gave yourself a body. You gave yourself the color of your eyes, the color of your hair, your height, your weight, and all that you think you have, that which you, through the illusion of I, identify with, you have given yourself in keeping with the laws of evolution, in keeping with your own efforts. Look at the temple in which your eternal spirit is residing this moment. That is what you have earned. Now you won't stay there, because the Law of Evolution that governs all form, is change. So even this instant it is in a process of change. But you are not that which you think you are, for if you were, you would not be. Think, my friends, what a simple truth.

In your evolution, as in mine and everyone else's, that that you have earned, you are. But you're not destined to stay at that stage of evolution. You are changing moment by moment. You can be what you desire to be. If that desire is freed from the judgment and the limit of your mind, then you are in what is called divine grace and freed from creation's Law of Payment and Attainment.

There are many ways to accomplish that which we, in our evolution, are destined to accomplish. All experiences we alone will into action. We will the experiences of our attachments into action. We will the experiences of our disasters into action. We alone will it. There is no God, the sustaining, intelligent, infinite Energy, that wills it for us. There is no one we can turn to, to blame. Because, you see, my friends, it so quickly does—our mind—blame something when things don't go the way we think they should. But oh, look what our little minds do when something goes great: we're the first one to leap on the bandwagon and take all the credit. We're the first one to say, when things are going what we think is good for us, "Well, I merited it. I merited it." But when they're going bad, "Someone else did it to me." Now when we bring into balance those two extremes by accepting each moment of personal responsibility, then we begin to be the captain of our ship of destiny. And we alone become consciously aware of how we are directing the great power that flows through us to literally will these experiences into our life.

Remember, because God, the sustaining power, is the power that sustains all thought, man makes the choice of his thought, God sustains our choice. We have never been left without choice. Because the power that sustains thought is the power of God, called good, when we make the effort to see good in all things, we will pull the goodness or God within us up through the seeming disasters in consciousness. And like attracts like and we will attract from the universe the good in the seeming disasters that we experience through our errors of ignorance. And so, as the Bible teaches, "In the midst of the Philistines, I will deliver thee." We are delivered moment by moment when we make the effort to see the good in all things. Because if we will make that effort, because the good, or goodness, is ever within us, because it is the very power that is sustaining our thoughts and our feelings, we call that forth within us and nothing can stand against it.

Surely ten years of experiences in this church have been a wonderful thing, not only in my life, but the lives of many people. Here is an opportunity to grow, not that opportunity doesn't reside everywhere, because you are never without opportunity. It meets like the hands of the clock every so often because only every so often is your mind still that you may see it. But opportunity is ever present, never absent or away. It is ever with us, if we will still our mind. Nothing is impossible. What makes things impossible is the judgment which we give a higher priority than God, our God.

Remember, it's our God and your God; it's my God and everyone's God. But I can only experience that God inside of me. You may experience it inside of you. Once you have experienced it inside of you and I experience it inside of me, then we recognize it when we see it expressing itself. And we can see it expressing itself when we free our self of judgment, when we separate truth from creation. Now we are here in this world of creation to separate our true being from creation. [That] doesn't mean we leave creation. We are in creation and not a part of creation. When we free our self from the need to attach to the thought that comes into our consciousness, when we are freed from that need, we separate truth from creation. We are no longer bound by limit, for we no longer have judgment.

Now when we are still, we see very clearly the bird. It chirps. It sings. It expresses itself. But we must be still to see there are other birds [who] don't like the chirping of the robin. The sparrow doesn't like the noise of another bird and on down the list of all creation, for creation is the Law of Duality. It is creation that offers us the likes and dislikes. It is creation that is the king, that is the judge. God, the true God, of which we are an inseparable part, does not judge. Only creation judges. Our mind is a part of creation. It is a part, inseparably a part, of duality. Our mind knows good and bad. Our soul does not, for our soul is the perfect note of harmony, the perfect balance. There is no opposites in the Eternal Being. There is only one truth. There is no duality to truth. So when you understand that you, in truth, are above and beyond the duality of creation, then you'll be freed from what creation offers, which is bondage. You will use creation as you drive your automobile: to take you where you want to go in the plane of consciousness in which you are, but you will never again be controlled by it. That, my friends, takes a little bit of daily effort. Do what you have to do in life, care less what the world thinks of it and you will be freed from the thought of man.

We all know what we're supposed to be doing. No one really needs to tell us. All people ever do is remind us, hopefully, of what we're supposed to be doing. It isn't that we don't know. Oh, we do know, all right, but it's rare that we still our mind long enough to allow that truth within us to come up and say, "Just a minute. You know you haven't been doing what you're supposed to do. How much longer will you take?" You see, it's the illusion we must someday free our self from.

We are above and beyond what we think we are, but we think in limit and we're bound by limit. That will not always be. That is in a process of change. And this is why I said to you earlier, many come and many go. Many of my students, they understand one thing or they understand another. And I have said for many years I'm so grateful that it's on tape. It's recorded. They change this. They change that. But the tapes they can't change. That's the way that it is. Because we all are on different levels of growth. We all understand things a little differently.

Many people come to the Serenity Church. They don't understand why this regulation, why that regulation. We have a multitude of regulations. But we have a multitude of thoughts and judgments from our people. Each regulation was given birth by a law of transgression, by someone, somewhere deciding they wanted to do a certain thing without an ounce of consideration for other people. And so, regulation was given birth. We began without all these different kinds of regulations. In fact, wouldn't it be nice just to come to church and forget the hour, but who would be here to serve? It would really be an interesting type of church. So our doors were opened for a 10 a.m. service. And even in those days somebody wanted it at 2 in the afternoon, because they felt that was a little early to have to get up on a Sunday morning. I told them very nicely I didn't care for people to come to church that felt it was too early to get up. I would rather they would stay home in bed. I had enough work to do.

I love you all very much. Thank you very kindly for supporting Serenity.

Thank you.

MAY 3, 1981

Church Lecture 100

As our chairman has stated, [there are] a couple of weeks left before our annual bazaar. I know that many of you are not aware that this church has less than twenty-four members; that it has, of the twenty-four, less than twelve who actually do the work. Therefore, it is of critical importance that those members of the church, numbering less than twenty-four, make arrangements with me this day on the time that they will be here to do their annual, selfless service work in order that these church doors may remain open for those who are yet to come and benefit for the twelve years of its organization. To those of you who are friends of this church, I encourage you personally and collectively to offer what help you can on that once-a-year time in order that we may continue to rent this hall, to bring these services to you, to pay the just debts that the organization existing in a material world must incur. To those of you who are visitors and to everyone, I will come to all of you this day to see if you wish to support this organization and make your reservation for this bazaar, the Saturday, two weeks to be.

For many years—forty-four at the present time—I have taught to the best of my ability the teachings that I have received. And one of those teachings [is] the Law of Personal Responsibility, another, the spirit of spontaneity. So few people seem to understand what the spirit of spontaneity means. And so in keeping with the teachings I have brought through for these many years and the demonstration being the revelation, we all receive the golden opportunity to experience the spirit of spontaneity, which is the willingness, the ability to respond to instant change without thought, without concern, without judgment.

And so after twelve years of weekly Sunday services, a change was brought today in our regular scheduling of our service. A change that my students were not informed about in order that they, personally, may experience the truth that is within them. The willingness, the ability to respond to instantaneous change without thought, without judgment, without fear.

Many people come to Spiritualism with the motivation of establishing contact with another dimension. A wise person, with that motive, prays for the full awareness of the soul faculty of discernment. For we all know from our personal experiences that we communicate and are in contact with many, many mental realms of consciousness. Some of them we judge to be beneficial, and some of them we judge not to be beneficial. As it is a mind that communicates with a world of mental substance, so it is a soul that communicates with a world of soul substance. So the motivation to communicate with another dimension must never override the desire to awaken the soul faculty of discernment and the spiritual faculties of personal responsibility, the light of reason. For of what benefit is it to any of us to communicate with any dimension that we do not understand and even in the knowledge of its existence, to make no effort to apply the laws that it reveals?

Truth is not something we gather. Truth is something we are. And it has been and continues to be my desire and responsibility to reveal to those, in keeping with the law, who are attracted to our organization, to help them to help themselves to see whatever they seek is wherever they are. And wherever they are is always dependent upon how much effort they choose to make to control their thoughts, their mind, their desires, their hopes, and their fears.

Those of us who experience fear—and rare is a person that I have found who doesn't—reveal to themselves and to the world where their faith truly lies. We can only fear what we doubt, and we can only doubt what we think we do not control. And so man doubts and man fears the existence of God and the light of truth. For man knows from his own efforts that he cannot control it and therefore, man fears what he knows he cannot control. And that fear becomes a doubt; doubt, a denial: and so, to many God does not exist. And, of course, if God does not exist, there is no possibility that his ministering angels could possibly exist.

It is not, nor has it ever been, my purpose in life to prove to anyone the existence of God, nor the work of his ministering angels. For it is only the mind that requires proof. And the mind is never satisfied and proof, therefore, is never sufficient.

So we go through life ever seeking and searching for what we call truth and what we call freedom. And as opportunity knocks constantly at the door of our conscience, we turn away when we sense and see the payment for what we desire. As recent as moments ago, I watched, as a teacher, the upset, the trauma, the fear, and the concern of people because of a change which was brought about by the authority of this humble church. And so it only proves to us in the moment of our experiences how far we have allowed our self to go on the path of light and reason, that will transfigure and transform us.

I spent my very early years in life here on earth in nightly seances with spirits materializing in physical form, for that was the phase of my mother's mediumship—one of them. And I can assure you from those many years and early experiences, the materialization of any spirit or any other manifestation of any spirit is not sufficient proof to any mind. For it will satisfy, temporarily, one level of consciousness, but it will not satisfy all levels of consciousness until man judges he can control God's angels. And folly is the judgment in any mind who thinks it can.

And so along the path of spiritual awakening, as man sees and finally accepts that he cannot control that which is outside, he begins to doubt, to fear, to deny. And life within us becomes miserable. The need to control is the need within us to control our thoughts, our judgments that stand in the way between that which we truly are and the Source of which we are an inseparable part.

We live in want, we live in need, we live in unfulfilled desires only because, through an error in our thought, known as the thought of I—the thought of independence, the thought of individualization—do we separate in consciousness our self from the Source, which we are an inseparable part of. And because of that error of ignorance in our mind, we experience the lack of the good of life. Because many of us are yet unwilling to face that truth, we insist on blaming others for the experiences that we encounter, and that reveals, of course, to us the truth of where we are.

No one need tell us where we are. We all know where we are. We all know what we are. We all know who we are. And there are times, through our lack of self-discipline, through our lack of facing personal responsibility, that we don't like to see who we are and what we are and why we are. Because we do not like something in no way implies nor guarantees that it is not good for us. For all things are sustained by the same intelligent divine Energy that man calls God.

And who is so great—greater than God—to dictate that one person's lifestyle is wrong, while their own is right? Who is so great to dictate what is best for all humanity? Usually it is the ones who dictate that they know what is best or right for themselves. But there is something inside the consciousness of one who knows what is best for themselves and for everyone else. There is something inside in their own consciousness where they experience insecurity and fear and, therefore, an insatiable need to force everyone they meet and everyone they can find to reform them to their way, in order that they may prove to their own uneducated egos that they are right and the rest of the world is wrong.

Religions for untold centuries have taught and demonstrated the benefit of fear, for fear is nothing more nor less than faith in the vehicle known as the human mind. And because the religionists of old have known that, because they have known, and do know—many to this day—that man's greatest weakness, his faith in the thought of I, the illusion which is but the shadows of the judgments of yesterday, the religionists know that man's faith is so great in the illusion of the thought of I that fear and fear alone will help him to make the changes. Though under duress, they're made, for man serves the realm of fear. For his faith in the illusion known as the thought of I is so great, his fear of what he does not know is not willing to pay the price to investigate to understand. They know; and so the religions of our world are filled with fear.

We know in the Living Light Philosophy what fear is. We know it is not necessary to teach a person to fear, for we know whenever any person believes he or she is the illusion called the thought of I, fear is guaranteed. You don't need to teach man the fear of death, the fear of things he doesn't know. Man already has that in his belief that he is the illusion, the separation, the thought known as I.

And so it is that as long as we insist on living the lie, we must accept the payment of the lie. We must continue to want. We must continue to need. We must continue to suffer. For that is the payment of the lie that we insist on believing is the truth.

And so, my friends, we teach to suffer senses not in vain for freedom of the soul is gained. And if it is your choice not to make the conscious, moment-by-moment effort by controlling your own mind in the illusion, be of good cheer, Life herself will extract the payment from you, and you will understand it as struggle, as suffering, as discord and disease. Man cannot experience discord until man believes he *is* discord. And man believes by his living demonstration that he is discord because man believes the discordant thoughts within his consciousness are himself. And so we are a house divided. We believe in love one moment, only to believe in hatred the next. We believe in peace one moment, only to believe in war the next, ever dependent upon what past experiences are controlling us by the opening of the thought of I, the identification with self.

We believe in our right to live our own lifestyles, and we believe it is our right to deny others their choice. We believe it by our demonstration. We believe it by our prejudgments. We believe it by our prejudices. That is the living demonstration. If we take a few moments each day to be honest with our self, then we will know our self, but until the day comes that knowing our self is a greater value than chasing the things of yesterday that we have created in our mind, the effort, the twenty minutes in twenty-four hours will never be available to us.

There will never be enough time until we face what man calls death. Let us be reasonable with what we call death. We see it all around us. We see a person one day; perhaps the next, they have died. Many of us, if not all of us, have experienced watching, hearing people leaving the physical body. And we see the body lay there, cold as ice. Something's gone. We know that something has gone. We know because the body does not look the same. It does not move. Its flesh is cold. And so we have to ask our self the question, "That something that caused it to move, what happened to it? I must ask myself that question because life is revealing to me that the same thing is going to happen to me."

A few weeks ago I gave a class, a private class, on the aging process known to man as senility. The light revealed in that private class was so great, the cost to our church so phenomenal, the classes, private, had to be discontinued that the organization may continue to serve the public. And so in keeping with our teachings, if the light is too bright, it is best that man see it not now. The light must not be [so] brightened that the soul, struggling through a mental world, shall leave the light. For it is better to have the light of one candle in the darkness than no light at all. And I have found in my forty-four years of service that, usually, the ones who are kept on the fringe of the light are the ones who remain. Rare, indeed, rare is a person able to enter the full light of truth and remain. It has always been my wish and desire to share with the world the many higher teachings that remain to this day locked in the vaults that, because of their light, I am unable to share with even my closest students.

And so it is that we shall all face death, for we face it each day whether we know it or not. And so the body goes into the furnace or into the ground. Dependent upon our identification with that body reveals where we will be. The students closest to me know that I never attend the graveyard. They also know the reason. Because look at the demonstrable laws, my friends. If our identification with and belief that we are the body that our soul is now expressing through, that identification and that belief does not change when we move out of the physical body. The more concern we have with the wrinkles on our face or the bags on our knees or whatever concern we choose to have of this physical flesh is the attachment to and the bondage to wherever the physical body lies, be it burned or be it buried. And that demonstrable law, that applies to a physical, material world, applies to the mental body, to the thought that we think and believe we are. So I see over these many years the astral forms that hover over the graves century after century after century. The astral forms earthbound in houses, in buildings, in places, in things. And God only knows I am not the only one that sees and hears them. And then the pathetic souls bound and attached to the mental realms that are all around and about us.

And the easiest thing to communicate with are those so bound to earth where we have permitted our self to be. What teacher with any sense of personal responsibility would open the doors to any soul to communicate with those earth-bound dimensions and not day-by-day work with them seven days a week that they do not lose their mental balance and become known as mentally diseased from the inability to cope with the forms they've opened the door to. Is it not enough to work with the uncontrollable thoughts that we have in the course of one day than to add to that the millions of mental forms that we potentially open the door to?

And so each of my students, that are students from their demonstration of personal responsibility to the organization through which the light flows, those students I spend seven days a week with.

If it had been my interest over these many years and my desire for the gold of earth, I assure you I would not limit my students to twelve. I assure you the requests from people to enter classes is, and has been, by the thousands. My interest is not in the gold of this earth. My interest is in the gold of heaven and that gold is the light of wisdom. For only through wisdom shall man become qualified to gain control over his own illusion and, in so doing, do what the Bible teaches: "Over all creation have I given you charge." The prophets were not speaking of the dogs and cats. They were speaking over the creation of the thoughts of man.

Thank you.

NOVEMBER 7, 1982

Church Lecture 101

[The Laws Governing the Continuity of Organization]

This morning, instead of speaking to you on the thirteen-year history of the Serenity Church, I wish to speak to you on the laws governing the continuity of organization, for that is not only of interest to all of us, but is, indeed, personally beneficial, for we all are an organization unto our self. Our awakening to that demonstrable truth is ofttimes very confusing and chaotic, to say the least. We are filled, in our lives, with so many desires, known as temptations. We understand, of course, a temptation reveals to us the areas of weakness of our own character. For one cannot be tempted to be the victim of anything unless one is weak in that particular area of consciousness. And so we find ourselves going through life tempted by many things, frustrated by our seeming lack of fulfilling these many desires that we permit to bombard our consciousness.

The Lord's Prayer clearly states, "Lord, lead us not into temptation." And in a sense, to the uninitiated, it appears to be a contradiction. However, upon further study and investigation, we clearly see that "Lord," as spoken forth in that prayer, is revealing to us "law." So if we study the Lord's Prayer as the Law's Meditation, then we can see that the law is what leads us, so to speak, into an awakening of our own weaknesses. That can and does, in time, serve us very, very well, for one cannot begin to control, nor to strengthen, anything that they are not first aware of.

We ofttimes take our many acts and activities as a very normal and natural thing. It is when these seeming desires, thoughts, and activities begin to interfere with the reasonable balance of our life, our health, our wealth, and our happiness—and it is at those moments that we pause to consider what laws have we, in our errors of ignorance, permitted ourselves to follow. And in that awakening we make conscious, reasonable choices of what it is we truly wish to accomplish in life. Is it the daily, temporal satisfactions of the many desires that we expose our self to or is it an accomplishment, a fulfillment, an awakening of a purpose of being? For surely, we all know that we have not entered this earth realm, with all of the multitudes of experiences that it has to offer, to simply be the victim of one desire after another and finally leave this world with the feelings of regret and discouragement because for some unknown reason, we tell our self, we never did really accomplish anything lasting, enduring, or worthwhile.

Footprints on the sands of time is the purpose of entering this realm of illusion.

For in keeping with this philosophy and its demonstrable application of the law, we know beyond a shadow of any doubt that heaven is not only a state of consciousness we are in process of growing to, but it is here and it is now; that this so-called God or infinite intelligent Power is constantly being used by us. It is constantly available to us. And in keeping with the Law of Personal Responsibility, it is our job, our effort to awaken to the very process through which we can become most receptive to an intelligent, neutral Energy that supports and sustains whatever it is we choose, through the vehicle of our mind, to direct this intelligent Energy to.

Now the world is filled with a multitude of positive thinking philosophies and teachings. For some, they seem to work, for a time. For others, they do not seem to work at all. Now, is the problem with what the teachings are, that work for some and seemingly do not work for others or work for a time and then fail completely when we need it the most—where does the problem truly exist?

We all, I'm sure, will agree when the need is sufficient and we have tried everything, that is when we enter the court of last resort. That is when we've passed through the many courts of judgments and dictates of our own mind, until finally we are ready and we are willing to accept the possibility of something that will work that we, with our minds, cannot control. It is there, in the court of last resort—where no judge exists—it is there, where will, the total acceptance of the human mind, the Divine enters and we are freed from the various problems, disasters, and discouragements that our minds seem to place us in for a time.

For it is when we, at any moment, free our self completely from all judgment, that is when we leave the mental world and enter the spiritual consciousness, where to God or good all things are not only possible, all things good are demonstrable. Now we may enter that state of consciousness whenever we choose to enter it. It, however, seems to be that we only enter it when everything else has failed.

This philosophy, for many years, has taught to all the listening ears who have come to hear it, it has worked to apply the very laws it has revealed, that a law, being a universal law, is not dependent upon anyone. It just is. When we choose to have the effect or the experience of the law, then we must apply the rules that govern that particular law. That choice is with us moment by moment.

We find it difficult to let go of what we think we have. This is why we find it difficult to change our thought, to change our judgment, to change our attitude. It is because we believe, unfortunately, that our thought is something we own; our judgment is something we possess. Therefore, we must nourish it, cherish it, and protect it. Yet the Law of Evolution clearly reveals that evolution is not possible without change. We look around all creation: the trees change; people do change; the animals change. All things that the eyes can see, the senses can sense, and the ears can hear, all things of creation, all things of mental substance, which is nothing but a reflection, not truth—[creation] never can be truth for it reflects what is. It never was and it never will be what *is*. And so it is in that realm where judgments exist, where thought exists. And they are subject to the law that governs a world of illusion. They're subject to the world of the mind, therefore, in spite of our judgments, in spite of our attitudes, in spite of our thoughts, and in spite of our own beliefs, they change. They change in our consciousness. Because they are not truth, because they are reflecting the Light, they are not the Light. For the Light is formless; being formless, it is timeless; being timeless, it is eternal and it is infinite. All other things, *all* other things are reflections and, therefore, in truth, they are illusions.

We look at our life and we see judgments of many years ago. Some of them have fallen by the wayside and have been replaced with other ones. From more experience, from more judgments, the changes do come about. However, there comes a time in our evolution when we say to our self, "Enough is enough. I have spent too many years going through life and not experiencing what I know is my divine birthright." For it is our divine birthright to experience or reflect—for that's what experience is—to reflect the goodness that we truly are.

What keeps us from reflecting that goodness is our belief that we are what we think. It is our belief that our judgment is us. It is our belief that our attitude is us. And yet we know from our own experiences that our judgments are not us, for we change our judgments in time. We know from our own experiences that our attitude is not us, for our attitudes change. Ofttimes, in a split second do they change. Therefore, in honesty, pausing in our thought, we see that it is an over-identification with our mind, with our thoughts, and with our judgments. And that over-identification is known to us as belief.

So man looks out in the world, he believes one religion for a time, changes, and he believes another. He believes in one political way for a time; various experiences happen and he believes in another. Is it he, the true being, that's made the changes? No, it's only a redirection of intelligent, infinite Energy that he is receptive to, that he has directed to that judgment or to another. Now in time all of that falls by the wayside.

We know beyond a shadow of any doubt that we have come here to this planet, Earth, to fulfill a purpose in this great evolutionary process. We did not come here to this Earth planet ignorant, just beginning. The only thing that begins in life, anywhere, is that which ends. So, if you ask anyone do they believe in total annihilation of their consciousness and their identity, something inside of them knows absolutely and positively that that is the furthest thing from the truth. That which fears death is that which fears change, for death, so-called, represents to the mind change. And because the mind cannot control it, it fears it. So those who have faith in the thoughts and judgments of their mind, have great fear for death, ever in keeping with their over-identification with their own thoughts and judgments. But those who fear death, they also fear life. They fear birth. For what they fear is what they cannot control. And so we cannot, with our limited earth mind, control the coming to this world, nor the going.

But we can do something far greater and far more important than our fruitless efforts to control the uncontrollable. For the coming to earth and the leaving [of] earth is not dependent upon the thought of man.

There is an intelligent Power that sustains the thought of man and whatever it is that sustains a thing is greater than the thing itself. For when the sustaining, intelligent energy is removed, it no longer exists, but returns to the substance from whence it has been created. And so our thoughts, given birth by our own minds, they come from a substance called mental substance. They are destined to return to it. Only a fool would believe they are their thought. Only a fool would believe they are their judgment. For they have risen only to fall. We look at the history of mankind and we see many judgments have risen, and we see many have fallen. So the rise and fall, the emotional trauma, the struggle, the stress, and the discouragement that we at times believe we are, is not, in truth, us.

And we can experience the truth we are when we take control of the human mind. For the mind, a vehicle designed by Infinite Intelligence to serve that which we are—not that which we believe we are, but to serve that which we are—has risen supreme time and again. It deludes and deceives us through what is known as our own belief. And our belief is only an effect of our over-identification with our own mind, with a mental world. So when we experience these emotional upsets with our automobiles, with the things of creation that are designed to serve us, not to control us—because we tempt to control that which is beyond our responsibility of control, we are controlled by that which is beyond our responsibility of control. Because of our own belief, we're controlled by other people. Yet we think, for a time, that we are free. We are always controlled by what we are dependent upon.

So we look at life and be honest with our self, ask our self the question, "What does my survival mean to me? Does it mean I must have a house, an automobile, and the financial security to support it? If so, who or what am I dependent upon?" If your answer, in your honesty, reveals to you [a] person, place, or thing, then beyond a shadow of any doubt you can clearly see that by your own choice you are controlled by something beyond your personal responsibility. You have made that possible in keeping with thoughts, judgments, attitudes—belief. And that is the mental law that has been established.

Now no one, when they pause to think, wants to be controlled by anything or anyone. There's something inside of us that revolts at the thought of being the victim of something or someone that we cannot control, for it is contrary to the Law of Individualization. It is contrary to it and, therefore, is in discord with it. And so we have these many problems in life. We move from being the victim of one thing, to another thing.

We try to change the people that we become involved with, because we've made the judgments of how they should react in order that we may experience the fulfillment of the many desires of our own mind. This process goes on moment by moment, century after century in a world of creation. And it is one way, in these many years—forty-some years now of counseling, and I still say the same thing to the many people with domestic problems: you can change your mind, you can change your thoughts and your judgments, for they are within the realm of your right of personal responsibility. Your effort and temptation to bring about a change in another person is not only foolhardy, but it is self-destructive. For the law reveals clearly whatever changes we make within our consciousness, that which is in harmony with us shall grow or shall go.

On the first day, thirteen years ago this day, of opening this the Serenity Church, I spoke to the congregation at that time and to my students. Many, many, many people will come and go through the doors of Serenity. They will grow or they will go. That is the very principle upon which the Serenity Church firmly stands. We do not ask people to come and we do not ask people to go; that is not the purpose for which I serve. Those who are seeking shall come. They shall go to the river. And it is our responsibility only to show them where the river flows. It is not the responsibility of anyone to dunk them in the river, for a wise man gives what he has to give, caring less what the world does with it, for the bondage is in the attachment to the fruits of action. There is no freedom to the mind that is concerned about what someone does with one's efforts. It is our motive that we must examine. What are we doing what we're doing for? Are we doing it for someone? Why, of course, then we're concerned what they're doing with the fruits of our action. And therefore, we are bound by that chain. But the truth of the matter is, we are, in truth, doing it for our self.

The law clearly reveals we always get what we really want, for we always do what we really want. Oh, we like to say we'd like to do this and we'd like to do that, but we can't do this and we can't do that because our wife won't allow it, our husband won't allow it, this one won't allow it, and that one won't allow it. That's the great con artist within our consciousness. For in the final analysis, life clearly reveals we always get what we really want because we always do what we really want. The problem is, after we've done it, we forget that we wanted to do it. For we have lost, over these many years, control of our mind. Losing control is an effect of losing our perspective, our true awareness of the thoughts and the judgments that we are serving.

Now we don't like to serve anything. In fact, we don't even like to serve what some of us don't even like to call God. Well, my friends, stop and think. We have no problem serving our self. So what it is, is an evolution and an awakening of what our true being is. It's not this little package called selfishness. That's what we believe we are. We believe we're that and time marches on and we believe we're something else. And we keep going through that karmic wheel of illusion, 'til finally the wheel spins so fast, it spins us right off into the universes.

Now, in the Law of Continuity, there is nothing in our life that we haven't already, and still are, demonstrating that law. Oh, yes, many people demonstrate clearly the Law of Continuity. The expression may be different than what we think it should be. Fickleness—I know many, many people who demonstrate the Law of Continuity in the area of fickleness. In the area of a good start and a poor finish, the Law of Continuity is revealed. It just doesn't happen to be what we judge the Law of Continuity is. Law is impartial. How we choose to express it is something else. Some people demonstrate the Law of Continuity religiously in being late for their own commitments. They are very dutiful in demonstrating that Law of Continuity. Then, we have others who demonstrate the Law of Continuity in the area of consciousness known as promptness.

Now that's important, for what does promptness reveal? Promptness reveals the Law of Consideration, for it respects the rights of another individual. It respects those rights. When you have a commitment in life and you establish the law by your own voluntary choice, you have a responsibility. You commit yourself to a time and a place and if you do not demonstrate your value for your own commitments, you guarantee the law to return unto you when someone, someday, somewhere shall have no value for commitments made to you.

Now the law, you see—this is what's important, for law is life. It's important to realize that when, through a lack of effort and control of your own mind, that you make commitments in life and you do not fulfill those commitments, you are narrowed in consideration of your own responsibilities. And you establish a law within your own consciousness. For all laws have no beginnings or endings. They're great circles. All spiritual laws are circular laws. We step onto the circle, and we step off. They have no beginning or ending, not spiritual law. It just is. So we step onto that Law of Commitment and it goes out into the universe. We try to break the law and we live to see the day it does a fine job on breaking us, that which we believe that we are. For whoever tempts to break universal laws of consciousness, that are unbreakable, shall be broken by them.

So life reveals to us, if we are honest with our self, it clearly reveals and demonstrates what we alone have done, are doing, and tempted to do. This moment reveals what we are tempted the next moment. All we have to do is to be honest with this moment. Remember, the moments past are shadows. And whoever chooses to live in the shadows can never see that light of goodness, for they are blinded by what has passed.

And so on this the thirteenth anniversary of the expression of the Living Light Philosophy through the Serenity Church, let us remember the benefits of the Law of Encouragement. Whoever permits themselves the sanity of encouragement awakens within their own consciousness the soul faculty of courage. Now what happens from the expression of the soul faculty of courage? And all faculties are triune in nature, as all functions are triune in nature. They permit this soul faculty of courage to impinge upon the mental substance. That impingement is known to us as determination. Now a person finds, when they have a desire, that they are very determined. They are determined to fulfill their desire, to experience the reward of their so-called need.

But let us pause in this great determination, which is an impingement of the soul faculty of courage. What [do] we do with it? Do we pause? When this determination we experience within our mental substance, do we pause? Do we look at the law clearly? Do we honestly speak to our self and then to our mind and say, "All right, I am determined to have this." If we are so foolhardy as to say, "at any and all costs," then believe me, the price is very great. But if we're reasonable with our self, we get what we're determined to get, and we do not tempt to hold it when it's ready to go. Then, we have a chance to free our self from a great deal of grief and suffering.

It is the demand of the human mind to control whatever it permits to enter its mind that is the bondage of life. It is the nature of the human mind to gather. It is the very nature of the human mind to preserve and to protect what is in it. We can free our self from the basic design and nature of the human mind by not over-identifying with it and believing that it is us.

Thank you kindly.

MAY 6, 1984

CHURCH QUESTIONS
AND ANSWERS

Church Questions and Answers 1

As our chairman has stated, beginning as a new format today, I will indeed be grateful to be receptive to the spirit and answer the questions that you have submitted, which are of interest to you. I'm sure that you all understand that your personal questions have been placed in the billets—the envelopes on the billet table—but these are questions of a spiritual and general interest to our congregation. And so I will ask our chairman, this morning, to read off the first question.

Thank you. Would you please comment upon chiropractic care as an aid in removing obstructions to the flow of energy in the body?

In reference to this question concerning the treatment or care of chiropractic, we must understand that many people do not readily make changes in their thinking. And chiropractic care is really only seventy years known to us today in this world, but it is not a new treatment. It is not new to the world. It was well known to ancient civilizations. In reference to its benefit, that, of course, is dependent upon each individual.

These vertebras of our spine carry thousands upon thousands of nerve cords from our brain that affect each and every part of our anatomy. Whenever there is an obstruction, created by the misalignment of the spine, there is, of course, an effect in that part of our anatomy that is controlled by that particular nerve. Now these obstructions or misalignments of our spine are not just created by a physical fall or a blow to our back, but the spine, carrying these various nerves to the parts of our body, moves in its alignment depending upon the degree of peace that we experience in our lives. For example, if we find our self extremely emotionally upset over a period of time, it has an effect upon the alignment of our spine.

Some children come into this world with spines that are already misaligned. If you understand anything about the process of evolutionary incarnation, then you can understand that the individualized soul, in its evolution, has earned or merited that type of a body. It can and is beneficial to those people who have a sincere desire to accept the possibility of a different type of health care than they have already experienced. Within the coming thirty years, chiropractic care will be more readily accepted by the medical profession. Thank you.

Thank you. Please explain the saying, "A dog in court is a friend to God." [This is a saying from the Serenity Game.]

Well, first we must understand what we mean by the word *dog* and what we mean by the word *court*. If we understand the word *court* to mean a seat of judgment, then we can understand this allegorical statement, "A dog in court is a friend of God." A dog is an old symbol of friendship. And so, when friendship is called to the seat of justice, you can be rest assured that there is, for the friend or the dog, there is a justice greater than the minds of men, which base their justice upon the limited experiences that they have already had. And so, that is, basically, the meaning of that saying.

Thank you. What does the card in the philosophy game [the Serenity Game], "The guest will never quest," mean?

Whenever we are a guest of anyone, we experience a broader consideration, if we are a guest of a host that knows how to be a host. And so it says, "The guest will never quest." When we understand that we are, in truth, the guest of the Divine Host, that we—our lives—are sustained and maintained by this infinite Divine Spirit, then we will never quest, we will never want, and we will never need.

Thank you. How can one review the past without attaching oneself to the past?

Well, of course, that could be easily answered in the simple word of objectivity. But when we attempt to review our past experiences, until we learn to control our mind and to control, at least to some degree, our emotions, we cannot, in truth, be objective in reviewing past experiences. For we have all had the experience of thinking of past events and when we do so, 90 percent of the time we reexperience the negative events that have taken place in our past. And in so doing, instead of learning the lessons that were offered from those past experiences, we review them and become discouraged and depressed.

In keeping with that understanding, we all, I know, are interested, to some degree, in success. And I have yet to meet a man—a human being—that is not successful. I will admit that it does seem that most people are successful in the principle of failure, but that does not deny that they are successful. Thank you. Yes.

Thank you. It occurs to me, in this instance, that a question is synonymous with a judgment, predicated upon preconceived opinion and, therefore, must be balanced with spontaneity, which may or may not be forthcoming upon demand.

That, of course, could be very true. That depends entirely upon the questioner. If we understand that there is a vast difference between a judgment and a decision, then we may ask a question and not be bound by the limits of a judgment. A judgment is a bound decision—a vast difference from a free will or choice decision. For a judgment demands and dictates what the effects of its bound decision or judgment shall be. A decision has the acceptance and total consideration that, whatever the results are, they are ever in keeping with the law that the decision itself has originally established. Thank you.

Thank you. Please explain how someone on the earth realm holds classes for spirit children.

It's very simple, my friends, if you understand that our spiritual body is in the process of growth. Because it is a body, it has a beginning and has an ending. Now many people, I am sure, think that our body, our so-called spiritual body, is something that is eternal. It is only the Divine Spark, the Divinity, that is eternal. The vehicles or bodies that this Divine Spark or

Infinite Intelligence uses to express itself is not, is not eternal. Your physical body reveals that it is limited because it is form. Anything that is form has beginning and, by the very Law of Beginning, has its own ending. And so it is that we are not, in our present thinking, we are not the people that we were twenty years ago, for we have made changes and we constantly make changes. That that changes is not eternal. Only the principle that sustains that which changes is eternal.

And so, my friends, when religions speak of the individualized soul and they speak of eternal life, they are, in truth, speaking of that which is formless and free. All of nature teaches us each and every day that form is limit; it is limitation, that it is born and that it dies, only to be born again. Your individualized consciousness is ever in a state of growth and progression. Let us not be concerned about being annihilated, for we annihilate thoughts which we find our self attached to each and every moment of our being. But in the annihilation, they only return to the substance from which they were given birth. So that that was, can be again. But remember, it is only the formless and the free that is eternal. Thank you.

Thank you. If we are supposed to be free of desires, doesn't that cause a person to react by feeling action is without use, causing a feeling of despair?

I don't recall in the Living Light Philosophy any statement ever made for us to be totally without desire, when desire is, in truth, the divine expression, the expression of the infinite God or Infinite Intelligence. In reference to desire, it is not a matter of being freed from the principle of desire. It is a matter of being freed from the judgment that immediately takes control of desire the moment the mind senses desire. It is the judgment of the desire which creates the attachment to the desire, which in turn creates the bondage and the difficulties in our life. Thank you.

Thank you. If one sets a law into motion, is there any way to know if it is in the best interest of our soul's evolvement?

Oh, yes indeed. Of course, there is a way to know whatever law it is that you set into motion whether or not it is in your best interest. There is one word and one faculty that will help you in that and that is the faculty of honesty. Thank you.

Thank you. How does one know the difference between self-will and divine will?

How does one know the difference between self-will and divine will? When you experience will and are freed from judgment, then you can be assured that it is divine will and not self-will.

Thank you. How can all levels of consciousness be in agreement when making a decision?

By knowing thyself. We understand in this philosophy that there are eighty-one levels of consciousness. In order for all levels to be in unity and in accord, we must first know those levels; we must first know our self.

Thank you. What are the laws, please, governing twinship and other multiple birth of souls?

Well, that is indeed a long discussion. I will try to make it as brief as possible. You hear in this world about so-called identical twins. They are not identical. There are no two forms that you will ever experience—be it a plant, a tree, a human, or a rock—that are, in truth, identical. They may appear to be identical, but they are not, for that is contrary to the Law of Individualization. There are no two forms, whether those forms are created by the divine laws of nature or whether those are forms created by man, there are, and never will be, any two forms that are identical. Thank you.

Thank you. What are the best ways of helping self and others in being a fruitful citizen in community and broader society?

When one is no longer concerned about helping oneself. And I'm sure we will all agree—frequently agree—that we haven't done too well of a job about helping self. When we're interested in helping another, we are freed from the concern of helping self. And in so doing we are helped by the only Intelligence that really knows how to help us, and that's called, in Spiritualism, the Infinite Intelligence or God.

Thank you. When you die, do you always see your loved ones from earth that have gone before you to heaven? And have some already reincarnated?

Well, in reference [to] when you pass from this physical body, for the physical body returns to the elements from whence it was composed and man calls that death. No, there is no guarantee that you will see the loved ones that you knew while on earth. That is entirely dependent upon your own evolution. If you have evolved to the plane of consciousness on which your loved ones reside, then, of course, you will reside with them. It is true, however, that many of those who have passed to the other world before us will descend to these other dimensions, lowering their vibration to greet us as we cross over from this blind, earthly world into an awakening world of our spirit. But there is no guarantee. That is ever dependent upon our own efforts to evolve ourselves.

Thank you. Sometimes I am absolutely certain I am in principle, but after counseling or discussion, I see that what seemed to be principle is actually personality. How can a person learn to perceive correctly when it is principle and when it is personality?

By not making the judgment that they are certain that they are in principle. Because if you are in principle, number one: you are not concerned about principle; and number two: you are not making the judgment that you are in principle because being in principle, truth, which is principle, needs no defense. Thank you.

Thank you. It is stated that as we evolve upon the path of light that the temptations from the world of creation will tempt us even stronger to leave the light. Yet, I have found that the experiences I have had have not been as profound within my consciousness to keep me tied to creation as when I first started studying this philosophy. Would you please clarify in what way the temptations are stronger?

Well, to clarify to the questioner, who already appears from the statement to be well illumined, would be for me most difficult, I think. However, whenever we make any effort to achieve any goal in life, whether it's playing basketball or golf or anything, we are often distracted from the goal that we have set for our self. It is the very nature of the human mind to attract, through attention, many things into its sphere of action. As you walk down the street, headed for a particular store on a particular goal to do a particular thing, your mind is constantly filled with many thoughts, many distractions having nothing whatsoever to do with going to the store and purchasing whatever it is you have chosen to purchase. And so it is that same principle that applies to this mundane, earthly world applies to our spiritual endeavors to attain the goals that we have set for our self.

The temptation is a process that is taking place within us. We think that we are tempted from without. We think that it is the various experiences in life out there in creation that are calling and tempting us, but that is far from the truth. That, out there, is ever the effect. Our bodies, our minds, and our physical bodies and our astral bodies are composed of the substance of this planet. And therefore, we, being a part of all that this planet has to offer, are tempted inside of our self. There is one word that I have found in my life that is most unattractive to most all people: and that word, simply, is called *discipline* and personal responsibility. Everything that we seek, we alone must pay for. Often we don't like the price tag. But if we don't like the price tag of the things we desire, then we should consider something that is more reasonable for us and grow, perhaps, a bit more slowly.

When we accept personal responsibility for all experiences in our life, we establish the very law by which freedom and abundant good can be experienced by us. But because of many years of habit of giving power and control to things outside, to so-called circumstances, to so-called accidents, because of that habit pattern, it takes great effort, moment-by-moment effort, to remind our self that we indeed are the captains of our ship, that we alone are the masters of our destiny, that God, the Infinite Intelligence, will sustain and does sustain any and every thought that we choose to have. But no one thinks for us when we accept personal responsibility. No one controls us when we accept personal responsibility.

We are successful, all of us. Whether we like the success we have or not is our personal choice. If we look outside and we see others and what we judge their success to be is desirable for us because we judge we don't have it, then we do not see how successful we really are. Thank you.

Thank you. How do you set new laws into motion?

A law, set into motion in a mental world and a physical world in which you live and are most aware, is set into motion by our own attitude. For vibration, of which all things are in truth, is attitude of mind. Our attitude of mind *is* our rate of vibration. Now our rate of vibration can be easily viewed by those who see into the astral realms in which the aura expresses itself. It can be seen by various colors. Now our vibration changes according to the changes of our attitude, which create our emotions. Our thoughts and thought patterns, they create this attitude and aura of ours.

Now like attracts like in the universe and becomes the Law of Attachment. Therefore, all of our experiences are the light in our world revealing to us what we're sending out. Now whatever goes out from our aura is what we experience back. If we want new experiences, then the very simple way is to have new attitudes. But if we're not willing to have new attitudes, then we're not going to have new experiences. We're only going to repeat the experiences of yesterday. However, we must be of good hope and encouragement because the law clearly states that repetition is the law through which change is made possible. In other words, when you've had enough, you make a change. Now all of life reveals that to us. Look at how many divorces there are in the world. And remarriages, of course, too. Take a look. So when we've had enough of anything—whether it's ice cream or marriage, it doesn't matter—we will change. Thank you.

Thank you. How do we account for remembrances of past lives on earth? And is this, for some, the last incarnation on earth?

This philosophy has always taught, and still teaches, the Law of Evolutionary Incarnation: that we pass through this planet, usually, one time, and we move on to other planets and other spheres and other universes, that we came from other planets to this planet. I know that there is the belief—and has been for many centuries—of a return to this planet. Well, personally, for myself, I think one time around here is enough. But anyway, regardless of that, this planet offers to all of us what is known as faith. And we come here on varying grades of evolution and we pass through this planet and move on.

Now the question is, How do some people, if they do, become aware that they have lived on this particular planet before? There is such a thing as universal consciousness. And whoever becomes receptive to universal consciousness has the awareness of everything that has ever been, that is, and will ever be, for the only limit to that awareness is the over-identification with the present incarnation.

The more attached and the more identified we are to this particular incarnation in this particular experience, the less we view of what really is. Now you take a person that becomes extremely attached to their husband or wife, their world begins to shrink until all they have is that particular person. Their interests shrink and their world shrinks. And it becomes a very difficult process to grow through.

We are here in our evolution to expand our consciousness, to become aware of the eternal moment of now. As long as we identify in this limited view that we have chosen for our self, then that's all we can experience—is what can exist in that limited view. Time and space is only the delusion that we have created for our self. But because we have created this delusion of time and because we have created this delusion of space, because it is our child, we can change it. Thank you.

Thank you. What do the fingers and toes represent?

That has been given in one of our classes, but I will say this: each and every part of our anatomy is represented by a sense function and a soul faculty. Thank you.

Thank you. What does the elephant represent?

The elephant is a very eternal symbol, if the trunk is up, of spiritual work. Now by that I mean work for the light of reason and good for all creation. It is not a new symbol. It is a very ancient, ancient symbol. The elephant in the world of animals is the most evolved at this time on this planet. Whether we think so or not does not change that demonstrable truth. Thank you.

Thank you. How can people allow their creativity to flow without the interference of the mundane, such as paying the rent and other bills?

Well, that depends on what the person with their creativity—and by that I believe they mean their artistic talents—it depends not only upon what they identify [with] in this life, but especially upon what they depend upon for their life. Now if, in the expressing of a creative talent, we become aware of an obstruction to our existence, then, of course, we have to work with a very basic principle known as survival.

If you, whoever wrote that question, is truly interested in the unobstructed flow of their creative talent and is willing to make the effort to reidentify in reference to their survival and is willing to change their beliefs in their survival from a weekly paycheck and another person to the Divine Infinite Spirit that sustains their very breath and accepts that every servant is worthy of their hire and truly makes that effort to believe that God is the only source of their supply, yes, perhaps they will struggle for a time—for many great artists have, in reference to the material supply of this mundane world. But they have struggled not because of someone else, not because they did not have a sponsor, but because, through an error of ignorance, they denied the greatest sponsor of all sponsors, known as faith in God. Thank you.

Thank you. Who will be the next president and will there be a war?

By war, if you mean world war, there won't. At this time. By president, unless there is a drastic fiasco with the present President of the United States, which is not foreseeable today, then, whether we like it or not, he will be renewed in office. That's not my choice, believe me. And it's not my choice that he isn't renewed, believe me. I'm trying to remain impartial and neutral. But that's the way it is viewed. Now six months ago, it would have been something entirely different.

But let us take a moment and speak on that interesting question. The present President of the United States is not the first, nor will he be the last, to use the age-old tactic in politics of turning the attention of the people to foreign crises when things are so bad, it seems, at home. This is a very old tactic used by many, many, many presidents and many leaders of many countries. It's not only used by governments, it's used by institutions, it's used by corporations, and just about everyone else who works in that type of a world. As the attention of the American people is directed to a crisis and an attack from without, it unites the people from within. How many parents have used that tactic in raising their children? So it's not new. If we think it's new, then we've been sleeping for a long time.

As long as the crisis can be kept alive and the threat and the danger from without be predominant in the minds of the masses of the American people, the voters, then you guarantee a renewal of your present President. Unless, as I said a moment earlier, he really makes a great fiasco which is not foreseeable.

We all know when anyone has directed its people to a crisis from without that it is not only not popular to attack the leader at that time, it is [an] absolute guarantee of disaster for the one who is doing the attacking. Now that's just plain, old common sense. If those—his opponents—have awakened to that truth and will support the efforts being made in the present crisis, then there's a possibility you will have a different President for the new term. Yes.

Thank you. We are taught to educate desire or to fulfill it, but not to suppress it. How can we deal with desires as they rise while we are between the educating and fulfilling states since fulfilling them is ofttimes not in one's best interest?

Well, it's like the child that burns his hand once. It's usually not enough. It takes a little more experience than that. And so while we're in the process of making some effort to educate our desires in life, especially when we know that they are not in our best interest, when we've had enough, when we have been burned enough times, we will make the change, and that change is known as educating the desire. Thank you.

Thank you. How may we develop our own attributes for communication with the spiritual world?

The attributes, in that question, you already have. It is not a matter of developing anything. It is simply a matter of becoming aware of what you already have. The only reason, if you are not yet aware of the attributes that you already have, the only reason that it can be that you are not aware is because of over-identification with the experiences in life that you already, presently have.

Most people think it's so difficult to make the slightest change. So difficult to change our judgments, to free our self from them. So difficult to change our thoughts about anything. It is, in truth, as easy to change a thought to something else as it was to give the first thought we want to get rid of, that first thought, birth. The difficulty or struggle is what we have done by believing that we are the thought patterns that we think we presently are. We are not the thought patterns we think we are. True, we are using those thought patterns. True, we are experiencing the effects thereof, but we are not them. No more are we the color of our hair or the color of our eyes or the height of our body, we are not those things. We are not the thoughts we think. We experience the reaction from them, but we are not them. When you accept that truth, you are not your hair—if you were, you would be in terrible straights when you start to go bald. You really would. All of us would. You're not your hair unless you have so attached your mind, through over-identification, to your hair that you finally believe that you are your hair. And when your hair goes, a very good portion of you goes along with it.

So if we want to be free—and that's what we all really want—then let's just wake up and accept the truth. We're not the foot. Because if we are, when the foot goes, we go. We're not the hand. Because if the hand gets damaged, we're damaged. We are blinded only because we have yet to make the effort to understand and separate truth from creation. We are not things. We are not forms. We use things. We use forms to express. When we believe we are things, then only by having many things, do we experience what we call happiness. Therefore, we become dependent upon creation for our peace and joy. And creation cannot offer us peace and joy, for creation is a duality. It offers the light and the dark. It offers the right and the wrong. It offers the day and the night. So we cannot have peace as long as we are attached to creation, to duality. Not until we reach the neutralization within our consciousness, where there is no wrong and there is no right, where there is no day and there is no night, not until we reach that neutralization in consciousness will we be free. Thank you.

FEBRUARY 3, 1980

Church Questions and Answers 2

I am indeed grateful to be able to share with you my understanding of some of these questions you have submitted during the month concerning spiritual matters that are of interest to you. And so we will begin with the first question. Mr. Chairman.

Yes, sir. Man is his own enemy, dog, his friend. Would you please comment on our contemporary relationship to the nine levels of awareness?

Well, in reference to our understanding of the nine levels of awareness or levels of consciousness, we understand that man, this divine spark within him, which is formless and free, is expressing through several bodies here and now. We are consciously aware of our physical body. We are also consciously aware of our emotional and mental body. Some of us are aware of our spiritual body. A few are aware of our cosmic body and our universal body and etc. As man makes the effort to become aware of the motivating force within him, then he will slowly, but surely, become aware of these different levels of consciousness and more aware of these bodies through which he is expressing. We understand that our spiritual body—as our mental body is garnered up from the mental substance, our spiritual body is garnered up from spiritual substance. We do not automatically, when we enter this earth realm, automatically have all of these bodies in full motion or action. We enter this earth plane and slowly, but surely, we see the physical body that we have entered into, it gradually grows and matures ever in keeping with the mental body, as it makes its imprint upon the physical substance.

Now in reference to the question, which should be, "A dog is man's best friend," we are not speaking exclusively of the form of the animal. We are speaking in that reference of the attributes of the animal. Unfortunately, for many centuries so many have thought that the only form on the planet that has a soul or this spirit expressing through it is the two-legged form.

As we broaden our horizons and we take control of the judgments that we have made, by awakening our own faculty of reason, we can clearly see that the soul, the individualized soul, is not limited to the two-legged animal species known as man. As we make that awakening within our self, we open the doors to communication and through communication, we gain a broader understanding, for without communication there is no understanding. Thank you.

Thank you. Please comment on the dieting responsibility to the soul.

I have never been aware of a dictate by any soul concerning what diet one should have or have not. When we find our self dissatisfied with the experiences that we encounter in life, which are, of course, the effects of our own judgments, then we justify, and unfortunately ofttimes with a so-called spiritual justification, our reason for making changes. We know deep within ourselves what is right for us. But because we know deep within us what is right for us, we must never forget the right of all. For it is, surely, an error of ignorance when we awaken our conscious conscience within, when we awaken that and do not demonstrate the soul faculty of duty, gratitude, and tolerance for each and every other individual in the universe. I am not aware of any particular diet or system that awakens the soul within. It is indeed very individual to each and every person, for our soul has entered earth along the evolutionary path and we have all come to this earth with many, many differing experiences from our past incarnations in other worlds, in other spheres, and other planets. What is right for one does not, by its right for the individual, guarantee in any way that it be right for all. Thank you.

Thank you. Have people who are born into rich (money-wise) families earned this richness somewhere else or do they choose to simply be born into richness to experience richness in this lifetime?

Well, I am sure that we would all agree, if it was a matter of choice, then we would be rich, so to speak. *[Many in the congregation laugh.]* But this matter of choice, you see—we all have this 10 percent free will, called choice. Once we have exercised that free will in anything, called choice, then we must follow, we must follow the choice that we have made, for we establish a law, as man is a law unto himself. It is my understanding that whether we find our self in wealth or poverty is an effect of a choice made not to experience wealth or poverty *per se*, but it is an effect of our own merit, that we have merited making that particular choice. For example, we walk down the street and we choose, we look in the stores and we choose to purchase something or we choose not to purchase it. But what is it within us that prompts us to make that so-called free will choice? That 10 percent free will choice, what prompts us to make that choice? Why, it's very simple, my friends: it is the 90 percent law of cause and effect of the experiences of our past and how we have judged them that prompts us to make the 10 percent free will choice. Now I don't mean to imply predestination, but I do mean to, perhaps, broaden our horizon on so-called free will. Thank you.

Thank you. Please give your understanding of the saying in the Serenity Game, "It is better to have no shoes and have understanding, than to have shoes and return with them to the elements."

Yes, my friends, of what benefit is it to have shoes for feet that no longer serve their purpose? Now we know, all of us really know, that without understanding there is no purpose to life. Without understanding there is no purpose to life. For God, the infinite, divine Intelligent Being, is ever equal to our understanding. So without understanding we do not have the sustenance for life itself. And because we all have and demonstrate moment by moment this sustenance of life, we all do have some degree of understanding. Now we may talk with another and it may be the judgment of another that to them we have no understanding at all, only because it doesn't appear to be in harmony with what they judge is their understanding. But we all do have and we all do express, to some degree, the soul faculty of understanding. Thank you.

Thank you. What is meant by universal consciousness?

Universal consciousness very simply means a universality in our own acceptance. Now our world is ever dependent upon our acceptance. Our reality in life is what we create. We can't blame God for our reality, for we have that so-called free choice and moment by moment we establish our reality. And because it is our own personal responsibility, our reality, our reality is the effect of our own acceptance. It is the effect of our own belief. And so it is stated in this philosophy that truth is individually perceived. Truth is not individual. It is only individually perceived.

Thank you. Are there any laws set into motion for a big earthquake in San Francisco?

Well, that has been, of course, of much interest to many people over these past five years. If we look at the many experiences of our planet, we see that there are cycles to so-called disturbances in nature. And so it is that the many prophecies concerning this great earthquake in California, there is no question, there is no question that it shall take place. But I can assure you of one thing: you need not be concerned. Why need you not be concerned? You need not be concerned unless your faith, your faith in disaster is greater than your faith in God. Now if your faith in creation is greater than that which sustains creation, then, of course, it is your right and your choice to fear. But remember, my friends, that fear is known to us as negative faith, for fear is the mind's control over the eternal soul. So we all have this choice in this moment.

We're all going to the so-called spirit world in some day, in some moment. We are not the ones who can consciously dictate how that shall be or when that shall be. But we are going, of that we can have great faith in. Surely, we all want to go peacefully, whatever *peace* means to us. But that, of course, is dependent upon our own evolutionary path.

I would not direct energy, through concentration and concern, to something that does not bring benefit and good into your life. When we place our attention or direct our energy to that which is good, to that which is divine and peaceful, then that sustains and supports the peaceful, the good that is within us and, in so doing, creates our reality. Thank you.

Thank you. Don't souls really know when they are about to pass? Isn't this knowledge available in sleep?

The knowledge, the awareness is available, of course, to all of us, for our soul knows not only how long in years the journey will be on this planet or the planets yet to be, but it is a matter of stilling our own mind in order that we can become conscious in our mental world of that simple truth.

When you ask a person to concentrate upon anything, the usual answer is they have such a great struggle because they cannot hold their attention to one thing until they perceive the essence of it. That simply reveals that effort to self-discipline of the mind is yet to be truly made. We cannot be aware consciously in our mental world of this soul, which is our true being, until we still the mental activity. And when that happens, which is known as peace, the power of the universe, we see, is not something outside of our universe. It is something that we are in. We are in the universe. We are inseparable, therefore, from it. It is only when we deny the basic law of survival that we enter the realms of illusion and delusion and believe that God or the cause of *anything* is outside of our universe. And so by first accepting the first law of survival, the Law of Personal Responsibility, do we start upon the path of inner awakening and we know beyond a shadow of any doubt why we're here, what we have to do, how long we will be here, and in what way will we leave.

Thank you. How would substance be defined and could it pertain to matter?

In reference to the question of matter and substance, there is a vast difference in the thinking of the world today. We look at a chair or a wall and we say that is matter. Now some might say that it has substance and, in a sense, of course, that is true. But remember that matter and substance do not exist in all dimensions of consciousness. Matter, the belief therein, and acceptance of substance creates it for us in our mental world. It exists for us because the matter that is within us believes in it. When we no longer believe in it, then we rise in consciousness from the realms of matter and, for us, in those realms it does not exist.

Thank you. In regards to the [lyrics of the] offeratory song, why is it, "from lack I set it free?" [During the devotional services of the Serenity Spiritualist Church, a song, which contained those lyrics, was sung as the ushers passed the donation plates among the congregation.]

Because the only obstruction, the only obstruction to the experiencing of abundant good, to experiencing the health, wealth, and happiness of life, the only obstruction to that goodness is the false belief in lack. And so you hear in our "Offering Song," "from lack I set it free," because there is nothing else to set it free from. Only the belief in lack is the bondage, the obstruction to the abundant good which is ever before us, knocking at the door of our conscience that we may open the door through acceptance and experience what is our divine birthright. My friends, we all believe in many things. Let us take stock of what we believe in, because in taking stock of what we believe in, we can then make a wise choice, hopefully, of believing in that which opens the doors of abundant good in our life. That is our right. That is the proven, demonstrable path. If you want something better, you must first believe in something better, and your belief in something better must become greater than the judgments that we already have.

Thank you. I would like to know what is the meaning of the levels of consciousness in Spiritualism.

Well, the meaning of the levels of consciousness, at least here, in this the Serenity Church—the levels of consciousness are attitudes of mind created by thought patterns. Now our thought, any thought, repeated in the mental world becomes an established pattern. It garners up like kind throughout the mental universe. It becomes a level of consciousness by becoming an attitude of mind or rate of vibration. Now the final strength of a level of consciousness, the ruler of any level of consciousness is the extent of judgment.

Now let us, for a moment, think about judgment. Is judgment a limitless total consideration, a limitless total acceptance? We all see that judgment is a very limited total acceptance. We all see that judgment is a very limited total consideration. Now because all judgment is limited, it expresses into the universe what is known as denial. And denial is our destiny. As we become attached to our own adversities—that our adversities grow into attachments, so our denials become, in life, our destiny. Therefore, it behooves us, it certainly makes life more fulfilling to broaden our horizons through greater tolerance of the rights of expression of others and make decisions, not judgments, for judgments bind and decisions, they free.

Thank you. Please define vertical direction of thought and horizontal direction of thought.

Well, I think in an effort to define a vertical thought or a horizontal thought that we might get more than confused in limiting the direction that thought can take. Now I think what the questioner is referring to is thoughts that are limited to a mental world or thoughts and aspirations that rise to a higher level of consciousness. Thought is a vehicle through which man expresses his feelings. Now you may think that feelings can be expressed without thought. I assure you, they cannot. Thought is the vehicle through which feelings are expressed. Whether or not the thought is spoken is entirely up to the individual.

What happens with people who have difficulty in communicating with other people? They bottle-up these thoughts. These feelings burst open periodically, usually in anger, because there is no expression. They allow no expression through the vehicle of thought and communication of their true feelings.

Now remember, thought is not limited to man. I never found an animal that didn't express its feelings, that didn't have the vehicle of thought for those feelings to express. Just because the dog's language we call barking—that's the way the dog speaks—doesn't mean that the dog does not have thoughts. It doesn't mean that the bird doesn't have thoughts. I know many people believe that the animals are limited and are not thinking beings, but animals are thinking beings. It's when we think in a more broadened horizon of our universe that we will understand there is nothing on this planet that is not thinking. We may disagree with what it's thinking, but that doesn't stop it from thinking.

Thank you. Please discuss what is meant by the terms soul mate, Oversoul, individualized soul, and the soul's expression.

Well, now that's a question that could take a long time, but I'll try to be as brief as possible. That that is individualized, we will all agree, must have form; otherwise, it cannot be individualized. So we understand that the individualized soul, being individualized, has form. And that it is the covering of the divine, neutral, formless, free Spirit.

Now I know that a lot of people here are not agreeing with me, but that's not why I'm speaking, for them to agree with me. But if the soul is individualized, it must have form. Now what do we understand are the laws governing form? I'm sure we'll all agree from all the forms that we view that it is the Law of Creation and that creation is the Law of Duality. Therefore, we understand that our form—we view our physical form—is both positive and negative because it is of dual creation. Therefore, it follows that our soul, being form, governed by the Law of Creation, in higher realms, must also have this duality.

And so we now move on to what we call soul mate. Now I do hope that you will understand I'm trying to put a simple teaching into a very few, brief minutes. When this formless, free Spirit enters form, it is under the Law of Division, as all duality is under the Law of Division. And so we then understand what is commonly referred to as soul mate, I hope. If you don't, I'll have to have you at a private class for about six months, because that's how long it'll take for some.

Now, this Allsoul that has been referred to by many philosophers—we understand that our soul, individualized, comes out anew—that means again—in each incarnation. That once we have passed through, for example, this Earth planet, we leave this physical body. It goes back to the elements of the planet from whence it has been composed. And we express through these other bodies, these astral bodies, mental bodies, spiritual bodies, hopefully, and in our evolutionary path return to what is referred to as the Allsoul, to come out again to enter another experience in another time.

Try to understand that the true you is not what you believe in any given moment. You all know that you are not the person that you thought you were twenty years ago or more. You've changed your judgments, changed your beliefs, changed your attitudes, and therefore, if you look back twenty years ago, you'll find some difficulty in recognizing that that person who did those things was really you. Well, that's a sure way to slowly, but surely, gain some understanding that though we are personally responsible for the thoughts we think, we are not the thought. We are never the thought, for we are never the feeling. We are the idea. We are that which uses the thought, the vehicle. We are not the physical body. We are that that is using the physical body. We are not the feeling. We are that which is using the feeling. And if we will make that effort to simply understand that, we will separate truth from creation. And in separating truth from creation, we will use creation as a vehicle, for which it has been designed, but never again be bound by it.

Thank you.

MARCH 2, 1980

Church Questions and Answers 3

As our chairman has already stated, the first Sunday of each month is set aside for the questions that you have presented. And I will be more than happy to share with you our understanding. And we will begin with the first question, please.

Thank you. Please explain why "God's sadness is nature's joy." [This saying is from the Serenity Game.]

In reference to that statement from the Living Light Philosophy, "God's sadness is nature's joy," when we think of the word *sadness*, we usually associate that with a feeling of despair, certainly one that is not pleasurable to us, one of dissatisfaction with our efforts or endeavors. And so man's understanding of the word *sadness* is indeed very, very limited. Man cannot, of course, be sad, if man does not judge the fulfillment of his desires. In that statement, "God's sadness is nature's joy," we understand that sadness and joy, being the opposite of the same pole, are not different to us until we make them so by our own judgment. For example, man desires; and if man's desires are fulfilled when man judges they are to be fulfilled in the way that he judges it is to take place, then man is, usually, seemingly happy. But desire, being a divine expression, is totally neutral. It is only when we make the judgment when it is going to happen and how it is going to happen, that's the only time that we experience what is known as sadness. Thank you.

Thank you. Please explain why "Fear is the fulfillment of desire," when desire is the expression of the Divine. [This quote is also from the Serenity Game.]

Fear indeed is the fulfillment of the desire of our mind. It is not the fulfillment of the divine desire, for divine desire is fulfilled within itself. Our minds are controlled by what is known as fear or negative faith. This experience of fear is the effect of our own mental judgments. And so man fears many things only because man judges many things. We can never fear what we do not judge. When we make the effort to be freed from judgment, we will indeed be freed from fear; and desire, the divine expression, will be a fulfillment within itself at the moment of desire, not the effect thereof.

Thank you. How much, if anything, does location and vocation have to do with building a soul body?

Vocation or—and location is nothing more, of course, than an effect of laws that we alone have set into motion. As our physical body is created from the elements of this material world and our mental body is created from the elements of mental substance, so, of course, is our spiritual body created or brought together from spiritual substance. Now our vocation or our location in life, wherever it may be, is an effect of laws we have set into motion and offers to us the necessary experiences to unfold our soul faculties, which, of course, does create our spiritual body.

Thank you. Would you please explain the spiritual significance of the word fate?

To my understanding the word *fate* is restricted exclusively to the realm in which it was created: that is the mental realm. Now many people say that it was their destiny or their fate to have certain experiences, removing themselves completely from the Law of Personal Responsibility. We understand that man has 10 percent free will at any given moment, that there are the laws of cause and effect, which are 90 percent, which have been set into motion by the laws we have established before. But we do have that 10 percent. When we accept whatever experience we encounter as that being our destiny or our fate, then we remove our self from the Law of Personal Responsibility and we give up this 10 percent free will. We resign ourselves to things the way they are, rather than face the possibility that we can change them by making a little effort to change our thought, our attitude, and our rate of vibration.

Thank you. What is the first step to learn to recognize divine guidance?

Personal responsibility. Without personal responsibility, without the acceptance of personal responsibility, we cannot, in truth, experience divine guidance.

Thank you. What level are people expressing through when they are a people-pleaser?

There is a great need, with some, to please those people that they choose to please. But we must go beyond to find the cause of that great need to be liked, to please and to act and to think the way others want us to act and to think. Deep within us, of course, is the awareness that we all are a part of one infinite, eternal Divine Principle. That awareness is within all of us. When that awareness arises up from our soul and strikes a blow to our mind, we react in keeping with the limited, mental experiences that we have already had. And so this need to please others, this need to be wanted, this need to be liked is nothing more nor less than a distortion of the divine awareness within us that we are, in truth, a part of everything, everywhere, at all times, that we have always been. And because we have always been, we will always be.

Thank you. How does the soul faculty "to ignore" relate to the soul faculty of "in action" and how is their use beneficial?

Well, my friends, that that we ignore, we do not identify with. And when we do not identify with something, then it has no power, no effect, and no control over us. And so there is a principle to ignore that which we choose to ignore, for we do have that divine right of choice. The things that disturb us in our mental world are the things that control us. Only that that we allow to control us can ever disturb us. And so by the very principle to ignore, we no longer identify with that which is disturbing us and, therefore, we no longer experience it.

Thank you. Please elaborate on how one patterns when determining the qualities in another when interested in selecting a spouse.

Please repeat the first sentence of that question.

Please elaborate on how one patterns when determining the qualities in another when interested in selecting a spouse.

Well, my friends, I think we have a very simple answer to that very complicated question: like attracts like and becomes the Law of Attachment. Now if you are interested in marriage and concerned about what your spouse is going to be like in the years yet ahead, then make the effort, through the Law of Personal Responsibility, to become aware of your own patterns. For if you become aware of yourself and in keeping with the demonstrable, divine law that like attracts like and becomes the Law of Attachment, you need not be concerned with what your spouse is going to be like because you already know what they are like because you already know your own patterns and attitudes of mind. Thank you.

Thank you. What does the statement mean that we are all mediums?

Well, that's very clear. We are all mediums and communicants to some dimension. What dimension that may or may not be is ever, of course, our responsibility to become aware of our self. Now we can't become aware from what dimension or levels of consciousness these experiences enter into our life unless we are aware of our own levels of mind and we are aware of our own self. So, of course, the first step is to become aware of our self, but we can't even make that step until we first accept the Law of Personal Responsibility.

Thank you. Please give your understanding of the soul faculty of dignity.

Dignity is indeed an expression of self-respect. If we do not care to respect our self, we cannot expect to receive respect. You see, my friends, we can only receive what we have given. And when we give respect, when we think well of our self, then we will experience the return of that attitude and vibration. Most of our problems that we find in life are because we do not think well of our self. And not thinking well of our self, we set a law of judgment into motion and we experience everything necessary to guarantee to us that our judgments were right all the time. Let us learn this moment to think humble, yet well of our self, because if we don't learn it this moment, it only guarantees a more difficult struggle in the moments yet to be.

There is a part of us that is whole, complete, and perfect. That part of us we call the divine Infinite Intelligence or God. Now all these other expressions are nothing but the vehicles that this perfect Intelligence is using to express itself. If you do not think well of yourself, then your vehicle, your mental vehicle, your physical vehicle becomes distorted and the infinite perfect Intelligence cannot express itself fully and wholly and completely.

It is our responsibility to think well of our self. If you don't think well of yourself, you don't encourage yourself. If you don't encourage yourself, things don't change; they don't get better. They do, of course, get worse. It's ever in keeping with our attitude. Now we have been given that divine right of choice: to choose an attitude that will bring us the peace, the harmony, the abundant goodness that is, in truth, our divine right. You see, no God, nothing outside, can bring the change. That change is in keeping with natural law. We can change the image that we have of our self. We can, once again, express that divine soul faculty of dignity: to think good of our self and, in so doing, in keeping with the law that like attracts like and becomes the Law of Attachment, experience the return of that goodness.

If you are not satisfied with the experience in your day-to-day activities, you know where to begin. Stop looking outside. Make whatever changes you know—because all of us know, in truth, the changes that we need to make to remove the errors of ignorance in our mind, to remove the obstructions so that we can indeed experience that state of consciousness called heaven here and now. This is the place, my friends, to experience heaven. Not sometime after you leave your physical body. Your mental body will not change in that moment and, therefore, whatever you have already rejected or accepted is all that you will experience. This is the moment in which you can experience the state of consciousness known as heaven. It is entirely up to us. It is not within the power of anything or anyone outside of our self.

Thank you. Please give your understanding of the word reverence.

When man experiences what is known as reverence, when he feels reverent, he first has some degree of respect. Respect for himself. You see, my friends, one cannot experience dignity without reverence because they are both inseparably related to respect. When you have respect, then you can experience reverence. And when you have respect, you can know the character-builder known as dignity.

Thank you. On an intellectual level there exists the age-old debate over influence of heredity versus environment. At a scientific level of understanding, a student of biology, for example, may propose a theory of genetic memory, mutations, and throwbacks. At the theological level of understanding, a student of ethereal progression will speculate on reincarnation, personal responsibility, and earning that which we merit. There are those who believe that if one is right, the other must be wrong. My own suspicion is that these differences are the different language of different levels of growth of understanding, rather than a matter of being right or wrong. My question is, Is there not a correlation between these different beliefs and what percent of our attitudes are imprinted upon the genes that are passed on through inheritance from one generation to another, as was recently mentioned unto three generations? And what percentage of our will is of the formless and free?

That's a most interesting statement there. *[Many in the congregation laugh.]* I am not very intellectual, but I will try to get, hopefully, to some basics. First of all, our soul in its evolution enters a form that ever is in keeping with the laws that we have set into motion in our prior incarnations throughout the universes. This is not the first time our infinite, divine, eternal soul has had experience on a planet in the universes. And so if that soul has merited or earned a certain body that has genetic defects or benefits or whatever you wish to call it, or environmental experiences, they are ever in keeping, ever in keeping with what our soul alone in its eternal journey has earned.

Now the lessons that we have here in life, that we have already experienced and are yet to experience, are always in keeping with the unfoldment of our own soul, with our own spiritual, mental, and physical growth. I have yet to see an experience in life that did not offer to the person experiencing it, including myself, a golden opportunity for growth. You know, my friends, the more we dislike an experience that we are having, the greater the opportunity [that] lies within it: the greater the opportunity to change, to improve, and to grow our self. No matter what you find in life, it has within it a golden opportunity.

Now when you fight the experience that you have earned and you fight it with all of your being, it simply reveals to you that that lesson, that that growth step, you have faced many times before you ever got to earth. Sooner or later, you will find the good that is within it. Sooner or later, that is guaranteed. And so in reference to hereditary or environment or all of those other intellectual thoughts, be rest assured they are only vehicles. They are only effects. They are not causes. But they are serving the purpose for the soul's eternal evolution. Thank you.

Thank you. How may I get in touch with my dog's spiritual levels?

Well, that's very simple. Man cannot understand, let alone communicate [with], spiritual levels of consciousness expressing through an animal until he makes some effort to understand and to communicate with the levels which he is expressing through. And so it is that effort at self-awareness, some effort to communicate with oneself, so little time is spent—we are all mediums. We're all communicating with something. But if we will make the effort to do a little more communicating inside of our self, then we won't have so many problems communicating outside.

There's a simple statement about computers that one of my students told me a long time ago: garbage in, garbage out. Well, if we experience garbage outside, then we've got to stop dumping it inside. Now, only we can make that change. So if we make that change, then we're going to have the experiences that we really desire. The desire to be fulfilled, to be complete, to be freed from want, to be freed from need. No one enjoys the frustration of want and need and desire constantly plaguing them. No one really enjoys that. There is a way out, but it's up to us to take that step. Yes.

Thank you. What is happiness?

That depends on what level is asking the question. Now, you see, happiness is something that is very personal to each individual. Some people sitting here in the congregation, just a few, however, are very happy that it rained today. Most are very unhappy. But let us be grateful we have a roof over our head. And so, you see, we are happy depending upon our desire and what we have judged the way things shall be. Now when things don't go the way we judge they should go, then we usually experience what is known as unhappiness. But you just take anyone and give to them what they desire at the moment—you must be sure it is the desire of the moment—and you will see the smile of what man calls happiness.

That is not the soul faculty of happiness. The soul faculty of happiness and the spirit of joy is known as a total acceptance. Whatever comes and whatever goes, it will not change the sea of serenity on which you sail. Think of that, my friends. It's within your power at any moment to sail serene on the sea of time. To go through this illusion, called creation, for that's what it is. All effects are but illusions. They are not the true principle of the cause, but they are illusions. And the illusion changes in keeping with our own dictates. So happiness can be with you at every moment of your life, if you're willing to accept your right to the happiness and bow that desire of the moment for the moment. Yes.

Thank you. What is the effect of lingering on the telephone?

Well, the effect is quite different to different people. I have never been one that is overly enthused, or enthused in any way, of hanging on the telephone. It has been my experience over many years that conversations on the telephone that go over 60 seconds, or 90 at the most, reveal almost immediately the destructive force of self-concern. It is very rare that one will speak on the telephone over 60 or 90 seconds, very rare indeed, that they're not totally controlled by the concern of self. Unfortunately, it is a very negative, negative, negative experience. And I am afraid Pacific Telephone wouldn't make any money off of me at all, if I had my choice. *[Many laugh.]* Thank you.

Thank you. Will daily meditation assist us in knowing ourselves?

That depends on what you understand, number one, by meditation and, of course, number two, what you do with it. Unfortunately—but out of the mud of earth grows the lotus of heaven—unfortunately, millions of people involved in some types of meditation are really experiencing a type of self-hypnosis. It is indeed unfortunate, but out of that some good cannot help but come.

When man goes into what he calls meditation without making great effort, great effort to become aware of himself, to become aware of his suppressed desires, and goes into a state of meditation, those suppressed desires rise up in the consciousness with great force. And so for many centuries there has been great difficulty and misunderstanding concerning meditation. If the effort is not made to first become aware of your suppressed desires and, second, to work with them intelligently, then those suppressed desires will rise up out of the subconscious and will, unfortunately, misguide you. So I do not recommend meditation to anyone who is not ready, willing, and able to look inside to see where their struggles and problems are, to see where they have suppressed their own personal desires, so that they can be freed from those subconscious patterns of mind that are the first things that man experiences in his efforts to meditate. Yes.

Thank you. Is there a tangible relationship between intelligence and physical matter?

Why, indeed, of course there is. Without intelligence, there would be no physical matter. There is no physical matter that intelligence is not contained within it. Now, usually when man thinks of intelligence, he thinks of only, of course, one species, one thing: the human race. Not too many grant the animals the intelligence expressing through the animals, or the birds, or the insects, or the rocks, or the trees. It's indeed unfortunate. But what does man think? How does the tree grow? How do these things take place without intelligence? Does man really believe that it is some outside intelligence that is shaping the tree? That it is some outside intelligence that's causing the bird to fly. No, my friends, it's an inside intelligence. It's an intelligence expressing through the bird. It is an intelligence expressing through the tree.

You see, until we make more effort to understand a little about nature, then we're not going to have this ability express, that is within us, to communicate with these different forms of life. [If] you cut the limb of the tree, of course, the tree has a reaction. Of course, the tree has feeling. Of course, the tree has emotion. Most of us have accepted that the dog or the cat has some degree of emotion when they don't have their way or they're hurt. But few of us have made the effort to study the tree or the blade of grass. Now that doesn't mean that we shouldn't use nature, for nature is there to use. Because we should be a friend of nature. And friendship, true friendship, being use and not abuse, respects the rights of difference and weathers any storm.

You see, my friends, everything that you have out here in the world is inside in your world within. And so to communicate and to understand it, the effort must be made to communicate inside. You can go through untold centuries making an effort to communicate outside and you will face, each and every time, the obstructions that are inside. You see, the outside is only a reflector. It's reflecting where the obstruction lies. If you have difficulty in communicating with an animal, stop and find the obstruction that is inside.

The intelligence in the animal, expressing through the animal, is identically the same intelligence that is expressing through us. The intelligence expressing through the tree is the same intelligence that expresses through us. The vehicle is different. The form is different. There is no difference to the intelligence. You see, the dog is limited only by the vehicle. This Infinite Intelligence expressing through the dog is limited by the form of the dog. That's the only limitation.

And [if] we have difficulties communicating with the dog, the bird, or the tree, that difficulty is not within the dog. That is not where the difficulty is. That difficulty is in our mind. It is a judgment. We have made a judgment that the animal does not have the intelligence that we have. We have made a judgment that the bird in the tree does not have the intelligence that we have. And because we've made that judgment, we have built up within us an obstruction that keeps us from truly communicating with these other forms of life.

For centuries the masses have had difficulties in communicating with what we, in Spiritualism, know as the spiritual world. It is not the spiritual world where the problem lies. It's our world within. If we're honest with our self, we will find our judgments and we will find our own obstructions.

It's like a man who works so hard to try to get ahead, to have success, and success comes to the door and then blows away. Well, how does that happen? That happens within. If we will only be honest with our self, if we will be honest and look within, we will find every obstruction that's in our path. And, you see, when we find our obstruction, we accept that it's ours. If somebody else finds that obstruction for us, it's rather difficult. It's helpful, but it's difficult. But when we find it our self, be rest assured, we move it out of the way if our desire to change to something better is great enough at that moment.

Thank you very much. Thank you.

APRIL 6, 1980

Church Questions and Answers 4

As our chairman has stated, we would be more than happy to share with you our understanding of the questions that you have submitted. And so, if our chairman will please read the first question.

The first question: What is evil?

That, indeed, is a most interesting question. Because, ofttimes, we find in our understanding that which is evil to one is good to another. And so we must have an understanding within ourselves of what causes the decision or judgment for what we understand to be evil or good. This philosophy teaches that so-called evil is nothing more nor less than undeveloped good. If we understand, first, that there is one God, one Intelligence, infinite and eternal, expressed throughout all form—and by form, that also includes the mental forms created by our thought—if we understand that this one, infinite, intelligent Power is sustaining everything, then everything that is sustained by this Power has the potential of good. And so we do not spend our time, our efforts, and our energy on that which is undeveloped, but on that which is in the process of developing. And by that I mean that energy follows attention, and we and we alone are the creators of all the experiences in our life. So if we place our attention, which is directing this infinite, intelligent Energy, to the good, then the good, indeed, shall be our constant experience. Thank you.

Thank you. Please give your understanding of integrity.

Integrity is, indeed, a soul faculty. It is inseparable, inseparable from character. Integrity considers the all of anything and everything that is within its sphere of interest at any time. And so we see clearly that those who make great effort to consider the rights of others are surely demonstrating the soul faculty of character and integrity.

Thank you. It is sometimes said of our children that when they are small they step on our toes and when they are grown they step on our heart. Is it natural enough for subsequent generations, both individually and collectively, to resent one another and what can be done about it?

Well, ofttimes we, unfortunately, it seems, resent people or things that we decide are not harmonious with our own personal interests and desires. It is only an error in our own thought, it is only a limitation created by our own mind which keeps us separated from the universal consciousness of which we are, in truth, an inseparable part. If we decide and judge that our children or anyone are to do certain things and be certain ways—that we have made those rigid judgments in our mind—and they do not fulfill those desires and judgments, then, of course, we make the next step: that they step on our hearts. They step on what we have judged is the right path for them.

Now truth is taught through indirection, demonstration, and example. If we want someone to make changes which we believe is in their best good, then we must become the living demonstration. We must be the example. As like attracts like and becomes the Law of Attachment, when we set the example by working on ourselves, one of two things take place with children or people: they grow in harmony with our efforts or they go. We need not be concerned whether or not they're going to grow or whether or not they are going to go, for that is contrary to the Law of Personal Responsibility. If we take care of our self, if we truly become the living light, then we can be rest assured that our children, in keeping with the law established, though different from our own views, will be the light to the world that we have made effort in being ourselves.

Thank you. When the soul enters its spiritual body, does it no longer use the emotional body?

In reference to that question, When the soul enters the spiritual body, does it no longer use an emotional body? I have to first explain the understanding of the Living Light Philosophy. First of all, we are, our eternal being, expressing through many bodies at this very moment. We are aware of a physical body. We are aware of our thoughts—some of them—and a mental world and a mental body. Some of us are even aware of a spiritual world and a spiritual body.

Now this infinite, divine, formless, free Spirit, which is the true being—formless and free, it has no beginning and, therefore, has no ending. It enters form as it individualizes itself to what is called soul. Around this soul is garnered up substances from many dimensions. And so we find ourselves with physical bodies, mental bodies, astral bodies, emotional bodies, and on down the list.

When we are expressing through a spiritual body, if a spiritual body we have fully garnered up from spiritual substance through the expression of infinite, intelligent Energy through our soul faculties, we have a feeling body. There is a difference, and a vast difference, between a feeling body and an emotional body. The vast difference between a feeling or sensing body and an emotional body is that one is controlled by the function of judgment and the other is controlled by the faculty of consideration. Thank you.

Thank you. May I request a description of the stages in meditational practice in their order and a short definition of each stage?

I have never been one to encourage or promote meditation for all people, for all people are not ready for meditation. And what do I mean by that? It's very simple. Many people are not yet ready to make the daily effort to gain some degree of control over the thoughts of their mind. And when a person is not ready for meditation, it can be and has proven to be, on many, many times and many occasions, to be most detrimental to their mental and physical health. Because those who are not willing or ready to make the daily effort to gain control of their mind become controlled and are controlled by their mind. So when you open up to what you call meditation, the greatest danger is to be controlled by the suppressed desires of your mind that are lying waiting to express themselves. Some people call that a type of self-hypnosis. And ofttimes that is the effect. So the first step for anyone interested in a spiritual path of peace and harmony is the daily effort to gain control of the thoughts of your mind.

Now I'm sure you will all agree that at sometime in your life you have had thoughts in your mind that have taken control of you in the sense you have tried not to think about something that disturbs you, yet the thought and the disturbance continues to have an effect upon you. That simply reveals a lack of self-control, a lack of controlling the thoughts of your mind.

And so if you go into a meditation without making that effort to gain that control through the power of concentration, then you become the victim of the multitude of desires that you have suppressed in your life and that are waiting for their fulfillment. I have taught for many years and continue to teach never to suppress a desire, but to educate all desires or to fulfill them. Because anytime you suppress desire, you direct infinite, intelligent Energy to the desire and it grows and grows and grows in your own subconscious realms. Someday it is destined to come to the fore and ofttimes that happens when you consciously want it the least.

Thank you. Please explain why "Fear is the fulfillment of desire," when desire is the expression of the Divine. [Again, this quote is from the Serenity Game. This question was also asked in CQA 3.]

Yes, indeed. Desire, the divine expression. Whenever we entertain the thought and the feeling and the emotion of desire and we permit our thoughts to judge how, when, and where the desire will be fulfilled, we immediately, in that moment, limit the divine expression. We have, in that moment, stolen the divinity from the expression, for we have risen and become the dictator over its fulfillment. By so doing we lose, in that moment, the power of its fulfillment. What comes in place of the power of its fulfillment [is] but the fear, which is nothing more nor less than faith in what our own mind can accomplish. And so the fulfillment we experience, if you can call it fulfillment, of the desire is only in keeping with the limits of our past experiences. It can be no greater and it can be no lesser. For we have taken control by our mind and only what our mind already has in it can we experience.

The step from the mental realms to spiritual realms is a step that is easily accomplished. It's known as total acceptance. Try to totally accept one thought of good in your mind. You will very quickly see the limitations of judgment that rise with the thought that you hold. Our philosophy teaches to put God in it or to forget it. It's an easy and simple enough teaching. It is extremely difficult to accomplish unless we are willing to accept something greater than the mental world and the limited experiences that it has to offer us.

Thank you. How does one cope, emotionally, with sudden traumas that enter one's life?

Sudden traumas that enter one's life. Sudden traumas or disasters that enter our life are not sudden at all, only in the sense of our sudden awareness to them. Nothing grows overnight. Whether it is good or it is so-called bad, whether it is peace and harmony or it is disaster and despair, it did not come to us suddenly. We suddenly became aware of it. Now why did we suddenly become aware of our disasters? Simply because we were not making the daily effort to be aware of what we were thinking and what we were doing.

When the desires of our mind run rampant in our consciousness, we become blind and deaf. We cannot see what is around and about us, nor can we hear, nor can we sense, nor can we feel. For desire, once controlled by the mind, becomes total blindness and total deafness. Talk to your friends, your husbands, your wives, and your relatives and acquaintances. Talk to them in the moments that they are controlled by desire. You will soon learn they do not hear what you say. They don't even see what's really around and about them, because desire, controlled by the mental world, is total blindness and total deafness. It doesn't have to be that way.

I know it is not, seemingly, not easy when we are so used to our minds controlling so much of our life, but that's only a delusion that we have created. Our minds cannot sustain our thought. It does not have the power. Our minds do not bring us the eternal good of life, for they are limited vehicles. They're designed to serve our eternal being. They were never designed to control our eternal being.

Now, it's a very simple thing, when we look at our minds like we look at our automobiles. They're quite well designed, to say the least. And we should use them, not abuse them. When you do not use something for the purpose that it was originally designed, it's kind of like using a saw for a shovel. It does not last very, very long. And it does not serve us very, very well. Now when the tools of life, which includes our minds, our hands, and our feet and our senses, when the tools of life no longer serve the worker, then the worker begins to serve the tools. When your mind no longer listens and responds to your eternal being, when it is no longer under the guidance of the soul faculty of reason, then we become the victim. The tool becomes our master and we experience what is known as bondage to creation to the tools. Creation never, ever was designed to be master. It's to be used. No one would seriously consider permitting their automobile to dictate to them when it wants to go somewhere and where it wants to go and how long it wants to stay. No one in their right mind would consider using, let alone possessing, such a vehicle. And yet, my friends, through lack of thought, through lack of effort, through lack of consideration, we have permitted that automobile, known as our mind, to do that to us.

Think, ofttimes you want to do something. And you feel very good about the very thought of doing it. It doesn't take very long before your little mind gives you all the excuses, all of the justifications, and all the so-called reasons why you should not. Or, even more common, you have a thought and a feeling to do something and you tell what you consider to be a friend. And the friend, having their own frustrations and suppressed desires, tells you all the reasons why you couldn't possibly do such a thing. And as you listen, for you have judged them to be a friend, as you listen, those levels of consciousness within yourself, those negative, limited levels, they rise up and tell you how right your friend is; you'll just have to continue on in your miserable life and your disasters because that's the way circumstances for you happen to be.

Or your employer's about ready to consider you for a promotion or a raise and you get so excited that you have to tell all your co-workers. The next thing you know, you get bypassed. And the ones you told it all to get what was meant for you. This is what is meant by the statement that the secrets of the universe are never given to a blabbermouth. When you have earned something good in your life, cherish it and care for it until it's really yours. Because if you don't, if you have that need to tell everyone, what was meant for you, in keeping with the Law of Merit from what you yourself alone have earned, will go to someone else. Now that, surely, no one really wants that to happen.

Remember that friendship, being use and not abuse, respects the rights of difference and will weather any storm. It doesn't mean a friend should always agree with you, because if they do, they're not a friend at all. But it does mean when you have a thought of something that you want to do, then take it to the only source that knows how to keep its mouth shut. And most of us call that source God.

Thank you.

JUNE 1, 1980

Church Questions and Answers 5

As our chairman has stated, this time is set aside on the first Sunday of each month for the questions you have submitted. I will indeed be grateful to be receptive to the spirit to answer the questions to the very best of my ability. And so would you read the first question, please?

Yes, sir. What is the best way to control thought?

That is a problem that all of us seem to have in our lives: to control thought. Without the use of concentration, which is, in truth, the key to all power, there is no ability to control thought. As man makes the daily effort to establish that Law of Concentration, to place his mind pointedly and fixedly upon the object of his choice until only the essence of it remains, then man will indeed, through that daily effort, gain control of his thoughts and, in so doing, become once again the captain of his ship and the master of his destiny.

Thank you. What advice would you give or how can you help a person who very much would like to believe in life after so-called death, but needs scientific evidence to do so and cannot find any scientific evidence to support that there is life after death?

Man, in and of himself, is the living demonstration of the continuity of life. As our minds demand so-called scientific evidence to prove to our satisfaction anything we are interested in, each person has different requirements from different judgments of what, for them, will constitute proof. I personally, myself, am not interested in proving anything to anyone, for each and every person is proof unto themselves of what life really is: the effect of our thought, the effect of our attitude. And so we go out into the world and we decide that we need the scientific proof for this and the scientific proof for that and the scientific proof is in a constant state of change and evolution.

Facts, my friends, are never truths. They are only satisfactions to our minds for a time. For it is the mind that judges and decides what is truth. And, unfortunately for us, those judgments are constantly in a process of change. Truth is not something you will find with your mind. You will find a multitude of facts and you will add them up with the so-called function of logic and you will go throughout eternity in a constant process of frustration, being forced, it seems, from within to change from one fact to another. Life has already proven to us what facts have to offer to us. So if we will truly understand that when we ask for so-called scientific proof, we are asking for facts that will be satisfactory to the judgments that we have already made. Remember, my friends, a petrified opinion never freed a human soul. And that's what in truth our facts become. Thank you.

Thank you. The Living Light Philosophy teaches to think humble, yet well of oneself. Why is it that often those who don't think well of themselves are proud?

The teaching is to think humble, yet well of thyself. Man cannot experience humble thinking without the recognition and acceptance of a power greater than the mind that is doing the thinking. Now the questioner has stated why is it that people, some people, who do not think well of themselves are proud? That, of course, is a judgment that has been established by the questioner in their statement. I have yet to meet a person who truly is proud and doesn't think well of being proud. There is no person that is expressing pride that doesn't think well in the expression thereof; otherwise, they would never bother to express it.

This philosophy teaches to think humble, to recognize that there is a Power sustaining your thought, that [with] that intelligent Power, by your divine right of birth, you have choice. It doesn't matter what you think to the infinite, divine Intelligence, for the infinite, divine Intelligence, known as God, is neutral. It will, it does, sustain any thought that you choose. You may choose the thoughts that free you, that bring back to you, like a magnet, the goodness that you are truly seeking or you may give away your divinity and cast your pearls before the swine by constantly judging the acts, activities, and thoughts of other people, by constantly judging what they are doing and what they are not doing, by constantly judging what is right and what is wrong for someone else without first making the effort to qualify oneself in doing what is right for one's own self. The Bible clearly teaches, "O physician, heal thyself." If you have healed yourself, mentally and physically, then you will not be concerned about the individual rights of others. You will do what you know is right for you, and in so doing, you will establish that law that like attracts like and only right shall return to you. Thank you.

Thank you. How does one achieve more tolerance?

By making the effort to tolerate the levels of consciousness within ourselves that are difficult to view in others. Now in reference to this soul faculty of tolerance, which is one of the many triune soul faculties—this one being duty, gratitude, and tolerance—when one views, in others, what they find in themselves to be intolerable, what it is, in truth, revealing is a denial of that level of consciousness within oneself that one is unwilling to face. Now when we accept the divine right of expression, we will be on the first step of recognizing that whatever exists in one human exists in its potential in all humans, including our self.

For example, we often see, as we look out, we make the judgment that people, places, and organizations are always in lack. What it simply reveals to us is that we are always in lack and we are not willing to face that level within us. Therefore, we attract all of the adversities necessary in life and guarantee that they will become our attachments in life, for the law is totally impartial. Whatever you cannot tolerate in another, you establish, in that intolerance, the law that brings that very thing into your life in order that you may gain in understanding, through the first soul faculty of duty, gratitude, and tolerance.

Thank you. How do we change our bad habits into good habits?

By first freeing our self from the judgment of what is bad and what is good. You see, so-called bad, as we see in life, is nothing more nor less than undeveloped good. And this is why a so-called bad experience can and does produce excellent results if we will take the essence from the experience, which is the indispensable ingredient for the reeducation of our own senses. Now, my friends, we all can say that we've had bad experiences. We have made them bad by our own judgment. It is bad because it has not brought to us what we judged it should bring. Of course it did not bring to us what we judged it should bring because we did not demonstrate the Law of Continuity of effort. We did not first be still and understand the motivation of what we were setting into motion.

We are all here this day. We cannot say that we have all come through the doors only from good experiences that we have had in our life. If we only had so-called good experiences in our life, then all churches, religions, and philosophies would go out of business. And I think that's very understandable. So we do see that so-called bad experiences ofttimes bring to us good results if we and we alone will make the effort. And furthermore, what is a bad experience to one person at one time is a wonderful experience to another. Of course, it is ever dependent upon our own judgments, which are the effects of our limited experiences here on this earth realm. Thank you.

Thank you. Is it true that rain and the oceans give off negative ions that have a beneficial, healing effect and do the negative ion machines produced by man really work?

Well, in reference to water and its benefits of ions, of course, there are benefits. But there are benefits in the air you breathe. But there are, yea, even better and greater benefits in the thoughts that you think. Be not concerned about machines and how they will benefit you. Everything you need for your greater good, everything you think you need for your benefit is within you this moment and every moment. The only obstruction between us and the good that we seek is the judgments in life that we entertain in thought. For we have been given everything to demonstrate the fullness, the greatness, the goodness, and the joy of life. We deny that goodness when we experience something contrary to our judgments. Ofttimes, my friends, we deny God, which means goodness, because we judge the channel or person, through which the goodness or God is flowing and expressing to us, is not in keeping with what we have judged it should be.

Let us be still and honestly think. God works through man, and that includes us. God does not work directly to man. God works through man. And God's expression is not limited to working through man, for God, the divine Infinite Intelligence, is flowing through the tree and the dog and the animal and the insect. It's when we become free from the dictates of our mind that we experience and receive the flow of goodness, or Godness, through everything we sense, through everything we feel, through everything we see, hear, and touch.

You see, it's ever dependent upon us. It's not dependent upon some machine unless we alone make it so with our thought. We have to have, we think, these automobiles to move, physically, from one place to another. The only reason that we have to have them is because our judgments have made it so. It is not necessary, nor was it or is it, in the divine plan of the Infinite Intelligence that man be limited and restricted. Man alone has limited and man alone has restricted. We don't have to stay that way. But if only through struggle and strife and suffering is the way to be free from that limitation, then that and that alone is the path we have a right to choose.

Thank you. What does the very warm sensation over the forehead and eyes during the healing service mean?

It could, of course, mean many things. It could be an awareness of the energy that is flowing through the healer, as a channel, and through the person who is being healed. It *could* be that. It also could be an effect of emotional trauma. That, of course, is dependent upon the individual. One cannot say that everything that happens in life is spiritual. One cannot say that everything that happens in life is mental or physical. It could be either.

Thank you. What is the principle of organization?

Well, something that we all are not looking forward to hearing, and some of us—my students—have heard it before. The principle of organization is so simple: personal responsibility. The one thing we don't want to hear.

And in speaking of personal responsibility, I would like to share with you this morning, before we conclude, a most interesting experience I, personally, have had this past three weeks and two days. For several months, perhaps a year or two, those of you who have been attending our church, I'm sure, have noticed, for I've certainly heard your thoughts, that I was getting a bit stocky, to say the least. And today, of course, I agree with you. I probably would have agreed with you if you had come up and spoken to me before, but no one had done that.

However, like anyone else, we don't move to make changes, of course, until we get inspired. And it always seems to take someone outside to inspire us inside. So I got inspired by a very fine doctor who's been with me for many, many years from the spirit world: Dr. Waltham. He told me in no uncertain terms, a bit over three weeks ago, that I could lose at least, at least thirty pounds. And I said, "Well, I really don't like diets." I have some kind of a—seems it was born in me—adversity to such foolishness. And so he said, "You don't have to worry about diets. There's a very simple plan. You follow it religiously. You can eat everything you want, whatever you want, and you're going to lose at least a pound a day." And so I went on this simple plan. Simple, I thought. It does take a little effort. So I'll share it with you because for forty years I have listened to clients interested in weight, which they've made a problem.

Now let us first look at weight with a different attitude of mind. Remember, weight, or so-called fat, is stored energy. Oh, by the way, I've lost twenty-two pounds in twenty-three days. I didn't want you to go without noticing. *[Many people laugh.]* Fat or weight is stored energy. Forget about diets. Don't use the word. Don't even think it. And forget about so-called calories. Don't think it. And don't worry about exercise, that comes in the next stage. And so, my friends, if you will think of this so-called excess weight or baggage you're carrying around as stored energy, and if you will go on a simple plan—you may eat everything you want twice a day, but only twice a day. You can have no snacks. You can have no lunch. You can have all you want for breakfast. You can have all you want for dinner. Absolutely nothing in between. Now it is critically important that you do not eat breakfast past the hour of 9:00 a.m., that you do not eat dinner earlier than 5:30 nor later than 8:00 p.m.

Now there's a very good reason for this. You eat and it's converted into energy. There has to be a number of hours in between the two times a day that you eat, that you are active, that you will use up the energy you have taken in, plus you will use up some of the energy that you have in storage. You don't need any pills. You don't need any medicine. You don't need all these salons, unless that's what you think you need. If that's what you think you need, then that is what you must do. But I can assure you—oh, by the way, of course, you will feel hungry; so you drink V-8 juice. Now, you can do whatever you want, but if you want to lose pounds—and I had to make that decision, because it was for my own best health. If you want to lose 20 or 30 or 40 pounds, and you want to lose it and stay healthy, then it's a very simple program.

You see, by telling a person—which I found out three weeks later—that you can eat anything and everything you want for breakfast or dinner, you will find at breakfast and you will find at dinner, you're not as hungry as you thought you were going to be. You can only eat so much at those two times a day. Don't worry about the V-8 juice. It passes on through. It adds no pounds at all. You can be rest assured of that.

Now after you feel the hunger and you take a little V-8, it will not remove the thought, my friends. It will fill you up, but it will not fill your thought of being hungry. You will very soon become aware of what your thought has been doing to you. You will also become very much aware of where the pounds have been coming from. *[This simple plan came to be known as the Serenity Plan, which can be found in the appendix.]*

So, you see, my friends, whatever you want to do, there's always a way to do it. Part of that simple program, which I gladly share with you—especially my students, who have decided to free themselves from some of the extra weight they've been carrying. You see, we must first make the demonstration. I would not think of telling a person to go on a plan that I had not first experienced myself, that I had not first made the effort to see whether it worked or it didn't work. That does not mean that I doubt the spirit who has been with me for so long and has repeatedly proven his wisdom as far as the field of health is concerned. It does mean, after forty years, I still have a mind of my own and I have no problem exercising it.

Thank you very much.

JULY 6, 1980

Church Questions and Answers 6

Good morning. If you will kindly read the first question, I'll be happy to share in my understanding for the answer.

Thank you. What is The Living Light Philosophy's understanding of reincarnation?

Thank you very much. In reference to that question of the Living Light Philosophy and its understanding of the belief of reincarnation, the popular understanding for the term *reincarnation* is to return, specifically, to this planet Earth after once having lived upon this Earth. That is not the teaching of the Living Light Philosophy. The Living Light Philosophy teaches clearly the law of evolution, progressive evolution. It teaches that man, the eternal soul, passes through on an evolutionary path throughout the planets of the universe. Thank you.

Thank you. How can one tell if they are meditating correctly or if they are in self-hypnosis?

It is quite easy to determine whether or not one is experiencing what is called meditation or whether or not one is experiencing some type of self-hypnosis. One of the easy ways to determine the difference is when you find that you are in what you believe to be a state of meditation and the duration of time being spent in what you believe to be a state of meditation is no longer determined by your faculty of reason, which flows through your conscious mind. Now many people, I know, seem to believe that a type of meditation for them of three, four, five, or ten times a day is most beneficial. But I believe upon thorough investigation that you will find that is not meditation, but is, indeed, a type of self-hypnosis. Self-hypnosis, of course, is the control of the mind by the subconscious self. It has nothing whatsoever to do with spiritual meditation. A spiritual meditation is a complete removal from the thought of I. And only by a freedom from the thought of I can one truly meditate and become an inseparable part, in consciousness, of the Divine Whole.

Thank you. What is the essence of peace?

The essence of peace is the Law of Responsibility. Without responsibility, without the ability to respond, one cannot experience consciously the essence of peace. We all understand and we all know that within us there is the perfect peace that goes beyond the understanding of the human mind. But to be aware of that perfect peace, one must have the fullness and the totality of personal responsibility: the ability to respond personally to the vibratory wave of one's own eternal spirit. Thank you.

Thank you. How are illnesses in animals caused and is it connected to their subconscious?

Discord, disharmony, also known as illness—the law applies to all forms. Whether it is the form of the human being or it is the form of the animal or it is the form of the plant, the same law, being a divine law, being a natural law, applies to all forms.

Thank you. Recently it was stated in a church lecture that when man lets go, God takes control. Would you please explain how man lets go?

When man lets go, God indeed takes control. God, we understand to be an infinite, eternal, intelligent Energy. An Energy, when freely flowing unobstructed, is not only a perfect peace, [but also is] a perfect balance, a perfect beauty, a perfect harmony. Whenever we choose to permit our minds to dictate how, when we shall experience the goodness that we are seeking, our mind, being composed of mental substance, being subject to the Law of Substance, which is duality, creates an obstruction to that which we seek. Therefore, when man lets go of the thought of I, man is no longer separated from the divine, infinite, eternal truth, for there is no obstruction in his universe and there being no obstruction, the balance, the harmony is once again restored.

Ofttimes we have had the experience, when we are so concerned about a problem or a seeming obstruction in our life that we seem to forget it or we go to sleep on it. And we awaken ofttimes in the morning with the solution. What we have, in truth, done [is] we have removed the thought of I and, by removing the thought of I, are no longer identified in consciousness with the obstruction and with the difficulty. We can only experience in life that which we identify with. And if we do not identify with the problem, then the solution, which is hidden within the problem, appears before our view. We identify through the principle of the thought of I. The thought of I separates us, our eternal being, from the universal whole. It separates us by building a mental wall between our soul and the Allsoul. Therefore, when we do let go, God does take control because there is no obstruction to the flow of goodness or God in our life in that moment.

There is no greater destructive force in the universe than what is commonly referred to as self-concern. In order to be concerned about oneself, one must first have made judgments about oneself. And whenever the mind is permitted to make judgments, it places the soul into a world of creation and, in so doing, must experience the laws of creation. It is one of the basic purposes of the Living Light Philosophy and the Serenity Church to help man to help himself to clearly see the difference between truth and creation. Although it is the divine, infinite, intelligent Energy, known as truth, that sustains creation, truth shall never be creation, for it is contrary to the very nature of truth, which is a oneness. It is only when we permit our minds to identify—and our minds only identify following a judgment or judgments—only then do we separate our self from the wholeness that is our birthright. When we become aware of that simple truth, we will clearly see how we can separate truth from creation and experience the oneness which is the true essence of life itself.

Thank you. What is your understanding of persons who become addicted to alcohol or drugs?

Persons—we are persons and we become addicted to many things. There is no person identifying with creation that is not addicted, or perhaps better said, attached to something in creation. We slowly, but surely, begin to realize how much we are attached to our mental form, the effect being our physical form, when we start to lose a few pounds of weight. I have yet to meet a person, having lost weight, or gained weight, who has not had some type of emotional trauma connected with it. Of course, the reason being is our identification with the way we *think* we are. But we have proven to ourselves repeatedly that we are not the way we think we are, unless we are willing to accept that we are in a constant state of change. For one moment we think we are one way, only to meet someone else and think we are some other way. Surely, we've had this experience in our lives, in our courtships, and in our marriages.

And so it is our mind and creation, of which it is a part, is not something that we can rely upon, for we have already had sufficient experiences in our lives to prove beyond a shadow of any doubt that our minds, a part of creation, are not reliable. We desire one thing one moment, only to encounter another experience and desire something different. But we rarely pause in the course of our many activities to see what we are doing to ourselves. Because we are, in truth, the captain of our ship, because we are, in truth, the masters of our destiny, we see how we establish these various laws in our life, how we rise to heights of joy only to descend into depths of sadness, as long as we permit our minds to deny the demonstrable truth of personal responsibility—that we and we alone have established the laws and are reaping the harvest, known as the experience, the effect of what we alone have chosen.

It is, I know, difficult for the mind to accept experiences which it encounters which it finds distasteful. And yet the experience, like all experience in the universe, is only an effect. When we accept that truth, then we have the fullness of the experience of personal responsibility, then we become, as we have been designed to become, intelligent captains of our ship, intelligent masters of our destiny. And by that I mean we become consciously aware of the natural, immutable laws of life and we know, we know what our future holds, for we know the laws we're setting into motion in the present. For each thought we have this moment leaves our universe and returns to us.

There is no such thing as a secret. It is a delusion we have created from fear for ourselves. For in the universe, of which we are an inseparable part, everything past, everything future, of course is known. For in that universe of which we are a part, there is only eternity. Eternity is only the present. Whatever has been and whatever is yet to be is only experienced by the illusionary substance—mental substance—of our mind. It already *is*. When we accept that—but we cannot accept that until we accept the truth, which is responsibility, personal responsibility. When that takes place in our life, we will no longer fear the future, nor worry and concern our self for the past, for we are in the moment of eternity. We are in that moment now. If we do not experience that moment, it is only because we are over-identified with the illusion, known as the thought of I, for it is an illusion.

As long as we believe that we need the illusion, we will continue to deny the truth or God. But we cannot forever and ever deny the truth. We cannot forever and ever live in the illusions, the effects of our mental creations. We already have experienced that principle of being free from illusion. For our past is past and only the need of over-identification with the thought of I keeps the past before our view. Because without the thought of I, without that imbalance and over-identification, we could not experience concern. And we only view the past, the illusion, and we only view the future, the illusion, when we are concerned, which reveals our identification with the thought of I.

For all there is, is available to us. We need not move, except in consciousness, for everything is right where we are. As long as we believe in the illusion to attain what we seek we must go through certain steps, then we are bound by the illusion; we are bound by the judgment that we alone have made. That is not the true purpose of our life. And when we leave the limits of the physical body, we will find a greater freedom. We will find a greater freedom because we have lost, we believe, a part of our self, and our cup overfloweth. So when we lose a part of our self, there's room for greater good to come in. We all know that the greatest gift that we can give to the very Intelligence that sustains our very thought, the very greatest gift we could ever give is the gift of self. It is the greatest gift that we can give because it is the greatest bondage. And so that that we free, of course, unfolds us. And that that we hold, of course, binds us.

But remember, my friends, it's not a physical object that causes us the grief in life; it is a thought. It's not someone else's thought that causes us to suffer. It may well be our thought of someone else, but it's still our thought. Because it is our thought and because it is taking place in our mind, think of the opportunity that we have. You tell your hand what to do and your hand responds. You tell your foot what to do and your foot responds. But when you start to tell your eyes what to see, you find difficulty. And when you tell your ears what to hear, you find difficulty. Why is it, when they're all a part of the sense function, that we have more difficulty in telling our eyes what to see and our ears what to hear than we have in telling our hand where to move and our foot to rise? It's quite simple, my friends. The more refined the function, the more complex it is. And so in keeping with this statement: Truth is simple and unconcealed; 'tis falsehood that's complex and deeply hidden.

Many a prophet has taught that we have eyes to see and see not, we have ears to hear and hear not. The only reason we have those problems is because somewhere in our mind we have a judgment that blinds us to the beauty of life. We have a judgment that brings a deafness to the goodness of life. But it is ours. It is something in our evolution created from the error of ignorance. But because it's ours, because it is our judgment, because it is our thought and because it is our mind, we can, when we are ready, do something with it. But we cannot do something with it until we are ready. And how do we become ready to make any change? Indeed, it's a miracle, it seems, for survival is the miracle of life. And when everything fails, when our mind has exhausted itself from its efforts, then the miracle of life, called survival, brings about a change.

Long ago the teacher of this philosophy stated, "O suffer senses not in vain, for freedom of your soul is gain." Remember, my friends, whatever gives pleasure, also gives pain, for that is the Law of Creation. So what you find in life that's pleasurable, remember, it's only your view. And whatever you find in life that's to you painful, remember, it's only your view. Oh, indeed, is it true, you may find a lot of company to support your view, if you don't feel secure in your judgment. And so we move on to that beautiful truth that misery not only loves company, it is indispensable for its existence. We all know that we—none of us—appreciate being around anyone that's miserable all the time. No one appreciates being around anyone that is in self-pity and self-concern all the time. Why don't we appreciate having friends that are in constant self-pity and constant disaster in life? We can only grant to another what we are granting to our self and if we are not granting the glorious depths of self-pity to ourselves, then it is evident we cannot grant to another what we do not grant to our self.

We all have these levels of the mind of expression. We all have the conscious right to choose which level our soul, eternal, will express through. But we have, many of us, become attached to patterns that served us when we were little children. When we were three and four months old, we cried because we had a desire, a natural instinct; [we] were hungry. And so we cried to be fed, to have our bottle. And if the bottle did not arrive the moment we thought it should, we cried louder. And if it still didn't arrive, we soon found our whole body in movement—our arms, our hands, our feet, our head. And finally our desire was fulfilled. The crying stopped. The trauma stopped.

And then the years have passed since we were three and four and five and six months old. The years have passed, but for most of us the patterns of mind have not. As adults we no longer kick our feet. We no longer shake our arms and our fists. We no longer scream. We grew out of that. Now we rant and rave or we clench our teeth and tighten our jaws. We still have the same experience, but we've added something to the experience: it's called pride. And pride will not allow us to walk down the street crying, screaming, ranting, and raving. And so pride closes the door so the energy cannot express itself in that way. And unfortunately for many, the energy still rises to express itself. Unfortunately for many, it is suppressed. It is not educated because we are not consciously working with it. So we find that we still have these problems that we had in our early months in this earth experience. We still have the problem because we haven't worked with it. We haven't sat down and talked to that level within us to educate it that it may learn beyond a shadow of any doubt the wisdom of patience.

You see, my good friends, we always get what we really want. I know a lot of us, not having received what we really want at this moment, may disagree. We always get what we really want, sooner or later. And by the divine Intelligence and the divine grace, it's later for most of us. Because if we got it when we wanted it, we really wouldn't know what to do with it. Because, you see, we're not yet ready. When we're ready, of course, we get it. But who's going to tell us when we're ready? Why, it's a very simple thing that's going to tell us when we're ready: it's called personal responsibility. A word we love to hear when we're sitting on the top and our mind tells us how successful we are and how great the universe is and how everything is just working out fine. That's the word we all want to hear.

Well, let us move forward in consciousness and let us find the joy and the greatness and the goodness of that word in the here and now. Remember, my friends, whenever we permit our mind to blame outside, to blame a person, place, or thing for any thought that we are entertaining in our consciousness, we immediately become the victim of the very person, place, or thing that we blame. A mother raises her children. They grow up. Perhaps they do things that are not in keeping with her judgments and her experiences of the past. She makes the judgment, the child does not change, and she does the suffering. She only does the suffering because, through an error of ignorance, she has made herself—and the father has made himself—the victim of someone else's thoughts, acts, and deeds. Why think, my friends, you could make the President your God. You could be the victim of anyone you choose to be. And we all have to agree, unless we make great effort in the here and now, we are already the victim of someone. Usually they number in the thousands.

No one truly wants to be a victim. And the only way we're going to be free from being a victim is to accept personal responsibility. Because by accepting personal responsibility, then we will not permit our mind to say, "Someone else is making me unhappy when it's my thought that's doing whatever it's doing to me." What a wonderful world this is, the moment we tell our self that simple truth. And if there's nothing else that you accept in life, try accepting it's your thought, it's your mind. You have been granted the divine birthright to do with your thought and your mind what you choose. But you cannot do with your thought and your mind what you choose until you accept personal responsibility. And don't become the victim of blaming outside, for it is indeed a sad way to live.

Thank you.

AUGUST 3, 1980

Church Questions and Answers 7

Today, as I'm sure you're all aware, the first of the month, of course, it's become our recent tradition to speak to the questions that have been submitted concerning this philosophy and spiritual matters in general. I can only share with you the answers to the questions that you have prepared in keeping with my own receptivity to the spirit guides and teachers who are with us.

So often people visiting or investigating Spiritualism become a bit confused, to say the least, in reference to what its true purpose really is. Spiritualism, when we study the religions of our world, we quickly see is the oldest religion known to mankind. For there has never been a time on this planet when man has not communicated with higher dimensions, known to us as a world of spirit. Unfortunately or, perhaps, fortunately, for out of the struggle and mud of earth grows the lotus of heaven. However, for over a hundred years now many, many people, attracted to the light of Spiritualism, have been confused in their motivations, for they look to the answers for everything and they look not within, where the truth really lies, but they have a tendency to look without. And when it is that we look without to answers, then, of course, it is that we look without for question. And so man goes farther and farther from his true spiritual destiny by escaping the basic principle of truth, known as personal responsibility.

Spiritualism has, since it was brought to the world as modern Spiritualism in 1848, it has striven diligently to help mankind to realize that God does not work to us, that God's work takes place through us. And that we never know when God is going to speak unless we're free from the greatest obstruction we'll ever know, unless we're free from judgment and free from intolerance.

Whatever question enters our mind guarantees, by the process of questioning, its own answer. It may or may not come directly to us, but it will in time pass through us. Remember, my friends, everything, every thought you think, every feeling you have, every physical object that is in your possession this moment, is in a process of passing through your life. It is only when we make the judgment that we own, only then do we lose. For man cannot lose what is loaned to him for a time. Man can only lose in the realm of delusion that possesses and owns. We have already experienced [in] our lifetime today of viewing the many things that come our way and go their way.

Everything, even the tree that bears its fruit, does so for a purpose. There are no accidents in the universe. There is nothing that happens by chance. We see it that way because we, yet, have to understand its purpose and fulfillment in life itself. And so it is many thoughts come to us and many thoughts leave us. The thoughts that bother us are the ones we try to hold. And we all know whatever bothers us in life is that which controls us. We are controlled only when we hold, for that that we free unfolds us, and that that we hold controls us. Now none of us appreciate the thought of being controlled. We don't appreciate it because we feel deep within us that we are, in truth, a formless, free spirit. Knowing that intuitively in the very depths of our being, we become most upset at the very thought that someone or something is controlling us. Yet, all we have to do is to pause for a moment and to think and we can take stock of all the things we think we own, of all the things we think we hold, for it is those things, those people that control us.

Spiritualism has revealed—long ago—that a thought in our mind changes the very chemistry of our body, that our body reacts to our thought and our thought reacts to our body. So when we have a thought of holding to a person as our security, as our happiness, or to an object or to anything our world has to offer, as we entertain that thought of holding, we establish the Law of Loss, for we set into motion what is known as negative laws, the negative faith of force. Now the negative faith of force is known to man as fear. The positive power of the Divine, called God, is known as faith. And so as man entertains the thought of holding, he guarantees setting into motion the Law of Force, known as fear, and the loss is inevitable. We can never experience the loss of anything until we have entertained the delusion of gain.

When we awaken our spirit within we quickly view the truth: there is nothing to lose for there is nothing to gain. Our formless, free spirit is everywhere and everything. What can it gain, for it is already everything? It is our educated mind, only our educated mind, that views gain and knows loss. We are here in eternity. We are not going to eternity. We are *in* eternity. We have always been *in* eternity, for eternity is what we are. It is our educated mind that believes one thing one moment only to deny it the next moment. Surely our world here on earth reveals to us, with such a high divorce rate in the world today, that it is an illusion; to hold to people, places, and things only brings us and guarantees the so-called karmic wheel of one experience after another.

When our minds believe that everything is gone, when we have truly hit the bottom, when our minds accept that there's nothing left, when that happens to us, we will find everything. It is only when our cup is emptied that it can be filled. We cannot fill the cup we hold because in filling, it's overflowing. It is not what we need to put into our mind to free us. It is what we already have in our mind that we must empty out to free us. You cannot introduce a new idea into the mind unless the mind already contains, through the Law of Association, a similar experience, because that is the very nature of our mind. When we encounter a new idea, a new thought, it goes through the censorship process of what already exists in our mind. If there is something similar, there's a possibility of it entering. If there is not something related and similar, the king of kings, the false god, known as judgment, immediately kicks it out and declares, "It is not possible." When we declare, by our mind, that anything—no matter what it is—is not possible, we deny God for us. Because we all truly believe that to God, the power, the intelligence that sustains the universes and everything in it, all things are possible. So when we say to ourselves or another that this or that is not possible, in that moment we deny God.

Now when we deny God, we deny goodness. And it is our denials in life that become our destiny. Now if we want to know where we're going, all we have to do is take stock of our denials, and we will see the road map of where we're headed, for truly, our denials are our destiny. How do our denials become our destiny? To be adverse to anything does not mean to accept. It does mean to reject. Now God, we understand, supports and sustains everything, rejects nothing. So when we reject, we become controlled by the mental world. And in so doing we must follow the path of our rejections, the path of our denials, that we may gain through that process an understanding that there is something greater than the thought of man. That something greater is the power which sustains it.

We look about from a very narrow view, so often, and in so doing we suffer the consequences of our intolerances. It is a desire of all minds that are not secure—think, my friends, that are not secure—it is a desire of all minds to have everyone do things and be ways that we have accepted for our self. And when we experience people who do not do things and act the way that we have accepted for our self, we find within us, welling up in our emotions, what is known as intolerance. As we experience the fullness of that feeling known as intolerance, we become rejected by the wholeness of life, for we are the ones who have set the law of rejection and denial into motion. Remember, what you do not tolerate in life, tolerates you by controlling you.

Now if you see a person that you don't like the way they do things, each time you think or see that person, you have a feeling that is certainly not godly because it's not a good feeling.

You don't appreciate the feeling, but you have the thought. Now, of course, it's our thought, created by us, existing in our cranium. It's not someone else's thought. The person we cannot tolerate, they have no problem at all. We are the ones, therefore, that have the problem and have become the victim.

Now think of the world we live in. Think how easily it would be, and is, to control the masses. All you have to do is to do things they cannot tolerate. And by so doing, you have control over their emotions and control over their life. Think of what we're doing to our self. And because the masses of people believe that the problems they experience are caused out there in someone else's head, you even have more control over them. And so we live each day—I'm aware now, friends, we're supposed to have questions and answers, I hope we can get to that. But I'm a firm believer in evolution. Without change, there is no evolution. And I want to evolve like everyone. But think of how we are controlled. By all the things we cannot tolerate are we controlled. We are never controlled by the things that we tolerate. We can only be controlled by the things that we are not tolerant with, because the opposite of tolerance, intolerance, is denial and is destiny.

So no matter where you go and no matter what you do, remember, how you think is the way your life will be. Not the way someone else thinks, unless you have judged that the way they think is intolerable to you. And if the way they think is intolerable to you, then they have controlled you. Think of our daily work. Think of the employers, the companies, the corporations that we have allowed our self to be the victim of. Think of the philosophies and the politics that we have allowed our self to be the victim of.

My friends, every mind desires to succeed. Success is ever dependent upon your degree of tolerance. Look how many times you've worked so hard to get so far to have it all collapse. The only thing that created that—sure, it was someone else. It was the someone else that you couldn't tolerate. It was the someone else that you judged was wrong. He who grants the right of tolerance to himself, by the law that we can only give to another what we have given to our self, has tolerance wherever they go. If you find it difficult in tolerating things and people and places, remember, you are not tolerant with yourself. So we begin on making some effort inside our self.

Now tolerance, surely, we will all agree, is the effect, the effect of understanding. The moment we understand something, we have no problem with tolerance at all, because we understand it. And the reason that we have no problem with tolerance the moment we understand it is because man cannot entertain judgment with anything that he truly understands. When you understand, there is no judgment. But how does man gain understanding? Surely, we agree we cannot experience understanding unless we have some degree of communication. We cannot understand our many different attitudes and feelings and thoughts and levels of consciousness if we don't communicate with them. And if we don't communicate with them, we cannot understand them. If we cannot understand them, we certainly cannot tolerate them. We all know that we do things, and after we've done them, we don't understand why we did them. Well, we would understand why we did them if we had communicated with those different motivations that are within our self. So here we go again, of course, in the universe right back to our self.

But our life, really, is beautiful, if we will only pause to think, if we will free our self from dependence. You know, we entered this earth in our evolution formless, free spirit with a covering of so-called individualized soul. It is not our purpose to be bound, but we are bound because the moment we depend, the moment we depend on people, places, and things, that is the moment that we are bound. For it is in that moment that the Law of Judgment is established. And so we suffer when they're gone. We think we're happy when they're present and in-between, only God knows what's really going on. I ask you, my good friends, is that the way we really want to live? To have a week of so-called happiness and ten years of the opposite? Or to be going through that process just because someone doesn't do what we want them to do, because that's what *we* want, when most of the time we're not really quite sure of what we do want. One moment we're hungry and the next minute, we're full. One minute we want to go to the beach and the next minute, to the mountains. We're really never quite sure. And so, you see, my friends, whenever we depend upon our mind, we become bound by our mind. We're not sure whether this is going to work and we're really not sure if that's going to work. Well, how can we be sure? There's no possible way that we can be sure, because our effort is not being made to know our self.

Now if we knew our self, we would know that level 24 wants to go to the beach, while level 12 wants to go to the mountains. Level 10 wants to buy a new car and level 3 wants to lease it. Then we would gradually, slowly, but surely, begin to know our self and we'd say, "Now, let's see. Here are 81 levels. Now, I want you thoughts all to get together here because this is what I'm going to do. That's all there is to it. There is no doubt; therefore, there is no fear. That's the way that it is, no matter what comes or goes, because that's what I am doing. Period."

Now they say men get married and they always have cold feet. Well, what's cold feet? We understand, of course, feet is understanding. And their understanding gets a bit chilled. Well, they better work on the understanding before they go to the alter so they can get themselves warmed up a bit.

Now I'm going to get on to your questions and answers. So, you read your first question, please.

Thank you. Why are the consequences of procrastination regret and self-pity?

Because, my friends, we all have what is known as a conscience—a spiritual sensibility with a dual capacity that knows right from wrong and it doesn't have to be told. Now when we procrastinate, we reveal to our self and, obviously, anyone who is aware of our procrastinations, that we are not yet able to control our mind. And therefore, we do need a great deal of help. Because, you see—what is procrastination? One level of our mind decides we're going to do something and we commit our self to doing what we want to do. But a few minutes, a few hours, a few days, or a few weeks pass, there's some other level in control in our mind. It is not concerned about what commitments we have made. It is only concerned with the desire that it has at the moment. Now we see this happening all around us all the time. People commit themselves to being on time for something, and they have to be late. But they have to ask themselves, "What inside of me, O God, makes me be late when I commit myself to being someplace for an appointment at a specified time? What is it inside of me that does that to me? Help me become aware, for surely it is not a mark of a good and strong character."

When we say we're going to do something, let us have enough self-control to do it or let us not speak and say we're going to do something. And so, what happens to us? We experience pity. We feel sorry for our self for making such a fool out of our self. And we have all these regrets because we do know inside that we are still waiting to grow up. No matter how old we are physically, emotionally we're waiting to grow up, that we may speak our word forth into the universe, knowing that it shall not come back to us void, but accomplish that which we send it to do. Now, when we speak our word, it cannot accomplish what we send it to do because we may or may not be home when it returns. Because we're not prompt. We're not considerate. Promptness, in a commitment, is a true mark of our character, for it considers something and someone besides the limited self-desire that we entertained at the moment of our commitment.

Now even the procrastinators in our world don't appreciate being procrastinated upon. They're most intolerant. Perhaps they've been late their whole life, but you just let someone be late when they have a desire and a commitment and you will see the full blossom of intolerance. Because they do not understand themselves and why they procrastinate, how can they grant to another the understanding they are yet waiting to have? Thank you.

Thank you. What is meant by, "on earth as it is in heaven?"

Well, that depends, of course, [on] what people think heaven is. Now if, of course, we think it's angels playing harps, it's not the heaven I'm going to. I am aware of that and I am so grateful, because I love harp music for a time. *[Many in the congregation laugh.]* But I do have my limits, I have to admit, in tolerance with it. And to visualize myself sitting at the knee of some angel playing a harp day and night, I don't think my tolerance is anywhere near that expanded. So if I'm to go to you know where, then they'll be playing harps day and night, but I don't think that's in order.

"On earth as it is in heaven," I'm sure most of us, surely, do believe that there's a place of peace and harmony. Not void of excitement, of course, because, you know, we don't become saints overnight and our senses do need some challenge and stimulation. So, a little bit, perhaps, of surprises. But at least where we're free from the constant thought of how horrible and miserable life is.

Now heaven, of course, is this moment. Heaven is the moment that you choose that is not dependent upon anything outside of you. If your heaven, a state of consciousness, is dependent upon anything outside of you, then your heaven will always be in need. Now we already know that from the experiences that we've already had. We already know if we permit that wonderful, good feeling inside of us to be dependent on a person, place, or thing, that wonderful, good feeling doesn't last, because the person, place, or thing doesn't always do what we want them to do. And when they don't do what we want them to do, we become intolerant because we make a judgment and we lose the good feeling. So whether you're married or not married, whether you're dependent upon your employer for money or you're not dependent upon him for money, when you free yourself from dependence, you're freed from bondage. And when you're freed from bondage, you enter heaven. Truly, a state of bliss.

But let's change our thinking about what bliss really is. Some people in thinking that heaven is a state of bliss, they want to go in the opposite direction. Because to them bliss means they can't do what they want to do and that, certainly, is not where they want to go. But anyway, remember, if you allow yourself to be dependent on anything outside of you—for God is within you—if you allow yourself to be dependent upon anything outside of you, then you are not in a state of consciousness known as heaven. You're just moving from one level of consciousness to the other and you guarantee the depth, for you've reached the height. Thank you.

Thank you. Is there another implication to the saying misery loves company from like attracts like and becomes the Law of Attachment?

Absolutely. I never have yet met a person expressing what is known as a level of consciousness called miserable that didn't demand attention. Misery not only loves company, it has to have it in order for its existence. Now, if you want to help yourself and you encounter a person that's miserable, you make very sure that you're strong enough to stay in a level of reason that they, through you, may face that beautiful, simple truth called personal responsibility. That no one made them miserable. That they are there by a conscious choice. It is their right to choose to be dependent upon something outside—person, place, or thing. That is their right. It is not their right, nor yours, to support the level of consciousness that is so destructive.

I can assure you, in forty years in this work I have been blessed with meeting many, many, many miserable people, but they did not stay that way around me. Now you people are wonderful souls. I see no misery this morning, so I don't want you to feel bad. But they did not stay that way because I will not allow myself to stay that way. No matter what comes and no matter what goes, I see the good that's in it. It may be, by my own choice, a great test of my own tolerance. Of course, we test our self. But I am very happy, for every morning I open my eyes and see the beauty of the world. I know that everyone can do it, if they want to. So misery does not find a home with me. It hasn't for many, many years.

And if you have that problem, there's a way that you can help yourself that really won't take any great amount of effort. All you have to do—that's all you have to do—is to make the effort to help someone else. Because God helps those who help themselves by helping others. It's the "by helping others" we forget. We all totally accept, I'm sure, that God helps those who help themselves, but we leave off the most important part and that's the part that really works, you know. You just can't bake bread with flour. You have no yeast; it doesn't rise. So, you can't speak a truth and only give half of it. God does help those who help themselves and we've all accepted that part of the truth. Now let's accept the other part: by helping others. Because, you see, what happens—energy follows attention. The energy flowing through us that got locked in the level known as miserable gets redirected into helping some other soul, who's in a level, and by doing that, this level and this experience within us of being miserable, it just melts away. It disappears, until we think about our self again.

You know, it's so beneficial, really, it's so practical—it really is—to stop thinking for a moment about our self. Because what happens when we stop thinking about our self, God starts thinking about us. But when we're so busy thinking about our self, our cup overfloweth. So, you see, this great goodness cannot get in. We all know how beneficial it is to have a pet or an animal or a bird or something. Because, you see, that gives us a few moments to stop thinking about our self. We have to think about them eating. We have to think about their health and care. And in those moments, we just feel wonderful. But now, all of us cannot go around in the work we have with twenty, thirty cats or dogs that we live with, you see. So we've got to do something else. Now, some of us, we have enough plants that need watering that in the moments we're doing that we have an opportunity to get freed from self. I say opportunity. I didn't say it was guaranteed. I know a lot of people who water a tree and still think of themselves and the tree reacts accordingly, of course. [It] doesn't grow as well, you see. Because it's not just the water that it needs. It needs a little bit of consideration, a little love and care. That's what all of life really needs. I'll go on to your next question, please.

Thank you. Please comment on the saying figures don't lie, but liars can sure figure.

I don't recall ever making that statement, but if you'll repeat it, I will ask somebody who must have made it. "Figures don't lie."

Please comment on the saying figures don't lie, but liars can sure figure.

Are you sure that's from our philosophy?

It does not say it's from our philosophy.

I don't recall—that is an interesting—it sounds to me as though it came from the mental world. But you be patient and I'll see what I find out about that. Figures, you say, don't lie?

But liars can sure figure.

I don't think that's true. No, I will have to disagree with that statement that figures don't lie. I've seen too many figures lie, not to say that they don't. Now if the person means by two and two adds to four and that doesn't lie, then we're talking about logic. And there's a vast difference between logic and truth. There's a vast difference between facts and truth.

Knowledge, we all agree, it knows much. But there's something else called wisdom that knows better. Our knowledge of anything is in a constant process of changing. And it's in a process of changing based upon our own acceptance. And our acceptance is based upon our judgments; that's what limits it. So, you see, knowledge is not what we're seeking to be free. It is wisdom we are seeking. It is understanding we are seeking to be free, not knowledge. Because where is reliability in knowledge, when knowledge is in a constant process of change, based upon our judgments of the moment? A lot of people say they know a lot of things and you meet them ten months later and they know something else totally contrary to what they knew the ten months previous. Surely, we cannot find reliability in knowledge. Yes.

Thank you. Can the substance of heat be explained?

For what purpose? And what type of heat is the questioner discussing? Is he talking about the heat of the body or the heat of the universe?

You see, my friends, heat or cold is subject to the laws of creation. And you cannot have heat without cold. And you cannot have cold without heat. Now think about that for a moment. In order to have facts, in order to have knowledge, in order to have judgment, you must have comparison. And in order to have comparison, you cannot have truth. You cannot. You may have facts. You may have knowledge. You may have logic, but you cannot have truth. Because truth is indivisible. You cannot compare truth. Truth is individually perceived. When we separate creation, when we separate, when we move from our mental world into this other world—and we do do that. Unfortunately for our minds, they get very upset when it happens to us—most of us—but we do do it periodically. Truth is all encompassing. And logic and facts, they are dependent upon the Law of Creation, called duality, known as comparison.

Now, when you no longer compare, you no longer have problems with intolerance. You see, we only have problems and we only have intolerance when we compare. When we look at a person and what they do, we compare. Unfortunately, we've done it so many times it's habitual and we're not even consciously aware anymore that [when] we meet a person, we instantaneously compare that person with our self. And they either fit into our self or they don't fit. And if they don't fit, we're not tolerant. Now that happens *[The Teacher snaps his fingers.]* like that, because we've done it so many times. It's a habit. Thank you.

Thank you. Please explain the significance of color.

The significance of color. I think we've discussed that many times in our classes, but we'll discuss it once more. Color is vibration. And vibration is sound. Now, whenever you make a sound, whether you speak or you knock on wood or whatever you do, color fills the atmosphere. Science, slowly, but surely, has moved into the realm of that simple truth. Now each of us has our own sound inside of us. People who have opened their clairaudience, they hear that sound. A person doesn't have to speak, they don't have to move, for there is a sound, for there is color. Color is sound and sound is color. Now, our color, our aura is in a process of changing, fluctuating, dependent upon our thoughts and our feelings and our emotions. And this goes on all the time.

And so we move in the universe and our color, our vibration, our sound is either harmonious with the person we meet or it is not harmonious. And if it's not harmonious, we have problems. If it's harmonious, we don't have problems. But we are the ones that are doing this, not someone else. Now if we meet a person and we have this feeling [that] something's not right [and] we don't feel good inside, we know, intuitively, that our vibrations are not blending; they are not harmonious. Well, what we have to do, through the faculty of consideration, is be still a second and become aware within of what the color, sound, or vibration is that we have just entered into. And then *we*, through our own self-control, we change our vibration, we change our color to a neutral color that will blend, you see, with the aura we have just met. Because to force one's will upon another to change them is no change at all. But it's a lot of trauma for our self. We have time for one more, please.

Thank you. What is the substance of thought?

The substance of thought. I see our questioner is really in the vibration of substance. So I would like to first consider discussing what is substance. Is there such a thing as substance? We think there is. I'm sure we'll all agree with that. We do think there's substance. Does the substance exist in truth? Or is it only the effect of our belief? Now those who are informed on the many so-called phenomena that take place in our world, even today, have had experience that has proven to them beyond a shadow of any doubt that substance is dependent upon thought. Thought is not dependent upon substance, for substance, in truth, does not exist. It only exists in a realm of belief. You believe it exists and therefore, for you, it does exist. When you no longer believe that it exists, for you it will not exist.

And so man can, through a change in his beliefs, surely, a man can fly. He is no longer dependent upon so-called airplanes or anything else. Certainly he can walk through fire. Certainly he can walk through a wall. But that's up to man. Man has entered this earth with all those abilities or so-called talents. But his beliefs have bound him to the fabric of illusion and delusion to where he believes that substance exists. And if you try to help him to educate his mind that it does not exist, then you have a very delicate psychological problem, which reveals that we are totally dependent upon our beliefs. And because we are dependent upon our beliefs, when our beliefs become wiped away, we have nothing. Absolutely nothing. And it is that nothingness, the very thought of nothingness to the mind that causes it to go into a trauma—emotional turmoil—which tells us, each one of us, so clearly, that our dependence is not on the formless and the free. Our dependence is only on that which we believe has substance. The great trial of so-called death, the great trial is the false belief that substance is. That's the great emotional trauma.

Let us entertain, at least for a moment, that substance, a dream, is only a dream. Long ago our teacher spoke and said, "Dreamer, dream a life of beauty before your dream starts dreaming you." Now, as we believe in the existence of substance, the dream, you see, we have become the victim of the dream. But we're the dreamer. We used to be. Now those dreams that we have dreamed, they're dreaming us, because they're created by the intelligence that flows through our mind. It doesn't have to be that way. It was not designed to be that way. Let us, once again, take hold of the reins. Let us, once again, become the dreamer and not the dreamed. Let us, once again, become the observer and not the observed.

I have yet to meet a person that appreciates being observed. No one likes to feel they're in a cage with all these people passing by, looking and examining them. So, my friends, think. It doesn't matter whether you believe in extraterrestrial beings or you just believe in astral beings. Whether you like it or not, and whether I like it or not, we're all being observed. Because we became the victim of the dream, our dream.

Now I don't like being observed. And I haven't liked it for the forty years that I've been aware of it. But I feel much more comfortable today, knowing that everyone else is being observed. Not necessarily, now, by the people that I know. Not necessarily, unless they're students; that's something different. But everyone's being observed. So when you observe the little ant that crawls on the ground, when you observe the snake and the crocodiles and the little, dinky lizards, when you observe them, remember, there's someone who never stops observing you. *[Some in the congregation laugh.]*

Thank you.

SEPTEMBER 7, 1980

Church Questions and Answers 8

In keeping with the evolutionary spirit of our philosophy, we will have a slight change this morning, which our chairman, obviously, was not aware of. Rather than answer the questions that have been submitted, we will have the spirit of spontaneity, and I will be happy to share with you our understanding of any questions that you have, if you'll be so kind as to raise your hand. Now the questions that you have, please let them not be of a personal nature, but of general interest to all of us, of a spiritual nature and something that really has interested you. So if you will kindly raise your hand, I will share with you our understanding concerning your questions. *[After a short pause, the Teacher continues.]* Now if you have no questions, obviously I won't have to work that hard this morning; I can spend more time resting. *[Many in the congregation laugh.]* Yes, will the lady please speak.

Please explain spirit lights.

The question the lady has asked is, "Please explain spirit lights." Let us first have the understanding that as our spirit perceives spirit, our minds perceive minds. We must never forget whatever is a spiritual experience, whether our minds call them spirit lights or our mind calls it the presence of spirit, it is perceived by the spirit within us.

This is so important in understanding communication between these dimensions, for communication is indispensable to understanding. And without understanding, the soul faculties do not awaken; we do not have truth, let alone, freedom. And so it is, my friends, that great effort should be made by all of us to communicate with our self, for we know that we have many seeming difficulties communicating with others that we desire to communicate with, which, of course, is the revelation to us that we have difficulty communicating with our self. So as we make greater daily effort to communicate with our self, we will grow in understanding of our motives and our feelings and our thoughts in life. And the result will be a greater understanding of what we call spirit lights or spirit presence.

Remember that all communication is censored by the acceptances and rejections of our own educated mind. As man believeth, so he becometh, is ever in keeping with the denials and rejections that we have established by our past experiences. As long as our past experiences continue to control our thoughts, that is as long as we will remain in the bondage of any experience that we encounter in life. Remember that we are, beyond a shadow of any doubt, we are a law unto our self. So all the experiences that we have, they are only revealing to us, if we find them unpleasant and not beneficial and good in our life, they simply reveal to us that a change in our thought, in our attitude is necessary.

I know we're discussing the question of spirit lights and I am sure before we finish you will perceive the answer.

It is so very important, my friends, to understand why it is so difficult for any of us to make a change. We must pause and ask our self that simple question, Why? when all of nature reveals to us that change is the very Law of Evolution, that change is absolutely guaranteed for all form, including our own. We resist the Law of Evolution, and by so resisting do we suffer. We see that, day by day, we go through what we have made: the Law of Aging. We look around at nature. We see an oak. We see it age day by day and moment by moment. We have made that judgment that that is an aging process. We and we alone have decided that that change is known as aging. Yet, as the tree goes through the many changes of evolution, it becomes more mature, more beautiful, and more expressive. Yet, when that very process is taking place within our self, we resist and we struggle. We work against our self. We do those things because of an error in our thought.

All things, we see, are born and pass. All things, including thought, they come and they go. And so it is with that that our soul is presently experiencing, this little vehicle, this form called our body. We came to earth in keeping with the laws of evolution that only we alone had established, and here we are today. When we deny, when we alone deny that we are an inseparable part of a universal whole, when we make that judgment and we make that denial, we move from freedom into limit, into bondage, for this body that we have this moment is only going to be with us for so long a time. It has been designed by the Great Architect to serve that purpose. It is changing, but because our mind, our mind resists change, we experience discord in our body. Because the discord, the disharmony is in our mind. Our thoughts, our desires are not united. They are frequently, in the course of one hour, frequently are they discordant. Demanding that we follow different paths. Demanding that we have different things.

When we awaken within us the simple truth that we own nothing, that we never can own anything, when we accept that demonstrable truth, that we have been loaned many things for certain times, when we accept that truth, we will no longer resist the inevitable Law of Evolution in our life. For we never know the moment that that we desire will come to us, and we never know the moment that that which we hold will leave us. For there is demonstrated to us, moment by moment, a greater Intelligence in the universe that is the law that either we follow or we resist. When we resist that law that considers all, when we resist that law, we begin to suffer. For by the illusion, the illusion of possession, that is the only way that we can ever experience struggle, suffering, poor health, or poor wealth. It is our denials of the truth that become our destinies in life. If we free our self from that illusion, we will be the instruments through which the living Intelligence transforms our being.

But we forget so quickly that it is an infinite, eternal Intelligence that sustains the thought we choose. And because it is an Infinite Intelligence that sustains the thoughts we choose, it is that same Infinite Intelligence that sustains the form that the thought has created.

Now, perhaps, we can move to a greater understanding of heaven and hell. The same Intelligence that supports our thought of good, supports our thought of its opposite, called bad. So when we pray to a God to free us from bad experience, we must understand it is the same God that is [supporting], and has supported, the bad experience that we alone, through an error in our thought, have created. We create. God, the neutral Infinite Intelligence, sustains. But we and we alone are the creators. So when you have the experiences of hell in your life, remember, the same God that will free you is supporting the bondage that you, by your error, have chosen. There is not one formless, free, infinite, divine Spirit for heaven and another infinite, formless, free Spirit for hell. It is our minds that create those things. But they exist when we are in the mental world. It is when we are in the mental world, when we are in the greatest denial we will ever experience in eternity, that's when we see, feel, sense, and hear the opposites in life, called good and bad.

We open this door of hell by one thought and one thought alone and that thought, that very thought, is the greatest denial we will ever experience. It is the greatest denial we do experience. It is the greatest denial we have ever experienced. And that denial, that illusion, is known as the thought of I. It is the thought of I that moves our eternal soul, through the vehicle of mind substance, from the universal whole of infinite good to the limit of error of the past mental experiences in our life.

If you find a struggle in any area of your life, I assure you, you cannot continue to experience the suffering or the struggle if you will make the effort to gain control of your mind and free your true being from the illusion of the thought of I, which is the denial, the separation that takes you from the formless, free spirit that you truly are. For it is the thought of I that moves your soul into the realm of all past experience, guaranteeing for you a repetition of what has passed. You cannot repeat the experiences of yesterday unless you enter that realm in consciousness and you cannot enter that realm in consciousness unless you establish the Law of Illusion, which is the denial of the Infinite of which you are inseparably a part of. So does it not behoove us to pause and think? Do we consciously, in the light of reason, desire to continue the experiences that we have already had?

You know, it is so interesting to note: there is a simple way of seeing for ourselves whether or not we have had a similar experience as another. All we have to do is to become aware of whether or not we have tolerance towards that person that is having that experience. You see, my friends, the experiences that we have had reveal to us whether or not we've learned our lesson. If we have learned our lesson, our soul faculty of tolerance is expanded, and we enter the soul faculty of reason, where the light of God shines eternally. But when our eyes look around and about us and we find we have no tolerance, but much judgment—you see, my friends, you cannot be intolerant unless you be a judge. You must judge to experience intolerance.

And I am so grateful to this understanding of the Living Light that reveals so clearly that God is not a judge, but an infinite, intelligent, neutral Divine Power. And let us pause and think. If God, the very Intelligence sustaining our life, does not judge us, what do we do when we judge us? You see, we are the ones who judge our self. And because the law clearly reveals that we cannot grant to another what we have not first granted unto our self and because we judge ourselves all the time, we have no problem in judging others all the time. And because we do that to our self, we guarantee the intolerance to those around and about us, for we have already guaranteed the intolerance to ourselves.

Make friends with your adversities. Be kind and good to yourself. For guilt of that that has passed—and remember, you never experience guilt of that which is yet to be. You can only experience guilt of that which has passed. Guilt is nothing more nor nothing less than rejected desire. Think, my friends, a person says, "Well, I experience guilt of a thought of what I am going to do." No, you do not experience guilt of a thought of what you're going to do. You experience guilt of what you have already done and once again are thinking about doing it again even though you may have changed the way in which you're going to do it. It's really that simple.

Yesterday and the moments of yesterday have no effect upon you until you make them so. And when you permit the greatest of all denials, the greatest of all rejection, known as the thought of I, you move, in that moment, to the mental world of yesterday. The illusion known as the thought of I cannot see your tomorrows, for its realm is the darkness of what has been, not of what is, nor what is going to be.

We all can clearly see, if we so choose, what we insist on repeating. But be of good cheer. Repetition is the law, for man has made it so, through which change is made possible. When we have had enough, we will make the change in consciousness. And then we say, "Now I'm ready." We are ready when we remember that we have come to earth to serve a purpose, for we are a unit of it all. We are not separate from everything, everywhere, on every planet. Let us not be so bloated in the nothingness of our ego to think that we are the only intelligent beings in these vast universes. Let us no longer live in such illusion.

All the good your mind seeks, your mind can bring to you. It only has to do, your mind, one thing: be still that you may forget, for a moment, your mind, that you may forget the denial, the thought of I. And in so doing you move into the universal intelligent Being in all of its fullness. There, no denial exists. If you're short of money, your denial is great. If you're short of wealth, if you're short of health, your denial is even greater. If you are short of peace, then your denial is the greatest of all. It doesn't have to be that way. It doesn't have to be that way. What is so valuable about the thought of I that could have a greater priority in our consciousness than the peace that passeth all understanding?

And so, my friends, in conclusion, we shall return, like the great circle, to our beginning: the question concerning spirit lights. That that our spirit perceives knows and does not have to be told. It is only our minds that want to know, for our spirit and our soul already know. And why do our minds want to know everything? What do our little minds do in life? They do one thing: our minds control us. That's what our minds do to us. They control us. And the only reason our minds, which are vehicles for our eternal being to express through here, in this planet, the only reason our minds control us is because we became lazy. We became so lazy we no longer made the effort to think.

A good example is what has happened in this great electronic, computer age. We went to school, most of us, and we learned to count. We learned to add and to subtract, to multiply and to divide. We didn't need to use a physical object, like our toes, to count upon or, God forbid, our fingers or our teacher would have helped both our fingers and our toes. And now we look around and about us and we see in the stores where we go, the clerks have to carry a little, mechanical box. They can't add 275, 16, and 34 in their mind anymore. They've got to move their fingers over a keyboard. And even if they still try to make a little effort, they still use that box to guarantee to their mind that their mind still functions. Think of where we are headed. You see, because we did not stay on guard, the vehicle has become the master. We have become the slave of the form. Whether or not the form is a calculator or a vast computer, no matter what the form is, through our lack of effort, we have become its slave and its victim. That's what we've done to our self.

But we can change that in this moment. That is the great power that is really within us. But to do that we must awaken to the truth, which is separate from creation. When we awaken and the thoughts and the patterns of yesterday, the judgments rise in our consciousness and demand we do such and such and demand that we sit at a table and eat and eat until we cannot hardly move from the table, when we awaken to what we've done to our self, be rest assured we're on the path of freeing our self. No longer will we be dependent upon a little box to tell us whether we have added correctly or not. No longer will we be spiritual cripples, the victims of laziness.

My friends, it's so easy to see where we are, and it's really so easy to see where we're going. Just try the daily effort of self-discipline. Perhaps you'd like to be slimmer and trimmer. Perhaps you would like more good health in your life. Perhaps you would like to be wealthier. It's going to take some effort. It's going to take some self-discipline. Because the thoughts you're used to have not yet brought you what you seek. And because that has not yet worked, it simply reveals you must introduce something different. And what happens when we experience something different? What happens when we tell the mind, "Your thoughts, that you've filled my head with for a lifetime, I'm setting a portion of you aside, for I have a new idea. I'm tired of living the way I have lived. I have a new idea and this is what I'm going to do." That's all you have to tell yourself and then you will have the glorious experience of what your mind will do to you. Then you will awaken to whether or not your mind is still the servant of your free spirit or you, your free spirit, is the slave and the victim of a created mind. Such a beautiful choice to make.

It is important to all of us in our evolution when there is something to be done, to do it quickly, for it is the procrastinators in life who seem to love the experience of pity. I never met a successful man who told me how great yesteryear used to be. Oh, I have met many so-called failures who have told me how great it was in the days of old. How interesting our little minds really are. I assure you the greatest moment of your life is the moment of now. That is the moment of heaven, for in the moment of now is your true eternity. It is what you do in this moment, moment by moment, that places you in heaven. For, you know, when you go through life moment by moment, that little, dark shadow of illusion known as the thought of I, it just kind of melts away. The I rises when you think of what's gone and you hope what is to be. But take this moment in which eternity is—the very moment of now—then, my friends, if you do that for only a moment, take the moment of now, you will experience the paradise known as peace.

Thank you.

OCTOBER 5, 1980

Church Questions and Answers 9

There will be a slight change in our format this morning. We will still, of course, have our questions and answers, but rather than the prepared ones you have submitted, we will give you the opportunity this morning to simply raise your hand and ask any question of a general interest. Please refrain from questions of a political and strictly material nature, and I will be very happy to share with you the understanding that I receive. So any of you who have a question, you kindly raise your hand and I will be happy to give the answer that I get. Yes, in the back please.

Morning.

Good morning. *[After a short pause, the Teacher continues.]* I'm sorry, I didn't hear your question.

Work.

Work? In what reference are you questioning that word?

In the sense that there is no day that one should skip.

Well, our understanding of the true meaning of the word *work* is love made manifest. We look about all of nature; we see that every creature is designed to serve a purpose, that includes the creature known as man. And so when we find that we are not fulfilling the purpose of our life in what is known as work—the work, of course, of our own choice. We must remember that whatever work we have is an effect of the laws that we alone have set into motion. And if we experience a lack of work in our life, it is still the same law that is working for us.

Unfortunately, so often we give power over our lives to false beliefs. And the first thing that creates a false belief is a denial of the divine truth of personal responsibility. For all of us, including all forms in creation, have entered this earth realm to fulfill a purpose. And if we find our purpose for being here, which, of course, high on that list of purposes—there are more than one—is work. If we find a lack of fulfilling our purpose for being here on earth, it is simply because of an error of ignorance in our own attitude and thought. That can easily be corrected by becoming honest with our self and when we do, we will see where the error in our thinking is and take corrective measures. And there will be plenty of God's love made manifest for us, known as work. Does that help with your question?

[Thank you.]

You're welcome. Yes, the gentleman here, please.

Can I have a definition of good and evil in a social context or what is justice?

Yes, the question is could he have a definition, in a social context, of good and evil and what is justice. We understand in this philosophy, the Living Light Philosophy, that there is only undeveloped good, and that undeveloped good is ever dependent upon our educated conscience. Now we all have two consciences. We have the educated conscience of the human mind, which is involved with the mental realms that most of us experience. Our educated conscience is what we are taught is right or is wrong. That is not necessarily the conscience that many of us live by. There is a higher conscience, known as a spiritual sensibility. It accepts the Law of Personal Responsibility. It is the demonstration of divine truth.

Now an educated conscience creates many psychological problems for untold millions of people. The reason that it creates so many, many psychological problems is that man experiences, moment by moment, the divine expression known as desire. Unfortunately for man, until he learns the difference between the suppression of desire, the education of desire, and the fulfillment of desire, man will continue to live in the mental realms of frustration. The divine expression becomes limited when it is received by the human mind, and it is limited by the judgments that we alone have created that limit the Divinity. Now the spiritual conscience, having accepted the demonstrable Law of Man [that states man] is responsible for all his thoughts, acts, and activities, is not dependent upon the mental, educated conscience.

And so what does that have to do with justice? It has a great deal to do with the justice of the mental realms. It has a great deal to do with how man permits himself to look at life from a very limited perspective. When we truly understand and accept that every experience that we encounter is only an effect of a law that we alone have set into motion, that we have the power within us to make decisions and not judgments—the difference being that judgment is a rigid rule established by our mind that has no possibility of change or consideration upon its own limited motivation. A decision has the full consideration not only of the decision made, but all experiences that the Law of Decision may encounter. Therefore, it has total consideration, which is the divine love or the love of God. Now when we make a decision, we, in making the decision, have accepted the possibility of change, for we understand, in making decisions, that the Law of Evolution is the Law of Change. Judgment, like decision, is a created form in a mental world. Judgment cannot change the form of its original creation. Decision is a flexible form, ever moving, ever evolving. So when man makes decisions, he expresses not the judgment, not the justice of a mental world, but he makes a decision and is the living demonstration and expression of divine justice—not the so-called justice that is blinded by the limit of form. It is flexible and it is evolving. It has total consideration. It has understanding.

And so, my friends, if we believe, if we permit ourselves to believe that our thought and our judgment is not only right for us, then we guarantee the law that will impose our judgment upon another. For, you see, my friends, in keeping with nature's divine, demonstrable laws, we cannot grant unto another what we have not first granted unto our self. If we grant unto our self a small, limited, rigid judgment of a God to whom we serve, then that's the only thing that we can ever grant unto another. If we believe in a limitless, divine Spiritual Essence that is ever present and available, ever dependent upon our acceptance of it, then we can be rest assured, the goodness that is within us—for there is that spark in all form, known as the infinite Spirit—will only manifest itself ever greater, ever more in our life and, in so doing, like attracts like and becomes the Law of Attachment. So, in truth, the justice we grant unto our self is the only justice we grant to another. The goodness that we grant unto our self is the only goodness that we grant to another. Remember, friends, our limits are only errors in our educated conscience. Does that help with your question?

Yes.

You're welcome. Yes, the lady here, please.

Can you explain about the soul faculties?

The lady has asked a question in reference to an explanation of the soul faculties. As taught by this church? Yes. For many, many, many years we understand that there are forty triune soul faculties and forty triune sense functions. There is one infinite, supreme Divine Intelligence sustaining all of them. And so we know from our experiences in life and our education that there are eighty-one levels of consciousness.

In the many years of teaching I have shared the first soul faculty and a few others, but only a few, for one very simple reason. Duty, gratitude, and tolerance is the first triune soul faculty of being. The foundation of all soul faculties is known as understanding, but understanding is not limited to that simple statement that says, "In all your getting, get understanding." For it ends there; it's only half the truth. We all know that we are, indeed, perhaps the most perfected getting beings known in the universe. Only God knows how much our minds get, get, get, get, get. But we must move on to the other half of that great truth, "In all your getting, get understanding." We must give the whole truth. And so in all your getting, get understanding and in all your giving, give wisdom.

Because, you see, another great truth clearly states, "Your cup runneth over." And therefore, there is no more room for more goodness. When you fill a cup, if you keep on filling it, the excess runs over the cup and on out to someone else. And so this is what has happened in our own life. We hold, we get so many things. Our minds are so filled with the getting and we do not empty our cups in order that something new and fresh and good may fill it. And so I have given this first triune soul faculty: duty, gratitude, and tolerance. But how can we apply this wonderful, simple truth, if we don't balance in our life the getting vibration with the giving vibration?

We have taught for many years, your greatest gift, the greatest thing that you could ever give is the gift of self. Now we all have heard that and we all have different thoughts on what that means. Some people think it's a total annihilation of the self. They'll no longer have an identity. They will become some type of a universal blob. That's not what it means. Unless you understand that you are a formless, free spirit and if you want to call that some type of universal blob, then, of course, that will be your payment for that type of a judgment.

What is self? What do we understand self to be? Surely, we agree that our greatest gift, the greatest thing that we have garnered would be the self. What is it that creates the thought of self? For remember, my friends, without the thought, there can be no self. Without the thought, there can be nothing, for nothing is. It is only for us when there is thought. Without thought, for us, it does not exist. And that is why truth is individually perceived. It is the thought of I, the first step, that creates the thought of self and then, by the denial, the thought of I—not the I, but the thought of I—is the denial of your true birthright. Think about that. The moment you entertain the thought of I, you deny, you deny your inseparable unity of the whole. Now if you want a part of the whole, then you must give up the created illusion that you are separate from it.

Now many people, they pray for many things. They pray ever in keeping with the illusion of the thought of I. And so only in that limited way has their door to the whole been opened. Therefore, they can only experience what will flow through that limited opening.

We believe that we are a separate, individualized soul. Because of belief, we are. Because of belief, we experience. It is only because we are not still with our mind. We must go beyond our mind to know the infinite, eternal, divine truth that is. We cannot find the source as long as we believe that we are it. Now many people—and this has much to do with this lady's wonderful question of the soul faculties, because if you will be still, you will hear them. We believe that we are, and because of our belief, we are. Without our belief, we would not be. We would only be to those who believe that we are.

Let us try to understand that we may go beyond the mental gymnastics that our mind has offered us in these many years here on earth. When we move beyond the belief, we move beyond denial. And when we move beyond denial, destiny is at our command. Destiny is only at our command when we go beyond the denials that create it. Do not look for things, for they bind you to the things that seek their kind. It is the things within us that seek the things of the universe. And because that law is infallible and divine—the like attracts like—it is only wisdom to go beyond the form, to go beyond the limit of our thought. For that which is beyond the limit of our thought is the infinite, formless, free, divine, intelligent Spirit that sustains our thought.

Now many people, when they've had a thought and they experience and are aware, by accepting the Law of Personal Responsibility, that they now are a victim of circumstances and conditions that they do not appreciate, stop at that point. And because they do not appreciate the circumstances and conditions and experiences that they alone have set into motion, and because they are not yet strong enough in character, a divine soul faculty, to accept the truth of the error of their own thought that they and they alone have created the experience, they immediately blame outside as the cause. If you ever want to know where you are at any moment, all you have to do is pause and become aware of whether or not you are blaming outside for the way that you feel. It is very rare that our mind will ever blame anyone else for feeling good. It is a very rare experience to have. But stop and think how often we blame everyone else for how bad we feel. We blame them if we're broke. We blame them if we're emotional. We blame them for this. We blame them for that. Because, don't you see, my friends, we are out of balance between the function and the soul faculty of character.

Character cannot exist, we cannot experience it without personal responsibility. You cannot express the divine, infinite, eternal soul faculties of your being without the acceptance of divine truth called personal responsibility. And isn't it interesting, when we look at ourselves and we see, "I feel just great." But we don't say, "Someone just said good morning and that helped me. I made the decision to feel good because they said 'Good morning' to me." But be rest assured if we were a walking stick of dynamite in the universe and no matter who smiled or said hello, no matter who did that, our little minds would explode and it's that person's fault for saying good morning. "The level from which they said good morning to me was a level that was not harmonious to me." It is so interesting to note what, my friends, we do constantly to ourselves.

Now when I say good morning to someone—and I try to make that effort because I like good morning said to me! And because I appreciate anyone I see saying good morning, I always try to make the effort to say good morning to anyone else. Because I want to grant to them what I enjoy for myself. That's the way the law works. Now, if we have made a judgment in our life that there are times we don't want people saying good morning to us, then we can be rest assured at those times someone is destined to say good morning to us. Then we can tell our self how miserable we feel because that person said good morning and they didn't say good morning from the right level of consciousness. Because, you see, we know so much; our king of judgment, it is so great we know where everybody else is.

My friends, when we know where we are all of the time, we will be so active and so busy with keeping track of our score, we won't have the time nor the energy to know where everybody else is. That's not selfish; that's plain, old common sense. Think about that. Think what we do to ourselves all the time. We walk down the street. Somebody says something to us and we're miserable. Sometimes for the whole day. Sometimes for weeks or months after. But think. They did not do it to us. We set our self up. Our judgments set us up. They go out into the universe, as man is a law unto himself. Look at the law, what we're doing to it, for our self. We make the judgment, we guarantee the experience, sooner or later. The law is infallible, whether it is the divine law expressing in nature or it is the law that man himself by his own judgments sets into motion. And to perpetuate that Law of Ignorance we continually justify that the problems we have in our life are the result and the direct effect of the way somebody else thinks, acts, and does. You see, it will always be that way, until we decide that we've had enough.

I agree with some of you—maybe with all of you—a part of me is as ignorant as anyone else. I try to stay on guard not to let that be the control in my life because I would just feel miserable. I come to church every Sunday morning. I stand at the door to say good-bye and some people are so mad at me that they won't even grunt, let alone say good-bye. *[Many of the congregation laugh.]* Then I come here to work to keep the doors open, like the rest of our people. I go through the week. I check out every single item on our brunches and our dinners. Everything is pre-tested that it may be of the highest quality. And then some of my own members don't care enough to support their church to even stay and split with $5. You know, I'm very down to earth. Many Spiritualist churches, when you put a billet in, you know, you have to include $1 or $5. They don't work for nothing. They firmly believe that every servant is worthy of their hire. But I also know the law and therefore I make great effort inside myself not to give them power over me. And I don't give them power over me when I speak the truth and I speak the truth more each and every day, I hope.

And I do hope if the question-and-answer session is not interesting, that you'll kindly stop whispering amongst yourselves. I know the time is getting late. I won't keep you very long. But we do have time for one more question. Yes. Speak.

How do you correct your thoughts or get beyond your thoughts?

Well, that's a wonderful question that we all need the benefit of an answer, I assure you. "How do you correct your thoughts or get beyond your thoughts?" Well, first of all, we cannot make changes in anything that we are not first aware of. We have no power within us to change anything that we are not first aware of. So the first step in making a change in a thought is to become aware of the thought that you want to change. That you have first made an honest decision with yourself that that type of thought has brought you no good, returns unto you negative experiences that you are very weary of. Once you have made that decision and you have fully accepted the responsibility of this thought that has caused you so many problems in life, whenever the thought arises in your consciousness, you immediately replace it, by the Law of Substitution, with a positive thought and total acceptance.

Now remember that thoughts are things. The thought, whatever it is that we entertain, creates a form in a mental world. Now many people have asked the question, "Well, how does it know what form to take?" Well, any of you that have studied some of the studies of psychology are familiar with what is known as the primitive mind. Now our souls have entered earth and have merited the experience of expressing through what is known—a layer of our consciousness—called the primitive mind. And why do we call it the primitive mind? Because we now know and understand that the primitive cultures of centuries ago had these experiences. The primitive mind was born and is born and continues to be perpetuated by fear.

What is fear? Again and again man asks the question, What is fear? Fear is absolute faith in the mental world. When you rely upon your mind, you guarantee the Law of Fear. You not only guarantee the Law of Fear, which is reliance on your mind, but you guarantee the experiences of yesteryear, for you guarantee the realm of judgment.

Now, if man wants to consciously move forward in life, he must understand his own mind, for it is, in this realm, only our mind that limits us. There is nothing but our mind, our mental body, that is our limitation here on earth. For we all know the mind can go beyond the physical form. We all know the mind can change the physical form. We have all had those experiences to varying degrees. So we cannot help but accept the demonstrable, personal truth that our mind, our mind alone limits us. If a person says, "My physical body limits me." It is their mind's belief in the error that it is their physical body that limits them. For it is only our mind that limits us.

And so this mind and these layers of primitive expression that we go through, offering us fear—for it is fear to rely on the mind, [which] guarantees the Law of Fear. And what is it that creates fear? We know reliance on the mind *is* fear. But what creates fear? Fear is created by judgment. Now our God is a God of love. Therefore, it is not a judge; it is not fear, for to be so it would be a created god of our mental world. When you believe in a god, a judge that hands out this and takes away that, then you have a created god that only controls your mental world, for it is created by mind substance.

So if you truly want to move ahead, you must understand fear, how it works, what creates it, and free yourself from judgment. For whoever makes the effort to free themselves from judgment moves in the divine love and flow of God, for God *is*. The will of God is total acceptance, for it sustains all things, no matter whether we think they're good or bad. God sustains even our judgments. But that Intelligence *is*. No one has to tell it.

You see, whenever we make a judgment, we base that statement, we base that law upon experiences of our past. Therefore, by permitting our mind to make a judgment, we guarantee the repetition of yesteryear's experiences in that area of our life. When we enter a new experience—and we have the opportunity right around the clock, seven days a week—if we would only pause and become aware of how quick our mind is and take control of our judgments by taking control of fear, which is the reliance upon our mind to fulfill our desire. Whoever relies upon their mind to fulfill anything guarantees the Law of Limitation, guarantees the Law of Judgment, guarantees the Law of Payment. The mental world is a Law of Creation governed by that which controls creation, known as the Law of Duality. Now when you rely upon your mind, you must ever and forever pay the price. For the mind being controlled by the dual laws of creation, there is the Law of Payment and Attainment. Whoever refrains from relying upon their mind for the fulfillment of the divine expression, known as desire, is freed from the dual Law of Attainment and Payment, is freed from the experiences of struggle and judgment, and experiences the fulfillment of the desire in the eternal moment, of which we all are, in truth.

And thank you very much.

NOVEMBER 2, 1980

Church Questions and Answers 10

Now, in the past we have always attempted to answer the questions you have submitted in writing, but with our new format it will be necessary, of course, for you to raise your hands with the questions that you have, as our chairman has stated, of a spiritual and general nature to all people. So if you'll be so kind as to raise your hand with your question, I will do the very best to be receptive to the answers that I am given.

Yes, would the lady speak, please. Thank you.

Yes, thank you. Last night I had guests in my home who were Baha'is, and I mentioned I was coming to church this morning. They said that in their religion they are not allowed to contact spirit. They believe in life hereafter and so on. And I said why? And they said because it keeps spirit from progressing. And I said well I thought that a lot of the masters elected to be close to the earth plane to help. And I know you can't grieve for people because it keeps them from progressing. But, can you elaborate?

Yes, I will be happy to share our understanding with that and with all of you. It is true, depending on the motivation of the communicator, that some spirit people, as some people here on earth—remember, my good friends, we are spirit here and now. We are not going to become spirit. We are becoming spiritual in consciousness, but we are as much spirit as we will ever be. Now there are, through a lack of understanding, many people who attempt to communicate with other dimensions for very personal, selfish motives and consequently, in keeping with the law that like attracts like and becomes the Law of Attachment, would be instrumental in helping those spirits close to earth to remain earthbound entities. That, of course, is something that one themselves will choose. It is not necessarily true, in any sense of the word, that all communication with other dimensions causes people in those dimensions to become earthbound. That can or cannot happen. It depends entirely upon the efforts of the communicator and it depends, of course, on the effort of the person in the other dimension.

Now, one of the first things that happens when we leave the physical body, one of the very first things that happens is we become aware of a feeling of great weightlessness. The heaviness of the gross, physical body disappears. That's one of the first experiences that we have in leaving this physical body. It is critically important in our spiritual path and evolution that we become aware of the priorities that we keep in our mind. If we find that our priorities are limited to what the physical, earth realm has to offer, we cannot and do not change those priorities by leaving the physical body. Because, you see, my friends, our physical body, composed of physical substance, returns to a physical earth. But our mental body is composed of mental substance and that is the body that we find our self in here and now expressing through a physical body. Leaving the physical body, we still find our self expressing through a mental body. So, my friends, the world around and about us, of course, is ever in keeping with our own mental attitudes, our own motivations. And so it is that a wise person makes some effort each day to free themselves from the bondage of creation.

Now, *The Tibetan Book of the Dead* put it very wisely and very clearly. When you leave this physical body, you see the multitudes of forms and creations of your own attachments. We know in this philosophy that our adversities become our attachments; it's a very subtle law. Now, think what we do with the thought in our mind that we judge to be adverse. We direct to it our consciousness, our attention. The law clearly demonstrates that energy follows attention. So, my friends, whatever we are adverse to, we are, in truth, attaching our self to. And sooner or later, we guarantee the experience. We can clearly see from the short years here on earth that we have already done that as we view our past experiences. Time and time again we make the judgments that we will never do this and we will never do that.

By having that attitude of mind, by entertaining that judgment, we guarantee the mental law of the experience yet to come.

And so it is in leaving the physical body, we find our self in the world in which we are most familiar. And because we have made so much effort to become familiar with a mental world, I assure you, that's where most of us find our self when we leave the physical body. Of course, there are those, and there are many, of course, who make the daily effort to entertain in their consciousness things of a spiritual nature. As we direct energy through the Law of Attention to anything, that thing begins to form. And so it is with the soul faculties and the sense functions. This philosophy clearly teaches and demonstrates a balance between the functions of the mental body and the faculties of the spiritual body.

If a person spends most of their time in soliciting the aid of those in other dimensions to help them through each and every mundane problem that they insist on setting into motion and if that becomes an imbalance and contrary to the Law of Personal Responsibility, then, of course, they are not benefiting those with whom they are in contact with, needless to say are they benefiting themselves. Spiritual communication or communication with other dimensions should be kept under the Law of Reason, and the Law of Reason clearly dictates balance in all things. We find if we over eat, of course, we pay the price of over eating. We find if we spend most of our time in self-concern, then, of course, we pay the price of an imbalance of self-concern. And so it is, what applies to one thing in nature, applies to all things in nature. But we must also see the other side of the coin and those who have evolved to higher realms of consciousness, who by their own divine right of choice have elected to return to this mundane world as part of their own spiritual evolution to help those who are struggling along the path to find the light of reason. Then, of course, there is balance as long as it's kept that way. I do hope that's helped with your question. Thank you.

Yes, the gentleman on the aisle, please.

Yes. On the day of Pentecost, the Holy Ghost, or as some refer to, the Holy Spirit, filled Jesus' disciples. How can we get the Holy Ghost or the Holy Spirit to reside within us and help us each day and guide us with our daily lives?

Thank you very much. As the gentleman has stated, on the day of Pentecost, in keeping with the Bible, the disciples of Jesus were filled with the Holy Spirit. It is the understanding of the Living Light Philosophy that on that day an awareness of the Holy Spirit was experienced. We understand that the Holy Spirit, the infinite Divine Intelligence, known to man as God, is never absent or away, that the so-called Holy Spirit is ever within us. For if it was not within us, we would not experience what is known as life itself.

And so it is the obstruction to the awareness of the existence of the Holy Spirit within us is an obstruction created by our own mind. You see, my friends, our mind, designed by the Infinite Intelligence, to serve as a vehicle through which our soul may express itself in a mental and physical world, our mind has forgotten the source of its own sustenance. And in its forgetting, it has established the Law of Delusion, for it believes—our mind—that it is the doer. It believes and by so believing in its own delusion, it denies the source and the sustenance of its own existence.

And so it is with great difficulty when we find our self in a mental world, which is most all of the time, we find great difficulty in accepting the possibility of something beyond the control of our own mind. The Holy Spirit is forever within us. It has always been. It will always be. It is simply our mind that denies the existence of that that sustains it.

The Pentecost is something that is this moment. It is in the very moment of our acceptance. The moment we accept something beyond the realm and control of our mind, in that moment do we become freed from the limits and the law of the mind, which is duality. Only in those moments are we truly free, for only in those moments there is no judgment. For God, the divine, neutral, infinite Intelligent Power, is not a judge in the understanding of Spiritualism. For God to be a judge puts God under the Law of Duality.

We understand that our thought is our divine right, but this great, infinite Holy Spirit will sustain the thought that we choose. Whether that thought be beneficial or detrimental to us is our divine right of choice. And so it is, my friends, this Holy Spirit, that is ever present, never absent or away, only waits for you, for me, for everyone to free our self from a mental world of limitation to accept the universal consciousness of which we are, in truth, an inseparable part. Thank you. That help with your question?

Thank you.

Yes. Yes, the lady right there in the back, please.

Reverend, can you give us some insight and guidance as to the person or persons who is murdering people in the wilderness nearby?

I have refrained, and on several occasions turned down calls, in reference to spiritually or psychically investigating such matters. That, of course, has been and is my divine right of choice.

The experiences being encountered locally that you have mentioned are in keeping with laws that have been established. Now, I will have to elaborate a bit upon that and still not get into personal messages in reference to it. We understand that there are no accidents in the universe, that what we believe are accidents are nothing more and nothing less than a lack of understanding the cause of the experience. When we understand the cause, we have the cure.

Now the Bible teaches, "The thing I fear the most has befallen me." And so it is, for fear is the great magnet of the human mind. Fear is the direction of faith to a mental world, and it absolutely guarantees the thing we fear the most. So if there's something you want real bad, just fear the dickens out of it and you'll soon have it. *[Some in the congregation laugh.]* Now we all demonstrate this beautiful truth of fear. We fear inflation, and so we have it. We fear the economy, and so we have it. We fear poor health, and so we have it. Why not fear abundant good? And let's experience a little of that. You see, my friends, it is our choice. We're never left without that divine birthright. Now some time ago you will recall there were certain experiences in this county and there was great fear in reference to what the lady has mentioned. And so the law clearly reveals itself and attracts more. Without saying too much, I can assure you within the coming five weeks those experiences will be well behind all of us and hopefully those who have opened their eyes to the spiritual truth that's ever with us will do their part to see that those experiences, be it in divine order, may never reoccur. Thank you.

The lady here in the aisle was waiting for a question. Yes.

I would like to ask a question about meditation.

Yes.

Usually, people take a seated position, and yet when the spirit leaves the body at the time of death, most people lie down. Could you answer two parts of this question? What part of the body does the spirit leave from? And also, why is it, is it ever, does anyone ever meditate lying down and is it recommended?

Thank you very much. In reference to what part of the anatomy does the spirit leave through, it leaves through what you commonly refer to as the soft spot in the top of your head. All mothers know where that is on their babies and it's always soft, believe me. But anyway, that's the part of the anatomy through which the divine spirit leaves. In reference to the recommendation never to meditate in the prone position, to always keep the spine in an upright position, it is a very simple matter. The human mind has made many judgments, all human minds.

One of which dictates what type of thoughts it shall entertain in the prone position. Because of those laws long established by civilizations, it is absolutely and positively not recommended to meditate in the lying down, prone position. Thank you.

Yes, the lady here, please.

What is the source and significance of our dreams?

Well, they are more than two-fold. There are the dreams which are the effects and the release of energy created by suppressed desire. That's the most common cause of our dreams: suppressed desire. You see, my friends, we have many, many desires. We make, usually, most of us, make no effort whatsoever to educate them. We make great effort to suppress our desires. By suppressing them in our depths of our mind, great pressure builds up. Sooner or later we find ourselves living in frustration. Some of that pressure is released whenever we go to sleep through what is called the dream process.

Now remember, all form dreams. Whether it is the human being, the animal, the dog, the cat, the horse, the elephant, or the blade of grass, all forms on this planet dream. They all release some of that energy. And we must also remember that animals, like humans, like trees, like flowers, like plants, all experience what the human mind calls desire. They all have those experiences.

Then there are those dreams which sometimes come through that are spiritual experiences, that the spirit within us is attempting, in any way it possibly can get through the human mind, it is attempting to help us, to guide us, and to direct us. If a person will make the effort before going to sleep to flood their consciousness with things of a spiritual nature, then they will not only sleep more soundly, they will awaken much more refreshed. It is critically important to flood the consciousness prior to losing conscious awareness and upon regaining conscious awareness immediately. For that helps you to stay in levels of consciousness that are not only more beneficial, but reap a better harvest for all of those people with whom you come in contact. Thank you. I hope that's helped with your question.

Yes, the lady in the back, please.

I understand that we all return unto the source. If the mind was created by the Divine Architect, then is it not true that our mental body is, in truth, then, part of the Divine? That it returns unto its source? Would not the mind also be returning the essence of it to God?

Thank you for your question. First, I'd like to clarify one thing in reference to the Living Light Philosophy, which is given here in this church. The Divine Architect, God, did not create the human mind. This philosophy teaches a divine, intelligent, neutral Power that sustains the human mind. The laws of nature are the creators, not the divine, formless, free Spirit, known to man as God. You see, that that is free is formless. That that is bound is form. It's that simple. Now, surely we will all agree and accept that our God, surely, cannot be bound by anything or anyone, for our God is a formless, free God, therefore, is not limited in its expression. It sustains our mind, our thought. It does not create it. The laws of nature have created it. God does not create the tree; God sustains the tree.

If we permit our minds to believe in a God of form, then we shall be limited by the form that our God takes in keeping with our own mental judgments. Now those are the gods that the Bible spoke about centuries ago. It's known as the false gods. The gods with clay feet. The gods created by the limited experiences of the human mind.

So many people, believing in a god of form, have filled their lives with the experiences of guilt. We understand that guilt is nothing more nor less than rejected desire. Now a desire—desire, the principle of desire is the divine expression. That is the expression of the divine Infinite Intelligence. Man forms the principle of desire. So when you reject a desire, you experience guilt. You are denying the principle of the Divine itself. Therefore, in that denial, you establish the law of your own destiny.

Now a person could say, "I have many desires. Many of which are not beneficial to myself or those around and about me." This is where we educate the form of desire. When we awaken and stop denying the principle of the Divine, known to us as desire, when we make the effort to educate the form that the desire takes by our mind—we must educate the form of the desire, not the principle essence of the desire—then we will no longer deny the limitless source flowing through our being and all good we shall awaken to. And in so awakening, shall we have that experience.

We have time for one more question. The lady here, please.

It's my understanding that as the spirit evolves on the other side, it also leaves the mental body. Can you speak on the mind of the spirit within the spiritual body as opposed to one in the mental body?

Thank you very much. There is no mind, as we know mind, expressing in a spiritual body. It is true that we evolve in this great eternity in which we are this moment from a mental body into what is known as a spiritual body. Now, what is a mental body truly composed of? Of course it is composed of the substance of mental. It is sustained, of course, we understand, by the infinite Divine Intelligence, known to man as God.

We enter this earth realm, our soul, at the very moment of creation in keeping with the laws of nature. Now, many people have to wait to enter the earth realm. Sometimes they will hover around a particular person three, four, five, ten, twenty years because they have established those laws in their own evolution. The moment the soul enters, at that moment of conception, the entire thought world, the mental world of the mother and of the father at the moment of conception marks the mental body that that soul must express through in its earthly experiences.

Someday our earth world will truly become aware of the great responsibility, the great responsibility of bringing a child into this physical world of ours. For every thought you think at that moment and every thought your companion in that act thinks at that moment establishes and imprints in the mental world on the vehicle that is being formed for the soul to enter. We think, unfortunately in our error of ignorance, that the mind of the child is something that is developing over the many months and years ahead. That is the farthest thing from the truth. The soul enters a mental body already formed at the very moment of conception. The soul, then, makes great effort to express itself through a new mental body. That takes months and years here on earth.

If the mother, in carrying the child, is filled with fear, as the branch bends, so the tree grows, so it is with the child. All one has to do as a parent is to become aware of their attitudes before it's too late. So often parents have come to me, as their children have grown into their teens, upset emotionally because of the things their children are doing, for they have forgotten the things they did from the moment of conception and the years that followed. And so the mental body fulfills its purpose here on earth and the spirit is ready to shed that mental body as soon as it possibly can. But our attachments, our false belief, to creation keep that from happening to many people, sometimes for many, many, many centuries.

The mind, as we know it, is dependent upon the illusion known as the thought of I—not the I of the individualization, no, no—the thought of I, which is the illusion. The intelligence of our spiritual body does not have the illusion of the thought of I. Because it does not have the illusion of the thought of I, it expresses the principle of I and is free to return unto its source in universal consciousness. We can, here while yet encased in form, become aware within us of universal consciousness, but it is only possible when we make the effort to forget the thought of I.

Thank you.

DECEMBER 7, 1980

Church Questions and Answers 11

Once again it is a pleasure for me to share with you our understanding in reference to questions that you may have of a general interest. And so if you'll be so kind as to raise your hand with your question, I will be happy to answer to the best of my ability as many questions as time will allow.

Yes, the lady in the aisle, please.

How does a person come under the Law of Compensation and supply?

The lady has asked the question in reference to, "How does a person come under the Law of Compensation and supply?" We are already under the Law of Balance or supply, for every thought we think is sustained by the infinite Divine Intelligence. When we permit our minds to judge what is to be or to judge what is, we immediately come under the Law of Denial. Now how that actually takes place is really quite simple: that that has been in our life, though limited that it might be, has, in truth, served its purpose. When we permit our mind to look at life and to make a judgment, which is only based upon experiences that we have already had, we, in that moment in consciousness, deny the possibility of anything greater than what we have already experienced. Now it is known as the Law of Repetition through which change is made possible. When we continue to repeat experiences in our life, sooner or later we begin to think more deeply. Slowly but surely, we begin to accept the demonstrable Law of Personal Responsibility. We do, in time, accept and experience that everything that happens to us is a demonstrable law and is caused by us. Though in our errors of ignorance, ofttimes we do not see it.

Now the Law of Compensation or the Law of Abundant Supply is something that we all have. We do not experience the fullness of that law simply because we judge, in our errors of ignorance, how that law is to be fulfilled.

This philosophy clearly teaches and demonstrates that the soul faculty of gratitude is the faculty through which the abundant, divine law flows. That is a soul faculty. The opposite of that faculty, a sense function, is known as the function of greed.

Now we all know that nature is indeed the most conservative principle that man can possibly view. Nature wastes nothing. The law clearly states that the lack of use is abuse, that more than we need is indeed the Law of Greed. But what is it within us that dictates to us what our needs are? Do we need one pair of shoes or do we need twenty? Do we need two coats or do we need two hundred? This, my dear friends, is based upon our past experiences, based upon our present judgments, and it is a very personal thing of what we have already experienced. If we believe that we feel good—a lady feels good by having ten dresses, that she feels better by having a hundred, then it is very natural for a person to desire to feel good, because good is God and feeling God is an expression of the goodness within us. However, how we experience that goodness is dependent, unfortunately, upon our limited judgments, which are based upon past experiences.

When we make the effort to free our self not from the infinite, eternal I of consciousness, but to free our self from the illusion known as the thought of I, we will then no longer experience the imbalance between the soul faculties and the sense functions. The law clearly demonstrates that whatever we place our attention upon we have a tendency, by the infinite law, to become it, because energy follows attention.

Now in this mundane and material world the minds of men are often filled with the need, the illusion, known as the need for material supply or money. But let us examine what money, like shoes or coats, really is. It is the effect of directed energy. It is not the cause, only the effect. Now if we permit our minds to place our attention upon a lack of something we desire, then we simply build the lack greater in our consciousness, for energy follows attention and by our faith shall we be known. Now unfortunately, most people take the word *faith* to mean something religious or spiritual. That's far from the truth. You have faith when you start your car that it will move in keeping with the judgments that you have made, which are based upon experiences that you have already encountered.

My good friends, remember, the only obstruction to the fulfillment of our desires of the present moment is nothing more and nothing less than the shadows of past experiences. Not the experiences themselves, for they have come and they have gone. Only the shadows of those experiences, which is the indispensable ingredient for creating the judgment in consciousness, only the shadows are the obstruction. Man—each and every one of us is a law unto our self. And therefore, because we are a demonstrable law unto our self, we must ask our self, What are we doing with the law that we are?

If we believe in the illusion that what we desire is "dependent upon" [anything], in that thinking are we the victim of so-called circumstances. Once we accept that the true and only source of all that we desire is within us in consciousness, we will demonstrate that within our own life and the law of like attracts like and becomes the Law of Attachment will surround our universe. Therefore, whatever it is that we seek, we must learn to knock, we must learn to ask at the door of our own consciousness, for our consciousness is God, the source. It is not dependent upon anything or anyone at any time in anyplace. It is only dependent upon the channel through which it is expressing. The channel in question, being our self, in reference to the Law of Compensation.

We all are in the Law of Compensation to varying degrees. Some of us have a great abundance of health and yet, we seem to have a lack of so-called material wealth. Some of us have an abundance of activities. We have an abundance of acquaintances and some of us do not. It is not dependent upon the world. It is dependent on what we are doing in the world.

Remember, nothing and no one affects us until we alone make the choice and the decision for that to be so for us. The government, the politics, the world does not affect us until we decide we have a need within us for it to affect us. And in that moment that we decide that we have this need for things without to affect us within, we establish the Law of Rapport and, indeed, we become the victims of the very games that we play. Though the games may be in our errors of ignorance, they're still the games of our own mind. Let us stand firm, in reference, then, to the question, upon the rock of principle: that we have, by our very birthright, we have the right not to be affected by what others think and do, but to be free to express and experience the abundant good that is, in truth, our eternal right. I do hope that's helped with your question. Thank you.

The lady next to her, please.

You've spoken of God's angels and then you spoke of guides. Are they the same?

Yes, God's angels and guides. There is no difference between ant (*a-n-t*) and angel in respect to the divine Infinite Intelligence is expressing through both forms.

Now when we leave this physical world, we don't gain something. If we have at this moment—we all have this eternal spirit within us, flowing through us. We all are an individualized soul expressing through a mental, astral, and physical body. We lose a body here; we don't gain one there. We already have the body. We're already expressing through it here and now. We shed the physical body, which returns to the substance from whence it was composed, namely the earth substance for this planet. As we express in the next form, the form of the mental body, which we're expressing through at the moment, we shed the physical body and we see the mental world. We see the thoughts, the forms, the shapes. Now if we have, in our evolution while yet on earth, we have garnered up the necessary substance for an astral and spiritual body, then, of course, that is what we express through in those realms. Now remember, we can only express through the form on any plane of consciousness through which the plane of consciousness is composed of.

Guides and angels, I know there are many different religious and theological views, but to the understanding of Serenity and the Living Light Philosophy, a person known as an angel is one, in their evolution, who has refined the forms through which the divine Eternal Spirit is expressing. By refinement I mean, through evolution and effort, brought within their consciousness a perfect balance, which is harmony. We all understand, or most of us do, that harmony is health. And we must understand that harmony is balance. That that is balanced is harmonious. Now by balance I am not referring to the varying judgments of what balance is of the human mind, because if the human mind knew what balance was or is we'd all be balanced, and we all know that we're not that balanced. *[Some in the congregation laugh.]* So we all have room, of course, for some improvement. I'm sure you'll agree. As the soul, in its evolution, becomes more refined into a state of balance or perfect harmony, man calls that expression angelic or angels. Those souls have evolved through the various planes of consciousness in order to be the angels that we now call them.

Some, by their own laws that they alone have established, choose to return to other levels of consciousness, through which they have already evolved, to help those who are yet struggling on the path. They're qualified because they've been there. And so the teaching goes, "The greater the sinner, the greater the potential of sainthood." That does not mean that I endorse sinning in order to be saintly, but I do want that clearly understood. *[Many in the congregation laugh.]* I do hope that you—perhaps, however, I should temporarily or momentarily endorse it, and perhaps, then, we'll have less reformers. You know, I never did have a great deal of tolerance for reformers, because, you see, the moment we try to reform another, it simply reveals we've yet to educate the level of consciousness within our self. We might have stopped drinking or smoking or dancing, but all we did was suppress the desire. We never did bother to educate it, because, you see, when we educate a desire, we no longer have the need to reform someone else, you see. We know better. I do hope that that's helped with your question, ma'am.

Thank you.

You're welcome. The gentleman in the back, please.

Can you touch upon cryonics or the freezing of bodies?

We must understand—and it's a most interesting, of course, question. It's of interest to many, many people. You want my view or understanding of what is taking place in reference to cryonics?

Yes.

All right. Well, personally, I can see no value or sense in returning to a body that has served its purpose. Now, I had a 1940—no, 1939 Chevrolet once, and I thought it was a real nice car. I wouldn't particularly care for it today and I long ago got rid of it. The reason being: that it had served its purpose for me.

Now, this is one of the great difficulties with our world today. Many things enter into our life and into our universe. They enter by a Law of Attraction. Whether or not we like the things that enter our life, we alone attracted them. So let's take a look at what we have in our life that we may learn the lesson of what not to do. So if we find something distasteful in our experience, go to work on our mind and make the changes necessary to bring something more tasteful into our life.

All right. I cannot see the benefit, nor the value, of returning to a body that's been frozen and thawed out, that has served its purpose, when the Divine Architect, the Infinite Intelligence, surely knows more than my limited mind. Surely,

I do understand and I do believe in the right of the many, many people who choose to have their bodies frozen in the hope that they may return to this earth body, even though that earth body has served its true purpose.

But we must understand, my friends, it is not easy for the human mind to accept what is beyond the human mind. It is not easy, but it is demonstrably possible. Our mind, composed of mental substance, cannot perceive the divine, spiritual realms in which we move and breathe. Oh, it can conceive in its hope, but it cannot perceive. And so it is the minds of men that offer cryonics and offer these different things to those who are without hope, that they may have the continuity of life because their minds, in truth, cannot believe in what their minds cannot experience and what their minds cannot control. The human mind will reject anything that it cannot control, whether that be a rejection and denial of God, the Infinite Intelligence, or anything else. You can be rest assured all minds in principle are identically the same, and the human mind rejects, denies anything it cannot in potential control.

I do not honestly see the value of freezing any body, except for scientific experimentation, because the Isle of Hist has separated in the human form. And therefore, there is no way possible, no way, *no way possible* for the infinite intelligence individualized divine soul to once again animate a body where the Isle of Hist has separated. Thank you.

Yes, the lady here, please.

What is meant by the word suffer *in "Suffer the little children unto me?"*

Well, the lady has asked the question, What is meant by the word *suffer*? And then has asked a second question, What is meant by "Suffer the little children to come unto me?" First of all, we'll have to clarify which understanding of which meaning of suffering did you wish to have first? We have our understanding of the word *suffer*. Then, of course, there is the understanding of those who believe in the particular passage that you are quoting. So, which answer did you wish first?

Our philosophy.

Yes, thank you. We have a statement in this philosophy that says, "O suffer senses not in vain for freedom of thy soul is gain." Now, when we hear the word *suffer* and *suffering*, I don't know of anyone who smiles and appears to be pleased at what it brings up in their mind. What does suffering mean to our mind? To most of us, if not all of us, it means deprivation, pain, doing without the things we desire—doing without the things we desire. That's what it means to our mind. What does it reveal to us? If in the experience of not having the things we desire in the moment we desire them, that causes us suffering, then it reveals to us that we have lost control of our mind. We alone have lost control.

We look at a child and the child has a desire. Perhaps it wants a new fire engine. And any mother, any parent knows when the child has the desire, you have to do something, because if you don't, the child will certainly do something to you. Because you alone allow it. Now we look at children and we justify, "Well, they're only a little child. They're just a child." They have a desire. They want it fulfilled this minute, the moment they experience the desire. Not next month and, God forbid, not next year. Right now. It doesn't matter whether or not you have the money to purchase the item to fulfill their desire; that means nothing to the child's mind. It doesn't matter that you can't get the money right away, that you'll have to work for several months to earn it; that matters nothing to the child's mind. The child only knows that it, number one, has a desire; number two: that something inside of its mind demands that the desire be fulfilled; and number three: the demand is now. Right now. So we justify and we excuse the children. For we say to our self, "Well, they're only little children. They haven't had the experiences of life as we have had."

But then we look around the world and we see these little, wild children in great, big, adult bodies, and we wonder what has happened. *[Many in the congregation laugh.]* Where did the growing stop? Was it at the second year? Or the fifth? Or the seventh? At what point did these people stop growing mentally, emotionally? When did they stop? We must ask our self that question. For the same experience, the demand for the fulfillment of the desire right now, without the slightest interest in how it shall be fulfilled is still taking place 40, 50, 60, 70 years later, because the effort to become aware of the mechanics of our own mind has not been made.

And so we see many adults filling the psychiatric couches in the world because of what is known as frustration. In this philosophy it's called the frustration years of the forties, for that's when, usually, man takes a look and says, "Look at all the desires I have and have had that are not yet fulfilled. I've got to go back to when I was twenty. Somehow I've got to get back there to make up for all that lost time. To experience the fulfillment of all these desires that I've had to be great." My good friends, there's something within all of us that's already great. What is there in the chasing of being great? That's the illusion. Our mind doesn't know what that greatness is, but that greatness is there. It's greater than anything in the universe, for it is a part of the Infinite.

And so, the one thing I'm sure we'll all agree on, we all need, badly need what is called discipline, so we don't have to suffer. Discipline, self-discipline. For without it, there's no self-control. And without self-control, there is no freedom, there is no fulfillment. So if you want to stop the suffering that you experience in life, start the self-discipline and the suffering you'll no longer experience.

We understand that desire *is* the divine expression. What man chooses to do with that divine expression could easily be called something else, but the desire itself is the Divinity. Now, if you will learn through self-discipline and self-control, if you will learn to educate all desire, then the day will dawn in your consciousness when your desires will be fulfilled. It is when man dictates how the divine expression will fulfill itself—the divine expression known as desire—that man establishes the mental laws of duality. That's when man pays the price. That's when man suffers. Man suffers by the law that he is, through an error of his understanding of how the law demonstrably works. So it is up to us.

All that you need, you already have. All that you desire is waiting in consciousness. If you will only gain control of your mind, you will experience everything necessary for the greatest fulfillment of life itself.

But first we must gain control of our mind, for our mind judges. Our mind constantly returns us in consciousness back to yesterday. Hell only exists in past event. There is no hell, except in review. That's where hell is, my friends. It is in that that has been. Hope is in that that is yet to be. And freedom is in the eternal moment of now.

Gain control of your mind that you may never again view that which has gone and served its purpose, and then you'll have two avenues left open: that which is to be and that which is. And I can assure you, knowing a little something about the human mind, you will accept that that is and make it better. And in so doing, your tomorrows, you'll never worry about, for your tomorrows will always be increasingly better because you finally accepted the eternal truth, the moment of now. And if you have any question in reference to the existence of hell, think of what has been in your life and you'll have all the hell you could possibly desire. *[Many in the congregation laugh.]* Why carry that shadow in front of you? It has already been, my friends.

When we enter the other realms—and so many philosophies and religions teach of this great judge sitting on the throne, waiting to let you have it. Yes, indeed, the great judge is there. He's right in here. Right inside, my friends. We have two types of conscience. We have the spiritual conscience which is a spiritual sensibility with a dual capacity, knows right from wrong, does not have to be told. It is above and beyond the mental realm. And then we have an educated conscience, and this is where the king of kings waits on his throne for us: in our mental world, in our educated conscience.

You see, my friends, because the effort has not yet been made to educate desire, we have spent a lifetime suppressing it. And because we've spent a lifetime suppressing it, sooner or later—because it is divine, we forget the principle of desire, which is divine expression. So what we are doing with our mind, by suppressing and not educating our desires, we are swimming against the tide, for we, in our judgments, become greater than the Divinity. Sooner or later the suppressed desires rise up and they have their way. And what happens to us?

See, there's a better way: educate the desire and flow in the divine stream. No, we choose to suppress them, and suppress them until they're guaranteed to rise because in principle they are divine. And when that happens, we go contrary to our educated conscience. There on the throne of the educated conscience realm sits the judge of judges. Now we know in our minds that he's there, but we fulfill the desires anyway because we've suppressed them so long. And then we tell our self, "Well, it wasn't that good anyway." *[A great many in the congregation laugh.]* After the desire's fulfilled. Now we've all had that experience.

Then after that's over, of course, that puts more fuel on the fire of the judge of judges on his throne. And we go along for a while and once again we step over the cliff. And once again we put more fuel on the fire. And then the day comes, we leave this old mundane world. And we carry—we're still expressing through our old mental body, our mind, and we look around and we see we're in this realm with this king. And he has all these slaves working for him. And what is that realm? Most religions call it hell or purgatory. The Spiritualists only call it one of the closer realms to earth, because it's all composed of mental substance. It's the realm of judgment.

Because we ourselves judge so much and have—and the generations before us—we have created in mental substance the judgment world. Here, we experience the effects of the judgments, but we're blinded to the forms and shapes. But when we leave the physical body, we see the shapes and the forms, the kings and the princes, and all of the rulers of the realms of judgment. And we pay in that realm our dues in keeping with our own false beliefs and judgments. *The Tibetan Book of the Dead* has made it very clear, if you study it and you ponder it. And so has *The Egyptian Book of the Dead* made it very clear: what we face.

But, my friends, I tell you it is not necessary to enter the realms of judgment again. Those realms we go into here and now. We feel the effects of those realms of judgment, but we don't see the shapes and forms and we don't hear them. We only feel them. We don't have to live there. We don't have to, upon leaving the physical body, live for centuries—or whatever time it takes to make the change in consciousness—we don't have to live there for centuries yet to be. We can change this moment.

We understand that acceptance, total acceptance is the divine will, the will of God. For is there anything, even the flower, that God does not sustain? Does He not sustain the saint, as well as the sinner? Therefore, it reveals to us clearly that nothing, there is nothing in any universe anywhere rejected by God. When we, through our judgments based on past experiences, reject anything, we, in that moment, become greater than God. And because we have, in that moment, become greater than God, we pay the price of the fallen angel. All religions have taught the same thing. And I tell you once again, judgment is the fallen angel.

Thank you, friends. Thank you.

JANUARY 4, 1981

Church Questions and Answers 12

As our chairman has just explained, the first Sunday is set aside for the questions of a general interest; please, not of a personal nature—that is reserved, of course, for our message service time. So if you have any questions of a general interest to everyone, preferably of a spiritual nature, you may feel free to raise your hand.

Yes, the gentleman here, please.

My question is concerning the relationship and the interreaction between denial and discipline.

Thank you very much. The question the gentleman has is in reference to the relationship, if any, between denial and discipline. The Living Light Philosophy, which is presented by this association, teaches very clearly the Law of Personal Responsibility. We understand that our denials become our destiny, as we understand that each attachment guarantees its own adversity, and each adversity guarantees its own attachment. For they are, in truth, one and the same: they are the effect—not the cause—the effect of directed energy. We are all familiar, I am sure, with the seeming multitudes of problems with marriages, the problems, marital problems. And we can clearly see, if we remain objective, that to the degree of attachment to a person, place, or thing, we guarantee the day of our own equal adversity.

This philosophy teaches the Law of Balance between the natural laws of duality. We all are familiar, I'm sure, with the dual laws of nature: the positive and the negative; the light and the dark; the so-called right and the so-called wrong. We are all familiar with that Law of Duality and some of us have made the effort to become aware of the divine, infinite Law of Neutrality. Neutrality is not a do-nothing experience in life. It is the effort to discipline and to control the fluctuating desires of our own mind. We do not teach the denial of desire, for to do so is to place our self along the destiny of suppression. We teach the education or fulfillment of all desire, for desire is the divine expression, the expression of God. When we lack the expanded consideration of all people, places, and things that will be affected by our desires, then, of course, it is time to educate them. For we are not only responsible for all of our thoughts, acts, and activities, we are directly responsible for all those affected by our thoughts, acts, and activities.

And so the questioner has asked the relationship between denial and—what was the other part of your question?

Discipline.

Discipline. We must first understand what we mean by the word *discipline*. Do we mean by the word *discipline* our effort to bring into balance the contradictory desires of our own mind, to bring them into balance that the light of reason, which will transfigure us, shall flow through us? If that is what we mean by discipline—and that is what the Living Light Philosophy surely means by discipline—then man cannot experience, in that understanding, man cannot experience what is known as the destiny of denial, for there is no denial. There is only reason, patience, the wisdom of patience, fulfillment, and the joy of living. But if we understand discipline to mean a restrictive principle, then, of course, the relationship between denial and discipline is, of course, equal.

We all seem to have a negative thought, an attitude, in reference to the soul faculty of discipline. Yet we view nature and we quickly see that all of nature in her infinite wisdom is discipline. Nature does not waste. It is only the uneducated ego of the human being that wastes and, in so wasting, experiences need and want. The trees, the flowers, the grass, the animals, the birds, they do not waste. If we think for one moment that they lack, it is only our view limited by our own denials and acceptances that has such a belief, for even the lilies of the valley lack not, nor does the blade of grass, nor does the robin, nor does the ant that crawls the ground. It is only our lack of understanding the divine, natural Law of Balance that causes us to entertain such false belief. When the truth is everything, *everything* we really want we guarantee to experience. We believe that is not true because we do not make the effort to have the wisdom of patience. But remember that man is a law unto himself and therefore, in keeping with that demonstrable truth, we must honestly ask our self, "What are we doing with the law that we are?" Thank you. I hope that's helped with your question.

[After a short pause, the Teacher continues.] If there are no other questions, I won't have to work this morning. Thank you. Yes, the lady in the front row, please.

Could you please speak about our guardian angels?

The lady is asking for some discussion on our guardian angels. Of course, we must first consider what we mean by guardian. Does that mean some angel or some form in some dimension that takes over and takes from us the Law of Personal Responsibility? I have never, in these forty-some years, experienced any spirit, angel, mental or astral entity that did anything for me contrary to the natural law that like attracts like and becomes the Law of Attachment.

We experience in life the effects. Because ofttimes we are not aware of the causes, when we experience the effects, we look for a quick cure to free us from the laws that we have, through our errors of ignorance, set into motion. What does this have to do with guardian angels? It has everything to do with guardian angels. Because, my friends, no one, *no one* saves us but ourselves. No one can and no one may. We alone must walk the path, for teachers merely show the way, said by a wise woman many, many, many years ago.

It is the God within us, expressing through us, that if we are seeking what we think is salvation—and I assure you it is a waste of time, for we are already saved. We are saved by what we're doing moment by moment. If we are looking for salvation from the transgressions of natural law that we have ignorantly set into motion, then we must go within, be honest with our self.

We have two types of conscience. We have an educated conscience, created by mental substance, which guarantees the Law of Duality. Now that conscience dictates to us what is right and what is wrong. And we look around the world and we see what we have judged to be right, someone else has judged to be wrong. Therefore, who's right and who is wrong? That, of course, is dependent upon each and every one. Then we have a spiritual conscience. That is a conscience expressed in perfect balance. It sees that nothing is either right or wrong, but thinking makes it so.

Let us try to understand a neutral, divine, infinite Intelligent Energy, known by man as God. All things we see are sustained by some so-called invisible, intelligent, eternal Energy. Whether your thought is a thought that your educated conscience says is bad or whether your thought is a thought that your educated conscience says is good, it is the same neutral, divine, intelligent Energy that sustains both thoughts. But it is the mind that entertains the thought, a good or bad one, that must pay the price of the thought. It is only the mind that suffers. It is only the mind that struggles, for the mind is composed of the dual law. For mental substance is a creative force and a creative force is governed by the laws that govern creation. The Power that sustains all of it is infinite, divine, and neutral.

Guardian angels, of which I have never met a person or an animal that does not have what man refers to as a guardian angel. In some philosophies it's referred to as the higher self, the better part of oneself, the soul mate. It doesn't matter what you call it. It does matter that we all become aware that nothing ever in all eternity happens to us that is not caused by us. Now when we accept that very simple, demonstrable truth, we will begin to walk on the path of freedom, we will begin to walk upon the path of abundant good. It is when we permit our minds to continue to entertain the delusion that something happened to us by something or someone else—that, my friends, is when we continue on the karmic wheel of bondage. It is within the realm, of course, of all people to accept responsibility for the way their life has been, is, and shall be. It is when you permit your mind to think that because of something or someone else you feel happy or sad that you place your eternal soul in temporary bondage. But that type of thinking is only possible when you permit the mind to attach. One can experience all of the joys of living freed from attachment.

It is when our desire—whatever it may be—takes a higher priority in our consciousness than the intelligent Power that sustains that desire we have chosen, it is only then that we guarantee suffering, bondage, and struggle. For in the moment that any thought and desire becomes a higher priority than the very Power that sustains the thought or desire we choose, when that happens we fall from grace, for we fall from the natural Law of Balance into the dual laws of creation. And so this philosophy clearly teaches: learn to be with a person, place, or thing and never a part of the person, place, or thing. Learn to be in the world and never a part of the world, and you will forever be free. The abundant good that is constantly available to you is waiting right in front of you. It's waiting only for your acceptance.

It is so very important that we make some daily effort to remind our self that no matter what has happened, no matter what is happening, no matter what we think is going to happen, there is something greater than it. And because there is something greater, we can, when we choose to, we can move to that something greater in the eternal moment of now.

The human mind is designed to gather and to garner. It is the very nature of mental substance to increase by multiplication. Stop and see what one thought does in one mind. It is a very rare occasion that any mind on earth can entertain one thought, pure and unadulterated, for one moment. Because when we think of the simple word of *peace*, immediately our mind offers to us every feeling, every image that it has ever encountered in our earth journey. That is because, my friends, it controls us. Designed by the Infinite Architect to serve as a vehicle through which the eternal being may express, it has become such a priority—what we think we know is right and wrong—it has become such a priority in our mind that our mind has become the master and we have become the slave.

If you want to know, for your own personal experience, how much bondage we're truly in, then stop and tell the mind to be still and see how long, if at all, you can experience the stillness of eternal peace. That will tell you by your own personal experience who is really in charge. Does your foot tell you where it will go? It is a part of this vehicle designed to serve you. Does your hand tell you what it will do and will not do? Do your eyes tell you what they will see and not see? Do your ears tell you what they will hear and not hear? Think, my friends, they do. For God, the Infinite, has given us eyes to see and we see not, ears to hear and we hear not, for if it is not in keeping with the experiences we have already encountered, if it is not in harmony with what man calls his judgments, then the eyes see not and the ears hear not, the foot moves not, nor does the hand. It is because we have given so much of this divine, neutral, infinite Energy, have given it by direction, by choice to the importance of our mind, that our minds are now in control.

We all, I am sure, will accept the simple truth that the body is an effect of the mind. It is the mind that tells us whether our foot hurts or it doesn't hurt. It's our mind that does that. It's not the physical flesh of our foot. It is our mind that does that. And our mind does that in keeping with the laws that we alone have set into motion. But be of good cheer, because we set the law into motion, we, in truth, are still the captain, for the father is greater than the son. We created the thought; therefore, we can change the thought. We created the laws of yesterday for our life. We entered the earth realm in keeping with laws already established by us. Therefore, they were established by us; they are still subject to us.

God will sustain the choice you make. God is not a doer. God is not a giver. God is not a taker. God makes no choice. God, like truth, just is. It doesn't matter, the color of your eyes, whether God will be kind to you or not. For that's not the God of Spiritualism; that is not even the God of truth. No matter what you do or don't do, God will sustain what you choose. It is your spiritual conscience that you face, like we all face. It knows; it does not have to be told. But remember, there's a vast difference between your spiritual conscience and our educated conscience.

A good thought returns to the sender in keeping with the natural law that so does a so-called bad one. If you believe the times are tough, if you believe it, for you they will be. If you believe there's prosperity in the land, if you believe it, for you it shall be. No matter what your neighbor does or doesn't do, no matter what the government does or doesn't do, for you can only experience the law that only you have set into motion. And so we look over the world and we see those who seem to have it all and those who seem to have it not. And even the Bible teaches, "To those who have, yea, even more shall I give. And to those who have not, yea, even that shall I take away." What does that simply reveal? As we believeth, we becometh. When you believe you have it, you establish the law through which you may experience it. When you believe you have it not, you establish the law through which it may all be taken from you. How simple, how demonstrable it is for all of us.

Why would we—anyone—choose to be without the goodness of life when it's just as easy—in fact, it's easier—to be with the goodness of life? Why would we spend days, hours, weeks, years, months, or centuries desiring the goodness of life and being frustrated because, like a shadow, it keeps moving away from us? The only reason that it does that is in keeping with our own belief. There's no other reason, there's no other way that it happens. As we believe our employer pays us so much money, therefore we can have only so much good in our life. That type of god I do not believe in, for that is a god created by mental substance, that gives and takes ever in keeping [with] what we believe we must do. If we believe that freedom, for us, can only take place in keeping with unbearable suffering, then, of course, that's how we will attain our freedom. If we believe by being poverty stricken we will be more spiritual, in keeping with our belief we will be more poverty stricken and we, in keeping with our belief for us, will be more spiritual.

Don't you see, my friends, the key, we've always had. We've never been without the key that opens the door of truth. We all have it. It's time, of course, that we all use it.

Thank you.

FEBRUARY 1, 1981

Church Questions and Answers 13

As our chairman has already stated, if you will be so kind as to raise your hand, I will be happy to serve as the channel to share the understanding regarding your question.

Yes, the lady in the front row, please.

Can you tell us if the etheric body and the astral body are one in the same in this philosophy?

Thank you very much. The lady is asking in reference to the astral body and the etheric body. In the understanding of this church and this philosophy, they are not the same. Thank you.

Yes, the gentleman here, please.

I'm wondering how should a person make choices in life that will help speed up their evolution, when, for me, it seems impossible to know what I must do here and now, when right and wrong can seem so relative.

Thank you very much. There is a vast difference—the gentleman is asking the question how can one make choices to speed up their evolution when it seems so difficult with the thinking of right and wrong. My friends, the difference between decisions in life and judgments is quite simple: decisions free us and judgments bind us. Decisions have total consideration with the full acceptance of the possibility of change. Judgment has limited consideration without any acceptance of the possibility of change.

As long as we entertain the type of thinking of right and wrong, we are controlled by the dual laws of creation and cannot find the peace that passeth all understanding, for peace is the Divine Neutrality. So the first thing we consider is whether or not we are willing to give up what is known as our judgment of right and wrong. Granting unto each their right of personal responsibility, a wise man learns early in life to make decisions that he may remain free and truly serve the purpose of his soul's journey here on earth.

The fall of Lucifer, in these ancient stories, is when an angel, a servant of the Divine Spirit called God, fell from decisions to judgments and entered the realm of right and wrong. The infinite Divine Spirit, known as God, is a neutral, eternal Intelligence, without beginning or ending, that flows through all life. It is not limited in and of itself. It is bound and limited only by the form through which it is expressing. If it is truly man's desire to evolve and to awaken, to experience the peace that passeth all understanding, to experience the harmonious flow of good or Godness through his being, then he must free himself from the level of consciousness that rejects the cornerstone of a firm foundation on the faculty of reason.

We understand that God works through man, never to man. Because, you see, my friends, we never know when God is speaking unless we have entered the realms of judgment. When we enter the realms of judgment, we lose the divine, infinite, eternal, free spirit that is within us. We lose it only in the sense that we no longer accept or recognize it. And it is in those moments that we create in our life the false gods of clay feet that are ever destined to crumble for they have been created by mind stuff, by mental judgments. Judgments do not exist in realms of the spirit. They only exist in the minds of men. And therefore, if we truly wish to be free, if we truly desire truth and the only faculty that will transfigure us, the faculty of reason, then we must make the conscious, moment-by-moment effort to make decisions in life, never judgments, that we may truly enjoy our divine birthright. Thank you.

Yes, the lady in the aisle, please.

You've spoken about the eighty-one levels of consciousness. And do they have names and how does one realize the need to change one's consciousness, other than the obvious?

Thank you very much. In reference to the question of the eighty-one levels of consciousness, Do they have names and how does one know what they should change in their consciousness?

Let us understand, my friends, that, first of all, in these eighty-one levels of consciousness, of which we are all—our souls—expressing through, there are forty functions of the mental realms of creation. There are forty divine soul faculties. There is one Infinite Spirit that sustains all of them.

It is of the utmost importance to become aware of how one truly feels. So often we spend most of our time in life making great effort to give a certain impression to a certain person or persons. When we have that feeling, when we have that need, we must reassure ourselves, we must know that we are not in decision, but we are in judgment, for only from judgment do we make the effort to appear a certain way to a certain person or people. Therefore, the levels of consciousness will reveal themselves to us if we will make the effort to become aware each moment of how we feel and why we feel the way we feel. When we begin to accept the demonstrable truth of personal responsibility in life, the first thing that begins to happen to us is an inner awakening, an acceptance that the way we feel is directly the effect of thoughts we are entertaining. When that takes place we slowly, but surely, have the inner knowing of the various levels of consciousness.

We look at life and see that in many respects we have changed in many ways in the past 2 or 20 or 30 or 40 years. We have made some changes because evolution is the Law of Life. Whether or not we like changes, change we shall and change we are. For without change, evolution and growth is not possible. Though we are, all of us, aware of some changes that we have made in our life, we are yet to be aware of how lazy we really are. Now we physically work and mentally work, but we live with that which has passed. Our daily experiences reveal to us that our judgments are based upon experiences of years ago. We are not yet aware of the difference between a decision and a judgment. Because we are, unfortunately, through our own errors of ignorance, we are lazy in our thinking. We are not consciously aware that what we think we think, we are not thinking at all. It is only a pattern, a tape that has been recorded in our mind in many years past that simply is set and starts to play. We are honestly, unfortunately, not aware that that is not conscious thought, that is simply, wholly, and completely subconscious reaction to the experience we are having at the moment.

None of us appreciate, I know, that in thinking, indeed, we are lazy, but all we have to do is to be honest with our self to see whether or not we accept or reject new thoughts and new ideas. If we find that instantly we reject any new thought or new idea, that we immediately have a negative reaction, then we know beyond a shadow of any doubt that we are not thinking. We are in what the Spirit has termed the "robotical level of consciousness." We react automatically because the experiences of yesterday we still are controlled by. This is the very thing that makes it such a struggle in life. Such a struggle to grow. Such a struggle to find peace of mind. Such a struggle to have the abundant good of life that is our divine birthright. That is our suffering. I can assure you of that. That is not only our suffering, it is our struggle. It is our grief. It is our sadness. It is our deprivation. It is our poor health.

It is demonstrable to anyone who makes the effort to experience for themselves the direct relationship between the faculty of harmony and perfect health. Perfect health is our right. It is not something that we should seek, for it is something we already have. If we do not think we have perfect health, then what we are, in truth, doing is making a judgment, giving power and control over our life to whatever we judge is the cause of our illness. I can assure you, my friends, that when harmony flows unobstructed through our universe, perfect health, wealth, and happiness is the law that we will experience. We know, for we demonstrate it moment by moment, that man (all humanity) is a law unto themselves. Therefore, we must ask our self the question, "If it is demonstrably true to me, if I have made the effort to awaken, then I cannot help but accept the truth that I am a law unto myself. Having accepted that demonstrable truth, I must ask myself the question: What am I doing with the law that I am?" There is nothing, my friends—and I am answering the questions on the levels of consciousness, the names, you alone will find. What are we doing with the law that we are? We are casting our pearls before the swine of creation, for in our minds we are giving our freedom, our goodness, our birthright to a judgment that only we have made.

Some time ago in counseling with a married couple when they came to my home, the wife said she brought her husband because he had a problem. The Spirit revealed to her at that time, "Your husband has no problem." She said, "Oh, yes, he has a problem: he drinks." I asked the man, "Does your drinking bother you? Does it create for you a problem?" And he said no. I said, "You see, ma'am, it is evident that you have the problem, for it bothers you." And that that bothers us in life, controls us. That is the Law of Personal Responsibility. Now if a man and his wife are having problems, you must go to the one who is having the problem, to the one who is bothered. That's the only way you can ever help them. Because the one who is bothered is the one who is controlled. And the one who is controlled is the victim—the victim, my friends, of their own judgments.

How do people get along? It's very simple: accept the Law of Personal Responsibility. That that is around you will grow or go, for the law is very clear: like attracts like and becomes the Law of Attachment. What so few people realize is that our adversities in life become attachments, that our attachments in life become adversities. It is the divine law, in order that we may experience the freedom which is our right. And so we have people, they marry, and they divorce. And they marry again, and they divorce again. They come, and they go, because they move from attachment to adversity to attachment to adversity, until finally we accept personal responsibility. Take a look at life, here. Take a good look. One moment we love them, the next moment we hate them, and we move back and forth constantly. We love them when they do what we want them to do. We hate them when they don't do what we want them to do. My good friends, when you desire to control another, you establish the law in the universe to be controlled. And when we are bothered, we know we are controlled.

And so the great circle of life, the great, clear, beautiful reason of life, clearly states all things shall return unto their source. It is only when we become aware that we, indeed, are the source and that that is returning unto us we are not happy with. Instead of growing up and accepting responsibility as adults, we react with the trauma of little children.

How beautiful life is, if we permit our self to accept it. There is no limit. There is no shortage. There is no struggle until we make it so. God did not make it so. And because God, the divine Neutral Intelligence, didn't make it, God can't take it. Only the created gods, the gods that we have created (the "Santa Claus" gods) can give and take. Let us use our simple reasoning faculty. If we believe that God is a giver and we believe that God is a taker, what a miserable life we have to live, for we look around the world and see, "That one has everything. I have almost nothing. God has given them all of that. What kind of a God am I believing in?" My friends, awaken. God gives nothing, and God takes nothing. The law, the law that we set into motion, that one, that is what gives and that is what takes. Unfortunately, frequently we forget that the Divine Spirit is flowing through everything.

If we have difficulty with people, if we have difficulty with communication, the only difficulty is that we do not communicate with our self. I've never had a problem talking. Hopefully, not many problems listening, and yet some people think I'm very shy. As I mentioned, here, to some of my students from my birthday party—which I thank all of you for. It was a wonderful experience to be twenty-seven again. *[Many in the congregation laugh.]* But anyway, a lady said—who attends our church—that, "Why, Mr. Goodwin, you're terribly shy. You're awfully shy." So I mentioned it to a couple of my students, and they said, "Hmm, that's only because she doesn't really know you." I said, "Yes, I think so, too." But anyway, I do hope that's helped you with your questions.

It's very important, friends, we are as good as we will allow our self to be. And we are the opposite as much as we want to be. Let us, if we take care of our self—remember, God helps those who help themselves by helping others. Let us not forget that. We can't help someone else, my friends, 'til we [have] first qualified our self. I wouldn't think of lifting my voice on the divine, abundant goodness of life if I didn't make some effort to have some of it for myself.

I have to admit my tolerance for hypocrisy is a bit short, but I'm working on it. I believe in a demonstrable religion. I believe in one that works, and if it doesn't work, then for me it's time to change it. And this is why I am a Spiritualist, because it offers to me the opportunity, the freedom, and the growth to express ever in keeping with my own efforts and evolution in life. I do not believe in anything being a certain way without possibility of change. Because if that were possible, why bother in the first place?

You know, I must take a few moments, with your permission, to speak on something that has been so interesting to me, especially in Spiritualism. So many people come to Spiritualism with many different motives. And some stick around for a while. And that is fine. I freely receive; therefore I can freely give. So I try not to hold to people, to places, or things. I try not to hold to students. They come, however long they are to be, they shall be and their day shall come to go. Or some will stay, long after

I am gone. But it's always been interesting to me to watch the evolutionary growth of people involved in spiritual study, especially in the religion of Spiritualism. Coming in with various motives, if they don't have, after varying periods of time, a personal experience of some spirit materializing and sitting down and having lunch with them, they become an atheist! *[Many of the people in the congregation laugh.]* So we find the level moving from the depths of spiritism to the depths of atheism. And so it bounces back and forth until we become free from this thing called the king brain.

My friends, the only veil between us and God, the only veil between us and His ministering angels is the veil of self. If our minds are so filled with self-thought, how can anything else penetrate the barrier? It's when we're free from self that our eyes open and our ears hear, in those moments that we're truly free. I cannot give it to you. I spent enough years of my life in what they call physical seances and materializations. I spent enough years with that. It didn't bring one single soul to God's eternal light. It certainly did entertain the senses of the phenomena. Long ago I asked, I sincerely prayed that I may merit being receptive to some teaching that would benefit not only myself, but mankind, for it is more important to me to have an understanding that works in this moment, than a hope that may never manifest. We must accept the truth, my friends, we cannot prove God to anyone, for God is beyond proof, for God is beyond the mental needs of man. God *is*, as truth *is*. It doesn't matter what we believe to the Divine Spirit. Of course, it matters to us.

So we can bounce back and forth. It's just like judgment. And I do want to finish on judgment—I'm not supposed to lecture. I'm supposed to answer questions. But I'm—long answer to this question. *[Many laugh.]* Anyway, it's just like, you know, we spend so much of our time in rejection. We feel terrible, rejected by this, rejected by that. Surely, we all know we can't feel rejected by our wives, the husbands, the brothers, the sisters, or anyone else, or our employers, we can't feel, nor experience [being] rejected, until we've made a judgment. Rejection doesn't precede judgment. It follows judgment. So if you make a judgment that your employer gave your co-worker a raise and bypassed you, well, of course, you're going to feel a little rejected unless your little mind can justify that that co-worker really did deserve it and you really didn't deserve it. Now if you use that type of thinking, that's one way of not feeling too bad. One way. And so you see what judgment has to offer. It offers us the feelings of rejection. Our wives reject us, our husband rejects us, the government rejects us, everybody rejects us, when they don't do what we judge they should do, in keeping with our personal, selfish desires. Is that what marriage is all about? May God ever save me then.

But anyway, from these judgments, we have these rejections. Now from the rejections, this is what happens. When we feel rejected, the first thing that happens to us, we experience self-pity. How bad we feel for our self, the way somebody else has treated us. And so after we spend a little time in the depths of self-pity—the Law of Creation is always working to balance—we move from that depth, that pit of rejection over into belligerence. So if you're working with a person you try to help them, first you experience how bad they feel for themselves, how tough everything is, the way everybody out there treats them. They'll only stay down there so long. Then, the next time you won't believe the demon you see; they're at the heights of belligerence.

Tell me, friends, is that the way to live? Is it really the way to live? When we no longer have a need for servants to wait on us to do the things we want them to do when we want them to do it, when we no longer have the need, then we'll no longer have those problems. When we move to a level of consciousness where we do what we know is right for us to do, we are not concerned with all these other things, because we can only, in truth, take care of our self and God will help us in keeping with that Law of Responsibility. That that is around us is going to harmonize with us.

If we want to know where we are, don't bother to look in the mirror; look at the people around you that bother you, for those are the people who are controlling you. Now once you know what's controlling you, study it very well. Then you will see the level of consciousness that you are in. And I think it's wonderful. My students are a beautiful barometer for me. And for them I am extremely grateful. From the self-pity to the belligerence, it's back and forth; the miracle of miracles is there's a church at all. *[Many in the congregation laugh.]* The greatest miracle is that it's successful! I love them all, even though they hate me most of the time. *[Some in the congregation laugh.]* But that's not important. If I was attached to them, I would be terribly miserable, I can assure you. They're beautiful souls and they're growing. And a wise teacher pays the price of his student's growth. And if he's not willing to do that, he never should lift his voice as a teacher in the first place. So let's think—I hope that's helped you with levels of consciousness.

We have time for one more question. Yes, please.

Can a person really speed up or slow down their evolutionary process when they're born on this planet?

It's an excellent question. Can a plant grow slow or fast? Is a plant part of the divine laws of creation? Of course it is. And so is man. You see, we've separated our self from the demonstrable laws of nature itself. We think, why, it's not possible for a human to grow fast or slow. Yet, we see a plant grow fast or slow. And as science continues on with its research and development, we'll see animals grow fast and slow. That is not some miracle. Miracles are only lack of understanding natural law. Science is moving at a great speed in the universe. We must make great effort that our spiritual understanding will catch up.

There is no law and no dictate from any God that I've ever been aware of, or any Divine Spirit, that man cannot grow slow or fast. Man is already demonstrating varying speeds of growth. Some people, they learn quickly. Some people, they learn slowly. Some babies grow hair faster than other babies. Some babies walk faster than other babies. Some babies do many things that other babies don't do. How does that all happen? It's in keeping with natural law. Just because we now have what is known as hothouse plants, that in the dead of winter we can have the summer blossoms, it's in keeping with natural law. And so it is with cloning. And so it is with all these other things that all you hear about as science fiction. Today's fiction, my friends, is always tomorrow's fact. Let us face that simple truth. Let us not hold on to the horse and buggy. It served its purpose. We're now in a different age, hopefully with broader horizons.

So what's going to happen? God did not dictate that man shall take X number of years to grow on earth, or any place else. God did not dictate that a baby must wait for several months before it runs and plays. God did not dictate that a child cannot learn at the age of one or the age of a day. At the moment of conception—and a wise mother awakens to know that truth—at the moment of conception, at that moment, the law is established: the Law of Growth. Depending on your motive, depending on your thinking, depending on your emotions, and all the other things that affect the form in which the soul has entered from the moment of conception, the child reveals where you were. Your attitudes as parents, your feelings, your thoughts. Indeed, it is a great responsibility. If God is in the moment of conception, then goodness is the greater percentage of vibration that will be in the child. If the mother in that nine-month time makes effort to be happy, to be free from disturbing thought, to be balanced and harmonious in her emotional realm, the child, that soul, will merit a form of health, of wealth, and happiness.

For our thoughts, they heal or poison the temples of our soul. And because our body is the temple of our eternal soul, we have a great responsibility to keep it in good working order. Someone said to me the other day that they never saw a group, as this Serenity group, that had such good health. I said, "Well, I'll be glad when it gets better." Right now, I happen to have two of my students with sniffles. I don't tolerate it very long. I can assure you of that; ask my students. Because I know that it is an error that we must correct deep inside of us. And because I know that and because I teach that, I have to work very hard on my own errors that I don't run around here with colds while I'm correcting them or even after I have finished. So anyone here knows that it's rare, and hopefully will be a lot rarer, that I'm sick, that I'm puny, that I have colds. Asiatic flu, Russian Flu, or just plain, old Communist flu, it doesn't make any difference, I have to stay free. *[Many in the congregation laugh loudly.]*

Thank you very much.

MARCH 1, 1981

Church Questions and Answers 14

As our chairman has already stated, if you will be so kind as to raise your hand if you have a question of interest to all of us, I will be more than happy to share with you the answer that I receive to your question.

Yes, the lady on the aisle, please.

Is man a reflection of God?

The question is, from the lady, "Is man a reflection of God?" Man is a reflection as long as man sees man. It is when man stills his mind that he becomes the living light in the world of God, which flows through man. You see, man, the mind, is not God, but is sustained by God. The God that is, is not that man of identity, but it is the power that flows through man. Does that help with your question?

[Thank you.]

You're welcome. Yes, the lady there, please.

When will the female of principle be known in the West?

In reference to your question of the female principle, if you are referring to Mother Nature, which is the female principle of the Divine Spirit, known in the West as Father God, when man frees himself from a god created by the human mind in keeping with the limited judgments of the mind, then man will find the true and only God of Divine Neutrality or peace that passeth all understanding. Therefore, as man constantly changes his concepts of God, he grows slowly, but surely, to the divine principle and precept of God and brings about, in his own consciousness, a balance between the duality of creation. At that moment man sets himself free by finding truth, separating it from creation—for that that is form is limit, and that that is limit is not truth. I do hope that's helped with your question.

Thank you.

Thank you. Yes, the little boy in the back, please. Yes.

I forgot. [Many in the congregation laugh.]

You forgot. Well, to forget is human and to forgive is Divine. Thank you. Or vice-versa.

Yes, the lady in the front, please.

Could you tell us the benefits of encouragement?

The lady has asked the question on the benefits of encouragement. Man spends much of his time in what is known by man as guilt. Now we understand that guilt is nothing more nor less than rejected desire, but we must also understand that we are the ones that reject desire in our own consciousness. For the principle of desire is the divine expression. We reject one desire after another until we find our minds filled with untold hundreds of desires being rejected in the course of one waking day. What is it within us that rejects the divine expression? It is the limit that our minds have placed upon the divine expression, known as desire. We have judged that this can be and that cannot be. We alone have made those judgments in our own errors of ignorance in days past.

We understand in the Living Light Philosophy of Spiritualism that eternity is the moment of which you are conscious. That is our eternity and that is our truth, as truth is individually perceived. That that has been, has been. You cannot change what has already gone in consciousness. You may reflect upon it, but you cannot change it. We can always be aware when we are in judgment for we are in that moment in the past, in that which has been. Judgment is not possible to the human mind without review of that which has been. We are bound not by tomorrow, for that is yet to be. We are bound not by the moment in which we are in consciousness in this great eternity. It is not the present that binds us. It is not the future that binds us. It is that which has been that binds us.

And so man, having many desires, when he looks at the desires recorded in his consciousness, he immediately reviews past ways that he has used of fulfilling his desires. And in so doing he becomes, in that moment, greater than the God, the Power, that is sustaining his very thought. For we understand that God is a divine, neutral, intelligent Principle and judges not. It is only creation, the Law of Duality, that judges. It is not the Power that sustains the Law of Duality that judges. Therefore, when we judge, we place our self in consciousness to that which has been. We are, therefore, bound by the laws that have been established in our own consciousness years ago and cannot move into the fullness and abundant good of eternity, which is the moment of the present.

Therefore, when we receive the benefit of encouragement, when we are encouraged in the thought and the act we are about to do—encouragement being a soul faculty through which the light of reason, the power that transfigures us, flows unobstructed—we benefit because we are not without hope. We seem to be, unfortunately, in many of our daily thoughts and activities, without hope. He who thinks he is without hope, you may be rest assured, is totally controlled by the past. I hope that's helped with your question. Thank you.

Yes, the lady in the back, please.

I understand that God is formless and free and sustains all. My question is, What was the creator of form?

Well, the lady is asking a question that the Power, known as God, is a formless, free Spirit. And what was the creator of creation? My friends, it's really, when you stop to think and think more deeply, when you ask yourself the question, "Who am I? And if this is what I am, how did I come to be?" [you find] the law, the divine, infallible Law of Duality, the positive and negative, is the very principle of creation. Now, if you believe that that which has form has beginning, then you cannot help but see the Law of Creation, which is a constant process of beginning and ending. When you have something that is formless and free, in order for form to be aware of form, then you must have beginning and ending. If you believe you are form, then you are beginning and ending. If you know in your consciousness that you have always been and, having always been, will always be, then you are freed from the limit of creation. In that moment you separate truth from creation.

The mind, you see, has to know. It has to know, but it is limited by the very nature of the mind. Formless and free is an awakening in our heart. It can never be in our mind. The only thing that can be in our mind is opposites. It is not possible to experience by the limit of nature, which is form, it is not possible to experience formless and free. The Living Light Philosophy teaches very clearly to still the mind. To still the mind is to rise in consciousness—because our consciousness *is* God—to rise in consciousness above the mind. Therefore, no mind can answer a question that is not within the power of the mind to form in the first place.

I will say it in one other way; perhaps it will be a bit clearer. The power of the mind to question predisposes and guarantees its own power to answer. But you have to understand, my friends, a circle has no beginning and a circle has no ending. So the moment you find an answer to a question that your mind entertains, you guarantee the next question and the next and the next. Until finally the mind stills and you return to what you think is beginning, which is not beginning and never was. I hope that's helped with your question.

Yes. The gentleman, please, in the aisle.

What's the significance of the number six?

Well, if you understand the number six—if you look at the number six, what does number six look like? Does it contain a perfect circle with a straight line? Most of us will agree that a straight line is representative of infinity, would we not? Pardon? Would we not?

I'm not aware of that.

Very well. Perhaps you would agree that a circle has no beginning or no ending.

Yes.

Then, perhaps, you would agree that a straight line leaving a circle must return unto the circle by the very law of the line itself. And so six is representative of divine love. There is no place, never was, never will be, where divine love is not. It's like truth, my friends. Truth *is*. You cannot defend truth, for the moment you attempt to defend that which is, you no longer have that which is. Thank you.

The gentleman in the back, please.

How does the divine Law of Responsibility work?

The divine Law of Responsibility works with the ability to respond. Man is never left without the ability to respond to anything that he encounters. We all have the ability of response. Though we may not ofttimes accept our ability to respond when it is an experience that we have forgotten that we were the cause of and it does not entertain nor please us at the moment of the experience, then ofttimes we deny the demonstrable, divine, eternal law known as personal responsibility. When we stand still in consciousness, we will accept—and acceptance *is* the will of God—we will accept that it is within our power, that there is something flowing through us that is the ability to respond to anything at any time in any place.

Remember, my friends, we are limited only by our denials, and our denials are nothing more nor less than an effect of our judgments of our experiences of the past. Our denials are the law of our destiny. Destiny is that which man creates. It is not something that some God somewhere has chosen that this or that shall be your destiny. Destiny is what *we* create. Destiny, destiny is the shadows of our path of evolution. Because destiny has no substance, it is only a shadow, for judgment is a shadow upon the light of reason. And so everything that happens to us, once we accept, has been caused by us. You see, my friends, the moment we accept that whatever happens to us is caused by us, we, in that moment, once again gain control over our destiny.

If you deny the demonstrable Law of Personal Responsibility, you become the victim of what you call circumstances and conditions. You give away in the moment of that denial, you give away your birthright, you give away your divinity. It's known in this day and age as selling out the principle that we know that frees us. It's entirely up to us. If we have experiences that are distasteful and we can see clearly they are not beneficial, it is very simple. Stop and declare the truth that is yours: that this is the moment of your eternity. That that has been can no longer affect that which is. All things to God are possible, but God does not flow freely in our consciousness when we establish the laws of denial, for that is contrary to the divine principle of formless, free Spirit, of total acceptance. And we must pay the price of nature, of creation. For every high there is a low, not to the divine, eternal spirit which you are, only to the form that you have created. I hope that's helped with your question.

Yes. The lady here, please.

When communications come through, how can you better determine whether they're things thrown up by your mind or they come from a higher source?

It's a wonderful question. It's a very important question. Man in his efforts to communicate must begin in the realms of consciousness with which he is most familiar, and that is man himself. First, man makes the effort to be honest with himself that he may clearly and freely communicate with himself. That is becoming aware of all his desires, suppressed and expressed, and especially the suppressed ones, for those are the loudest voice of all in human consciousness. Once man makes the daily effort to communicate with himself by being honest with himself, being freed from what others think or think not, then it's time to move onward to meditation, to an awareness of these other dimensions in which we truly live and act. No other way do I know of that man can discern whether or not it is the voice of suppressed desire that is calling as a voice in his consciousness or whether it is a decarnate spirit that is calling in his consciousness.

Because, you see, my friends, when we first make the effort to communicate with our self we establish the law. We, we alone establish the law that says clearly: You cannot grant unto another what you have not first granted unto yourself. As the Bible clearly states, "O physician, heal thyself." O communicator, communicate with thyself. Only then can we grant to another the clarity of communication and be able to discern that which is of the spirit.

Because we, our eternal being, is moving in many bodies of consciousness, so few are we this moment aware of. We know we have a physical body; we touch, sense, and feel it. And see it—we *think* we see it. And we know we have a mental body, for thoughts entertain our mind twenty-four hours day and night until the daily effort is made to still the mind.

So many of us think we go to sleep and we're resting from thought and all that it has to offer. I assure you, my friends, we are not resting from thought while we sleep. We are only in another dimension of which we, then, are aware of the different body that is within us. It behooves us to become aware by establishing the law before going to sleep which one of these bodies we're going to let be active, for there are the realms of fascination. There are the realms of the astral. There are realms of the mental, and there are the realms of the spiritual and, oh, so many other realms.

And so as we make great effort to know our self, through honest communication with our self, then we can grant that to those who are close to us. Because, you see, my friends, when we go to become aware of our self, we become aware of the judgments, of the throne of pride that restricts us from being honest with our feelings and our true being. And when we make those growth steps, it doesn't matter whether someone likes us or dislikes us, because that's not who we're working for. There is no other way to be free, as long as we are concerned what people think about us, whether they're going to smile or scorn when they see us, for to live that way is to live in a realm of consciousness that is not pure, that is not clean and certainly does not offer clear communication. So, first, let us begin by standing firm on what we believe is right in our consciousness, regardless whether others think or think not and then we will qualify our self to communicate with another in the realms of which we are so familiar: this old mundane world. After we have got that cleared up—and we work on it daily so it can stay that way—then it's time to be still, to meditate, and become aware of these other dimensions around and about us.

Spiritualism did not come to the world as a door through which man can escape from his thoughts, acts, and activities. It came as a light unto the world again in 1848 to show man that heaven is not a place we're going to, but is, in truth, a state of consciousness that we are growing to, ever dependent, of course—our growth—upon our own effort. Let us not forget that, my friends. Take care of the world with which you are most familiar and be rest assured those realms you seek to view will take good care of you. We must take care of our self. Our physical, mental, and other bodies are the temples through which our soul is expressing. If we do not keep the temple, the house in good working order, it cannot express clearly, nor fully. So let us take care inside, then all things around us will be harmoniously arranged. As we know our self, we will know without being told what is of the spirit within us and what is not. Because only by knowing within can you ever, ever flow in the light of eternal truth. Thank you for your question.

[After a short pause, the Teacher continues.]

No more questions? I won't have to work any longer. Yes, the lady here, please.

Can you explain the term used, the magnetic body?

Would you repeat your question, please?

Can you explain the term that is in The Living Light *book . . .*
Yes?
The mental body? I mean, not mental—the magnetic body?
Magnetic body? Why, I will be happy to share our understanding with you. I'm sure that you have already had experience in your life when you felt magnetically attracted to what you would consider to be strong desire. Is that not correct? Pardon?
Yes.
Yes. Like a great magnet, when some desires flood our consciousness, we feel forced or compelled to fulfill them. The magnetic body is the body through which our emotions flow. Now what are emotions? Emotions are what we do with our suppressed and expressed desires in life. That's what emotions are. Now if we express all of them—some people do. They're over there in that place called San Quentin *[Some in the congregation laugh.]* or up there in a place called Napa. *[The Teacher refers to a state prison and a state psychiatric hospital, respectively.]* Because we live in a society, we must consider someone beside our self. But that's what emotions are, suppressed and expressed—what we've done, what we've done with suppressed and expressed desire. Desire being the divine principle.

A magnetic body can only be brought into balance with the soul faculties. Now the soul faculties—we have these bodies within us called the magnetic body and the electric body as part of the forms of nature. And so some of us find ourselves almost fully expressing emotionally, magnetically. Why, we become so so-called super-sensitive we can only sit in certain chairs and certain places. We can only have certain people talk to us at certain times. Sometimes when my students slip into the darkness of that great delusion, I ask them, "Just what in the—that I'm supposed to be doing?!" After forty some years I guess I'm not supposed to be sensitive, let alone have any emotion. Well, I can guarantee you I have plenty. I try to keep this magnetic body of mine in some degree of balance with this electrical side. So, only through that balancing can we fully enjoy life.

Now, when you accept all your experiences as effects—effects of your attitude, for that's what caused them in the first place—when you really accept that, you will find that you are, in that moment, freed from the magnetic pull, demand, and compulsion to have what you want when you want it, which means right now. I never met a person in their magnetic side of consciousness that didn't demand of the world that their desire be filled instantaneously. The reason that it be filled instantaneously is because they could not live with the frustrations of suppressed desires that they'd been entertaining for untold years. Patience, my friends. Let us be patient with our self. Let us know beyond a shadow of any doubt that to us all things are possible. But let's find out who the "us" is. You see, if I tell people to God all things are possible, they immediately put God out there and therefore, for them, it's not possible. So let us straighten out who "us" is—the infinite, eternal, free, formless, free Spirit called God, the Infinite Intelligence. That's what we really are. And so to that part of us, that which is, all things are possible.

It doesn't matter what your experience is today. It does not matter what your experiences were yesterday. If you really awaken within, all things are possible. Your little house can be repaired at any moment you choose it to be repaired. But if your faith in man and man's judgment is greater than your faith in the God that flows through you, then you will ever and forever be limited by your own beliefs. I am not one that ever believed that doctors or any of these so-called great scientists have some great mystic, some direct pipeline to God himself. I've never believed that.

A few years ago in our annual forecast, it was given that the day is dawning when everything from toilet paper to toothpaste will be blamed for cancer. That was given three years ago.

I've found and took an interest in yesterday's news when they revealed that the research back East had finally proven that coffee was now the cause of cancer, certain types, of course. And so I enjoyed my coffee more fully. *[Many in the congregation laugh.]* Because I really do know that as we believe, we become. And I do know that to God within us all things are possible.

When we believe in the mental realm of consciousness, we know fear. In this philosophy, it's called negative faith. The great magnet of the human mind of which the lady is speaking, that *is* the magnet of the mental world. And as Job said, "The thing I fear the most has befallen me." Why does the thing I fear the most befall me? Because this great, formless power flowing through me is under the control of what I choose. If I choose to direct this great power to the human mind, to the mental realm, then I shall be controlled and the victim of what creation has to offer: the Law of Duality.

My friends, whatever your experience of the moment may be, you have the right to choose. That is your divine birthright. You may continue to choose to direct the great power to the mental realms and pay the price known as payment and attainment. Or you may direct that great, infinite power to the source from whence it is flowing. But that takes the divine will called total acceptance, that takes the divine love known as total consideration.

I assure you if you will give that smallest of all gifts—it's called the gift of self—you will receive all that can fill your heart with joy and abundant goodness. And what is this great gift, so microscopic that we have such a difficult time in the very thought of giving it up? Why, my friends, it is nothing more than the warehouses that are filled to overflowing with the judgments this *[Mr. Goodwin points to his brain.]* has created in its days of darkness. We cannot receive that which we desire because our cup is overflowing with what we hold on to. To empty your cup that it may be constantly filled, does not mean giving gold to God, for God, the infinite, formless, free, Spirit, doesn't have any need. That's not what it means. It means giving all that you're holding in consciousness, all that has passed, whether it's ten years or ten minutes ago. If you empty out those warehouses, I assure you, you will have the abundant good as your mind could never dream possible.

Thank you.

APRIL 5, 1981

Church Questions and Answers 15

As our chairman has already stated, this is our time for your question-and-answer period, once a month. So if you will be so kind as to raise your hand, I will be happy to share our understanding with you.

Yes, the gentleman in the aisle, please.

Of what value does Serenity find in the gift of tongues? And, also, what place would speaking in tongues have in a Spiritualist church?

Yes, indeed, it's a very interesting question. What value do we see, if any, in the speaking of tongues? And what place does it have in a Spiritualist church, if we do find value? Many instances in history record these so-called speaking in tongues. There are religions in our world today who are based upon that very phenomena. The Spiritualist organization and the National Spiritualist Association of Churches is not based on that particular phenomena.

So often we hear the speaking in tongues and the listener has no understanding of what the communication, if any, is all about. The speaking in tongues, if it is genuine, is a phase of mediumship of which the Spiritualist organization is well versed. If, however, there is not proper interpretation, then it can be of no benefit to the channel through whom it is coming or to the listener. Ofttimes it is the attempt of decarnated souls, still residing in astral realms, who are yet to gain sufficient control of their minds to concentrate and put across to our world a clear, intelligent conversation. Therefore, it is not in the best interest of anyone to make themselves receptive to what has been known by many investigators as pure gibberish.

Now let us stop and think, my friends. If someone is conversing with you, here in this earth realm, and you do not understand what they are talking about, then what benefit can it be to you? There is, however, a speaking in tongues which can be interpreted and which does serve a most beneficial purpose. The sadness in the unfolding of mediumship, in its very early stages, is that our minds have a tendency to accept whatever communication comes through simply because it's a communication. Now we certainly would not stay on the telephone and listen to a conversation simply because it's a conversation. We would very soon exercise some degree of self-control and hang up the receiver. I do hope that's helped with your question.

Thank you.

You're welcome. The gentleman here, please.

I understand that the human body produces vibrations that are called electrical and electromagnetic. I was wondering regarding the cause and effect of electromagnetic compared to electrical.

We understand in this philosophy, the Living Light Philosophy, that man's conscious mind releases from his aura electrical impulses that can be registered and have been scientifically investigated for many years. We also understand that his emotional body, his feelings, release from his aura magnetic vibrations, which attract to us the very things that we, emotionally, experience.

Now I would like to clarify that for a moment. It is stated by Job that the thing we fear the most has befallen us. I am sure that we all accept the demonstrable truth that fear is not a conscious function. I'm sure we will all agree that fear is an emotional reaction based upon the seeming unknown. Now fear, being the very king of our feelings, our emotions, attracts to us the thing that we fear the most, for it is the realm of the magnetic field of our own aura. This philosophy teaches and demonstrates that our electrical vibration must become balanced with our magnetic vibration, that our conscious thought, in which the faculty of reason resides, must cast its light upon our feelings and our emotions, which are based solely, wholly, and completely upon past experience.

I'm sure we all understand that judgment in the human mind is not possible without the foundation of past experience. So we clearly see that whenever we make a judgment, that we have based that upon what we have already experienced in this limited earth experience. No judgment has in it the light of reason, for no judgment has in it total consideration. Therefore, my friends, whenever we permit our minds to experience and to express judgment, we are flowing in the magnetic field; we guarantee the principle of fear to return to us the very thing that we judge, the very thing that we fear. This, of course, is in keeping with the teaching that our adversities become our attachments, for our adversities in life are based upon past experience and express through judgment. Therefore, they return to us through the magnetic field of our aura.

Our electrical vibration, which is emanated by our conscious thought, by our faculty of reason, once balanced with the magnetic field, we will experience the peace that passeth all understanding, for that is where neutrality, that is where God truly exists. God is not magnetic and God is not electric. God is the perfect, neutral balance between the poles of opposite. A god that is either magnetic or electric is a god of creation, for that is duality, that is the pair of opposites that only exist in what the Hindu philosophers have called the world of *maya*. For man to experience the abundant good and the joy that is his true divine birthright in entering this earth realm, he must make the conscious, moment-by-moment effort to balance his electric and magnetic vibration in order to flow in the divine flow and the principle of what we call God. And in so doing we will truly fulfill the purpose of our journey here on earth. I hope that's helped with your question. Thank you.

The gentleman in the back, please.

What laws govern the science of numerology? And would the speaker cite or recommend a book on the subject?

In reference to the laws governing the science of numerology, I can only say that mathematics is not only the key to the universe, it is the very lock itself that opens the door to reason, which will transfigure all of us. For mathematics is the principle of perfect balance. Numerology, as it is known in our world today, is not based upon the true principle of mathematics, but is based upon superstition and the magnetic field of emotion. Therefore, unfortunately we do have the experiences in our world today of what is known as self-prophecy.

In order to understand the laws governing anything, whether it is numerology, astrology, or phrenology, we must first demonstrate the law inside of our self. We cannot understand what we have not first accepted, and we cannot first accept what we do not make an effort to understand. Therefore, man is a law unto himself. And being a law unto himself, he must ask the question, "What am I doing with the law that I am?"

Our bodies are known to be the temple of the living Spirit or God. We have a responsibility to the Divinity that is expressing through this temple, that is risen from creation. When we demonstrate, through daily effort, a balance between our sense functions and our soul faculties, we will begin to understand the principle of mathematics, and in so understanding the principle, we will have no problem in recognizing and accepting the scientific basis of the science of numerology. I hope that's helped with your question. Thank you.

The lady here in the front row, please.

Class tape 160 [CC 160] *speaks of controlling the air we breathe through the control of the air centers, which are in the neck. I'd like to know where it is, if the purpose of controlling it is for controlling our thought.*

Thank you very much. It is not possible physically, psychologically, mentally, or spiritually to entertain a thought without the motion of air through the system. If a person is interested in improving their life, if a person is truly interested in demonstrating personally their divine birthright of abundant good in their life, then we must first demonstrate the greatest power we will ever know. And the greatest power we will ever know is available to us through what is called concentration: placing the mind, which is a vehicle for our soul, pointedly and fixedly upon the object of our choice until only the essence remains. If we cannot or will not make the effort to control our breath, then it is of no benefit to attempt to control our thought, to control our mind.

We all know that we would not permit our automobiles to dictate to us when they want to go, where they want to go, when they want to stop, and when they want to do something else, for they are a tool that we have designed to serve us. And when they do not serve us in keeping with our judgments, we become upset and we're not happy. That's the way our emotions react to tools that we have designed.

Now our minds are not us, for we, in truth, are eternal. We are formless, free spirit. That that is formless and that that is free is above and beyond the limit and changes of evolution, for it is the essence of life itself. We know that our minds are in a constant process of change. We do not think exactly the same way we did a year ago. We don't entertain exactly the same thoughts or feelings. We are aware that our minds are changing. Some of those changes we judge we like. Many of those changes we judge we do not like, but they are happening anyway. Whether we like them or not, we are evolving. Even our physical bodies are evolving; we call that aging. It doesn't matter what you call it. All things in creation must return by the Law of Creation to that which gave them birth; [it also] gives them death. Birth and death are creation. They are only creation, for they are limit and they are form. He who lives in creation must pay the price of birth and death, whether or not it is a birth of a thought or it is the death of a feeling. Therefore, a wise man does not become attached to creation, for he knows the attachment to the Law of Duality, the attachment to form, which is birth, death, and change, guarantees pain and suffering.

So, we look at this Law of Duality. We look at form and we look at creation. And we see the true intent of our divine, eternal being: to be in it (creation) and never a part of it, to be with creation and ever free from it. For creation is a tool. It is dual. It is limited. It is born and it dies. It changes and it suffers. That is not what we are. We have never been, we will never be creation. It is like our automobile, designed by the Infinite Architect to be used, not abused. We abuse things, like creation, our minds, our bodies, and the things that we make, we abuse them by improper use. When we awaken to that error of ignorance, we will begin to use creation the way it was designed to be used: as a vehicle for our eternal soul to express on this particular planet. When we believe we are the body, we suffer the pains of the body, for the body is creation. When our hair is golden and it turns to gray, we suffer and we try to prevent or change the natural process of creation. How foolhardy we are to run uphill only to slide down again. That is not life; it is experience. Our life, and all things around us, is beautiful when we make the concerted effort to see the principle of life and not the effect of life.

And so in keeping with your question, when we make the effort to control our breath, we will control our thought. And then this vehicle, designed for our soul to express through, will move where our soul inspires it to move. It will do what our eternal being knows that it should be doing. It will no longer be the captain nor the master of our destiny. And we will see clearly the path before us, not concerned of that which has passed. For he who is concerned with that which has passed lives in a realm of delusion. You can only call it forth like a shadow before you. You cannot change it, but it can change you. Thank you.

Yes, the lady in back, please. Yes.

Would you please explain the left path and the right path referred to in Spiritualism?

All things in which we insist on being attached have two paths, for we can only attach to creation. It is not possible to attach to that which is formless and free. We are the formless and the free spirit; that is what we are. But we have permitted our minds to dictate who we are, what we are, and why we are. And so our minds, being in control, have before them the path of form. That path is the left path of that which has been or the right path of that which is to be. But then between the left path of yesterday and the right path of tomorrow, there is the divine path of the eternal moment of now. That is the path of neutrality. It has no thought nor interest for that which has been. It is not concerned with that which is to be, for it already knows that which is. And so it is stated when our hindsight becomes our foresight, we will in truth gain insight. Thank you.

Yes, the lady in the aisle, please.

Who is the agent of days?

Would you repeat your question, please?

Who is the agent of days?

In reference to that question, which has been covered many times in occultism, I do not feel that it would be of a general interest to our congregation today. I do realize you understand. Thank you.

Yes, the lady in the back, please.

Could you please explain duty?

Duty. Yes indeed. Duty. We'll begin with a soul faculty inseparable from gratitude. Inseparable. Without gratitude, duty cannot express, for duty is based upon the Law of Personal Responsibility. When we are not grateful for what we are, then we do not see, nor can we recognize if we did see, our duty in life. We desire constantly, for desire is the divine expression. But when our mind, composed of the elements of creation, registers desire, then the light from whence it comes goes out, and we are blinded by what we think we need. When we are not awakened to the faculty of duty, then we do not see what is. We live in what we think we need based upon what we thought we had. Man cannot experience need until he judges what he had. Therefore, duty does not live in yesterday and does not serve in tomorrow. Duty is this moment. Duty is a faculty, and it is in the light of reason.

When we gain control of our mind and we consciously choose our thought—for when we consciously choose our thought, we consciously establish the laws governing our lives. It is when we no longer consciously choose our thought that our feelings seem to rise spontaneously from the emotions and experiences and judgments of yesterday. It is stated in this philosophy that gratitude is the door through which abundant good doth flow, that if we are grateful for the crumb of life, that Law of Gratitude will guarantee us the abundant loaf. And that works hand in hand with duty and is known to man as personal responsibility.

We always get in life what we really want. We ofttimes don't think we do, because what we wanted last year we no longer want this year. We've even forgotten that we even wanted it at all. Stop, pause, and think more deeply and we will see these multitudes of experiences that we encounter are in keeping with the laws that we alone have established. But we have changed in many ways from the years that have gone, and we no longer recall, "Oh, yes. I had that desire ten years ago." And here it is being fulfilled today—fulfilled in principle, not in form. This is why we are blind to the law that is ever in our hands. Here we are this moment, forgetting the laws we've set into motion, disturbed and upset because things are not going our way. But they are going our way; it just took the law a long time to return, and we forgot we wanted this and we wanted that. But if we are honest with our self, we will quickly see, "I did want that, but not the way I'm getting it." So, you see, my friends, we always get what we really want.

It's like if we live in the cold and we want to move to California, where we judge that it is warm. And finally the day dawns, circumstances and conditions help give us a push and we end up in a warmer climate. And we're not happy because we got there not the way we wanted to get there, but we did get there. So let us really be honest with our self and let us see, "Yes, I did get what I really wanted."

It's like a woman, she wants to get married. Now there's a lot of desires along with the marriage. It comes as a whole package. Sometimes a whole warehouse cannot be large enough to contain the desires. But the principle is there. So she wants to get married. So she gets married. The honeymoon sometimes is a little longer, a little bit shorter, depends upon our judgments, of course. But she gets married. The days pass, and slowly, but surely, she begins to awaken—or he begins to awaken—or they both begin to awaken—and realize they wanted to be married, but not that way. *[Some in the congregation laugh.]* Now that has nothing to do with the principle desire of being married. That has an awful lot to do with judgment, but it has nothing to do with the law that the individual established. They did get married; it's what they wanted. Now what they did with what they wanted is something else.

A little boy can get a new, red fire engine for Christmas, and the day after Christmas it's all smashed and destroyed. And so he's all upset, but he did want the fire engine. He did get the fire engine. He just never took care of it.

So, you see, my friends, let us enjoy life and let us accept the demonstrable truth, whether we like it or not, of personal responsibility. Because, in so doing, we no longer are the victim, the slave, and in bondage to that which we think is our God. Let us accept personal responsibility and let the God within us free us. Let us have no desire greater than the Power that brings us truth.

Thank you.

JUNE 7, 1981

Church Questions and Answers 16

As our chairman has already stated, this is the time of the month when you have the opportunity to ask your questions of general interest. So if you will be so kind as to raise your hand with your question, I will reach as many people as time will permit.

The gentleman here, please.

How can one use mind to discriminate in living everyday life without also judging?

The question is very well put. How can one use the mind in their daily activities to discriminate, I believe the word was, without judging? Well, first of all, discrimination is a function of judgment. So one must learn to discern to be freed from judgment. Now to discriminate is to limit the Law of Possibility, for it is a limit of the vehicle of mental substance. To discern, being a soul faculty, has total consideration. Not only does it contain total consideration, but it contains the indispensable ingredient known as understanding. Whenever we understand anything, there is no judgment. There is, however, discernment. For it is our divine birthright to choose the path that we find before us. Of course, the path being ever in keeping with the laws that we alone have established.

Because man is an eternal being, because man is spirit, formless and free, because he is that eternal being, he can reach a state of consciousness in an eternal moment, known as the moment of now. It is only when we use the function of the mind that we are limited. It is only when we use the function of the mind that we judge, because in the function of the mind is the function of review. We look at our eternal moment and base it upon that which has already been. It is when we base our eternity on what has been that we discriminate, that we judge. We understand that God, the divine, neutral, infinite Intelligent Energy, is not a judge, that judgment exists only in creation. It only exists in the function of the mind and is totally dependent upon experiences that have already happened.

How does man, then, keep himself free from judgment, which is bondage? How does man discern and not dictate? How does man choose and not discriminate? [It is] very simple, my friends. It is only when our mind entertains the thought of I— not the I which we truly are, but the thought of I. When we permit our mind to entertain the thought of I, we are then subject to, bound by, and dependent upon that which has already happened in our evolution. That is the great trap of creation. That is when man no longer is master of his ship. That is when the tools no longer serve the worker. That is when the worker begins to serve the tool.

The mind is a vehicle, an instrument of form, of the laws of mental substance subject to the dual laws of creation. In the mind, you cannot have right, without wrong. In the mind, you cannot have light, without darkness. Man, however, can move in the eternal moment of now to realms of consciousness above and beyond the dual laws of payment and attainment and, in so doing, truly experience his divine birthright. The first step on the downward path is not the I of eternity; it is the thought of the I of individuality. I do hope that's helped with your question. Thank you.

Yes, the lady here, please.

Yes. It seems that the aura on certain individuals extends farther out than others. Can you explain the nature of the aura and what it is?

We understand that man, like the insect, the ant, and all creatures, lives within a sphere that he calls aura. It is a radiation from his inner being. It is changed in vibration and in color and in sound dependent upon the obstruction through which the energy must emanate from the source within. Now there are no limits to what is possible for the being that we are—not the being that we think we are, but the being that we truly are. Limitation is totally dependent upon mental substance. Physical substance moves by the laws of mental substance, for physical substance is the effect of mental substance. Therefore, mental substance has a higher vibratory rate of expression than physical substance. And so on, 'til we finally go to the source that we are within. The aura of varying animals and people is limited by the mental activity through which the emanation must pass out into the universe.

The scientists, most of them, have finally accepted—that is, the physical scientists—the existence of [an] electromagnetic field that man has, for untold centuries, called the aura. He has photographed it and accepted its varying color. He has yet to accept its varying sound. Now, my friends, you cannot have what you call color without sound, and you cannot have what you call sound without color, for, in truth, they are one and the same.

This philosophy clearly teaches that man is a law unto himself, that everything that happens to us is, indeed and in truth, caused by us. To attempt to work on the effects of the law is a total waste of one's energy. Therefore, when we accept that whatever is taking place is the effect of what we alone, in our errors of ignorance, have set into motion, we will once again not only declare our divine birthright, but experience it.

The tendency of our mind is to blame outside for the unwillingness to grow inside. The reason that that is a tendency of all mental substance is very simple: the mind, by its very nature, gathers, garners, and holds not only physical and material substance, but mental substance. The greatest difficulty for the human mind is to give up a thought that it cherishes. Even greater is the difficulty for the human mind to change a judgment that it has made. The reason for that is quite simple: mind and mental substance is totally, wholly, and completely dependent upon the divine energy not only for its sustenance, but for its continuity. It knows that if you, as an eternal being, change your thought or your judgment that it will die, for it does not contain the eternal source which you are. Therefore, when you permit your mind to entertain the illusion known as the thought of I, in that moment you direct infinite, eternal, neutral, intelligent Energy to all the experiences and judgments that you have ever had. And in that moment you support, sustain, and maintain the forms that your mind has created in days long ago.

A simple teaching is, "When we harbor a thought, we are feeding a form," for thought cannot exist in a world of creation without form, for it is dependent upon limit for its very existence. This is why, my friends, that that is truly us is formless and that is why it is free. Anything that is form has birth and death. The greatest trauma we will ever face is the trauma we have faced before and have long forgotten: the trauma of shedding one of the bodies through which our eternal being is expressing. If in the passing from this dimension we entertain the thought of I, we find our bondage from our attachment from that which has been and we hover in what is known as the Shadowland. There we see the forms, and there we live. In different philosophies they are known as different realms, but it is in keeping with the law of what we alone are setting into motion. It is the thought of I that is the chain of bondage, known in Eastern philosophies as attachment to the fruits of action.

We have difficulty—and this in keeping with the question on auras—we have difficulty with our work, we have difficulty with taking orders because we are so busy taking orders from realms we alone have created and are no longer aware of. My friends, show me a person who believes they are under great time pressure and I will show you a person whose desires are by the billions and I will show you a person who makes no effort of self-control. For it is the uncontrollable thoughts and desires of our mind bombarding the door of our consciousness that we call time pressure. And so it is, whatever it is that you desire, give the desire back to the source that you have stolen it from, for desire is the expression of the Divinity. We make it the devil when we judge it is ours.

The moment we judge we own or possess, in that moment do we become the victim of that that we think we possess. Instead of it serving the purpose for which it has been designed, we begin to serve it. We know when the tool no longer serves us. We know when we begin to serve it. All we have to do is pause and think. When we tell our car to move and it's broken and will not work, whether or not we are in control, whether or not the car is a tool to serve us or we have become the tool of serving it, is revealed in the degree of emotional trauma when we want something to do something and it doesn't do what we want it to do. If we have permitted our self to be the victim, we know from moment to moment. It is such a simple, demonstrable truth.

All of us have the tools of creation. In fact, many of us have so many tools of creation that over 90 percent of those tools are serving no purpose at all; they're in cold storage. And we don't yet have enough sense to move them on so that that which would serve us well may enter our life. It's known as our cup overfloweth. And when the cup overfloweth, the good that is waiting for you is poured into the cup and runs on to someone else, for that is the law. We cannot change it because it is not a law of creation. It is an immutable law of the Divine.

And so let us be more interested, not in whether our aura, from bringing control to our mind, extends five feet or five inches. The demonstration in life is always the revelation. But let us be interested in how we, in this moment through some very simple, daily effort, can improve our life.

How interesting it is to note whether or not, when we are someplace, whether we are sleepy or awake. It is always dependent, of course, on where our thoughts are drifting. And those of us who have drifting thoughts can be rest assured, can be rest assured we are serving something; we don't know what, but we're drifting here and there and everywhere.

My friends, when we think we sleep, we are not sleeping, for we have yet to learn what sleep is. We have yet to learn that simple truth. Most of us think we close our eyes and we wake up miserable or we wake up feeling good. And we think we have no control over how we're going to feel when we open our eyes from what we think is sleep. And indeed that is the demonstration of the masses today. They awaken and sometimes they feel great and sometimes they feel terrible. Sometimes they feel encouraged when they awake and usually they feel discouraged, "My God, another day!" What is taking place while we think we're sleeping?

We know, if we have studied and we have made the effort to awaken within, that our eternal being is expressing through nine vehicles or bodies in this the moment of now. We, unless we make the effort to awaken within, have no conscious awareness of which body is active at any given moment, for we have yet to make the effort to become aware of what thoughts that we are thinking. How many of us can recall the first thought that we entertained at the moment of so-called awakening this morning? It is indeed a rare person who can recall what was their first thought, let alone the second or third. I assure you, my friends, that so-called sleep is designed by the Infinite Architect not for the lapse of consciousness, but for the awakening of consciousness. Our body, for the sake of our good health, does not require the hours of so-called sleep. It requires minutes of total consciousness for total rejuvenation. And what we are experiencing in what we call sleep is really the thing we shudder at the very thought of, for we are working very hard in many dimensions serving the forms of creation that we have [not], from the lack of effort, taken control of.

There is no freedom without discipline, for there is no freedom without self-control. You see, my friends, either we control the self or the self controls us. And the choice is very simple. Every moment we have that divine choice. We experience many things that we enjoy and we experience many more things that we don't enjoy. That's when we know whether or not we are controlling the self or the self is controlling us. Now if we have had sufficient experience in what that vehicle called self has done to us, then we will have value on what we will do, finally, to it. For it is created by our mind and our mind is designed to serve a good and useful purpose. But remember, our mind, like any mind, like all creation, is a robot. It does only what it has been programmed to do. It is limited by the programming you have allowed it in your evolution. You can reprogram it. You can expand your consciousness, but it is not the easy step if you are attached to the fruits of action. If your mind entertains the illusion known as the thought of I, then reprogramming of the human computer, the robot known as mind, is then most difficult.

However, we are given that opportunity each and every day. We know how we react to our acts. We know from our own experiences if we blame outside for the lack of effort inside. No one has to tell us whether or not we blame outside for what we're doing inside. All we have to do is pause a moment and we all know where we are and we all should know where we're going. For if you know what you're doing this moment, you can be rest assured there is no question about the next moment. We have time for another question.

Yes, the lady here, please.

I'd like to ask a question about—sometimes we see people and there is a light about them. And it may not necessarily be a spiritual light. It may be a light of fascination, but there is a very strong pull. And sometimes people see us that way, too. Would you give me your understanding of this light?

Thank you very much. I'm sure we will all agree the light we see is the reflection of the light within. It may be the light of the twilight zone of the shadows or it may be the eternal light of truth, but it is the light we see without [that] is the light that's glowing within, in keeping, of course, with the great demonstration of personal responsibility. If we find in our experiences in life, as we look around the world of creation and we see the shadowy light of fascination, then we know, in those moments, where we are. For, my friends, the good in life is the good we are. When we allow it to shine within us, it returns unto us. And as someone has once said that, of course, that goes around comes around. This is why we all know where we are. We all really do. We all know whether or not the light we see is the light of fascination, the glow of creation, or the eternal flame of truth, for it is a mirror that is reflecting back to us. But he who sees the goodness in all, experiences the God within. For there is no right or wrong to that which is neutral and divine.

The glow of fascination is only the pause before the victory of the realms of imagination. It is only that we got lazy before we walked through the door of victory. Because, you see, my friends, you cannot enter the spiritual realms of consciousness without passing through the realms of creative imagination. And you cannot enter the realms of creative imagination until you pass through the realms of fascination. So we have paused when we are in that shadowy world of fascination and we have paused too long, and because we have paused too long, we have become the victim of the forms we have created. And we are there serving those forms until we once again stand up and we exercise the lord of our universe known as the will power. For all things to man are possible when man directs his will and that that he has directed it to, he does not, from the realms of fascination, begin to serve.

We create many things with our minds. Constantly we are the creators. All of life reveals to us that we, mankind, we are the creators. And so we create many forms, but let them be forms that work and are constructive and accomplish some good in life. To have a thought is to create a form, for it is the Law of the Realm of Thought. Now if you have a thought of goodness, you may say you see no form. But all of the many forms created from the thought of goodness, they come knocking at your door. If you do not see them, that is your evolution. Someday you will, for it is guaranteed in keeping with universal, divine law. But are they going to serve you? You have created them. Or will you be their victim and serve them? You are their parent. So ask a parent; they are the instruments through which the child is born to creation, through which the soul enters. Do they nurse and serve the baby? Do they continue to do that when they're 20, 30, 40, 50, 60? No, we don't want to do that, for we see by the animals in creation it is contrary to the law of nature. Even the mother bear drives her cubs out, for she has that much intelligence.

And so we, being creators through which the divine spark enters, and we have the child. And it grows up and we make a judgment: it's time they went to work. It's time they did something for themselves. We begin to awaken within. Hopefully before it's too late and we're in the bondage and slavery of the form that has been created. We, as parents—for no one is exempt from parenthood. You are the mother or the father of a thought and a form. That is the law. No man made it. It is the Law of Mental Substance. Therefore, all people, all creatures are creators, are mothers and fathers. What will we do with the children we have created who are now adults by the thousands that we are still serving? For by us serving them, they are not serving the purpose for which they have been designed. That, my friends, is known as quitting at the gate of victory, locked in the realms of fascination.

Thank you.

JULY 5, 1981

Church Questions and Answers 17

As our chairman has stated, if you have questions of a general interest, you will be so kind [as] to raise your hand, I will be more than happy to share our understanding with you.

Yes, the lady here, please.

Would you speak on how to balance the mental and the spiritual world?

Thank you very much. The lady's question is in reference to balancing our mental and spiritual world. I am sure we are all very familiar with the many things we find our self attached to. We must remember, my good friends, that whatever in life that we identify with, we establish the Law of Attachment. We cannot be attached, of course, to anything that we do not identify with, for what we do not identify with, we are not bound by.

In balancing our mental world with our spiritual world, we first must understand that our mental world is totally and completely dependent upon our identification with it. It is known in many philosophies as the thought of I, the over-identification with what is known as self. We must ask our self, then, "What is self?" When we ask that question, "Who am I? And what am I?" the first thing that rises in our consciousness are those things which we have already identified with. And so it is that the obstructions along our path in life are the things that we have identified with. That that is past is passed only when we permit it to be.

So often as we face the seeming new experiences in life, we find a direct relationship with those experiences to experiences that have long passed in our life. But we call them forth, these shadows, and once again experience similar events; that is taking place by the Law of Identification. Man has, at any given moment, the divine right of choice. He may choose the eternal moment known as the present and in so doing, [in] that state of consciousness and that state of consciousness only can he establish for himself new laws to reap a better harvest than he has already experienced. That takes daily effort.

So often along the spiritual path to bring about a balance between the formless and free, which is known as the Spirit, and the bondage of creation, which is known as the world of form, we find great difficulty and much discouragement. But we must also remember that discouragement, a sense function, a function of the human mind, rises up to protect and to defend the events and experiences of yesterday which we insist upon being identified with. It is because we identify that we hold and we bind. And we find in our lives, many times, there are things we would like to be freed from. The principle of identification is not limited. When we find our self over-identified with anything, we have established the Law of Over-identification with anything that brings interest into our life. And so it is that our attachments in our life, sooner or later they become our adversities in order to bring about the eternal freedom which is our divine birthright.

We have a simple saying in this philosophy that clearly states to put God in it or to forget it. Now it is indeed human to forgive, but we must remember that it is divine to forget. The human instrument is designed to record, to gather, and to garner all things unto itself. And therefore, it is not within the power nor the possibility of the human mind to forget. We must rise in consciousness and be free from the identification to creation or form to express our divinity, which is to forget. Because without forgetting, we cannot truly be free or ever experience the truth that brings us the heaven which is our birthright. I do hope that's helped with your question. Thank you.

The gentleman over here, please.

The thought of I. How do you get away from that, in applying discipline to get to concentration and peace eventually?

In reference to the question, How do we free our self from the thought of I and establish discipline that we may experience concentration, which is, of course, the key to all power? First, we understand, hopefully, or make the effort to understand that it is not the I, but only the thought of I that is the delusion that is created by the human mind. Now it is the thought, not the I, which is the eternal being, but it is the thought of it, which is created of mental substance, which gives unto the person the form. For we cannot have a thought without creating a form. All thought is the very substance from which form is created. First, it must exist in a mental world to be experienced in a physical world.

And so on the path of self-discipline, for only in the control of the self can we ever be freed from the self, which is the thought of I. We cannot be freed from anything that we cannot first control. Therefore, self-control, self-discipline, personal responsibility are inseparable. When man first becomes aware of what the so-called thought of I or self is offering to his life—first, we must become aware, because we cannot control what we are not aware of. And we must have self-control in order to experience the truth and freedom which is our birthright.

Now the thought of I is the very substance from whence the self is created. Self means, in this philosophy, separation. That which we separate from we are no longer a part of. Therefore, when we entertain the thought of I, we create the self-image. What has taken place in truth is a separation from the divine Infinite Intelligence—a separation only in consciousness, not a separation in essence, for it is the divine Infinite Intelligence that is sustaining even the thought that we entertain in consciousness. We make the effort to become aware of the self—we're already aware of the thought of I. We become aware of the self and in so doing, we slowly, but surely, gain control over it. Once having gained control over the self, we may place it in its proper perspective in our life and, in so doing, be freed from the bondage, the struggles, the disasters, and the limitation that self has to offer. Thank you. I hope that's helped with your question.

The gentleman in the next row, please.

To my understanding in this philosophy we are supposed to educate our desires. OK.

Or fulfill them.

Or fulfill them. All right. Well, I want you to explain or give me a definition for denial and also a definition for discipline and the correlation, if there is any, between the two.

Thank you very much. In reference to your question concerning the correlation, if any, between denial and discipline, discipline, if it is discipline, does not deny. It does not deny the right of expression of the desires entertained by our mind. It simply places them under the light of reason and puts them in their proper perspective. Now discipline has, as part of its expression, all of the soul faculties, especially the faculty of consideration. Denial does not contain the faculty of consideration. Denial is based upon experiences that we have already encountered in our life. It is totally dependent upon past experiences and judgments that have been formed from them. There is a vast difference between discipline and denial.

The things in life that we deny, we guarantee to experience. For we direct infinite, intelligent Energy to the form of our denial and as like attracts like and becomes the Law of Attachment, we guarantee the very experience. For what we have done, by our denial, is placed our self in consciousness above and beyond the right of the infinite Eternal Intelligence, known as God, to sustain all form, all thought, and all life.

If you have confused discipline with denial, then you have yet to experience discipline, for in discipline there are no denials. There is simply organization under the light of reason, which, of course, is inseparable and dependent upon the soul faculty of understanding. Consequently, when man makes the effort to understand himself, he knows beyond a shadow of any doubt the desires that he entertains in consciousness, the ones that are filled with consideration, the ones that will not only benefit himself, but by so benefiting himself will benefit others around and about him. Because we must remember, my friends, God helps those who help themselves by helping others, for God works through man, never directly to man. And so it is the stone the builder rejects becomes the cornerstone. For, you see, my friends, when we seek from God and we deny the channel through which that which we are seeking is flowing, then we have, in that moment, denied God's right of expression. Discipline, self-control, personal responsibility are indispensable to truth and freedom. Without them there cannot be, for us, in our consciousness either truth or freedom.

By having discipline in our life, we become aware of the self. And remember, desire is the divine expression. Desire is the expression of God, the Infinite Intelligence. It is what man does with the principle of desire that causes the problems in life. Man's mind experiences this wonderful flow of goodness or God in his life, and then he forms and limits how that goodness will be maintained and its experience will be continued. It is man's mind that causes the problems with the divine expression known as desire. It is not desire in and of itself. Desire entertained in the minds of men is the blindness of the world. It is the blindness because it dictates how it will fulfill itself. In the moment that it dictates, in the moment that the mind forms the principle of desire, in that moment is man bound by the law that he alone has established. Because he has stolen the essence, known as desire, the divine expression, from God, it must be returned. And because man, having experienced the goodness of desire, because his mind has taken it and has stolen it, that is where the payment is. For in the dictate of how, when, where, and what will fulfill it, in that judgment and in that dictate does man pay the price of the human functions of the mind. For in that moment of judgment, there are no soul faculties; there are only the functions of the mind. There is no wisdom of patience. There is no consideration. There is no love. There is no understanding. There is no duty or personal responsibility. That is why man lives in a world of creation known as payment and attainment.

When man rises in consciousness to the heavenly realms which are waiting for him in this moment—remember, my friends, heaven is here and heaven is now. If it is not within your thinking of possibility for the here and now, then you must pay the price hereafter. Because if your heaven is something that you believe you will experience upon changing your suit of clay, I can assure you from forty-some years of experience in those realms that is not what takes place. Our mind goes with us. It is a vehicle through which our soul is expressing. It is the same mind after we leave earth as it was the moment before we left earth. So unless we prepare our self for changing our suit of clay, then we will, by the very law established, the Law of Procrastination, then we will have to pay the price at the moment of going. We prepare our self for living by preparing our self for the illusion known as death.

You see, my friends—and this is in keeping with your question—everything that has form has birth. And everything that has form has death. Our thoughts are born, and our thoughts in time, they die. And so our bodies, they're born, they're formed, and they die, for that is the Law of Creation. We suffer and we pay the price as long as we are attached to creation. The teaching of old is quite simple: be in creation and never a part of creation; be with a person, place, or thing and never a part of a person, place, or thing. For all form goes through the process of birth and death. If we over-identify with our bodies, with our form, then I can assure you it is that attachment that is the pain when it's time to change our suit. It is only our mental attachment that is the suffering and the pain. We cry when we're born, and we cry when we die, but the crying is only the illusion that we are the suit we wear.

So often in our daily experiences we believe we are the thought that we have formed in our mind. Only moments later to form another thought and feel good. So here we are eternal; forever we have been; forever we will be. This is only one form, one suit of the many we have already worn and the many that we are yet to wear. To attach and over-identify with the form of which we permit our self at present to be aware is indeed a bondage, not designed by the Infinite Architect. It is an error in our thought that we have closed our minds and cannot see the universal, eternal whole which we truly are.

So, my friends, remember, from the Divine cometh the desire, and to the Divine it is destined to return. When we steal it, because we think it is ours, we pay the price. If we will accept the demonstrable truth that it entered our life to fulfill a purpose, that the purpose will be filled above and beyond the dictates of the human mind, that it is not necessary—in fact, it is extremely detrimental—to interfere in mental consciousness with the Divine expression. All things come and all things go, for things are form. We are more than form, for we are that that moves form. Let us not forget who we truly are. And if we will make that effort daily (not to forget who we truly are), then we will no longer pay the price tag of creation. Thank you. I hope that's helped with your question.

The lady at the back, please. Yes, please.

Long ago you made a short sentence. You said something that stuck with me and I can't remember how it goes, but it had to do with helping people and having it be a detriment. This is kind of . . .

Yes. Thank you. In reference to helping people, we must be still and honest with our self, for the motive of any intent, the motivating force will dictate the law that is established for us. Ofttimes we look out into the world and we see people in different straights. Some are hungry. Some are cold. Some are uneducated and some seem to have the wealth of a world of creation.

But we must pause in our thinking and in that moment, in that pause, enter the light of reason. We must see clearly the Law of Personal Responsibility. We have entered this earth realm, into earthly forms, in keeping with the evolutionary laws of life and according to the laws that we, in our previous lives, have established. We have come to this Earth, the planet of faith—the principle that governs the Earth planet—we have come here to once again face the lessons in life that we, putting it bluntly, have flunked before. Here, we have the opportunity to pass the grades of school that we are in here and now. If we do not make that effort, we guarantee the repetition of the lesson again, and again, and again.

So we look out into the world and we see the suffering and the struggle, but in that moment we must question the laws established. It is our duty to place our hand and help a soul that is sinking. It is our personal responsibility, if they are stronger than us, to save our own soul. That is our personal responsibility. And having accepted the personal responsibility of duty to one's own eternal being, we accept that right for others. Remember, we cannot grant to another what we have not first granted unto our self. If we have granted unto our self the Law of Personal Responsibility and we see the struggle of others, we are impressed often to help them to help themselves. If the effort is not being made by a person to help themselves, then we are instruments of misunderstanding and we only help them down, instead of up. It is one thing to feed a person until they have gained their strength to feed themselves. It is very detrimental to feed them until they are no longer able to feed themselves.

We must all face the responsibilities in our life. We do not help people by doing things for them. We help people in the sense that we are the living demonstration to show them the way. To do things for people does not serve a useful purpose, because by doing for them, we deny them their right to do for themselves.

A crutch is designed to help a person to strengthen their legs to walk again. Glasses are designed to help a person; they are not designed to take the place of our eyesight.

It is the abuses in life that cause the problems. It's not the uses in life. All things, all people are designed to serve a useful purpose. If things and people are not serving a useful purpose, then they are not beneficial to themselves, nor to others. Now we would not use a dinner knife for a screwdriver when we know that we have designed the dinner knife to serve the purpose for our dinner. But unfortunately in our life, ofttimes we abuse the thoughts that enter our mind. We do not use them to serve the purpose for which we truly desire them to do.

And so we help people by helping our self, for the physician must first heal themselves that they may be the living demonstration. We, by being the living demonstration, are a light into the world that they may see. But to do it for them is to deny their right to their goodness and their life. I hope that's helped with your question. Thank you.

Yes, the lady over here, please.

I understand that there is a saying in the Bible or something that it's not possible to serve God and mammon at the same time. Could you give your understanding of that, please?

Yes, there is that statement in the Bible. It is not possible to serve both. We all know that it's more than possible to experience both. For we all experience this old, mundane material world in which we're in, and no one can deny that there are moments they experience something above and beyond this old, mundane material world. If we recognize the cause and do not confuse it with the effect, then, my friends, we will not be bound by this mundane, material world, for we know beyond a shadow of any doubt that it is an effect; it is not a cause. That it comes and it goes and you never know when it's going and you never know when it's coming. And so it is that a wise man sees the world for what it is: an effect of his own creation.

This philosophy teaches a God that sustains all things—a sustaining, infinite, intelligent Energy. It teaches that man, the mental world, is the creator. We create our life. We are the creators of the thoughts we think, the experiences we have. Our health, our wealth, and our happiness is dependent upon our own efforts to control our own creations. But unfortunately we have, temporarily, forgotten that what we see out there is an effect of what we're doing in here. The most difficult thing in our growth through this earth realm, the most difficult thing to face, let alone to accept, is that all experiences are effects of our thought, that we can control what is outside by first controlling what is inside because what is inside is where it really is.

If a person enters your life and you decide, you judge that they are robbing you of your peace and harmony and your right to goodness, it is not the person that has entered your life: it is the law that you have established to call them forth. And compounded upon that, it is the law that you continue to live by that judges they're doing such and such to you. It all takes place in our own consciousness.

But we have deluded our self by the thought of I that it is taking place by someone else. That's not where it is. It never was there. It never will be there. Our lives, our goodness, our joy, our peace, our happiness, our abundant good is dependent upon what we have done with our thoughts, what we insist on doing with our thoughts and that's where it really is. Because it is our attitudes of mind, created by our thoughts, that establishes our vibration. It is our vibration that emanates out into the world and brings back into our life what we are sending out into it.

So if we don't like an experience, we know where to go. I can assure you, my friends, we quickly know where to go when we do like an experience. I tell you it takes but a split second for our egos to lap up all of the credit of how good this turned out and great that was because of what we had done. But, don't we see, the same law is working with all those negative experiences. It's identically the same law; the law didn't change. The experience changed because we changed our thoughts and that's what we sent out and that's what we got back.

Now stop and think of how qualified we all are. We are so qualified in the law. How clear: Man is a law unto himself. What are we doing with the law that we are?

Now we all know how we get all these experiences back, one disaster after another. Doesn't take any time at all. All we have to do is get into certain types of thinking and attitudes of mind and everything falls apart. One of my students told me here the other month it's called Murphy's Law. *[Many in the congregation laugh.]* [If] anything [can] go wrong, it goes wrong. But what a wonderful thing! That we have within us this great power that we can establish every disaster we could possibly desire, that we could have our marriages, our money, everything fall apart, that we could be without work, hungry, and cold. How beautiful it is that it only takes less than split seconds for us to establish those wonderful laws! *[The congregation laughs again.]*

Well, let's just direct it the other way. Now we all know we can do those beautiful things in the negative way. Let's turn it over and do it in a positive way. It's the same power at work. You know, God's not partial. The Infinite Intelligence is going to sustain your disasters just like He'll sustain your peace and harmony and abundant good. It's the same God, neutral, infinite and intelligent, that is supporting whatever it is you choose. You see, my friends—and it is time for me to go—but don't you see? It's that wonderful same God that's supporting everything!

Now, you want to choose disaster? Some need, emotional—you know, I know some people get a great charge if they're ready for the hospital. They think they've got cancer or go down the list of disasters. I've taught my students for many years: you show me one blade of grass that doesn't have cancer and I'll go over to the other side. Everything has cancer. Cancer is nothing but a name that some brains gave to the negative cells in form when they become predominant over the positive forms. That's all that it ever was. It's only recently we gave it this name tag. Think, my friends, that's all it is. So whether we like it or not, we're working with a delicate balance. Keep entertaining all the negative thoughts throughout life; they'll have an effect because they direct energy to the negative cells within us. So the more negative we are, the more we support the negative cells within and then, sooner or later, some great physician comes along and says, "Oh, you poor thing, you've got cancer." *[Again, some in the congregation laugh.]* We always had it; it's just starting to show. That's the only difference. The trees have it. The dogs have it. The cats have it. The ants have it. Even the cockroaches have it. That's the way it is in old creation.

There is no disaster unless for some psychological reason we have chosen that to make us feel good. Believe it or not, my friends, some people feel good if they have enough disasters in life. They feel good because people tell them what a terrible life they have and they receive this attention, don't you see? Now remember, feeling good is experiencing God. Man is choosing how he will let God in. Now if you have to go to the ball game to feel good, well, that's where you're experiencing your God. But why limit it to the ball game? You never know when they're going to strike. They just got back again. *[Many in the congregation laugh.]* So why would you want to limit God to a ball game? Or to a TV? Or to certain foods or anything else? You see, we're the ones limiting God. God didn't limit us. We have limited God's expression through us. We choose how we will let God in. Now we know what those experiences are, because we're the ones that created them. We know when we feel good, all right? So all we've got to do—we feel good, we say, "Ah, I just feel great! I feel really good! What did I do?" That's not what happens. You say, "Oh, look what somebody did for me." See? Not, "What did I do?" When you feel good, you've got to understand, my friends, that's when you let God in. Why limit goodness, or God, to the human mind that says such and such and such and such has got to happen? Your boss comes and says you did a good job, you got a $50-a-week raise. So you feel good. But why do you want to limit God to your employer? Think about it.

Thank you, friends.

AUGUST 2, 1981

Church Questions and Answers 18

As our chairman has just stated, whatever questions you may have of a general interest, you may feel free at this time to raise your hands and I will be happy to serve as the medium for these questions. And we will answer as many as time will permit. So if you will be so kind as to raise your hands, then I will come to you.

Yes, the lady, here, in the second row, please.

I would like to ask if you are born with guides and how you attract guides. And what about the forty-nine guides that some great teachers have?

Yes. Thank you. In reference to your question—when a person enters this earth realm, do they come with spiritual guides and teachers? And how does this teaching of the Living Light Philosophy of this church relate to the teachings of forty-nine guides of some philosophies?

Well, in reference to your first question, man, the eternal soul, is never alone. We have entered this Earth planet in keeping with the laws that we alone have established in evolution. Unfortunately, we are not aware of this evolutionary process. And the reason that most of us are not aware of it is because of over-identification with the earth realm.

Whatever man directs his attention to, his energy follows. And therefore, we become bound and blinded to the universe as a whole. We see a very small portion thereof. As our soul in its evolution entered this, the fifth planet in this particular solar system, here, granted the wonderful opportunity to awaken to the soul faculty of faith, he entered not alone, for man is never alone. Therefore, guides and teachers entered this realm with us in different dimensions. Guides and teachers, helpers—whatever we wish to call them—or ministering angels are attracted to us in keeping with the law that like attracts like and becomes the Law of Attachment. Now as we, in our interest in life, make varied changes, the guides and the teachers that have been attracted to us make similar changes or they go. That is ever in keeping with the demonstrable law.

In reference to the teachings of forty-nine guides, that is based upon the ancient teaching of seven planes of consciousness, based upon the ancient Babylonian theory of astrology, which knew of the seven-planet system. That is not the teaching of this church. We, our teachings, are of evolutionary incarnation, of the nine planes of consciousness and of the nine bodies in which we are truly expressing. So often in our over-identification with this physical, material world, we lose our awareness of the spiritual, the mental, the astral, and the cosmic worlds of which we are an indispensable part.

Man loses conscious awareness and he calls that sleep, but in that sleep, man does not lose consciousness. If man would make the effort to broaden his horizons by expanding the possibility of his identification, then man would be consciously aware while he sleeps. Because the only reason man is not consciously aware while he sleeps is simply because he is identified with a physical world in which he lives. And when he loses that identification, then he is blinded and knows that as sleep. Rejuvenation of our body is not dependent, and never was dependent, upon sleep. It is totally, wholly, and completely dependent upon a state of consciousness that we reach during what we call sleep. There, we are rejuvenated. It doesn't take an hour, six, seven, ten, or twelve. It's only a matter of minutes. So when man reaches that state of consciousness, commonly known in philosophies of the world, as the peace that passeth all understanding, then man will be totally rejuvenated and he will not have to concern himself about sleep, about so-called rest, and all these other things. I do hope that's helped with your question.

It did.

Thank you. The gentleman over here, please.

I was wondering if you would give your understanding of habit, the seeming good and bad habits.

Well, of course, I'm sure that we will all agree: nothing's either good or bad in eternity, but thinking makes it so. And as we change our thinking, so we change our view of what is good and what is bad. And so our goodness of today is not necessarily the goodness of what was yesterday. And our goodness of tomorrow will not necessarily be the goodness of which we judge good to be today. Therefore, goodness and its so-called opposite, the undeveloped good or what we refer to as bad, is totally dependent upon our own acceptance and rejection. Now our acceptances and rejections, we all understand, are dependent upon our own judgments, which in turn are dependent upon, unfortunately, our educated conscience. Now there is a vast difference between our educated conscience and our spiritual conscience. And that difference is, of course: one is the mental world which views life in a very limited, restricted way; the other is a spiritual realm which views the all of all.

In reference to what we call habit, they are nothing more and nothing less than patterns of mind established, maintained, and sustained by directed energy through the function of attention. The more attention we place upon anything, the more energy we direct to it. Unfortunately, what happens when we make choices in life and those choices are not under the soul faculty of reason, which will in truth transfigure us, we make what we think are choices [and] we make what we think are decisions, but they turn out to be judgments. Now judgment has limit. It has right and wrong. It has the function of creation. It has duality. It considers a very limited way. When we make what we think are decisions and they turn out to be judgments—we know the difference between a decision and a judgment because one ends up, in the final analysis, as freedom—that's called decision; the other ends up, in the final analysis, as judgment and that's called bondage. So we establish, by what we think is choice, a certain way of doing things.

For example, let us say something we're all familiar with: we establish a certain pattern of eating. Some of us, most of us, we eat very fast. We eat fast and we justify that that fast eating is necessary because we have so many things to do in life. Well, what that, of course, is dependent upon [is] the lack of control of the desires bombarding our own mind. And that is known to us as time pressure. So we make what we think is a decision. In order to do this, in order to do that, in order to do all these things that we desire, we must eat fast. We must spend less time in dining and more time in fulfilling the multitude of desires that bombard our consciousness.

Then, sooner or later, in life we find out that that so-called decision we made early in life is not serving us very well. We enter about that time the hindsight years of the forties and it's commonly referred to in our world as the battle of the bulge. And so there's a bulge here, and there's a bulge there, and there's a bulge someplace else. And we do not desire all those bulges. And so we make other decisions and we make great effort to win the battle of the bulge. And then we find out, when we begin to make that effort, who is really in control. And that rude awakening causes us great emotional trauma, known to man as frustration.

And so we go through life and we try this and we try that. It works for a time, but it only works for a time. Why does it only work for a time? Because the attention, the energy that we have directed to what we thought was a decision in our life and turned out to be a judgment has made us the victim. It became the captain of our little ship and we became the slave. And so man says, "That habit has got me!" That's the habit speaking. That's how habit defends and protects itself.

You see, thoughts are more than things. They are living forms created by a living substance known as mind or mental substance. And so when we think a thought, what we are doing in truth is harboring a form. So the more we think the thought, the stronger becomes the form. And someday, because we direct more energy, through attention, to the thought, we become the victim of the thought. And this is what we experience in our world today. It doesn't have to be that way. It wasn't designed to be that way. But we have forgotten the demonstrable law that all of nature teaches us: use, not abuse, is the path to freedom. All things in creation are designed to be used. No thing in creation is designed to be abused and that, of course, includes our own mind. Thank you.

The gentleman back here, please.

You say in this philosophy that the principle of mathematics is that of perfect balance. Do certain soul faculties correspond to certain numbers?

Why, yes, indeed they do, for mathematics is the key to the universe and the soul faculties of man are a part of that same universe.

You see, all sound is vibration. That, we accept. What most of us have not yet accepted is that all sound, being vibration, is color; that all color is sound and that both are number, for number is vibration. And so what we will in time, of course, all of us, consider with deep thought is when we speak our word forth into the universe, we establish a law, for man is a law unto himself. So it behooves us to consider the thought that prompts the word and what is done by us with the word, for it is the word that is the law that will return unto us. We need not question anything outside, for to so do is to bind oneself to the illusion and delusion that they can be controlled by external forces in the universe. It is not possible to be controlled by any thing that we do not first permit [ourselves] to be controlled by in our own consciousness. And so it is within our self where the power truly lies.

There is where the key to the universe, the key to freedom exists, the key to truth. It does not exist in the illusion that you call "outside," for creation and all things that we sense, that we smell, that we hear, that we view, they are an illusion that is created by our mind. They do not exist outside of the illusion of mental substance, which is totally dependent upon energy that flows through us and is directed by us. Therefore, whatever it is that we think we desire in life, we must first accept that we have it in order that the illusion for us of experiencing it may be created by us. I hope that's helped with your question.

The gentleman in the back row, please.

I'm not sure this is applicable, but I've been exposed to your church a short time, although I've been associated with many philosophies. The question keeps coming up in my mind, Spiritualist beliefs and philosophies appear to have been around for centuries, yet there seems a minuscule amount of people that either attach or attract or are supportive of it. And I keep coming up with why such evident truths, for me, are not more readily accepted throughout the world?

You wish an answer to the question, sir?

Yes.

Certainly. Well, I think if we will pause to think, we will clearly see that Spiritualism offers to the world a path of effort. There are no savior gods in the religion, science, and philosophy of Spiritualism. There never have been any savior gods in the religion, science, and philosophy of Spiritualism. Therefore, because it does not offer to the world an easy path, but it does offer to the world the truth of personal responsibility and in keeping with the evolution of the human species on this planet, it is most understandable.

If you take a child and you sit him in a chair and you offer him the fulfillment of desires without him making any effort to attain them, I'm sure we will all agree the child will take them. And here we have in our world millions of children. It is known by our mind as something for nothing. We do not value—man never values anything that he doesn't make effort to attain. The air we breathe, we do not consider whether it is there, that it is going to remain there, that it is going to be clear and in the best interest of our health until someone somewhere—and of course it's always someone else—begins to pollute it. And as we become aware of the pollution, we begin to make some effort to stop the pollution. And because we begin to make some effort to stop the pollution, we begin to have some value for the air that we call clean. But before that came about, we had no value; we had no thought.

How many of us and how much time have we spent in our life to this point in considering whether or not the ozone layer that protects our planet from total annihilation will be there for us before it's time for us to leave earth, will be there for our children, our grandchildren, and the many generations yet to come? Had we considered it before, there would not be so many holes in the ozone layer and we would not be facing a potential crisis today that so few of the world is even yet considering. And so it is with truth and freedom. We desire it, but when we see the price tag that it comes with, the price tag of effort, our desire wanes very quickly. Only to rise again, and again, and again.

Now many people, they look at the desirability of getting married. And perhaps after the first time, the second, the third, the fourth, or the fifth their desire for marriage has waned drastically. Why? Because they had experience that it takes some effort; for two people to harmoniously grow together takes daily, constant effort. And so we find a change in our society. We find marriages less, and less, and less, and less, and less! And what does it reveal? Less interest in paying the price, less effort, less interest. And so it has always been with religion. And so it has always been with philosophy. The more that it demands from you, the fewer people it will attract to it.

Until we all awaken in life and we truly understand and accept that there is no way that we get something for nothing. There is no possible way. It is a terrible delusion in life to think that we're going to get something for nothing, yet there's a part of us that keeps trying. It tries in marriages. It tries in jobs. It tries all over the world. There is no way to get something for nothing. It is contrary to natural, demonstrable law and man is not greater than the Law of the Universe. There is no way to get something for nothing.

And so when we seek truth and it knocks at our door and it's not in keeping with what's already inside our little house, we kick it out. Because it comes contrary to what we judge it should be and it doesn't fit. And besides, it carries a price tag with it. Though it offers freedom, for truth is freedom, the cost, we decide, is too great. But it will knock another day in another way.

And so it is with the religions of our world. They rise and fall, to rise again. And so it is with Spiritualism. Spiritualism, beyond a shadow of any doubt, not as an organized movement, but as a philosophy that has gone out into the world, taken on many name tags, is one of the largest—if not the largest religion—this planet Earth has ever known. It has been the instrument throughout untold ages of giving births to many religions. It gave birth to fourteen major religions that only one, today, you are aware of, called Christianity. The founder of that religion had visions and was a medium. Mithraism, the religion of the Roman Empire—the religion prior to Christianity—a savior god, born in visions, and on down the list. So Spiritualism, its science and its philosophy, has always been with us and always will be. It doesn't matter what name tag man gives to it. Its very purpose is to remove the barrier created by mental substance between our true being and this world we live in, known as spirit. I hope that's helped with your question.

[There was no audible response from the questioner.]

You're welcome. You see, we don't always hear what we want to hear, but we hear whatever law we've set into motion; that's what returns to us. The gentleman in the aisle, please.

You said that the system was designed differently and is not being used as it was designed. Why is that?

Which system are you referring to, please?

Earlier you referred to the system of mental substance and the energy is focused more on the earth realms and . . .

Why isn't it being used in keeping with its design? Is that the question?

Yes, that's the question.

Yes, my good friend, it is not simply because of our error of ignorance. Someday we will have to accept that we don't know everything. And when we accept that, our errors of ignorance will disappear into the nothingness. Everything is designed to serve a useful, constructive purpose. Every thought we think, every act we do. For God or good, the principle of perfect harmony and balance, is in all things.

Now when we look out in the world and we see something and to us we say [it] is distasteful, we have a moment in which we can choose to see the good that is in it. That that sustains it is good, for it is the principle of perfect balance; it is the divine, infinite, neutral Energy. Now whatever experiences we encounter in life, if we will pause in the moment of the experience and we will look for the good that is in it, we will find the good. And in finding the good, the good for us, inside of us, will grow. Because we are the one that is viewing it. And we are the one who has the choice. If we choose the good and we make the effort to see the good in all things, then the good in all things will be ours. It is entirely up to us. That is where the choice really is.

It doesn't matter what our minds say. Our minds are conditioned; they're like computers, but we are the ones that programmed our minds. We can reprogram. There's no reason why we can't. We're reprogramming anyway, the only thing is that most of us are not aware of the process. And not being aware, we are not doing it with a true, conscious awareness. But we can, if that's what we want to do.

Our life, it's ever as we make it. We make our life; that is our responsibility. We made our life and we came to earth. Just because, through our ignorance, we are not aware of the process does not exempt us from the law that we alone established. We made the law that sent us to earth. We are making the law that keeps us and we are making the law on which we shall go on. There is no power outside of us that pushes the button and tells us when we're going. That isn't how life truly is. We alone make the law and we alone change the law for ourselves. And that, you see, we have been granted in our evolution. It is up to us. If we don't like what we see, we can change what we see. It is our world.

So often, I know, with some students, they think, "Well, that's just the make-believe." Well, what do we think our life really is? Our life is an effect of our belief. It is an effect of our acceptance. It is an effect of our rejection. That's what our life this moment is. Now we made it that way in errors of ignorance. Why not make it the way we wish it to be in the light of reason? For it is entirely dependent upon us. As long as we permit the error in our thinking of believing this is our lot in life and that's the way it is, we have accepted that error and that error, therefore, is the law which we must follow. We don't have to live any way that we choose not to live. We are, in truth, doing it to ourselves. We always have done it to ourselves. We always will do it to ourselves.

What we know as God is a neutral, intelligent Energy, infinite, expressing through all form everywhere at all times. It is up to us what we do with that intelligent Energy. We can direct it, and are directing it, according to our thinking, for that is where our attention goes and our energy follows. Whatever we place our attention upon, we have a tendency to become. For the form that we create by thought is in a mental world and is the basic substance upon what a physical form must stand. There is nothing that we know in the physical world that does not have a mental duplicate form. And that's the way that it really is.

So we have, by our own right of evolution, we have that power within us. But remember, there are eighty-one levels of consciousness; there are nine spheres on which the nine planes express. And when we go to establish a law by speaking forth our word, let us not forget to know ourselves and eighty-one levels of consciousness is a full-time job.

Thank you very much.

SEPTEMBER 6, 1981

Church Questions and Answers 19

As our chairman has already stated, this is the time of month and the service at which you are free to ask your questions of a general interest. And if you will be so kind as to raise your hand, I will get to as many questions and answers as time will permit.

The gentlemen here, please.

I was wondering if you could compare the Serenity philosophy with the Seth philosophy as set forth in books by Jane Roberts.

Thank—

Particularly with respect to modifying the past.

Thank you very much. Whereas I am not familiar with the Seth philosophy, I am familiar with the Living Light Philosophy. But in respect to your question on modifying the past, I can only say that that with which man places his attention upon, he has a tendency to become. And so, of course, that does reveal to us, as we direct our thought to anything, past or future, we place our consciousness in that dimension. Whereas it is a past event, we cannot change what has been. We can only change what is. But by changing what is, we, in truth, are making and forming our tomorrows. The past, so-called, has served its purpose as a lesson in this great evolution, the school of life.

All experiences, we alone will into action, for that is a demonstrable, subtle law. If we make the effort to place our attention upon the eternal moment, known as the present, the now, by so doing we establish the laws which will govern our tomorrows. All of these experiences that we encounter are serving a purpose for us. The purpose they are serving is the purpose of, whether we like it or not, literally forcing us to evolve and to grow. That does not mean that we are deprived of the divine right of choice. It does not mean that we should justify our lack of effort in life by saying that this is the experience we need to grow, for it is not our mind that knows what experience we need to evolve. It is that part of us that has always been and will always be. That's the part of us that knows what is necessary for our evolution.

To look at the past, one must look from a level of consciousness known as objectivity. Because if one looks at the past and has any feeling whatsoever, they are in an emotional-magnetic realm of consciousness and will once again attach themselves to the experiences of yesterday, by so attaching, will repeat the same errors that have already passed in consciousness. Therefore, the Living Light teaches eternity is the moment of which we are consciously aware: that is the moment of now. If we use our energy, direct our attention to the moment of now, then we will evolve in that moment to what is called heaven: a state of consciousness that we can evolve to in any moment, not a place that we're going to. I do hope that's helped with your question.

The gentlemen, here, in the third row, please.

Mr. Goodwin, would you expound on the principle about likes attract likes as much as possible, please?

Thank you very much. The teaching of this philosophy clearly states that like attracts like and becomes the Law of Attachment. If we want to know where we are, we need but study the company that we keep. There's a very old saying, [from] long, long ago. It clearly states birds of a feather, they flock together. Like attracts like and becomes the Law of Attachment. Ofttimes, for example, in a marriage, we look at our partner, we see the weaknesses, we see the errors, we see, seemingly, their unwillingness to change. But what we do not see is the unwillingness of our self to change our view.

You see, we all identify. We look at a person and we create in our consciousness an image of that person. So when we see the person again, it is the image, limited and censored by the judgment that our minds would allow, that see the person. We see life in a very narrow way until we awaken to how our mind censors what we see depending on what has been. To introduce something new into the human mind, it is necessary, as long as we're in mental realms, it is necessary to introduce something that will relate to something that has already been in our consciousness. Otherwise, our mind, as a defense mechanism to protect itself, will immediately reject the new experience. It does it as a matter of self-preservation. When we are in the thought of I, the greatest of all delusions, we are controlled by this realm of consciousness called self. And when we are controlled by that, preservation is the first law of creation, so we work diligently beneath the conscious mind to censor, to limit any thing and all things that attempt to enter our mind.

We like to believe that we are in the will of God, that we are in total acceptance. And the truth of the matter is that in limited avenues of expression we most certainly are in total acceptance. A person sits down to have their breakfast or dinner, there's usually no conscious thought. They're in total acceptance to shovel in whatever's there, until something inside starts feeling uncomfortable and they push the plate away. And so it is with all things that we desire, we are, in those moments, in total acceptance, known as the divine will of God, for that is what desire is. When we are in desire, there is no limit, there is no extreme that we will not go to, to fulfill what we think in that moment we desire.

So let us pause a moment and consider that desire is the divine expression, the expression of God. It is only destructive and blinding when it is limited, restricted, and censored by the human mind, for it grants only unto itself and denies to others. Consequently, when of no thing, when of naught desire, the divine expression, is, in vain shall sorrow speak. The sorrow is only the effect of our effort to judge, to dictate, to censor, and to limit that which is beyond the control of our mind, known as the divine expression, or to man as desire. I hope that's helped with your question.

The gentleman on the aisle, please.

Would you please discuss the cause and effect and remedy of frustration?

Thank you very much. In respect to frustration, its cause and cure, we must first understand what we mean by the word *frustration*. If we mean by the word *frustration*, the unfulfillment of desire that swims in our consciousness, if we mean the emotional turmoil that we experience when we desire this and desire that and we do not get, we think, what we desire or, if we do get it, we don't get it when we think we should have it, if by those feelings and experiences you mean frustration, then we can go directly to the cause, where, in truth, the cure exists.

We are all receptive at all times to thought. What we have yet, most of us, to consider is that our thought, that we think, is not original. It never was original. It cannot be original. Only to us. For that that is, has always been. We are only moving along the stream of life, the consciousness, having a multitude of what we think are new thoughts, new deeds, and new experiences. There is nothing new under the light, the sun. There never was anything new, for all things that are, have always been. They are new to us because we limit; we limit the expression of the Divine Consciousness through us. This is why we believe that space travel is new, the possibility of intelligent beings in other universes and systems is new. It is not new. No thought is new. Therefore, we must consider when we have a thought not only that it is not new, except for us in our limited view, but it is thought and has been thought by untold millions of intelligent beings. And when we become receptive to any thought, then we must understand the force of thought. For the thought we entertain has support of minds that we know not and, therefore, becomes a great force in our life, unless we have made the effort, through control of our mind, to know our self. To know our self is to be the captain of our ship and master of our destiny.

Frustration is simply an unwillingness on our part to be honest with our self, to look at thought and desire for what it is, to separate truth, which is our true being, from creation, which is the vehicle it is temporarily expressing through. All things—remember, we always get what we really want. But by not making the daily effort to know our self, the things we get, we don't think we ever wanted. But we always get what we really want. But in our desires, limited by our minds, we work and we want this and we want that. But we never seem to want the payment that comes with the desire. Man cannot experience the fulfillment of desire by the dictates and limits of the human mind without paying the price of the desire; the price being the limits and the censorship that he placed upon it. For desire is no longer divine when the minds, the mental realm, dictate how, when, and why it shall be fulfilled. Therefore, we find ourselves in many desires. We find some of those desires, we *think*, being fulfilled. But we never seem to get them fulfilled without paying a price. And I'm not talking just about money. I'm talking about the price we pay with our own frustrations in our own mind.

When, through lack of effort, we have lost control of our mind, we experience what is known as time pressure. Our minds are filled with a multitude of desires and we judge it is not possible for us to fulfill all the desires that we have, and therefore we experience what is called time pressure and frustration. That's only an effect of the lack of organization. It is an effect of our refusal to demonstrate the divine Law of Choice. To choose this over that. To choose with a conscious awareness of what it will take to get what we desire. To accept, to be willing to face personal responsibility. You see, my good friends, all things to all people are possible. But all things to what people think they are, are not possible. And there is a vast difference between who we really are and what we think we are.

We know more today about outer space than we do know about the human mind, the vehicle that we use to express on this planet. Because creation is a reality only to a mental world, it behooves man to know the mental world that he has allowed himself to become a victim of. Whether we like it or not, when we free our self in consciousness from the mental body, creation, as we know it, does not exist. There are energy fields everywhere throughout all the universes. They are perceived to be the forms that our mental world, for us, permit them to be. That is known as reality: a conscious awareness of passing events.

They say that beauty is in the eye of the beholder. I tell you in all truth that form, shape, and all experiences are in the I of the beholder. And by "I," I do not mean *e-y-e*. I mean the letter *I*. All is in the I of the beholder. The I is the crown, the delusion of separation.

We *think* that we are, and it is only because we think that we are that we are in a mental world. And when we no longer think that we are, then we are no longer identified with a mental world. As long as we think we are, as long as the I is in control, as long as that is happening to us, we cannot and will not know realms of consciousness in which we move and breathe and have no conscious awareness of. We can only be aware of what we identify with, and we identify with in keeping and in rapport of what has been. This is why change is so difficult. We make it so difficult for us. Yet, the Law of Change is indispensable to the divine Law of Evolution.

In spite of ourselves, in spite of the thought of I, we are changing moment by moment by moment. Whether or not we like it, we can either get used to it or we can kick and scream all the way up the Mountain of Aspiration, for we're destined to go home. It doesn't matter what we think, the divine law is far greater than the self law of the human mind, for it is the divine law that sustains the thought you think. Think of that. Whatever thought you think, the power of God is supporting and sustaining it. Does it not behoove us to be aware and to choose more wisely?

We have a simple statement in this philosophy. It teaches very clearly: Put God in it or forget it! Well, how do we put God into a thought? Very simple. By removing the self. By removing the thought of I, we, in so doing, take away the censorship. We take away the judgment. We take away the dictate, and in so doing we are receptive to the power of the universes. That's when all things are possible to all men: when they no longer think the I and the self. Once again in this great eternity we will be consciously aware of the inseparableness of all life, of all intelligence. This philosophy is founded on that divine law: To love all life and know the Light. It is not possible to know the Light without the love of all life. And it is not possible to love all life and hold so tenaciously to separation, the thought of I. I do hope that's helped with your question.

We may have time for one more. Yes, the lady on the aisle, please.

Could you speak on the subconscious? And is there a means of controlling the subconscious?

Thank you very much. Only by working with the conscious mind can we ever expect to gain control of the so-called subconscious. For it is very simple. The subconscious is a storehouse that has stored that which our conscious mind has first entertained and, through the Law of Repetition, has become attached to. In so doing it enters that magnetic field and we say our habits and things are now automatic. We have to go to where it got its birth. And it got its birth in our conscious mind. And if we are honest with our self, we will take a look and we will see, "Oh, I now remember when I thought that way." So control of the subconscious is, of course, through the door of reason that exists only in the conscious mind. Thank you for your question.

Now I'm very pleased—of course, why shouldn't I be pleased?—I'm always pleased when it is my opportunity to serve the Spirit. I find it a bit interesting and I don't want you to think that we have restricted your questions of general interest to only spiritual realms of consciousness. I think that would be quite a limitation which we do not intend, and therefore I have not heard a question involving our economy and what's going to happen to all of us. I know, and I am well aware, that once a year you do receive your Annual Forecast. And it certainly was, over these past years, really encouraging. But because there is such great interest today in the economy, I will ask the question. *[Many in the congregation laugh.]* And see [what we receive] for an answer.

We have looked around our world and seen, repeatedly and with great frequency, ever-increasing costs, whether we go to a store to buy a pencil or we go to the store to buy clothes or especially we go to the grocery store. I tell you the cost of food, as it ever increases and will continue to increase, is our greatest blessing. Of all the countries in the world we have demonstrated for a long time the Law of Abuse. This philosophy teaches the lack of use is abuse. And so we are fortunate to have such great abundance in our life, but indeed are we unfortunate to be so wasteful. We look and we want to move ahead, and in so doing we cannot see very far. We can only see as far as that that we're holding to. We look in our houses and there are so many things. And we tell our self, "Well, someday I will have a need for that." And in that thinking, we establish the law. Someday we will have a need for that: we may have to sell it to buy groceries, because that's the law we set into motion.

Lack of use is the world's greatest abuse. And so we have, some of us—fortunately not all of us—we have become the world's greatest pack rats. And we want more! We are not free. Even though we have warehouses that we live in, we are not free from the desires of wanting more, and more, and more, and more. The pattern is so well established. But we can't seem to get as much "more" as we want, as we desire. The obstruction is our cup runneth over. And therefore, what by the divine law is coming to us is poured into our cup [and] flows along to someone else. Because we have so much that we are not using. Now if you want to fulfill the desires that you have, be honest with yourselves and see what you are not using. And by not using it, you are transgressing the very law of the Divine: the lack of use is abuse. There is no tree that loses its leaves that does not serve another purpose. All things rise to fall in creation. All things were designed for a use. They were not designed to be stored in warehouses for some possible rainy day.

Well, under the new "Reaganomics," they call it, it's time to use what we've been abusing because there won't be so much "more" so easily to get because we've stored so much from fear, we can only attract more fear. I assure you the stock market will not collapse in this coming year. I assure you the greatest thing that has ever happened to our country in 75 years is taking place. Our federal government is slowly, but surely, freeing itself from abuse. The lack of using wisely what it has: the taxpayer's dollar. Now we've heard much about people who will starve. People who will go hungry. People who will go cold. I assure you there is no one in this country today who has the willingness to work, and having the ability to work, will go cold or hungry or do without the necessities of life.

It is way passed time when we consider that our country was founded by our ancestors who, with great suffering and struggle, escaped the unbearable taxation in Europe. And so as we entered here in these past years, unbearable taxation upon our people, God, in his divine wisdom, has brought about a new vibration, not to deprive us of the goodness of life, but to bring the light of reason back to our world.

We have always stayed away from anything of a political nature. I don't interpret this to be of a political nature. I am not running for the Republican office, though I am a Republican. I am not supporting anyone for any reason. But I am sharing with you the light of reason that we will all clearly see before another six months pass us by.

Do not horde, my friends. Do not store up, for those laws will put you in deprivation. Do not fear that you won't have enough sugar. Do not fear that you won't have enough coffee. Do not fear that you won't have enough paper. Don't do that to yourself, because in so doing you establish the law not only for yourself, but for many others that are receptive to your vibration.

We all know that in the great difficulties of past years, there were two most important stores in our country. One was called, and is called, Montgomery Ward and one is called Sears, Roebuck. One chose to hold to every penny they had from the fear that the economy of our country would collapse; the other chose to spend, to expand and grow. Well, you can look today at the results. I tell you when your mind thinks times are the toughest, that's the time to spend and that's the time to grow. And if you think you don't have it to spend, then, believe me, you never, ever will! We must first accept that we have it before we can ever experience it. And if you accept that you have something, that establishes the law, and I assure you, in God's time and God's way, it will flow into your life. You don't have to be worried.

You know, it's like going out to the stores and you go to the grocery store and you see all these prices increasing almost weekly. It's like going to the stock market because it's constantly changing. But what an incentive. What an incentive. As we restore our health by eating less, we spend less at the store. We have more money to pay for the desires we want to fulfill. It's really quite simple. You know, I was in error as much as most of the people in the country. I was in error because I like many things to eat. I like chocolates, like about five pounds at a time. I didn't like those one pound—didn't seem to last very long. Five pounds of chocolates and perhaps all of the pastries that I could possibly eat, especially bread and milk and potatoes and all of those things that—I finally woke up—I had become addicted to. Ninety-two pounds later—it took me that long to wake up. *[At this time, Mr. Goodwin had lost ninety-two pounds on the Serenity Plan, which can be found in the appendix.]*

I'm not saying that everyone should go on a diet because I don't believe in diets. I never went on [one] myself. I never went on a diet. I do not believe in diets because I do not believe in deprivation. Self-control, the effect of which is freedom, is what I believe in. I do not believe in restriction and censorship and diets especially. If I believed in diets, I certainly wouldn't have waited 54 years to get off 92 excess pounds, now would I? So I think the demonstration is the revelation. I absolutely and positively do not believe in diets. Self-control, I believe in. Will power, I believe in. And I never met a person, not even a dog, that doesn't have will power. In fact, we have a dog that has phenomenal will power. *[Many in the congregation laugh.]* It's not a matter of annihilating our will power, for that is the lord of our universe. It's a matter of telling it which way it's going to go. That's all it is.

We don't have to pray for will power. We don't have to pray for faith. We don't have to pray for that that we have. And if we're honest with our self, we will quickly see that we have all kinds of will power, we have all kinds of faith. And we're using it all the time.

And the reason I'm mentioning this is because when I was waiting for church service to start—and I best not take too long, if we're going to have a service and brunch. But anyway, someone did mention to me that, you know, how many more pounds was I going to lose. Well, I am losing a few more, you know. I don't want to get too skinny, because then I've got to get another wardrobe and I just completed that last year.

But let's stop and think, for us whatever it is that we want, it's available to us. We must first accept that truth first. We have everything necessary to do whatever it is we want to do. It isn't as though we've got to go out and get something. It isn't as though we've got to rack our brains for twenty years to find something. Everything we need—that we think we need is always right where we are. So I want to assure you that there is no one in this wide, wide universe that doesn't have all the will power they need, all the faith that they need. There's only one thing, there's only one, little error: they're not pausing to think that they may say, "I choose to direct my will power here. And because I have so much will power, I choose to direct it in thirty other directions at the same time, because I have more than enough to spare." This philosophy has never taught the annihilation of the human ego, for the human ego is absolutely necessary to survive. For survival is indeed the miracle of life.

Thank you.

OCTOBER 4, 1981

Church Questions and Answers 20

As our chairman has already explained, this is the time of month to ask your questions of an interest to you of a general nature. So if you will be so kind as to raise your hand with your questions, I will indeed be grateful to share with you the answers that I receive.

Yes, the lady here, please.

Good morning, Mr. Goodwin. A lady in Connecticut asked these questions. How does one protect oneself from being influenced or possessed by diabolical forces? How does one recognize these elements for what they are? And is usage of the tarot cards a healthy means of expanding one's understanding or is this tool dangerous? Why?

Thank you very much for those three questions presented. And so we will take the first question, which is so-called diabolical forces. Harmony is the Law of Evolution. That which denies its source is discordant and is known to man by many names: disease, detrimental, and diabolical.

In reference to the recognition, one finds the answer to all questions within the consciousness, for it is our consciousness that is God. And there is no form on this planet, any planet, any universe that consciousness is not sustaining. When we first make the effort to recognize within our self that simple, demonstrable truth, then we will become qualified to accept what first we recognize.

In reference to so-called tarot cards, we must ask ourselves the question, honestly, simply, and clearly, "Is a physician who is yet unable to cure himself an instrument through which the cures we seek can be made manifest?" I am a firm believer of demonstrating unto oneself first, for not to make that effort is to support the error and the ignorance of so-called hypocrisy.

All things are possible. It is our denials of possibilities that place us under the law of a mental world. And a mental world, being a world of form, which, of course, is a world of limit, places us, through our error of ignorance, into what is called the bondage of creation. Whereas it is possible for man to demonstrate unto himself that which is yet to be to the mind, for man is not the mind; he uses the mind. Therefore, it is not necessary, nor is it advisable, to use a crutch to awaken to the simple truth that is within us. There is nothing in the cardboard of a tarot card. There is nothing in the crystal of a crystal. There is nothing in the rabbit's foot. It is in our own judgments that we need these so-called crutches. If we judge that we are more receptive to certain vibrations in the universe when we carry the rabbit's foot, the power that flows through us is limited to the judgment that we have made in our error of ignorance. To depend upon form for truth is to deny the very law through which truth may flow clearly and unobstructed, for we place before that which is that which is not. For creation and its Law of Duality is conceived by the minds of men identifying with a mental world. It is not perceived by the divine, formless, free Spirit which we truly are. I do hope that's helped with your question.

The gentleman on the aisle, please.

Yes. Would you please clarify the terms faculty, function *and the significance of triune. Thank you.*

In reference to your question of defining soul faculties and sense functions, we first must consider, before we can understand, let alone accept, that which we are aware of. Remember, my friends, our awareness is ever dependent upon our own acceptance of possibility. For man cannot identify with that that the mind does not first entertain the possibility of.

Many philosophies have taught that to God all things are possible. When that thought enters our human mind, the so-called defense mechanisms, known as judgment, always based upon that which has been—for it is not possible for the human mind to judge without the foundation of that which has passed, for that which has passed is an indispensable ingredient to forming a judgment by any mind. So when man, looking at the possibility of change, the demonstrable, eternal law of the evolution of form, he struggles because he limits because his attachment is to that which has been, not to that which is. To bring about a transformation of that which is yet to be, we must first let go of that which we think has been in order that we may enter the realm of eternity, which is ever the moment of which we are conscious of. Therefore, this process, known to the minds of men as judgment, is the bondage of a mental world.

A wise man, once becoming aware of that simple process, chooses carefully that which he identifies with. For the law is demonstrably clear in all things: we shall become that which we identify with ever in keeping with the demonstrable law that like attracts like and becomes the Law of Attachment. You cannot have truth, of which freedom is an indispensable ingredient, as long as you have attachment or form. Therefore, truth, not being individual, is individually conceived by the minds of men. Truth *is*; our soul perceives it. When it enters the dual law of a mental world, then it conceives it. Therefore, [when] one man speaks his truth to another, indeed it is false, ever dependent upon what judgments, what bondage of the moment is in control.

I know it seems to take a long time to answer your question, but we must first consider the basis upon which your question has been formed.

Now, we understand in this, the Living Light Philosophy, that the soul expresses through what is called triune (three) soul faculties, such as duty, gratitude, and tolerance. For duty is inseparable from tolerance, tolerance is inseparable from gratitude, and so it is with a triune soul faculty. The expressions of the mental world, of which we have chosen, fortunately or unfortunately depending on how you view your own evolution, in which we have chosen to over-identify with, the expression of that mental body is known as the expression of the sense functions. The teaching of this philosophy is not to annihilate that which is, but to understand the purpose for which it has been designed. All things, whether or not they are faculties of our soul or functions of our sense body, are designed to serve a useful purpose: that the divine, infinite, formless, free Spirit may express on the planet and in the realm of consciousness from whence a form has been created.

Man believes he's born. And man believes he dies. The error is the over-identification with the vehicle or form in which he is at this moment expressing. It is the belief which dies. It is the belief which is born. As thoughts are born, being form, they die, so it is with the form of all forms you identify with. We are not the form, but our error in thought causes us to believe that we are. As a little child growing up slowly, but surely, views the changing in his or her form, so there is a gradual, slow, but sure adjustment taking place within the mental world of the child. Then we enter a form, a growth process, in which we judge is what is known as the prime of life. And there, from our judgments, from our error in our thinking, we choose to remain. Because of our over-identification with the form, with the judgment, we struggle and we do everything within our power to sustain and to maintain that so-called image, known to the minds of men as the prime of life. Therefore, we do not evolve with dignity. We do not evolve with the faculties of graciousness and we certainly do not experience harmony, which is not only the Law of Evolution, but is what man calls health. Those are the struggles because of an imbalance between the attributes of our soul and the functions of our sense and mental body. I do hope that's helped with your question.

The lady here, please.

Good morning, Mr. Goodwin.

Good morning.

Is it right for a young man to join the American Army?

That entirely depends upon the responsibilities that the young man in his desire and choice [has] to join any army. We must consider the divine, demonstrable Law of Evolution. We must consider the motivation in the mind of the young man. Is the lesson they are choosing, is it for them necessary for their evolution, for their truth, and for their freedom? Now, if a young man makes a choice to join an army, any army, and that is contrary to the beliefs of the parents, to those who have reared the young man, then it is time for an understanding not only of the desire of the child, the young man, but an understanding of the desires, of course, of the parents.

We view the world and we view the armies of the world with different and differing understanding. If the experience is necessary, truly necessary for the freedom, the truth, the growth, the understanding, the peace, the harmony, the joy, and the abundant good of the young man, no one who loves the person would deny them their choice. However, first the effort must be made to understand what has prompted the desire. For we do know that desire is the expression of the Divine. It becomes detrimental or beneficial dependent upon the minds of men as they steal it from the Divine to dictate to the Divine when, if, how, and why it should be fulfilled. Therefore, I do hope that's helped with your question. If it hasn't, you're free to speak.

Thank you.

You're welcome. The gentleman here, please, on the aisle.

Mr. Goodwin. I would like for you to explain selfless service and when it becomes mental, when it's coming from a mental point of view, and when it's coming from a spiritual point of view.

Thank you very much. Selfless service, service less the self, can never, of course, come from a mental realm, for the mental realm is a realm of form and therefore a realm of self. To distinguish between selfless service and selfish or service of the self all we have to do is to pause in consciousness when we have, by the divine, demonstrable law, merited the experience, the opportunity to serve. If in the moment of the opportunity, our mental process becomes active and we place the opportunity at the convenience of the self, then forget selfless service, service less the self, and face the honesty which will free us and admit the simple truth: "Because I serve at the convenience of my mind, I serve my mind. I serve nothing else." Then we will not be concerned, for we will know and we will do. For all things that happen to us are caused by us. To entertain the delusion that the cause of anything that takes place within our universe is outside our universe, therefore, beyond our control, therefore we are the victims of circumstances, places us still waiting to accept the Law of Personal Responsibility. I hope that's helped with your question.

The lady, please, yes.

[The lady clears her throat and has some difficulty in speaking.] *Excuse me. In* The Living Light *book there's a—my throat likes this—there's a—it speaks in reference to behooving all of us to learn the art of giving. Is there such an art of giving in reference to our thoughts?*

Thank you. The greatest gift we can ever give is the so-called gift of self, for it is the belief that is the gift. It is that which we have created. We create the so-called self. We believe it is, because we have over-identified with it and, therefore, cannot see beyond the power, the intelligence that sustains it. As a drop of water maintains its form and shape only while it's a drop, and yet it contains all that the ocean contains. We are the drop only in that which we have created. If we have attached our self, from over-identification, to the drop that we believe that we are, then when we expand our consciousness and we broaden our horizons and we once again return to that which we are, the struggle, the pain, the suffering of the thought, the judgment, and the belief will indeed be very great. I assure you that there is no pain, there is no suffering, there is no struggle to so-called death, unless you believe you are the form that is returning to the elements from whence it has been created.

We cannot stop evolution. We can attempt, and ofttimes we do, we can attempt to stop it and pay the price. We are because we are. And one moment we think we're this way, only the next moment to think we're that way. And so the roller coaster goes on and on and on and on and on. But even the roller coaster serves the purpose for whence it has been designed. Sooner or later we will weary of that vibration. Sooner or later we will tire of the multitudes of thoughts, beliefs, judgments, prejudices, and on down the list of things we have created in our mental world. And when we are truly weary of all of that, we will slowly, but surely, awaken to what we are, not what we thought we are. For what we think we are, we only are in a world that has no eternity, in a world that only a fool would rely upon. For who would rely on that which is not tomorrow what it is today? For to do so creates within the mental realm a constant state of frustration.

When we make peace within our house of clay, our house of clay, known as a unity, no longer a house divided, will be the perfect manifestation of the divine law that sustains it. Be happy with the house, the home of your soul, that you now are aware with. For if you do not see the beautiful attributes and your identity, your identification, is only with that in your little house of clay that does not make you happy, be rest assured our adversities become our attachments; it is a subtle, but guaranteed, law. We have the little house of our soul, here, now, that only we have earned. No one did it to us. God is not a doer. God, the infinite, eternal, Divine Intelligence, is a sustaining power flowing through us. When we are unhappy with the house in which we reside, we are denying the wisdom of Infinite Intelligence. We are unhappy with what we have done to earn the house we've earned.

Let us no longer be so foolhardy. Let us not try to be in a house that is not ours. Let us make friends with the house in which we live. We bear a great responsibility, a responsibility to the temple of God and that temple is known as our house of clay, our human body. If we don't like it, be rest assured someday in eternity it will be worse, if that's what you judge what you have. If you place your attention on the beauty that is there—and no house ever created does not have points of beauty. Put your attention on the good, the beautiful, and the good and the beautiful will be, from this moment, the life you live.

Thank you.

NOVEMBER 1, 1981

Church Questions and Answers 21

Good morning, ladies and gentlemen. Before getting to our question-and-answer session, I should like to take a few moments to speak with you on the nature of thought. We often think that we have in our experiences new thoughts, but the very nature of thought is contrary to being new. As thought and its process is ever dependent upon that which has already been experienced, there are no new thoughts. There are, however, ideas, and ideas come from a realm of consciousness above and beyond the realm of thought of the mental world. As thoughts are dependent upon, by their nature, what has been, they are instrumental in causing the process of repetition of experience in our lives. And it is through this process of repetition that change is made possible.

We understand, I am sure, that thought is form created in mental substance through which neutral, intelligent, divine Energy is expressing in a mental world. We are, I am sure, understanding that when this process no longer takes place, when man no longer thinks, then man, in a mental world, no longer is. But because man is not a mental body, because man is a power, an intelligence, and a form that is sustaining a mental body, that is sustaining a physical body, when we sleep from lack of energy, which is attention, the vehicle through which it expresses, to a physical world and when we sleep to the form of a mental world, then we awaken to that which is, and we experience what man calls a spiritual world. For we cannot experience a world composed of substance that we ourselves do not express through in our own awakening.

And so it is that man goes through this mental and physical world, through a constant process of repetition, through pain and struggle ever in keeping with the dual laws of a mental world, ever in keeping with the positive-negative dual laws of a physical world. But those are only vehicles that man is using.

Therefore, when we awaken to the demonstrable truth, that we, someday in our evolution, shall separate truth from creation, the formless from the form, then we shall go beyond knowledge, of course, which knows much, to wisdom, which knows better. And so our world, of course, is ever as we permit it to be, for our reality is dependent upon what we are doing with our thought process.

As we believeth—the teaching is simple—we become. For what is the process of belief? The process of belief is quite simple. Man is constantly expressing what the religionists call faith. That means he is placing his attention pointedly and fixedly upon the object of his choice until he becomes in awareness that which sustains the object of his choice. He does not become the object. He simply becomes aware that he is the power of its life. As we awaken to what is, in truth, the power of our life, then we awaken to what, in truth, is the power of the life of creation or form. "For all these things of creation have I given for your good." Therefore, all these things of creation, man is responsible for, for man, in directing life-giving energy to it, becomes the father or the mother of it.

And so it is in our experiences with communication and relationship with others, it is the image that we have created in our mental world and that image is dependent upon, in its birth, what has been already experienced in our life. Therefore, we repeat and repeat and repeat the experiences of the past. But because we do know, we really do know, that it is all inside in our world, that it is our world that is our reality, because we really do know that, we can do something about it. And that something we can do is to make the conscious choice to change the image and images that we hold in mental substance in our mental world concerning another. He who sees the beauty in all things, becomes the beauty within.

So often we permit ourselves a constant panorama of distraction. We do this because in the quiet and the stillness we ofttimes do not like to see the thoughts of our own mind. But in that stillness and quiet we must consider. They are ours, created, if they are not beautiful, in our days of error, in our days of ignorance. However, because they are ours (our children, living in our house of clay), we have not only the right, but we have the duty to transform them into figures of beauty. For in beauty there is the Law of Harmony, for harmony is beauty, and the effect of harmony is health, wealth, and happiness. So what it is we seek with our mind, remember, it is within our mind. And because we have, through error, believed it is beyond our mind, we are the victim in our error of what our mind has already offered to us.

The law that works in what we call negative experiences is identically the same law that works in what we call positive experience. That that keeps good from us is identically the same law that brings good to us. It is up to us. Our divine birthright is the Law of Choice. Man in a mental world seeks often what he calls satisfaction, not knowing that satisfaction is not only a sense function, but is governed by a dual law and guarantees regret. So let us not be satisfied, for none of us would consciously choose to experience regret. But let us be fulfilled. And to be fulfilled, we must permit ourselves to be still that we may become the observer and not the observed.

This philosophy clearly demonstrates that man (mankind) is a law unto himself. And we must ask our self the question, "What are we doing with the law that we are?" We already know that we are having many experiences that we would not consciously choose to have. And as we look at those experiences, we see clearly the fulfillment of divine, natural law.

And now it is the moment of eternity, for eternity is only the moment that you are consciously aware of. It is not something that has been. It is not something that is going to be. It is something that is. And because we *are*, eternity *is*, and only because we are. So now this eternity is our moment. This is the time. If we are in a mental world, then we have awareness of time. If we are in a mental world, then we have awareness of space, we have awareness of distance, we have awareness of things. And so here we are in a mental world, awake to many things. Because a mental world ever seeks to garner and ever seeks to control, we find our self the victims of that which we have sought. Let us no longer seek. Let us *be*. Let us not become, for becoming is a mental world of thought. But let us be. And we cannot be until we awaken that we are. And when we awaken that we are, we will be. We will no longer seek for knowledge, for we will know there is something greater, much greater than what man calls knowledge. For when of thy mind thou seekest to know the truth, on the wheel of delusion shall we traverse. And surely no one would desire to walk a treadmill century after century after century.

What is it that places us in a world of things, in a world of duality, in a world of struggling, in a world of suffering, in a world of pain, in a world of pleasure? For as we seek pleasure, we guarantee pain. Therefore, it does not behoove us to seek, for we do not consciously choose to suffer. But as all religionists have known, that when the senses suffer enough, there is something that takes place within the human being that drives them on to greater realms of consciousness. But I assure you, my friends, it is not necessary to place yourself in a torture chamber of suffering to rise to realms of consciousness in the here and now that will free you from the pain and lift you from the bondage of so-called pleasure.

Fulfillment is a soul faculty that clearly is what it states it is. Man is filled and no longer seeks, and when he is filled and no longer seeks, he *is*. We think we have not because we seek to have. And by seeking to have, we cannot see what *is*. We view the world with mental eyes and by so doing our vision is clouded. We cannot see clearly in a mental world for the very process is dependent on the shadows of the past and the hopes of the future. Therefore, let us not concern ourselves with what has been. Let us not concern ourselves with what is to be. But let us *be*, and then we will be free from all concern, from all mental activity and we shall in the midst of the Philistines of creation be delivered in the here and the now.

So often it is spoken that our world is ever as we are within. Of course, it is, for that *is* our world. Our world is not what is out there. Our world is not what is beyond our grasp. Our world is what we identify with. And so the teaching goes, the greatest gift we can ever give, the gift to the Power that sustains us, is the gift of self, for it is the limited identification with what we think we are that binds us and keeps us from the awakening of what we truly are. We think we are this limited package. And slowly, but surely, pieces are torn away. Small, new pieces are added to the package that we *think* we are. But those pieces all contain, those so-called new pieces, they contain an essence of what has already been in the package; otherwise, they could not enter, for it is contrary to the very law of mental form. And so it is the package that we have identified with, that we call self that we want to open and free our true being from.

There is something within us that our minds call security. There is something within us—in the same mental package—that our minds call self-preservation. There is something within us that our minds call need. And when we permit ourselves to enter that package, we experience the treadmill of that world. What the mind seeks to have, by the very process of seeking, it denies it has. And the denials in our life are our guaranteed destinies. But there is a better way. We do not have to go through untold centuries to learn what the mental world has to offer. It does not take a set time for any soul.

We came to this, the fifth planet of this particular solar system to learn about directing the great power that we are, called faith. And surely we all direct it, and we direct it in many ways. And lo and behold, its power is constantly revealed to us. We tell ourselves how bad the economy is, and for us it is. We tell ourselves so quickly all of these things of limit, and so limit is our constant experience. Ofttimes I have heard students say that it is so easy to be negative; it is so difficult to be positive. The only reason for that has been the Law of Repetition, and in the Law of Repetition is man's security. We feel comfortable with that with which we think we are familiar. But the sadness in being comfortable with that which we think is familiar to us is that we enter that realm that knows it all. And when man knows it all, he loses respect. And when man loses the soul faculty of respect, he not only is limited to that loss, but he loses the faculty of consideration, the faculty of care, and the very foundation of all soul faculties—he loses the greatest thing of all—it's called understanding. Thank you.

Now it is time, we have some moments left, for your questions, if you'll be kind enough to raise your hand. Yes, the gentleman here, please.

In this association we hear the terms right *and* left. *Do those words have any special spiritual significance?*

They have significance only in the world that we are consciously aware of. And we are surely consciously aware of what man calls a mental world. Because they are dual, they are governed by a mental world. There is no top or bottom, left or right, good or bad, to that which is. That only applies to a world called comparison and a world of comparison is a world of the mind. And a world of the mind is a world of judgment, and therefore man suffers. Does that help with your question?

Thank you.

You're welcome. The lady over here, please.

When the senses of the body get bad, like the sight or the hearing, is this because there's an equal—I mean, because the soul faculties of perception have been neglected? In other words, is it a fault?

I would—I can publicly say this much in reference to our forms: in this philosophy, the Living Light, we understand that the soul is evolving, that it has already had, in forms, many, many, many centuries upon centuries of expression. We distinguish between reincarnation (or return) to evolutionary incarnation, which is progression—continued refinement of form. We enter in this world of creation what man knows as the temple of God, the human body. That house of clay is the effect of our own evolution. Whether the eyes are blue or brown or black or gray or green or hazel, it does not matter. It does not matter the color of the skin. It does not matter the height of the body. That is not what matters. That is only the book that's telling us what lessons we have passed and what lessons we have flunked in this great evolutionary incarnation process.

It behooves man to place his attention in this world upon those lessons in life that he has passed with flying colors, for to do so is to awaken within him the soul faculty of encouragement. And whoever is encouraged in any endeavor, of course, does better. By placing our attention upon the good, the good within us grows, for we can only give to another what we have first given unto our self. So it is extremely important in our spiritual awakening process to put our attention upon our assets, for none of us are without them. Everyone has wonderful, wonderful lessons in evolution that they have passed, and are passing, with flying colors. We need not concern ourselves about those lessons that we flunked; the law herself will fulfill herself. Because the tendency of the human mind is to blame what has been for what is and, in so doing, places us back in the bondage of yesteryear. The very place we're trying to free our self from.

It is important, however, that we not cover up what is, for to do so, to do so is to deny our truth. To place our attention upon that which is beautiful—and there is no one in form that is not beautiful—to place our attention and to see the beauty that we are, is to help that beauty to grow and to expand. And in so doing we will enter in consciousness that which is, that man calls heaven. Remember, my friends, the greatest effort is to accept the Law of Personal Responsibility. I am what I am, and that I am. So what you are, see clearly, and in seeing clearly, become clearly.

So often we hear people, they have a judgment about hair that turns, by the very laws of nature, that it turns white or it turns gray, that it is no longer youthful, because it is no longer beautiful. And, of course, for them it is no longer beautiful. How can it be beautiful when judgment is in front of it? There is nothing beautiful about judgment, for it is not a spiritual faculty. It is the very cell block of mental consciousness. It is the phenomenal need, the phenomenal need to feel secure, the phenomenal need to preserve what has been. That's the cause of judgment. And it limits and it binds us to the struggle of old creation.

Accept what you truly are and you will no longer be concerned of what you want to be, because by accepting what you truly are, there will be no desire to become. And when there is no desire to become, then you are what you are. And you are, in truth, free because you are the truth that is. You are not what you desire to become. I hope that's helped with your question.

Thank you.

You're welcome. The lady here, please.

We've been hearing on the media about nuclear holocaust on this planet. And I was curious as to what you think about all that.

Because I know to my mental world and am aware to my spiritual world, that what man calls nuclear holocaust shall not be. You see, we think, unfortunately, that we are the power—this one little, dinky, microscopic planet—that we are the power in the universe, that we can do what we want to do, that we can invent all these great things and create an unbelievable disaster in the universes. But we are a microscopic bit of intelligence. And we are not so greatly evolved in the intelligence evolution process. This is a baby in the universe, this planet. It is a baby that is just barely beginning to crawl. It hasn't even walked yet. It's still crawling. And for centuries yet to be it will continue to crawl. There are great intelligences, more evolved and less evolved, with physical bodies as dense as ours that live in the universes that surround us. They have their worlds to preserve. For a so-called holocaust of such magnitude does not limit itself to affecting only the planet Earth and its solar system. It affects many, many, many universes where many great intelligent beings are.

Therefore, I assure you—it's like your neighbor who lives next door. Say they decide, in some fit of anger or temporary insanity, that they're going to pour kerosene on their house and burn their house down. Because it's perhaps five to six feet from your house and the wind is blowing in your direction, I am sure that very quickly you would take corrective measures. Would you not? And so it is, my friends, with this little planet.

Let us not become so bloated, as Emerson said, in our nothingness that we think for one moment that we can cause such a great disaster and that untold trillions beyond number of intelligent beings will permit their houses to be affected in such a detrimental way. I assure you it shall not be. That does not mean, my friends, that one should not stop their efforts in helping to prevent it, if that is their path and work to do, you understand? But one must consider the greatness of the universes. One must consider that we do not have four or five corporations running the entire universes, that we may have, unfortunately, less than twelve who run the so-called planet Earth's people. But they do not, and will never, run the universes.

Thank you. Our time is up.

DECEMBER 6, 1981

Church Questions and Answers 22

As the chairman has already stated, this is your opportunity at this time, on the first Sunday of each month, to ask the questions that you have. So if you will be so kind as to raise your hand, we will get to as many as time will permit. The gentleman here, please.

Yes. I'd like to first ask permission to put some more energy into a question that was asked two years ago in reference to the substance of thought. It will take me about four minutes to explain my frame of reference.

Yes, well, I think at this time, with this particular session of questions, that would be more suitable for a class, whereas the answer will take much longer than the four minutes of the question. But thank you very much—unless you have another question.

Yes. The lady here, please.

The news media has made a big issue about arthritis and that they're trying to find cures and how many, many people seem to have it. It is our understanding that all things are caused by us. So can you please explain the cause and the cure?

Well, in reference to a particular disease, let us first, for the benefit of those who are not aware of our understanding of the word *dis-ease* or *disease*, which means not at ease, not in harmony, discordant. If we understand and accept that disease is a demonstration of a discordant effect, if we understand that we are an inseparable part of the divine laws of nature, that we cannot separate our self from the inseparable Source, only through an error of thought, a delusion of our mind, then we can understand more fully the word and the meaning of *disease* and *discord*.

When we lose sight of what we truly are, then we become, in the limits of our mind, what we *think* we are. We are what we think we are in a world of the mind, for mental thought is from the substance of mental vibration. But the substance of the mental is sustained by the essence of the Spirit, the Divine Spirit, the very essence of life itself.

When we in our own error and ignorance attempt to separate our self from the whole of which we are an inseparable part, we experience the opposite of the divine Law of Harmony. And in that error we suffer the consequences. And so the question must arise, then, "What is the cause of a child, of a new babe, being born that is not in harmony and, therefore, is what we judge not to be healthy and diseased?" Therefore, we must take the question farther and understand the laws of evolutionary incarnation: that this experience here on this particular planet is not the first, nor can it be the last of the experiences that lie before us and that are behind us. We enter the forms ever in keeping with the laws established in our own evolution. We understand, whether it's a so-called common cold, from a headache to so-called arthritis, to every other name that man has given to discord or disease, that it is an effect, that the cure does not lie in the effect. The cure of any discord only lies in the cause thereof. Therefore, we must go within, for we alone are the ones who are experiencing the effect. And because we alone are the ones who are experiencing the effect, we alone, in our own error, are the only ones that have established the law which we know to be the cause.

Honesty with oneself is not something that we suddenly decide to be honest. It doesn't work that way. Honesty is an ever-unfolding process. It is not what we must put into our mind to awaken us; it is what we must make the effort to remove from our mind to awaken us. For our mind is a cloud that lies in front of our conscious awareness and our true being. So often in life we just do things without conscious thought, but we must understand, habit was a conscious cause. It was never a subconscious cause. We set ourselves up to have many experiences in life. And those experiences we often term to be discordant or diseased, not in harmony, not fulfilling.

And so we look ahead in our life; sometimes we look ten minutes ahead of us. Sometimes we wish ten years ahead. Sometimes it's ten days and sometimes it's two weeks. And as we look with our minds at what we think lies ahead of us, we immediately zoom in on the target of what we call responsibility. It seems to be a word that few of us like. It means the ability to respond when it is contrary to the desires that we may entertain at the moment. And so we look a few days, weeks, or months ahead, and we see, "I have this to do and I have that to do. I have made these commitments and at this time I don't want to fulfill these commitments, but I somehow feel guilty, which is, of course, nothing more nor less than rejected desire, about not fulfilling these commitments that I have, by my own voluntary act and thought, committed myself to." That type of thinking enters a level of consciousness in the deep, dark resources of our own subconscious mind, the greatest computer ever designed.

Man will never duplicate that which is the greatest of creation, the human mind, the human computer. Oh, he'll have many similar things, but he will never be able to copy it exactly.

And so that thought enters a portion of our mind in the subconscious, in the computer and there it goes to work to set up many experiences so when the day of our commitment arrives, it is not possible for us to fulfill it. And we wonder why we have so-called accidents. We wonder why we have so-called disasters in our life. We wonder why we have so much discord. And we wonder what's happened to peace. We wonder what's happened to harmony. We wonder what's happened to fulfillment and the joy of life, which is, in truth, our divine birthright.

And so it is, whether we call it arthritis, the common cold, whether we call it an accident, whether we call it unhappiness with our wives or our husbands or our children or our relatives or the politicians or anything else, it doesn't matter what we call it. It's still the same law that is working: the Law of Personal Responsibility returning unto us the error that we have sent out. So all philosophies of all ages have taught, "O man, know thyself, for only then shall you know the truth. And only then shall you be free."

To race around the universe looking for fulfillment is nothing more and nothing less than experiencing temporary satisfaction. And that that satisfies does not fulfill. And so the cup we try to fill never fills when we seek out in the universe for what has always been, will always be, inside of our self. If we decide that a certain discord, we have become the victim of, then we direct, through the Law of Attention, energy to it. And we continue to increase, in our experiences, the negative reaction in keeping with the Law of Energy that feeds any form.

An artist knows a thought is form. They know it and put it on canvas and put it on many things. They know the picture they paint is the story they tell. And the only difference between a writer and a painter is the form in which the art is being expressed. It's the same art. It's the same principle. And so it is with all of life. Whether the art is the words you speak, the pictures you paint, or the words you write, it is still the same.

And when we understand that we are not, we are not the life essence—our minds, that our minds and our bodies are but the effects. And a wise man goes to the source of harmony to experience harmony and to restore what we call perfect health. But until we truly understand that peace and peace alone is the power, and by that understanding grow to the becoming, which is the returning to the source in consciousness, only then can we experience our divine birthright. Thank you for your question.

Yes, the lady in the next row, please.

Could you give us your understanding of 10 percent free will and what it's in reference to?

Ten percent free will is in reference to the Divine Principle that sustains creation. Now we understand that there are, within us, these vehicles, which are called by most of us a mental body, an astral body, and hopefully we are growing slowly, but surely, and forming a spiritual body. Mental bodies are formed from the direction of mental energy. Physical bodies are formed from the direction of energy to physical substance. It's as simple as that. And when we take a look, we see it clearly.

And so in reference to your question, What do we mean by 10 percent free will? We mean that is the percentage, based upon 100 percent, that is the percentage that we have to change laws that we alone have established in a world of form or a world of creation. Now it doesn't seem like much, but if you place your attention upon it, it becomes everything. Because when you place your attention upon a thing—that's everything that is not the thing your attention is upon—that's known in this philosophy as true concentration, the key to all power. Peace is the power. Concentration is the key that unlocks the door of understanding in order that you may return home to the power that you truly are, not the thing that we think we are, but that which we truly are.

And there's a vast difference between truth and reality. Reality is that which we realize. It is that which we have created for our self. A person looks like they feel and—adjust the heat downward, please. Let us be conservative. A person feels and a person thinks and in so doing we create. We are the creators. The laws of nature, of which we are an inseparable part, are the creators. God is a divine, infinite, formless, free Spirit. It is the forms, the effects of the divine laws of creation, that are the creators. And so we constantly are in a process of creating. We create thoughts, which, in truth, are forms. And we create all manner of things.

Truth *is*. In order to give it some expression, I must give it some limit. Because to speak a word is to form, is to form energy that flows freely. But if we will consider that truth, which is freedom, which needs no defense because it is—there's nothing that you can do to truth, except temporarily deny your awareness of it. You cannot change truth. You cannot get truth. You cannot give truth, for you *are* truth. You cannot get, you cannot give what you are. What you are, that *is*. Therefore, truth *is*.

Now these percentages, as I have explained a moment before, are all in reference to creation, this 90 percent. They're in reference to form. But now remember, my friends, the moment you permit, and we permit, our mind to entertain thought, in that moment we become form. For thought is form. And therefore, in the moment of thought we are, in that moment, in creation and in that moment, we are bound by creation. And creation, being form, is limit, and, therefore, is not truth. So when of our mind we seekest to know the truth, on the wheel of delusion we shall traverse.

That that frees us is what we are, not what we think we are. Our minds, being form, our bodies, being form, are the effects of laws established. We believe we are the form because, through the Law of Identification, we become the form. We become what we identify with, for in the Law of Identification is the concentrated power of the universe which we direct and therefore become. I do hope that's helped with your question.

The lady here in the back, please.

Is one of the great dangers of taking drugs or alcohol that we are apt to attract those very addicts that have passed on and have a hard time getting rid of the attraction?

Yes, the teaching clearly states and demonstrates that like attracts like and becomes the Law of Attachment. Now like attracts like and becomes. It is not that like attracts like *is*. Like attracts like *and becomes* the Law of Attraction—of Attachment, rather. Like attracts like and becomes the Law of Attachment. It becomes it because we believe it. Now, if a person thinks a certain way and, in that thinking, sees that it is detrimental—and detrimental to one is that which is out of harmony with the natural flow of Life herself. They attract unto themselves all like kind and become, through the attraction, the attachment thereof. Consequently, if one wishes, using the same law, to live a life of abundant good, peace, and harmony, one, using identically the same law wisely, can become that in a world of identification. But in answer to your question, that is the reason one should consider. For we attract unto our self not what we are, for we are truth, but what we believe we are and, through that belief, become the thing itself.

You see, my friends, when the tools of life, the forms of life, no longer serve the worker, then the worker begins to serve the tools. That's the difference in life—and life eternal is the moment of our awareness—that is the difference between being the victim or the victor. We are ever faced moment by moment with being victimized or victorious. And as we pause to think, we soon discover to our minds, to our so-called selves, that we have been the victim and we do not appreciate continuing in life to be the victim when it is our right, our divine right, to be the victor. We are as victorious as our identification will permit us to be. It is not a matter of saying, "I'm better and better and better." It is a matter of being what we truly are and letting go of what we *thought* we were. But letting go is the awareness.

It is such a wonderful thing to pause and make the effort to forgive, which means to free, for in that process we become aware of how victimized we have become. Look at that [that] you cherish. All of us must pause and look, and in the moment decide to let it go. The things of physical form are much easier to let go of than the things of mental form. The reason for that is quite simple. Man will tenaciously hold to a judgment, but he will give a thousand dollars. But a judgment he cannot let go of, though it is possible. And the reason for that: all form is a physical effect of an original mental form. Once we have the mental form, the image in mental realm consciousness, and, through identification and the great power of the universe known as concentration, it is placed into physical substance, we have accomplished a part, not all, but a part of our ego need challenge. And therefore, [the mental form] has served as an instrument that we have judged is part of our need. It has then granted unto us, in keeping with that law, a bit of satisfaction. But the mental form that has yet to be released, the mental form that has yet to enter into the substance of what we call a physical world, it haunts us in our consciousness, in our waking and our sleeping state, ever waiting and ever wanting its fulfillment. Those are the forms, the thoughts, the judgments that are so difficult to forgive.

So our teaching is, in all your getting, get understanding; in all your giving, give wisdom. For when we have given every *thing*, what then is left? Truth, freedom, that which we are—no *thing*—that is what is left. As we entered the Earth planet truth, a no *thing*, except the shadows of yesteryear, so we must leave the Earth planet a no *thing* with only the shadows of yesteryear to haunt us.

Most people say, "Evolutionary incarnation? I can't even remember what I did when I was two, let alone an awareness of who I was with." So, you see, in the process from moment to moment and day to day, these things, they're slipping past.

What is judgment—and then we must conclude our meeting to get to the rest of our service. What is judgment? Of course we know it's a form. What is it based upon? Not on that which is to be. It cannot be based on what it knows not. Judgment is simply a form created by our mind based upon all past experiences that we can recall. And we recall many things that we think we are not aware of. And so judgment, based on that which has been, not on that which is, not on the possibility of what is to be, based only upon that which has passed, is death itself. It's dead. It is a dead form. The only life it has is the life we give to it by directing energy, through the Law of Attention, to it. Otherwise, it is dead and gone. And so the books, the holy books of our world have taught forever and ever and ever in very simply terms, judge not that ye be not judged. Die not that you die not yourself. Don't you see, my friends? We are entertaining the very thing we fear and know it not. We believe in death because we believe in that which has gone and cannot see that which is. And because we cannot see that which is, we have become that which was, that which has been. And that is called the living dead, the shadow of yesterday.

Thank you kindly.

JANUARY 3, 1982

Church Questions and Answers 23

As our chairman has stated, this is your opportunity, once a month, to ask the questions that are of interest to all of us. So if you'll be so kind as to raise your hand, I will get to as many of you as possible. Yes, the lady on the aisle, please.

Please speak to us of the formless One.

Well, in reference to your question to speak of the formless One, if we understand that to mean the Infinite Intelligence, the Divine Spirit, the Principle of all life, then I can speak on that. Fine. We must remember whenever we attempt to speak on that that is formless, we are attempting to speak on that which is free. Because we are yet in form, we are censored and limited by the form in which we are, of course, encased. Therefore, we can only be receptive to and limited by our own awakening consciousness. This is why this philosophy teaches that truth is not individual; it is individually perceived. To speak on the divine, formless, free Spirit, the listening ear must be as broadened in its acceptance as is possible for the ear. Otherwise, whatever is spoken, whatever is received is limited not only by the speaker, but by the listener.

If we understand that all things we see and all things we hear, all things we feel and all things we sense are restricted by what has been. The reason for that is the very nature of the mental substance. Its purpose is to gather and to garner. It is not its nature to free. Its nature is to gather and to bind. Consequently, we find, when we are in mental realms of consciousness, great difficulty, great, great difficulty in our efforts to understand anything. Because to understand anything at any moment is ever dependent upon what has already been, if we are in a mental realm of consciousness. Therefore, in my efforts to share with you our understanding of the formless, free Spirit, of the Infinite Intelligence, as called by Spiritualists, as the Divine Spirit, silence is the truth, for in silence there is no mental activity. And where there is no mental activity, there is no restriction, there is no judgment, there is only truth. I do hope that has helped with your question.

The gentleman in the row back, please.

It's my understanding in this philosophy that God is neutral and that God is goodness. Is this not a denial of God being the opposite of goodness?

That's an excellent question. First of all, the Living Light Philosophy teaches that God—we understand God to be a divine, infinite, neutral Intelligence. Neutrality, we must first consider what we understand neutrality to be. If we understand neutral and neutrality to be a perfect balance, a perfect harmony between the poles of opposites of the positive and negative, of so-called good and bad, a perfect harmony and a perfect balance of creation itself, then we do not have what seems to the human mind to be a contradiction.

When it is stated that God is good, that goodness is Godness, then we are speaking, of course, of that which is in perfect balance. Whatever is in harmony, we understand, by our minds, to be good. Whatever is discordant, we understand, by our minds, to be not so good. And so it is our minds and our minds only that are the judge. It is our minds that accept that this is bad and accept that that is good. That is what a mental world—our minds are composed of a mental world—that is what it has to offer to us, instead of the living demonstration of Nature herself: that so-called bad is undeveloped good. It is just a process of evolution.

It is our educated conscience, not our spiritual conscience, but our educated conscience that sees one thing as bad and the other as good ever dependent upon what we have denied and what we have accepted in our earthly experiences. The tree does not say that this is a good day or that is a bad day. The tree, like the animal, simply responds to what is. Now in that flexibility and in that perfect balance within itself, we find a divine harmony expressing itself. When we dictate how the tree should be, when we dictate how the animal should be, that is when we find discord, that is when we lose the Divine, for that is when we lose neutrality.

Now a person may say that passive resistance is neutrality, and therefore to do nothing is to do something. And the truth of the matter is, to do nothing is ofttimes doing something. In fact, when one does nothing, one does something by doing nothing. Now if we don't yet understand that by doing nothing we are doing something and by doing something we are doing nothing, then we have yet to understand the eighty-one levels of consciousness through which our eternal being is expressing itself at any given moment.

Unfortunately, as with all philosophies, when the mind attempts to perceive, limited by its very nature, it can only conceive. And in conception is duality; in perception is neutrality. When we take spiritual teachings and we make the effort by the mind to perceive them, we, in the final analysis, find we have only conceived them. And that conception, of course, is the ingredients and the very substance of the experiences of yesterday.

To be *is*. Truth is not something you are going to attain. Freedom is not something you are going to attain. Truth is what you are and freedom is what you be. Therefore, that is available to all of us at any moment of our choice.

But to our minds, you see, we must give to gain, and we must gain to give. So as long as we choose to be in a mental state of consciousness, we will forever and ever and ever go around and around and around on the so-called karmic wheel of illusion. Illusion is that which is dependent upon what has been. Illusion is not what is. Illusion is not what is to be. Illusion is what has been. And so we look at a world, we think it's a world; that, of course, is dependent on what in our life we have already accepted.

To experience what you are takes a conscious, moment-by-moment effort to be, for to be *is* the eternity; it is the moment of conscious awareness. So many of us wait and wait and wait to leave a physical body in the hopes of being free, to leave a physical body in the hopes of finding truth. I assure you, after over forty-some years of this work, that is not what happens. When you go home and change your clothes, you do not, in that change, experience freedom necessarily. You do not, in that change, experience truth. There is no difference between shedding the physical suit than shedding the suit of clothes that you put on in the morning. There is no difference. Our minds do not change by some seeming law of the universe. That does not change. It is only the physical body that we leave.

However, in leaving the physical body, depending upon our attachment to it, dependent upon our over-identification with it, that's where the possibility of change takes place. It's called the divine shock therapy. We die each moment and we're born each moment, for we die to thoughts that have been and we give birth to thoughts that are to be. And that's a birth and a death and it's happening moment by moment by moment. If you have made your judgments and firmly hold to your beliefs of what so-called death is, then I assure you, you're in for a little divine shock therapy. You're not going to be someone else when you take off your suit of clothes and your dresses. You're not going to be instantaneously free. You're not going to find the eternal light of truth.

If you find it this moment, when you change your clothes, it will be there for you. For it is always there, has always been, will always be. It is only the illusion that we alone have created that keeps us blind to it. We have, for many years, given that simple truth that heaven is not a place we're going to; it's simply a state of consciousness we are growing to. There is no law that dictates it will take 3,000 years to grow to heaven. That can happen in less than a second. That is dependent on what we want to do.

Remember, we always get what we really want, but because so few of us make the daily, moment-by-moment effort to know who we are, then we don't know what we want. We think we know what we want. And one moment we want this and the next moment we want that. Therefore, we must first begin with who are we, by knowing what are we. For we have made our self something. By making our self something, we have made something else in our consciousness nothing. And that's the great illusion that we entertain. I do hope that's helped with your question.

The lady over there, please. Yes.

Mr. Goodwin, could I ask you a question about animals?

Certainly.

So many times they're seen starving or abused and it's affecting me greatly. And I wonder—I've tried to seek understanding and I don't have any. And is it judgment or is there some good happening there? And at the time when they're experimented upon and abused, do they get spiritual help? Is something happening there? And what is—why are there such things?

Thank you so much for your question. We look about the world and we see a world of seeming contradiction, for we look from a realm of duality, and therefore can only see duality. We see the haves and the have-nots ever in keeping with where we live in consciousness.

There is something that we all know that is sustaining the forms of creation. That something is divine, infinite, whole, complete, neutral or perfectly balanced. It is limited by the form through which it is expressing at any given moment. The Divine Power, known as God, the Infinite Intelligence, affects the form through which it flows. The form does not affect the Divine Neutrality, for it is not composed of such refined essence.

And so we look and we see what we judge to be suffering of the form, but we must go beyond appearances and we must see the process, impartial, divine and neutral, that is refining the form. Do we cry or judge in the polishing of the diamond in the suffering that it experiences? Do we think for a moment when we saw the tree, we cut its arms, its legs, and we warm ourselves by the fire, do we ever stop to think that it has feelings? It has sensations. We do not consider that. We do consider that we want to be warm and we have judged it is an ancient source of heat. And so it is. All things in creation are here to serve a purpose. The tree, when it grows from its little acorn, from its seed, it does not pause and think, "I will last only a few years before some animal comes and saws me down." We don't even consider that the tree has any intelligence, let alone individuality.

Few of us even consider that the animal has intelligence, let alone individuality. But we all agree, I'm sure, that if we take fifty dogs or cats and we examine them thoroughly, we see there are differences. There are similarities, but there are basic differences: that each one does have what we call a personality. Now show me anything that has personality that doesn't have individuality. Because if it didn't have individuality, there could not be such a thing as personality. So we do accept—most of us—that the dogs and the cats have personality. And so we are on the path of awakening, to accept the inevitable, that they have individuality. Now that that has individuality, in keeping with ourselves—we certainly consider that we have individuality; that we are individual; that we are not identically the same as everyone else. We certainly have personality and we have individuality.

That that is individual is divided. And what is it divided from? It is divided from the whole. And in that division is established the Law of Personal Responsibility. And in that personal responsibility it is very clear: for every thought, act, and deed we alone are responsible. For every thought, act, and deed, so it is with all creation. Therefore, what we accept for ourselves, and so tenaciously fight to maintain, we must accept for all of

God's creatures, for the law clearly demonstrates they, in keeping with the divine, immutable laws of evolution, have personal responsibility. That, however, should not, in any way, keep us from expressing the soul faculty of compassion, of duty, of gratitude, of understanding.

So often in life we look around the world and we see a person and we see what they are doing and we say, "Oh, there they go. Are they going to have problems and a struggle in life!" And when their problems and their struggles come, if we don't say we told them so, at least we think that way. So we do accept, for them, the demonstrable Law of Personal Responsibility. And then the day comes from our own lack of tolerance, it happens to us and the struggles begin. That's when we start to deny the demonstrable Law of Personal Responsibility.

Our philosophy teaches to love all life and know the Light. But what do we mean by love? So often we think that word means attachment, when it means the direct opposite. That that we love, we consider. That that we consider, we have compassion for. That that we have compassion for, we have understanding of. That that we have understanding of, we certainly express duty, gratitude, and tolerance. Now those are the necessary ingredients of what man calls love. Love is not an attachment to something that is, by some miraculous law, supposed to serve you like a downstairs maid. That's not what love is all about. Love is not something that you're supposed to attach yourself to, that is the Lloyd's of London or some bank account that's supposed to take care of all your fluctuating wishes and desires in life. Surely, we are not so unevolved in our evolution to think for a moment that that is love.

My good friends, whatever in creation we love in that way, known as attachment, stands between us and the divine, eternal light within us that frees us. So if we want to know what to work on in our life to be free, to experience truth and the abundant good and joy which is our divine right, all we have to do is be still for a few moments, go through our list of desires to the world of creation, find out which ones we are so attached to in our so-called love that the priority is greater than our love of God, and we will see clearly in that moment the weight, our weight of responsibility. This is why this philosophy teaches, "The weight of responsibility must never exceed our love of God."

When we find in these attachments, called love, to creation, when we find the ones that are standing in our way from the joy of life, the ones that have a greater priority in our consciousness than God, we know in that moment where our weaknesses are. Now once we know our weaknesses, we have established the Law of Possibility. The possibility of making the effort to do something about it.

Let us not deny the divine right of personal responsibility. Let us not deny it to ourselves, to all humanity. Let us not deny it to the animal kingdom. Let us not deny it to the plant kingdom. Let us, in our own consciousness, awaken to a great, divine Principle, called God, that *is*. That has, in its divine grace and wisdom, granted unto all of life the divine right of choice. Because we cannot see the cause of a so-called accident, because we cannot see the cause of so-called suffering, let us not deny the Divinity. Let us not blame the Divine for what a mental world of duality, the very essence of illusion, has created in our consciousness. Let us see clearly that all things are in keeping with divine, natural law: that if man, in his ignorance, chooses to suffer, he is guaranteeing the law through which someday he will be free; that if a dog or a cat, a plant, or a tree, in its own ignorance in its evolution, has established those laws, it shall be free.

Do you think for a moment that the pine appreciates growing next to the oak? But they tolerate each other. They are different personalities. They are different trees. Do you think that all dogs appreciate having to live with cats? That depends on their evolution. Some will not tolerate them. Some egos are so attached to their own little ego they will not tolerate a cat to be near. And so it is with all humanity. So it is with all animals. They are here on this planet to serve a purpose, to evolve, to be free. Because they shed their little suit, like we shed our little suit, does not in any way automatically make them angelic. But some of them become quite angelic here on earth.

Now I've spent much time on these animals, because it's very important to all of us. We have, by laws we alone have established, brought these animals into our life. And in so doing we have attracted them unto us that they may learn from us, ofttimes what not to do, and that we may learn from them. And if we think for a moment that a dog or a cat, looking at its master, does not see clearly, ofttimes, does not see what not to do in their life, does not take a few examples of what to do, does not slowly, but surely, absorb the ego of its master, educated or uneducated, then we have yet to see clearly what creation really is.

When we go to train an animal, let us begin by training our self. So many of us, as they say of little babies, are waiting to be potty-trained; we are not yet emotionally trained. So what do we offer to the pets, the animals we bring into our life? We offer the same license, the same lack of discipline and we look at them and we become very upset of the shenanigans that they do. Then we get emotional and then we whip them or do whatever we think is necessary, which is no discipline at all. But that's what we've offered to our self.

When we make a mistake, instead of pausing and saying, "Now I've got to work on this weakness of mine so I do not repeat this mistake. I do not like the effects thereof." That's not what we offer our self; consequently, that is not what we offer our animals. If they do not do what we tell them to do when we want them to do it, we get very upset. But then do we do what we should do when we're supposed to do it or do we get upset?

My good friends, if you want to know where you are and you have a pet in your life, study your pet well. They'll tell you right where you are. And sometimes they don't even want to be near you. No matter how attached they are, because you feed them—they're not fools, you know; they know where to go. But remember, some of them, they'll even leave home and they'll find food someplace else. So stop and think. They're doing what you're doing, but you won't pause to see what you're doing. Therefore, you can only see what they are doing. So, my friends, I do personally and sincerely recommend that all people have what they call pets, because we all need a mirror. We need to see what we're doing and there are few of us who will spend the hours necessary looking in the mirror and being honest with the reflection we see. Oh no, we just deny this and deny that. In fact, we deny anything in that mirror that we don't like. We just think we ignore it. But get yourself a little creature. If you live where you can't have a dog or a cat, there's always a canary or a cockatiel or a turtle. I guarantee you, they will all reflect your personality. They will show you just exactly how you're thinking and what you're doing, for they know. And in that knowing, sometimes they don't appreciate it at all.

Don't beat your animals. Don't be so cruel to yourself. I guarantee you, those who have no tolerance for anything in creation establish the law necessary to live in an astral realm, after they leave this physical body, with the very things they cannot tolerate, for that is the divine, demonstrable law of Nature herself: that that you are adverse to, by the Law of Adversity, becomes your attachment and that that you are attached to, by the Law of Attachment, becomes your adversity. So let us not be so foolhardy. Let us not be attached that we may not be adverse. And let us not be adverse that we may not be attached. Because who wants to live on the roller coaster of life?

It's just like deciding you want to lose two pounds. So you go on a diet and you lose the two pounds and you go back and gain twenty. And up and down, up and down until finally you go who knows where. But such a waste of energy, when all things in life in our experiences are the effect of directed energy. Stop and think of that. No matter what it is you desire, the experience thereof is the effect, not the cause, of directed energy. How do we direct the divine energy? We direct it all the time. Attention is the law through which energy flows. So if you want to know why your experiences are the way they are, all you have to do is become aware, to make the effort [to] say, "Oh my God, where have I placed my attention?"—every day in every way—"What am I thinking about? Am I accepting in my ignorance the need of some kind of a sensational charge, that all I can think about is disaster and the negative? Is my need and my ignorance so great that I can no longer see the Divine in life itself?" Because, remember, we must see it within before we can ever see it without.

The good that we seek in life is the good that we are. It isn't something we want out there. It's something that we are. And it's clouded over with this illusion that we have created. But we can pierce through that veil any moment that we really want to. And all we've got to do is stop and think. We always get what we really want. [We can say,] "I don't like what I'm getting. God forgive me for my ignorance that I ever wanted it." And move on. Thank you.

The gentleman's waiting for a question. Yes, you had a question, please.

Dr. Goodwin, could you speak to us about fear? [Mr. Goodwin was a licentiate minister, but not a doctor.]

Yes, fear, indeed a most interesting device of the human mind. In fact, I think we spoke of that just last Sunday. Surely, we'll all agree that we have many judgments, that hardly a moment goes by that we're not creating new ones in keeping with the ones we already have. Now fear's a devise that the human mind uses to defend and protect the judgments that it already has. Now if we judge—and we've already judged the way life is; we're in a process of gradually adding something to it, slowly, but surely, subtracting a little from it—that realm of judgment in our consciousness. But whenever you face a change in life—change, the Law of Evolution—whenever you face a change that is a drastic movement from your established patterns from the judgments you already have and you face this change and it's not in keeping with what you already have in your judgment consciousness, fear rises up as a mechanism, a device of the mind. It rises up to protect what we think we have.

Now the reason that judgment is such a pain for all of us—it is, in truth, the only cause of suffering. It is, in truth, the only cause of lack of goodness or any of the other abundance of Life herself. Judgment is the cause. The reason that it is the cause is because judgment denies. Now we understand that our denials become our destinies. Stop and think of anything. Well, let's pick a politician. Let's pick the president and see how your judgments work there, especially at this time, you know. So when you say, let's see, "the president of the United States," all of a sudden your consciousness gets flooded with a multitude of judgments. And you will see, in this multitude of judgments, that that soul starts getting blamed for everything that isn't working just right in your life. Now this is the way all our minds work. Now if you happen to be a supporter, you say, "past president," then all those judgments come up. Now this happens in our mind, in our consciousness, all the time, moment by moment by moment.

And the device called fear is used by those judgments to protect itself. Because we have over-identified with what we call individuality—the self—because we have over-identified, we are bound by what we have over-identified with. Now, for example, if you over-identify with a particular pattern—say you over-identify with eating, all right?—which is our right, of course. Now we over-identify with eating and the day comes, we become the victim of eating. Take a look at the world. I agree with that. Or we over-identify with drinking or anything you want to choose. The moment we over-identify with form, we become the victim of form. Now we don't have to over-identify.

The very first words of this philosophy are, "Broaden your horizons." That's trying to help you to see that if you will broaden your horizons, you will not over-identify with anything. By not over-identifying with anything, you will not be bound by anything. Our bondage, our suffering, our misery, and our struggle is nothing more and nothing less than our ignorance of over-identifying with anything we choose to over-identify with.

Now, say we're already over-identified. We don't like the life that we are experiencing and we want to get freed from that. Well, the first thing to work on is a conscious awareness that you are not the thought, therefore you are not the thing. We must first separate truth from creation in order to be free. We cannot be free 'til we separate truth from creation. We cannot be free until we separate what we are from what we think we are. Because when we permit our self to identify with what we think we are, then we are bound by what has been in our life. Now we don't want to be bound by what has been in our life, so we must separate what we think we are from what we are. Now when we make the conscious, daily effort to separate what we think we are from what we are, we guarantee the very law that we will flow upon to free us. We will still have the good of life, but we will no longer be the victim of the good of life.

For many years, I have asked students—and tried to teach them—you don't have to deny any goodness, for to do so is contrary to the divine law. That is not the path to follow, for denial is destiny. You take a person that denies their right to enjoy the good of life, they guarantee someday, someday to live in that bondage for who knows for how long. So therefore, denial is not the path of freedom. It is and does create the Law of Destiny. You don't deny what you seek in a world of creation. You simply put what you seek into perspective that you may not be its victim.

You have the divine right to what you consider the abundant good of life; that is our divine right. It is not our divine right to dictate to the Divine that this is bad and that is good and this is how it will come. You see, whatever you seek, by the law of your seeking, is also seeking you. But when you permit yourself to over-identify with what you seek, you become the victim of what you seek and are ever in want, need, and desire. It is when we over-identify.

Now, if we will simply accept the possibility—say, we seek many things. So we accept the possibility of all things. To accept the possibility of what you are seeking is to establish the law that will bring it into your life far beyond the payment-and-attainment realm of a mental world, you see. Because if you seek it and you dictate how it is to come, if you put any specifics upon it, you have entered a mental realm of consciousness and that's a realm of duality and you must pay. Payment and attainment is the law of the world of creation. But there is a law far greater than the Law of Creation: it is the divine law that sustains all creation. So, when you seek, accept the possibility, for it is taking place—never out there! That's the first delusion to pierce. Whatever you want does not take place out there. In your mental world of illusion, you believe it takes place out there. It does not take place out there. It takes place in your consciousness.

So, when you are struggling and you desire to be free, when you are poor and your health is broken down or whatever the problem may be, if you will accept the possibility of something better, if you will accept that possibility, you will rise in consciousness where something better already is! You see, my friends, where there are eighty-one levels of consciousness, the first thing to do is to know yourself that you may know those eighty-one levels of consciousness and, in so doing, consciously choose to rise to the level of consciousness where fulfillment for you is. If you do not do that, then you must pay the price in a mental world of mental substance governed, censored, and controlled by what you know as judgment. And that price is very dear.

So, often with our mind we want something with such great desire and by the time it arrives and we've paid such a dear price we say, "Oh my God, I wish I'd never wanted that." And then finally, after enough of those experiences, we say, "The heck with it. I don't want anything!" And then we live the rest of our life in frustration. Now surely that is not the way of abundant good.

So—I see that our time, surely, has gone far—I'll try to get to just a couple more questions, but how very important. We must understand that there are the laws beyond the dual laws, and those are the laws to work with. But we can't do that, my friends—you cannot enter that realm of consciousness until you start walking the path of personal responsibility. There is no understanding without personal responsibility. There is no duty. There is no gratitude. There is no tolerance. There is no compassion. There are none of those soul faculties. The moment you deny personal responsibility, you leave the realm of consciousness of the soul faculties and you enter the realm of the sense functions, where all those payments have to be. I mean, it's a simple choice. Why choose a difficult path when the path of freedom, the path of truth is a path of harmony, beauty, and abundant good? Why choose that other foolishness simply from the error, simply from the error of ignorance of over-identification? You see, we pull our self from the source the moment we over-identify. You want a new car? You over-identify with a new car, you take it out of the Divine, and you put it a dual realm. And then the price keeps going up.

Yes, the lady to the back on the aisle, please.

Would you please comment on the Bible story of creation, the seven days?

Yes. I would be happy to share with you our understanding on the seven days of creation, as stated in one of many books, the Bible, the lady is speaking of. Seven is a very—for many centuries, long before the Bible, the number seven was a mystical number. That is, it had always been claimed to be a number of mystical power. The Babylonian astrology—which we have today, here, in this world is the Babylonian astrology—is an astrology based on the mystical number seven. But where did this number come from? Where can it be traced to? Well, if you go back through the centuries, you'll see the ancient belief of seven planets. Very ancient. But the belief [is] long and well established. But we know that that is not true. We understand in the Living Light Philosophy that nine is the number of totality; that long before there was a number seven as a mystical number, there was and still is the number nine. Now the seven days of creation that we understand in the Living Light Philosophy is simply a mystical number of this seeming miracle.

Creation is not governed by the Law of Time. It never was governed by the Law of Time, never will be governed by the Law of Time. Its expression, not its conception, is governed by the Law of Time. The positive and negative poles of creation, the Divine enters at the moment that they meet. It doesn't wait nine months. It doesn't wait seven months. It doesn't wait ten years. It doesn't wait seven years. It is spontaneous. Spontaneity is the Law of the Spirit, for the spirit is above and beyond the realms of illusion. It is the expression of creation that is governed by the Law of Creation. It's the expression and illusion of creation.

If we did not live an illusion in consciousness, we would have no conscious awareness of what we call creation. It is because we believe that we are. Without belief, without illusion, the formless, free Spirit cannot animate what we call creation. So illusion serves its purpose. The difficulty is when the illusion becomes—we become so identified with the illusion that we become the illusion. This is where all of our struggling and suffering really is.

Now how does that apply to these seven days of creation? Well, these seven, this mystical experience of creation is the illusion, but is not creation, the principle itself. It is only the illusion. Now in many religions and philosophies they teach this mystical this and mystical that. The "myst" is what we must remove. And the only way we can get the "myst" out of mystery is through the soul faculty of reason. As long as we need illusion, we shall have illusion. I'm only trying to share with you, you don't need it to the point that you become it. Now the illusion is serving the purpose as a vehicle in which we can experience this mundane world, for this is illusion. And if we lose the illusion, then we are no longer here. So it is serving its purpose in the evolutionary process. But it is when we over-identify with it that we become it.

Now we all know and we experience many times in our life, there are moments—say that we have a thought that is disturbing us. Well, we all know that that disturbs us controls us. So we are being controlled by a thought that we have permitted in our consciousness, and we don't appreciate it. Say, like the thought of being poverty-stricken. That's a thought, and that is the principle and the vehicle through which we experience poverty. Now, as long as we believe we're poor, we continue to support the very law to experience that illusion. Now, we justify and we defend that illusion because we have over-identified with it. By over-identifying with it, we have become it in consciousness. We are not it in truth, but through the illusion of our own creation we have become it. This is what we need to free our self from. To be in the world and not a part of the world. To be with a thing, person, or place, and never a part thereof. Because, my friends, if we do not learn that lesson here on this planet, the fifth planet in this great solar system, the ancient symbol of faith, if we do not learn that here, then we must learn it, I assure you, here, hereafter.

Thank you, I see our time is up. Thank you.

FEBRUARY 7, 1982

Church Questions and Answers 24

As our chairman has stated, this is the one time a month that you have to ask your questions of a general and current interest. So if you will be so kind as to raise your hands, I will be happy to share with you the answer that I receive to your question.

The lady on the aisle, please.

I want to ask you about the eighty-one truths or paths you mentioned one time.

Thank you. In reference to the question, I believe concerning the eighty-one levels of consciousness, it is the understanding of this philosophy that there are eighty-one levels of consciousness through which our soul is expressing. There are forty sense functions and corresponding forty soul faculties. It is our understanding that man is the divine, formless spirit expressing through the individualization of form. We all understand there cannot be form, there cannot be individualization without limit. The limit is the form through which the formless, free spirit is expressing at any time.

We also understand that harmony and peace that passeth all understanding is an effect and not a cause; that it is an effect of a perfect balance of the electromagnetic field of the aura through which this formless, free spirit is expressing. When we make the conscious, daily effort to bring the thoughts of our mental body, which are vehicles through which the formless spirit is expressing, into harmony or balance with the motivation of our soul, we are then instrumental in achieving and fulfilling the purpose of our journey here on this planet. I do hope that's helped with your question.

Yes, the lady here, please.

I believe there's something in the Living Light Philosophy in regards to souls who reside on other planets and also express through ours?

In reference to your question on the planets on which souls reside, we understand that intelligent life is not limited to the planet Earth. Indeed, it would take a very, very limited mind to so delude oneself, in an ever-expanding universe, to believe for a moment that the only intelligent expression of the divine Life Principle is limited to the forms which inhabit the planet Earth. I hope that's helped with your question.

Yes, the lady in the front, please.

Will you please speak on computer games, their effect on people, and on the accelerated evolution of robots to ultimately express human emotions and aggressions?

Thank you. It's quite a three-fold question. We'll begin with the first: video or computer games and their effects upon society. Indeed, a very current and very important topic of discussion. It is only in recent months that one of the countries in the world has outlawed what we understand as video games. In their decision in the best interest of their society, they have been outlawed. Now, throughout history there have been many societies and many laws passed by governing bodies in the interest of sustaining and maintaining their societies as they were. So it was in Biblical times, so it was in times long preceding Biblical times. Whenever there is anything in society that brings about a drastic change in the consciousness of the society, then it becomes a threat to the society, as the society, at any given moment, knows itself. So it is the very Law of Survival, so it is the demonstrable Law of Self-Preservation.

We understand that the preserving—first, we must understand what we think self is. If we think that self is how we think at this moment about what we understand self to be, then we are in a constant process of changing the image of self, for we do not think this moment as we thought the moments past. We only think we think the same. But as the years pass, we see that our thinking expands, changes, evolves, and refines itself from what we think is experience, which is only the effect, of course, of how we think.

And so it is with this that we face today: an electronic computer age. We first must understand that it is the minds of men who have created the computers, and the minds of men have done an excellent job at cloning themselves. So as we study the machines that the minds of men have designed and are using—or being used by, depending on the state of evolution of the mind—we see clearly that whatever is programmed into the computer is what comes out. What is not in keeping with what the computer already has stored in its memory banks is immediately kicked out. And so we see, by these wonderful machines that the minds of men have designed, we get to see slowly, but surely, how our minds work until we begin to make the conscious effort to become aware of our own thinking process.

The video games fascinate the minds of men. Now we must ask ourselves the question, "Why do we see in society machines designed by men that literally hypnotize a high percent of the society?" What is it that man has put into the machine that controls the one who is trying to control the machine they have designed? And we quickly see that the function known as challenge stimulates the human ego, and whatever stimulates the human ego causes a person to feel what they call good. Now feeling good is not a luxury of man. It is a necessity of Life herself. For we understand that what we call good is God. And without God, we do not exist, for God, the divine, infinite, intelligent Principle, is that which is sustaining us. So feeling good *is* a necessity.

But the question must rise—adjust the heat downward, please *[The Teacher requests the vice president to adjust the thermostat.]*—the question must rise, "In what way have we limited ourselves to feeling good?" Must we have video games that fascinate and entertain our senses to feel good, a necessity that we must have—feeling good? No, we alone, through our own thought process, through our own limited experiences, through our own judgments, have dictated to our own minds how we will permit ourselves to feel good, the necessity of life. Some of us have to go boating to feel good. Some of us have to hear certain types of music to feel good. Not the principle of music, only certain types of music, totally limited by our own judgments. Some of us have to fly in a plane to feel good. Some of us have to play golf to feel good. Some of us, many of us, have to over eat to feel good. It doesn't matter what happens to the house that we are responsible for, the temple of God. If we have made the judgment that this is what makes us feel good, then that is what we must do, for man is a law unto himself. The question must rise, "What are we doing with the law that we are?"

It is demonstrable that man, that we are a law unto our self. We dictate how we will feel bad, and we dictate how we will feel good, because we do not make the daily, conscious effort to become aware of our thought processes, to become aware of our own judgments, to become aware of our own bondage created by our own thought of yesterday.

Remember, my friends, judgments are the shadows that stand between us and the light of reason that frees us. They are the shadows, for they are experiences of that which has passed. Never are they that which is. All judgment—though you may think you make a judgment this moment, the very ingredient, that of which it is composed, is a past event. It is a past event, for judgment is the forming of experiences that have already gone. So the shadow is what we serve when we permit our mind to entertain what man knows as judgments. And so the philosophies of ancient time have taught, "Judge not that ye be not judged," for the shadow in which you live shall forever bind you. Eternity is the moment of which man is consciously aware, freed from all shadows, all experiences of what has been. Man is a law unto himself and is creating his own destiny moment by moment. The sadness is that destiny is created based upon what he has already experienced.

However, looking at the other side of the coin, repetition is the law through which change is made possible. Ask anyone who's married or been married, the constant repetition, the constant repetition guarantees the Law of Change, which is the Law of Evolution.

What does this have to do with a computer age in which we live? It is my firm conviction, and has been for many years, if man will make the effort to study, to analyze, and to investigate what he has created, he will begin to understand how his mind works. The only intelligence that an electronic machine has is the intelligence that you alone have given to it. When we seek to control—and it is the very nature of the human mind ever to gather, ever to garner, ever to seek to control. For, you see, my friends, the infinite part of you impinges upon your consciousness and tells you the divine, demonstrable truth that freedom and truth is an effect of self-control. But when it reaches the uneducated ego, that part of us that lives in the darkness and the shadows of the past, then it strives to control that which is out there, for it does not accept the Law of Personal Responsibility, that freedom, truth, and abundant good is an effect of controlling what's in here.

And so we go to the video games and the computers and we are challenged to control a machine that we alone have designed. And the moment that we succeed, we feel good. And because feeling good is a necessity, we become addicted. Not to a machine—that is only an instrument through which our judgments have permitted us to feel good. And we become so addicted that we no longer function in a society of balance, of work, of effort and we become the victims of the games that we play. The video games and the computer age are only a manifestation of the games we have played for a lifetime. They are the outward manifestations of our own inner attitudes of mind. Let us view them for what they are that the change may come in consciousness within ourselves, for freedom or bondage is not dependent upon that which is without. It is ever dependent upon that which is within.

And so we're living in an age when fear shall slowly, but surely, begin to outlaw that which it does not understand. None of us desire to be the victim. We all seek to be in control. But when we take the inward journey, when we make the effort, O man, to know thyself, we must face the victimization which is the effect of the lack of effort of controlling our own thought. I do hope that's helped with your question.

The lady over here, please.

Thank you for answering that question. I'm wondering about the eighty-one levels of consciousness, and wondering if you could change an illness by singing a lot, as Schlesinger did when he was laughing and playing old movies. Would you comment on that?

Absolutely. First of all, our understanding of the word *illness* or *disease* is simply discord. We understand discord is inharmony, the lack of harmony, and that is what disease is. When we are out of balance we experience discord, disease. Now, whatever the mind, which is the great obstruction between—you see, it is the mind that separates us from the Divine Source of which we are a part. It is our mind that thinks we are separate. We are, in truth, a part of the infinite, divine Principle of Life. We are inseparably a part thereof. It is the mind that has deluded us that we are separate from that source. Whatever the judgments of the mind will permit to allow the individual to experience the fullness of the divine Law of Harmony will restore their health. Now if that is singing, if for one person singing helps them to restore harmony in their universe, then they will experience its effect of health. For someone else, it may be gardening. For someone else, it may be sailing. Whatever your mind—not just your conscious mind, but the great computer here that has all the memory banks—whatever it will allow you to experience harmony, for that law to enter your universe, will restore your health.

You're welcome. Are there any other questions? The lady, here, on the aisle, please.

Mr. Goodwin, I'd like to really understand judgments, so I wouldn't judge it.

Thank you. It's a most interesting question.

And may I elaborate just a moment?

Certainly.

Just—I hear you talk about it so much but—and I really am trying hard to understand and maybe my effort's getting in the way of understanding it, but what I want to ask you is, if something happens, like we go somewhere and there are certain types of people there. And they're nice people, but we don't get the high from these people that we get from other people. Are we judging those people? Or should we equally experience, no matter where we go, the same good feeling everywhere? Because I find myself being select with things and people and places along those lines.

Thank you very much for your question. The law clearly states and demonstrates that like attracts like and becomes the Law of Attachment. Now goodness, or God, is always where we are. It is not where someone else is unless we permit our mind, *our mind* to make it so. Now, let us pause and think. We meet a person on the street, someone that we know, and we say hello and they respond. But they do not respond in our thinking the way that they should have responded. Is the person that we meet at fault? Or are we, in our error, at fault? The question is, Which comes first, the chicken or the egg?

And let us pause. Life is ever as *we*—think, now—*we* make it. She is always as *we*—and *we*—take it. Now, to permit it to be otherwise, to enter the realm of illusion and to permit your life, your goodness, your happiness, your abundance, your health, and your welfare to be dependent upon the acts, thoughts, and activities of something beyond your control is to be the victim of what man calls circumstances. That is not the design of Life herself. It is what the error in our thought has created. We alone are responsible, we alone, for our thoughts, our acts, and our activities. To permit our mind to tell us that someone else is responsible for whether or not we feel good, whether we are low or whether we are high, is to serve a very selfish, very selfish, ignorant level of consciousness. Certainly, it is not the abundant good which is our birthright.

But we alone must make that effort. We alone must become aware of our thoughts that stand between us and the goodness that is our right. We alone must become aware and not permit ourselves to feel good because someone else does what we want them to do when we want them to do it. We alone must stand in the midst of the so-called Philistines to be free. No one frees us but our self. No one thinks for us, but only in our own thinking and error do we permit it to be. To tell ourselves that we can only feel God when we are exposed to certain people, that we can only feel God when certain things are happening is to limit the God that we are trying to experience. And to limit the God, the formless, free Divine Spirit, is to serve the gods of clay feet, the false gods of which the prophets of old have spoken so many, many times. What were the false gods of which the Bible speaks? The judgments that we serve in our error of ignorance.

We can feel good, or God, no matter where we are and no matter what we be or what we do if we awaken in our consciousness and, in so doing, take control of our thoughts. I know that if we will make the effort to become aware of what the greatest sin of which the prophets spoke, the sin of pride—by sin we mean error. But let us understand what pride is. What is pride but the crown of the unawakened and unillumined human ego. That's what it is. What is it composed of? It is composed of thoughts and thought patterns that constitute what we call judgments. What is right and what is wrong is ever dependent on what we want to make it, for nothing's either right or wrong, but only thinking makes it so. Are we to believe that there are two gods in the universe? Or are we to believe there is one divine, infinite Intelligent Principle that sustains all of life? For if we are to believe that there is a God that dictates this is what you shall do and only that shall you do, then we will not have any longer God's manifestation known as variety. For it could not possibly live in such bondage.

Let us grant unto ourselves the right of choice. Let us be kind to ourselves and grant the right of choice. For if we do not grant unto our self the right of choice, there is no way possible that we can grant it to another, for man can only give what he first has. And if we do not first grant our self the right of choice, the right of difference, we cannot give that or grant that to another human being. That which we attempt to impose upon another is only the revelation of what we are imposing upon our self. Think, what kind of a God would it be, what kind of goodness would it be that would not permit the snake to crawl the ground, that would not permit the ant to be equal in principle to the angel? Do you mean to tell me there is any difference in the Life Principle between the insect called the ant and the divine angel? Of course there can be no difference! Only in the form through which the divine, infinite, formless Intelligent Spirit is expressing.

If we choose to see the limits within our self, then that's what our life shall be. And when we enter and meet anyone who is not in keeping with the limits we have set for our self, then we cannot feel good, for we have already limited our self on how we will permit ourselves to feel good. Let us not be so insecure, mentally and emotionally, that we must impose upon another the restrictions, the limits, and the suffering that we have imposed upon ourselves. I have said before and I will say again, may God in the divine, infinite mercy save me from the reformers.

Thank you, friends.

MARCH 7, 1982

APPENDIX

The Divine Healing Prayer

I accept that the Divine Healing Power
Is removing all obstructions
From my mind and body
And is restoring me
To perfect health, wealth, and happiness.
My heart is filled with gratitude
For the Divine Law of Acceptance
That is healing both present and absent ones
Who are in need of help.
Peace, the power that healeth,
Is guiding my thoughts, acts, and deeds
As God and I go hand in hand
Living a life of joyful abundance.

The Total Consideration Affirmation

I am the manifestation of Divine Intelligence. Formless and free. Whole and complete. Peace, Poise, and Power are my birthright.

The Law of Harmony is my thought and guarantees Unity in all my acts and activities, expressing perfect Rhythm and limitless flow throughout my entire being.

Without beginning or ending, eternity is my true awareness and sees the tides of creation, as a captain sees his ship.

As the Light of Truth is sustained by the faculty of Reason, I pause to think and claim my Divine right.

    Right Thought. Right Action. Total Consideration.

        Amen. Amen. Amen.

Divine Abundance

Thank
(Gratitude)

You
(Principle)

God
(Divine Intelligence)

I'm
(Individualizing)

Moving
(Rhythm)

In
(Unity)

Your
(Realization)

Divine
(Total)

Flow
(Consideration)

Serenity Plan
The natural way of weight reduction
(This is NOT a diet.)

Phase I
During this phase you may eat a full breakfast of any foods you desire, preferably very nutritious ones, no later than 9 a.m. You may also eat a full dinner of anything you wish, except beer or alcoholic beverages, between the hours of 5:30 and 9 p.m. This is important to allow the proper time span between breakfast and dinner. The entire meal should be consumed at one sitting.

Though you may be used to eating lunch and snacking in between meals, it will not be difficult to give up both lunch and snacking, as you may drink all the V-8 cocktail juice (not the hot or clam variety), tea or coffee you wish. It is preferable to purchase the 6 oz. cans of V-8 which may be refrigerated, but you should add no ice, lemon or salt. You should drink each can all at once. You may add milk to your coffee or tea, but no sugar, except with meals. It is recommended that you drink no more than two glasses of plain water each day. It is strongly advised NOT to drink liquids while eating, as this interferes with nature's chemical process in digesting your foods. Foods not properly digested produce fatty tissue.

Each and every morning upon awakening, weigh yourself that you may experience the conscious awareness and joy of your weight reduction.

Phase II
During this phase, a 20-minute daily Waltham walk is advised. The great benefit of this walk is to redistribute the fatty tissue in your body, and aid in weight reduction in the proper areas. The Waltham walk is a rhythmic walk on level ground where the arms are swung in unison with the stride. As the left foot steps forward, the right hand swings forward the same distance

as the stride, so the forward hand and foot are the same distance out. The left hand is swung back the same distance as the right foot. Flat shoes are necessary. This simple movement exercises every muscle in your body, producing a beneficial and invigorating result. No other exercises are necessary, though you may continue other exercises if you are in the habit of doing them.

Phase III
When you are ready to move into Phase III, you may speed up your weight reduction by skipping dinner one night, but NOT more than two nights per week. The nights should not be consecutive.

Phase IV
Now that you have progressed to this point, you will notice that your food intake has automatically reduced by two-thirds of your original intake. One or two times per week, but no more than two, you may eat two slices of bacon and two eggs for breakfast. And for dinner, you may have a SMALL tasty salad consisting of lettuce and tomato only, with the dressing of your choice.

Phase V
By the time you enter this phase, you will be chewing your food VERY slowly and thoroughly, savoring each and every morsel. Each meal should take at least 30 minutes to consume. Remember, the slower you chew your food, the less you eat, the more weight you lose, and the happier you become.

(Copyright) Serenity – June 11, 1980
[No weight loss program should be initiated without first consulting your physician.]

www.ingramcontent.com/pod-product-compliance
Lightning Source LLC
Chambersburg PA
CBHW020635300426
44112CB00007B/123